ED

THE MILIBANDS

AND THE MAKING OF A LABOUR LEADER

MEHDI HASAN | JAMES MACINTYRE

ED

THE MILIBANDS

AND THE MAKING OF A LABOUR LEADER

First published in Great Britain in 2011 by
Biteback Publishing Ltd
Westminster Tower
3 Albert Embankment
London
SE1 7SP
Copyright © Mehdi Hasan and James Macintyre 2011

ISBN 978-1-84954-102-2

10 9 8 7 6 5 4 3 2 1

A CIP catalogue record for this book is available from the British Library.

Set in Adobe Caslon Pro and Telegrafico
Printed and bound in Great Britain by CPI Mackays, Chatham ME5 8TD

To our parents

CONTENTS

ACKNOWLEDGEMENTS

Ed Miliband did not want this book. Nor did his brother David. This is an unauthorised biography of the Labour Party leader. The idea for it arose in the autumn of 2010, just days before Ed Miliband clinched victory in the Labour leadership race. But it was not until the New Year of 2011 that our work began in earnest, with the support of our publisher Iain Dale.

A disclaimer is due here: this is the first biography of Ed Miliband but it probably won't be the last. Nor is it intended to be a final, definitive account of his life and career. Biographers often spend years studying, exploring and examining their subjects; this book has been completed, often through late nights and weekends, over only six months.

The book would, of course, not have been possible without the help, advice, and co-operation of many people. Our first and biggest debt is to our sources. Many busy individuals, both inside and outside Westminster, have generously given their time to help us. The principal source material for this book lies in more than 120 interviews, plus countless informal conversations that we conducted, on and off the record, between January and May 2011. The transcripts of these interviews amount to around a million words.

Interviews are normally attributed in endnotes, though the majority of our sources preferred to remain anonymous – hence the extensive and unavoidable use of the phrases 'private interview' and 'private information'. The wounds from the divisive Labour leadership contest of 2010 have yet fully to heal.

It is worth noting that our interviewees include shadow Cabinet ministers, former Cabinet ministers, backbench MPs, civil servants, Peers, special advisers and trade union general secretaries. We also spoke to the Labour leader's friends from his Oxford and Harvard days, his university tutors, his childhood and family friends, and his former colleagues in the media.

We are very grateful to Ed Miliband himself for taking time out from his crammed schedule to grant us two interviews. Members of his inner circle were sceptical, to begin with, about this project but became less so as the months progressed. We are grateful, in particular, to Stewart Wood for his assistance and for clarifying factual issues.

We could not have completed this book, in the limited time available to us, without the logistical support and effort of Sirena Bergman, Caroline Crampton, Christopher Czechowicz, Jack Evans, Tobias Garnett, Clare Keogh, Sophie FitzMaurice, Eleanor Margolis and Meketaye Mesfin.

We would like to thank everybody at Biteback Publishing for the dedication, support and speed that they have applied to this project. Hollie Teague has been a tireless and patient editor. Iain Dale, our remarkable publisher, took a risk in commissioning two unpublished, untested authors to write the first biography of the Leader of the Opposition.

Mehdi Hasan would like to express his gratitude to the following:
My parents, who have always had such confidence and faith in me. So much of what I have achieved in my life and career I owe to them. My sister, Roohi, who has always been a source of strength and advice.

My friends and well-wishers, who have provided much-needed guidance and encouragement since the New Year. They know who they are. But a special mention must go to Sameer Abedi, who has pushed, prompted, urged and nagged me to write a book for the best part of the past decade. I could not have wished for a better friend (and I hope he will now stop calling me 'WOK').

My extended family, whose support and smiles have kept me going in recent weeks. I feel I must mention, in particular, Saif and Reshma Bilgrami, whose home in Scotland was my base in the final few days of this project.

Don Macintyre, who was a font of wisdom and insight, a brilliant adviser and calming presence.

My colleagues at the *New Statesman*, including but not limited to, Jason Cowley, my editor, who allowed me time off to complete this project, as well as Jonathan Derbyshire, who lent his expert eye to looking over draft chapters, Jon Bernstein, Sophie Elmhirst, Helen Lewis-Hasteley, Emily Mann and Daniel Trilling.

But the greatest thanks of all, of course, is owed to my immediate family, my wife and daughter, for putting up with an absentee husband and father since the start of 2011.

Zaynab, my beloved daughter, is the light of my life – and the most tolerant and understanding four-year-old that I have ever come across. I promise her that her 'Baba' won't disappear again.

Reshma, my wife and salvation, my best friend, has been my closest collaborator from day one of this project. She has been a constant source of patience and encouragement, reassurance and inspiration.

To her I owe my greatest debt. She makes me a better person.

James Macintyre would like to express his gratitude to the following:
I am very grateful to the editor of *Prospect*, Bronwen Maddox, who went out of her way to give me time to finish the book before starting with the magazine. For wise counsel over a long period in *The Independent*'s Commons office, Andy Grice and Nigel Morris, respectively the nicest and funniest men in the press gallery today, my first editor, at LWT, David Sayer, and two other lobby veterans, Peter Riddell and Michael White. As ever, I am grateful for all the information and insights provided by contacts, the majority of whom remain unnamed here as well as in the book.

I owe a very special debt to Lindsey Brown for going through large sections of the book with such care, and making many consistently improving changes; thanks too to Lindsey's generous husband Bert.

I am very grateful to relatives and friends for their support including, in no particular order: Ashley and Carolyn Meyer, Bobby, Jonathan, Lindsay and Lawrence Speelman, Vivian White, Archie Bassett, Adam Minns, David Houghton, Colin McGregor, Francis Campbell, Andrew Liddle, Michael Harvey, Stephen Khan, Lizzy Davies, Jessica Benton, Simon Baugh, Jenny Parks, Tim Livesey, Roger Liddle, Caroline Thomson, Stefan Stern, Denis MacShane, John and Sally Bercow, Chris, Gaby and Natalie Nash, Quique Kierszenbaum, Sabrina Dadd, Hilary, Thea and Lara Downie, Daniel Castagno, Sarah Spankie, James Corbett, Ofri Akavia, Oliver Dove, Chuck and Sandy Bartman, Naomi Hamill, Spence Quinn, Laura, Hilmar and Emily Hauer, Lucy and Hannah Griffiths, Beccy Gibson, Stephanie Dellner, Toby Knowles, Alix Jackson, Ned Williams, Maria Rejt Meg, Alex and Victoria Freeman.

I want to thank everyone at St Peter's church, Clapham, including George Gray, Rosemary Nutt, Glyn Paflin, Tricia Davies, Rachel, Elizabeth, Dario and Hannah Addy, John, Michelle and Sophie McCiver, Robert, Wendy, Rebecca, Alice, Isabelle and Thomas Willer, Henry, Susanna and Benedict Long, David Isherwood, Derek White, Tim Abraham and Jonathan Bird. There are too many to do justice to here but I am grateful to them all.

Elsewhere, thanks to Harriet Sherwood for years of priceless advice and friendship.

For steering me through every day of this intense project, and so much more, I am eternally grateful to Sarah Ormerod and her lovely family, especially Rosie and Nicky.

I want to mention here my beloved late grandparents Margaret and Kenneth Macintyre. I am also more grateful than I can express to my sister Sophie Meyer for encouraging me always and, for being my constant inspiration, my parents Susan Freestone and Donald Macintyre.

M.H., J.M., June 2011

PROLOGUE

The time had come to emerge from the shadows.

Just after 10pm on the night of Wednesday 12 May, Ed Miliband left his house in Dartmouth Park to make the ten-minute drive to his childhood home in Primrose Hill, where he and his brother David had grown up, and where the latter now lived. Earlier that day, David had announced that he was standing as Labour leader; less than twenty-four hours after Gordon Brown left Downing Street for the last time. Stung in the past by criticism that he had 'bottled out' of challenging Brown, David was determined to be first to declare, surrounded by supportive MPs outside St Stephen's entrance to the Houses of Parliament. For several years, David had dismayed his supporters by resisting challenging Brown. Now he was the frontrunner. He was ready. And he had to win.

Ed maintains that as he watched David's statement on television that day, he had yet fully to make up his mind. There is evidence, however, that on the previous morning, despite widespread hope in sections of the Labour Party for a coalition with the Liberal Democrats, Ed Miliband had already decided to run should the negotiating talks fail. Either way, at some point between the Monday evening – when Gordon Brown met the Liberal Democrats' key condition by promising to stand down as Prime Minister – and now, he had finalised the hardest decision of his life.

Only the future leader's partner Justine was in the house to see him off. Minutes earlier, two of Ed's closest friends, Stewart Wood and Gavin Kelly, had left the couple in peace. Kelly went home while Wood made his way to a nearby Indian restaurant, the Monsoon. He would wait there, like a crutch of support, for Ed to emerge from his nerve-wracking rendezvous with his elder brother. David's two children were asleep upstairs when their uncle arrived at the house, but his wife, the musician Louise Shackleton, was still awake. The brothers, however, spoke alone.

Ed, then forty, says he left his brother, four years his senior, with little doubt that he planned to stand for the Labour leadership. 'I'd rather you didn't run,' replied David. 'I'd rather have a campaign where my brother was supporting me, if I'm really honest.' But, with composure and generosity of spirit that impressed even Ed's most loyal supporters, David added: 'I don't want me to be the reason you don't stand, so I think you should do it.'

Round the corner, Wood – who had been expecting to linger over his curry for some time – was surprised to receive a text message at 10.45pm. It was Ed; he was going home and Wood should join him and Justine there. The younger brother seemed to feel the meeting had gone better than he had expected. Wood would later say that he could sense the relief in Ed's demeanour. The deed was done.

ooooo

Or was it? The tragedy of the Miliband brothers, and the consequence of their bitter struggle for the Labour leadership during the summer of 2010, is that today the two men cannot even agree when it happened: the moment that Ed Miliband confronted his older brother David with his decision to run against him for the leadership of the Labour Party.

Indeed it is remarkable that in the face of this detailed and persuasive account of the pivotal days after Gordon Brown left the premiership, offered by Ed and his closest allies, David is emphatic: there was no meeting that week between the two brothers.

For all the bitter political and personal fallout from Ed's decision to stand, David has in fact refuted the most damning rumours that some of his outriders have spread about his brother's 'betrayal'. He denies, for example, a belief widely held in Westminster that Ed rang David on the night James Purnell resigned from Brown's Cabinet in May 2009 and assured David that if he stayed in government the leadership was his for the taking after the general election. Many David supporters believe Ed persuaded David not to challenge Brown to prevent his brother's coronation and ensure a later contest in which he would be a candidate. Yet David does not recall such a move by Ed.

Indeed, David has told friends that he remembers a conversation at the turn of November and December 2009, when he interpreted Ed's refusal to join a move against Brown as a possible sign of his future intention to run. Back then, of the two brothers only David had been seen as a credible alternative to Brown. He further accepts that then, and in the following months, he had the chance to ask his brother to support his own impending leadership bid, but made no such demand. He does not even deny that at some point between the end of 2009 and Ed's declaration on Saturday 15 May, David Miliband told his younger brother that he would not 'stand in the way' of Ed running for the Labour leadership if he insisted on doing so. It is therefore all the more remarkable that David denies this meeting took place.

It is tempting to conclude that the truth must lie somewhere in the middle, that Ed went round to David's house but stopped short of making it 100 per cent clear he was going to run at the end of that week. Indeed Ed himself has modified his account – from saying that he told his brother bluntly he had decided to run to saying that he told him he was 'seriously thinking' about a leadership bid. And having originally thought that Thursday 13 May was the evening of the encounter, Ed and his team are now clear that it was Wednesday 12 May.

And yet David is adamant that Ed did not set foot in his house at all in that critical week; that at best, Ed must have his timings mixed up. And that in any case, in their various conversations Ed was never explicit about his intentions, until he telephoned on the Friday, forty-eight hours after David's declaration, to tell – not ask – his brother about the announcement he would be making of his own candidacy in central London the following day.

Unlike Ed, David will not put a date on when the exchange about not standing in Ed's way took place. But he points out that from the Thursday of polling day to Saturday 8 May, he was in his constituency of South Shields. He was obviously in London on the day he declared, but friends say he would certainly have remembered if his younger brother had visited him with such deflating news the very same day. The following day he was campaigning in Worcester and it was only on the Friday, according to David, that Ed presented his *fait accompli*.

The exact circumstances of this exchange are important because from the point of view of Ed, confident all along that he would beat his brother, informing David was the biggest hurdle of all. For David, this was his chance to assert himself, to ask – or tell – Ed to put family loyalty before political determination. Whatever the truth, this seemingly trivial discrepancy, which in fact has its roots in an unusual sibling rivalry going back decades, is the clearest demonstration of the dysfunctional distrust and distance that now exists between the brothers. And it shows that the reverberations of Ed deciding to run against his brother continue to this day.

The fact that the Miliband brothers, and their camps, have insisted on sticking to diametrically opposing accounts points to a difficult future for the relationship at the heart of Labour's recent history. And the competing narratives about just what happened between the two men in the days before nominations closed in May 2010 give more than a hint of the trauma that decision inflicted on both brothers, one that is still very far from being healed today, and perhaps never will be.

ooooo

Why did Ed do it? Why did this apparently kind, gentle man with strong emotional sensibilities, put politics and ambition before family and decide to stand against his own brother? Why didn't he, say, run David's campaign, seek to influence the leadership from within, avoiding any of the very real family fallout that was to follow? The Miliband brothers have in the past excitedly been referred to as the modern Kennedys of British politics. So why did Ed not follow the example of his hero Robert Kennedy, who proved to be his older brother Jack's staunchest ally throughout his presidency?

Ed must have realised that Westminster, and perhaps in time the country, would be divided over the rights and wrongs of challenging his brother for the same job after years of following in his footsteps. Some of his more hard-headed supporters would dismiss any misgivings as primitive nonsense. But he must have known that there would be others who saw it as an almost biblical act of fratricide.

The story of this determined politician cannot be understood without examining the context in which he emerged from his dominant sibling's shadow. If the brothers were close, it was not in the usual way. In the words of one rare close friend of both, they inhabited 'different worlds', personally – and politically.

Both had seen their father, the Marxist intellectual Ralph Miliband, as a 'lodestar'. Both moved quickly to the centre of mainstream Labour politics. Both attended the same school, the same college at Oxford, spent formative time in America, and worked as special advisers at the heart of New Labour before entering Parliament and, eventually, the Cabinet. Yet, crucially, the brothers found themselves on the frontline on either side of the hugely damaging Blair–Brown wars that besieged the party in government. It was, in the end, the issue of Brown that divided them most. David could not bear him; Ed's loyalty was total. And that loyalty had already caused him to choose between allegiance to Gordon Brown – which he equated with allegiance to the party itself – and loyalty to his brother, Brown's principal rival during his premiership.

ooooo

Ed Miliband has had several moments of inner-doubt over the years: over whether Labour could fulfil his kind of political ideals, whether to quit politics for a life in the media or academia, and whether or not to challenge his brother for the leadership. Yet he has never doubted his own abilities, his own potential.

He says he told David in his house that he was going to run; David denies this. But this was just the beginning of the dramas to come. And, having crossed the psychological Rubicon, Ed was now prepared to do whatever it took to win.

The Miliband family, if not the Labour Party, would be changed forever. But there was no going back.

RALPH

1969–1981

'**E**ach of us has our own individual story,' Ed Miliband told the Labour Party conference in Manchester on 28 September 2010, in his first speech as leader. 'And I want to tell you about mine.'[1] The story of Ed's background and progression is a one of tragedy, resilience, opportunity, determination and ambition; it is a story of seizing victory, sometimes ruthlessly, from the jaws of defeat. To understand his political journey, his beliefs, his values and – crucially – his decision to stand against his brother David in the 2010 contest for the Labour leadership, it is necessary first fully to understand his upbringing, his family, his parents and, above all else, his father.

Adolphe Miliband – later known as Ralph – was born in Brussels on 7 January 1924, the eldest child of Polish Jewish immigrants who had left Warsaw after the First World War. His arrival was followed four years later by his sister Anna, who would eventually become known as Nan.

Ralph's father Samuel, or Sam, had trained as a leather worker and sold high-quality leather goods from a small workshop in Brussels, but struggled to make ends meet during the Great Depression; his mother Renée, outgoing, gregarious and proudly middle class, had to travel the city selling women's hats, a role she is said to have found 'distasteful'[2] and tried to hide from her neighbours.

It was a close-knit family, in which both children were expected to succeed. It was also unashamedly left-wing. In a series of notes for a 'political autobiography' that he never published, Ralph wrote: 'My father had no strong political convictions, but was very definitely left-of-centre… The political climate in our house was generally and loosely left: it was unthinkable that a Jew, our sort of Jew, the artisan Jewish worker, self-employed, poor, Yiddish-speaking, unassimilated, non-religious, could be anything but socialistic.'

Prompted by news of the Spanish civil war in 1936, and aged just twelve, Ralph began taking a much greater interest in the world around him, in politics and political ideas. He became aware of Hitler and the rise of the Nazi Party in Germany, and noticed German refugees appearing in Brussels in the late 1930s. By the age of fifteen, he had 'discovered'[3] Karl Marx through reading a copy of the *Communist Manifesto*, lent to him by a close friend Maurice Tran (who would later be executed at Auschwitz for distributing Trotskyist propaganda).

On 10 May 1940, Nazi Germany launched its attack on Belgium. Sam and Renée gathered together their belongings and their two children and set out to try and catch a train to unoccupied Paris, but they were too late. Returning to their Brussels apartment, Ralph switched on the radio to discover that the Belgian army, on the verge of defeat at the hands of the invading Germans, had begun conscripting teenage boys – he was sixteen – to fight, and die. A stubborn Ralph insisted that he be allowed to try and walk to France; his panicked parents agreed that he should go but with Sam accompanying him while Renée remained behind in Brussels with 12-year-old Nan. Once they had left the city, on 16 May, Sam changed the plan and decided the two of them should head for England and not France, overruling Ralph's protestations. They walked more than sixty miles to the port of Ostend, on the Flemish coast, where Sam managed to get them onto the last boat leaving for England. The pair landed in Dover on 19 May, as penniless refugees.

Father and son arrived in a nation at war with Hitler; it was here that the young Adolfe changed his unintentionally provocative name to Ralph on the advice of a friendly landlady. Sam and Ralph got paid jobs helping to remove furniture from bombed out houses in the Chiswick area of west London. It was to be Ralph's first experience of the English class system. He later wrote that he 'found out about middle-class meanness and snobbery, and kindness; and I found out about the curious combination of kindness, cunning, ignorance, feigned servility and subordination, actual contempt which this particular part of the unskilled worker class had for their masters'[4]. But he also found the depressing work that he did to be an 'arduous business', seeing himself, instead, as a 'budding "intellectual"'[5]. In 1941 he applied to study at the London

School of Economics, where he fell under the spell of the socialist academic and Labour Party intellectual, Harold Laski; by 1943, the professor was describing his student as 'a grand lad – one of the best I have had in years'[6].

Laski was like a father figure to him. 'His lectures taught more, much more than political science,' Ralph wrote in a tribute to Laski, after the latter's death in 1950. 'They taught a faith that ideas mattered, that knowledge was important and its pursuit exciting...' In years to come, these were lessons that the elder Miliband would impart to his two young sons.

Infuriated both by class inequality and the rise of Nazism and fascism, the ideas that mattered to Ralph were Karl Marx's. In the hot summer of 1940, aged sixteen, and only a few months after he arrived in London, Ralph had made a 'private pilgrimage' to Marx's grave in Highgate Cemetery where he says he stood 'in front of t he grave, fist clenched, swearing my own private oath that I would be faithful to the workers' cause. I do not recall the exact formula-tion, but I have no doubt of the gist of it; and that I thought of myself as a revolutionary socialist or communist...'[7]

But Ralph's Marxism didn't, in fact, spill into Communism; he never joined the Communist Party of Great Britain and was a ferocious critic of the Soviet Union. Nor was he a Leninist, as he never accepted Lenin's claim that violent revolution was legitimate – or, for that matter, inevitable.

But he reserved his hatred for fascism. With his mother and sister still living under German occupation, Ralph was keen to enlist and fight the Nazis. In 1943, with Laski's help, he was allowed to join the Royal Navy. Ralph stood out from his fellow sailors – he was 'generally the only Jew and certainly the only stateless, Belgian-born, French-speaking LSE student among the enlisted men, and the only one trying to set aside time to read Marx's *Das Kapital*. Over the course of the next three years, Ralph was involved in the D-Day landings and the fighting to recapture Crete, and was on board one of the first ships to enter the port of Athens after its liberation in October 1944.

Throughout the war, Ralph spent much time wondering whether he would see his mother and sister again. Renée and Nan, trapped in Brussels under Nazi rule, had been forced to wear the yellow star and subjected to a battery of restrictions and indignities;

nonetheless, Renée would set out each morning to sell her hats in defiance of the daily curfew. Then, in 1942, mother and daughter narrowly escaped deportation to the labour camps by fleeing to a village near Mons, in the south of the country, where Renée had forged a close friendship with the Catholic farmers Maurice and Louisa Vos several years earlier. Mother and daughter hid on the Vos farm for the rest of the occupation. As Ed would later remark: 'Month after month, year upon year, they lived in fear of the knock at the door.'[8]

In total, seventeen members of the Milibands' extended family sought refuge in the village, which had become a resistance stronghold, and survived the war. But another sixty or so members of the family and close friends of Ralph were not so lucky in evading the Nazis and were killed in the Holocaust.

Once the war was over, Ralph set about trying to reunite his family in London. His own application for British citizenship, based on his naval record and support from Laski and the LSE, was granted in 1948. But Sam had been refused permission to stay on in the UK and had returned to his wife and daughter in Belgium in 1946, from where he applied nine times, between 1948 and 1954, to be made a British citizen or have a six-month visa extended. Sam said he faced 'Nazi' style anti-Semitism in Belgium, a claim dismissed by UK officials as 'very thin'. A hand-written Home Office report from 8 March 1949, obtained by *The Times* in 2008, cast doubt on Sam's (and Ralph's) honesty: 'Miliband, father and son, have so misrepresented the case in the past, I am afraid we can place no reliance on their statements.'

In the end, Laski intervened on Ralph's behalf with the Labour Home Secretary James Chuter Ede, and asked him 'as one socialist to another' to grant Sam residency to show the world that the UK had more compassion than the Soviet Union. Sam's application to stay was accepted in 1953 and he, Renée and Nan were able to naturalise the following year.

Meanwhile, Ralph had returned to the LSE where Laski helped him to secure an assistant lectureship in political science in 1949. He became a popular figure in the university, and has been described by former students as 'inspirational' and 'wonderful'.[9] He was a brilliant orator, despite speaking with a slight French accent that he never lost. In the words of his biographer Michael

Newman, 'His looks, his voice, his intelligence, and his vivacity combined to make him a magnetic personality.'[10]

Ralph's students adored him, crowding into the lecture hall to listen to him speak with wit, energy, insight and passion – and often without any notes at all. Like his mentor Laski, his friend and former student Leo Panitch has written, 'Ralph was, in fact, always exceedingly proud of his "Beruf", his vocation, as teacher'[11].

It is no surprise then that many of his closest friends and admirers were former students – including the woman that he married. In September 1961, a month before the publication of his most famous book, *Parliamentary Socialism*, Ralph married Marion Kozak, who he had met at the LSE in the mid-1950s when she took one of his courses. Marion was twenty-six, eleven years his junior, 'with questioning eyes and disobedient hair'[12].

Born in Poland in December 1934 to a prosperous Jewish family in the south of the country, she was originally named Dobra (Yiddish for Deborah), only becoming Marion upon her arrival in the UK. The elder of two daughters, her prosperous and settled family's life in Czestochowa in southern Poland was turned upside down with the arrival of the Nazis: she was able to escape in 1942, with her mother Bronislawa and younger sister Hadassa, 'sheltering in a convent and then with a Catholic family that took her in'[13]. Meanwhile, her paternal grandparents were shot by German troops and her father David Kozak, who stayed back to be with them, is believed to have later died in Auschwitz.[14]

Marion Kozak arrived on British shores in 1947, unable to speak English and with very little formal schooling, having been sent by a Jewish charitable organisation that was ferrying children out of Poland. Exceptionally bright and hard-working, however, she managed to gain entrance to university at the normal age, attending classes at the LSE where she would later meet Ralph.

The two secular Jewish exiles from Eastern Europe, passionate, intelligent and left-wing, complemented one another. Marion, in fact, would become a thinker and academic in her own right. As Newman notes, 'She was the more spontaneous, outgoing and hospitable while he was rather "private", despite his ability as an orator and conversationalist. He was the more theoretical, but she was a formidable critic of his work and had also commented on *Parliamentary Socialism* before it was published.'[15]

Parliamentary Socialism: a Study in the Politics of Labour was Ralph's first book and was published in 1961. It put him on the map and made him a major figure on the British left. In the previous years, and under Laski's influence, Ralph had been drawn towards the Labour Party and, specifically, the Labour left, personified in those days by the figure of Aneurin Bevan. By the early 1950s, he had joined the local Hampstead branch of the party, allied with the 'Bevanites' and even spoke as a delegate at the party conference in 1955, delivering 'an impassioned speech on nationalisation'[16]. But he left the party a few years later, disillusioned with the 'revisionist' direction that Labour was taking under Hugh Gaitskell, never to rejoin. Instead, Ralph became one of the leading British voices of the 'New Left', an intellectual movement consisting of those who had rejected the Labour and Communist parties and were trying to salvage Marxist, socialist tradition from Stalinism and the crimes of the Soviet Union.

Ralph's book, *Parliamentary Socialism*, was a product of his disillusionment: it was a scholarly and polemical case against the Labour Party. Its opening lines sum up the book's thesis:

> Of political parties claiming socialism to be their aim, the Labour Party has always been one of the most dogmatic – not about socialism, but about the parliamentary system. Empirical and flexible about all else, its leaders have always made devotion to that system their fixed point of reference and the conditioning factor of their political behaviour.[17]

Ralph condemned the 'sickness of Labourism', his term for the party's historic and, he believed, self-destructive attachment to the established order and the institutions of the British state – from the first-past-the-post electoral system to the idea that securing a Commons majority was the be-all-and-end-all of left-wing politics. In his friend and former student Hilary Wainwright's words, the book argued 'that the DNA of the British state – its deference to the financial interests of the City and to the primacy of the US in foreign policy – had become part of Labour's DNA, too'.[18]

It soon became 'widely recognised as one of the seminal texts of the British New Left'[19], and was absorbed by academics and activists alike. In the words of the journalist and campaigner Paul Foot, the nephew of Michael Foot:

> I don't suppose any book made more impact on my life than *Parliamentary Socialism*... I read it in 1961 when I was cheerfully contemplating life as a Labour MP. It put me off that plan for ever, by exposing the awful gap between the aspirations and achievements of parliamentary socialists.[20]

Intriguingly, in his first edition in 1961, Ralph acknowledged that he believed there was no real alternative to the Labour Party as a party of 'the working class', and the book even concluded by leaving open the possibility that Labour might yet become a fully socialist party able to implement a truly radical transformation of British society and the state.

Disappointed by what he perceived to be the Wilson government's failures between 1964 and 1970, however, Ralph became even more pessimistic about the prospect of Labour becoming a vehicle for social, and socialistic, change. In the postscript to the second edition of *Parliamentary Socialism*, published in 1972, Miliband called for a new 'alternative' to Labour, which he dismissed as 'a party of modest social reform in a capitalist system within whose confines it is ever more firmly and by now irrevocably rooted'[21].

Nonetheless, and perhaps in a twist of fate, between 1961 and 1972, Ralph had become the father of two boys, both of whose lives would become intertwined with a Labour Party that he had so thoroughly dissected and rejected.

ooooo

Edward Samuel Miliband was born at 2pm on 24 December 1969, in the maternity wing of University College Hospital in Hunter Street, London. The 'Swinging Sixties' – defined, politically, by the Cold War and events like the Cuban Missile Crisis, Vietnam, the Prague Spring and the 1968 student uprisings – were drawing to a close. Harold Wilson had been Prime Minister for five years but, just six months later, his Labour government would be ejected from office in a surprise defeat at the hands of Edward Heath's Conservatives.

Baby Edward weighed 8lbs and was Ralph and Marion's second son; David Wright Miliband (whose middle name was inspired by Ralph's friendship with the late C. Wright Mills, the renowned and radical US sociologist) had been born four years earlier in July 1965. Ralph told a friend that the decision to have a second child was driven by the poignant belief that 'no child should have to carry the burden of taking care of their elderly parents alone'[22]. In his forties when David was born, Ralph had earlier worried that he would not be able to cope with being a father and had told friends that 'neither he nor Marion had been feeling very excited about the prospect of parenthood'[23].

But, according to Ralph's biographer Michael Newman, 'The boys were to become precious to him and many people who found him formidable or daunting in public were amazed to witness his tenderness with his children.'[24]

The sons of middle-class, foreign-born leftists, living in north London, Ed and David referred to their parents by their first names, Ralph and Marion, and continue to do so today. Ed himself was called 'Edward' by the rest of his clan.

The family lived at 29 Edis Street, in Primrose Hill, north London, then a much less desirable area than it is now. Marion had found the house on her own in 1965, just after David's birth, and Ralph put down an offer without even going to see it.

As Newman points out, it was Marion who made the family home an 'open house'[25] where guests from across the world would join them for dinner and debate in their basement and – during crowded parties – on their narrow staircase. And it was she who provided much of the warmth and hospitality; Ralph could often come across as a more austere figure – in public, if not in private.

'It wasn't a cold house,' Ed would later remark. 'It was warm, full of the spirit of argument and conviction… the conviction that people of courage and principle can make a huge difference to their world.'[26]

That Ralph was a renowned and busy intellectual and academic did not stop him bonding with his sons. 'He was a fantastic father,' Ed has said. 'There were some people on the left who said that if it hadn't been for their children they'd have completed a few more books – Ralph was never like that and would never say he was too busy for us.'[27] Theirs was a 'paradoxical' household, says Ed,[28] both normal and unusual at the same time. Despite having little interest in sport or games, Ralph would go to watch David play in goal for his school team in the pouring rain and he would spend hours playing chess and backgammon with Ed.

But he would also include his children in political debate and discussion. The family would listen religiously to BBC Radio 4's *World At One*, with Ralph making pronouncements on whether Harold Wilson could have answered this or that question better or whether Denis Healey had flopped a speech or not. Ralph may have disagreed with the Labour Party and spent much of his life intellectually dissecting the so-called Labourist approach but he was totally immersed in the minutiae of party politics. 'You couldn't not be interested in politics in that household,' says Panitch. 'That's where the boys obviously picked up their interest in Labour.'[29]

Visitors to Edis Street included Joe Slovo, the head of the military wing of the African National Congress, and his wife Ruth First, the anti-apartheid activist and scholar, who had been a student of Ralph's at the LSE. In a speech at the start of his leadership campaign twenty-eight years later, Ed recalled meeting First in 1982, aged twelve, only to be told a few months later that 'she had been assassinated by the South African secret service – blown up by a letter bomb'. Her death affected him deeply. 'Some people will wonder about why I got to care about politics. When something like that happens, what kid wouldn't... It teaches you at the age of twelve that some things you cannot walk away from. It teaches you that political causes matter.'[30]

The Miliband home became one of the best-known and best-attended London meeting places for Marxists, socialists and radicals from around the world. Regular visitors included the cultural critic Raymond Williams, the historian and writer E. P. Thompson, the author and activist Tariq Ali and the doyen of the Labour left, the then MP and ex-Cabinet minister Tony Benn. 'Marion is a very good cook,' says Benn. 'We'd have a lovely meal and then we'd all sit and talk.'[31]

But it wasn't just radicals and revolutionaries who were made to feel welcome at Edis Street: Ralph and Marion entertained people from across the left and centre-left. Clive Jenkins, the 'champagne socialist' trade union leader and friend of the tycoon Robert

Maxwell, was a visitor to the house. So too was Giles Radice, one of the tribunes of Labour's pro-European, centre-right faction. The boys were exposed to a range of arguments and political opinions from a very young age.

'Their shared passion for politics and the unusually equal relationship between parents and children made them an extremely close family,' writes Newman in his biography of Ralph.[32] In fact, Miliband senior would encourage his sons to contribute to the highbrow intellectual and political discussions and question the views and positions of their high-profile guests, often having to jump in to defend young David or Ed's right to speak and participate in the conversations. Ed would later recall: 'Ralph's respect for our point of view was unflinching.'[33]

Some of Ralph's friends remember David being more voluble than Ed, with the youngest Miliband often listening intently to the contributions of his elder brother with his eyes wide open. One says: 'Ed was shyer, less sure of himself, more introspective.'[34] During the Labour leadership campaign, Ed himself encouraged the idea that he was slightly less engaged in the debates and discussions at Edis Street, telling a reporter how he had often alarmed his father by quietly sneaking off to watch *Dallas*, 'my secret vice… I think [Ralph] believed I was planning a future in Big Oil'.[35]

But Leo Panitch, one of Ralph's closest friends and another former student of his, who now teaches political science at York University in Toronto, disagrees: 'I just don't think that's true. I remember both David and Edward, at a remarkably young age, with a good deal of confidence, engaging in discussions.'[36]

'[They were] very, very fresh lively, intelligent… and I must admit Ed amazed me by being able to do the Rubik's Cube … in one minute twenty seconds and, as I recall, just with one hand too,' the socialist historian Robin Blackburn, an ally of Ralph's, has said.[37] 'The boys were treated as adults and equals and with respect from a very young age,' says Richard Kuper, a friend of Ralph and Marion's who is now the chair of Jews for Justice for Palestinians (of which Marion is a member).[38] It meant that both David and Ed matured much faster than other kids their age, and were more disciplined and driven. Ralph and Marion's ages were also a factor, with Ralph having turned forty-six less than a fortnight after Ed was born. 'One of the reasons David and I never rebelled is because we had older parents,' Ed has said, remembering how his friends at secondary school had been shocked to discover that his father was in his sixties. 'I had the oldest parents in the playground.'[39]

In February 1973, when Ed was just three years old, Ralph collapsed after suffering a 'moderately severe'[40] heart attack during a meeting at Leeds University, where he had moved from the LSE to become head of the politics department. Given Ralph and Marion's declining years, Ralph's heart problems and a turbulent family history involving death, dispossession and destruction at the hands of the Nazis, Ed grew up with a sense of his parents' – and, in particular, his father's – frailty and mortality.

Following Ralph's heart attack, Marion and the kids moved north to join him in Yorkshire and give him support. They lived together in a house on Clarence Road, in Horsforth, to the north west of Leeds city centre. Ed attended Featherbank Infants School.

Ralph, meanwhile, had tried to throw himself into his work to take his mind off his newfound fears about his health and his life expectancy, but he found the administrative aspects of being the head of a department 'boring and a waste of time' and missed being in London. It didn't help, either, that he considered Leeds to be an 'absolutely awful' town, with a 'provincial' atmosphere.[41]

In 1977, the Miliband family moved again – this time to the United States, where Ralph had arranged to spend the academic year as a visiting professor at Brandeis University, near Boston. Ralph and Marion rented a house on Franklin Street in Newton, an affluent suburb east of the city, and bought a car – and a cat. David and Edward joined local schools, where they thrived. Indeed, Ed has described his time in America as one of the happiest periods of his life; Ralph, the Marxist theoretician, would often take his two young sons to one of the icons of capitalism, McDonald's, to eat burgers and then on to the local bowling alley – for Ed, it was a 'big treat'.[42]

Ralph decided to stay on in America, part-time, but the following year, Marion and the children returned to the UK and it was not until September 1982 that Ed would return to the US. His mother had become interested in health care and childcare issues and accepted a job with the West Midlands Health Authority which required her to be away from London, and the family home, for several months. David was seventeen and could stay on his own but Ed was just twelve and 'they felt that he needed to be with one of his parents. It was therefore decided that he should go with Ralph'.[43]

Ralph was delighted to have Ed around. He wrote, in a letter to Marion:

> I find myself very gladly in the role of father and mother combined and spend a fair amount of time thinking about what needs to be done, and realise better how much you do and how demanding it is and how much more I should do when I am in London.[44]

Young Ed's presence in Boston boosted Ralph's spirits; he was much more positive about his teaching and his research with Ed around than when he was on his own and prone to occasional depression. Ralph was living in the home of the radical sociologist Kurt H. Wolff in Bennington Street, in Newton, where father and son would enjoy making and then eating spaghetti in cold sauce together.[45]

But Ed returned to London in December 1982 as Ralph began a peripatetic academic career which saw him spend the next decade teaching at Brandeis in Boston, York University in Toronto and the City University in New York. (He would not retire from teaching, and his annual trip across the Atlantic, until May 1993 – a year before his death.)

The absence of Ralph for nine months each year had an effect on a young Ed. 'I think it was hardest for my mum but it was hard for me too,' he admits. As a teenager, it was difficult for Ed to spend three-quarters of the year without his father. With David off at university between 1984 and 1987, Ed became 'the man of the house', supporting and helping his mother. 'My dad being away, and my mum working, made me a more self-sufficient person,' he says now.[46]

Ed is often asked by reporters and interviewers about his relationship with Ralph but some friends of the family have suggested that he had always been closer to his mother than his late father. Marion, a restless, curious, idealistic woman, 'always smiling', has been a huge influence on Ed, say both friends of Marion and friends of Ed.[47]

It is Marion who, after all, helped Ed to connect with the Labour Party that he would go on to lead – she, unlike her husband, had remained a party member. Ralph may have been the inspirational left-wing academic, but Marion was the inspirational left-wing activist. She saw the import and influence of social movements – especially women's groups – early on and threw herself into campaigns, lobbies and direct action. She protested against the wars in Algeria and Vietnam, joined the Campaign for Nuclear Disarmament (CND) and became a member of the anti-war Women in Black group, founded by female Israeli peace activists in Jerusalem in 1988, in the midst of the First Intifada, and with branches around the world. Marion is believed to have participated in the group's protests and vigils outside the offices of the Israeli airline El Al in the late 1980s.[48]

She was also a passionate and devoted supporter of the Miners' Strike, taking David and Ed with her to fundraisers for striking miners. She was in constant touch with Norma Dolby, a key figure in the mining community of Arkwright in Derbyshire, and later went to stay with her and help her publish and publicise her book, *Norma Dolby's Diary: An Account of the Great Miners' Strike*, in 1987.[49] Ed has described the Miners' Strike as one of his 'first political memories'[50] – he was fourteen when it kicked off.

A close family friend recalls: 'Ralph was a princely person, self-confident, sure of himself, with a loud voice. Marion was more impulsive and, over the years, became courageous enough to interrupt or contradict her husband. She was the driving force behind their marriage – much more down-to-earth, much better at connecting with people in an emotional, non-rational way.'[51]

The friend says he believes there is a similar division between the 'princely' and 'confident' David, who takes after their father, and the younger, 'more impulsive' and 'emotional' Ed, who takes after their mother. Ed himself has never hidden the close relationship he has always enjoyed with his mother: 'I know nobody more generous, nobody more kind, nobody more loving... than my Mum.'[52]

Such a distinction has merit but perhaps can be overstated. Overall, the mood in the house was rational and analytical. Take the family's attitude to faith. Ralph had ceased believing in God as a child – perhaps as early as the age of ten – and was an atheist for the rest of his life; so too was Marion. But they were also consciously and culturally Jewish and had been the victims of vicious anti-Semitism in Belgium and Poland, prompting their flight to the UK. It is worth noting that the first political organisation Ralph joined, as a 15-year-old, was the left-wing Zionist group, the Hashomer Hazair. Later in life, he distinguished between a 'low level kind of Jewish identity' – relating to birth, family background and culture – and the idea of a tribal bond 'with Jews as Jews', favouring the former over the latter. He himself never denied being Jewish – a 'non-Jewish Jew' – and liked speaking Yiddish. As Newman points out, 'it was not pure coincidence that Marion and so many of his closest friends, such as Marcel Liebman, Harry Magdoff and later Leo Panitch, were Jewish'.[53]

Despite sharing his parents' atheism, which he says he did not inherit from them, Ed was also aware of his Jewish roots from a very early age. As children, both David and Ed accompanied their mother to Israel to visit their maternal grandmother, Bronislawa, who had settled there. Ed also went to friends' Passover dinners when he lived briefly in America. But there were moments of confusion: when he was seven years old, and a pupil at elementary school in Newton, Massachusetts, Ed was asked by his American teacher if he was an Episcopalian. Hesitating, and unsure of the distinction, he told her that he was, only to return home and recount the incident to Marion who threw her hands up in the air and told him: 'No! We're Jewish.'[54]

Both Miliband brothers would grow up to be proud atheists, with Ed telling a journalist after his victory in the Labour leadership election: 'I don't believe in God personally, but I have great respect for those people who do.'[55] As for his Jewish identity, he has said that he feels Jewish 'because it's an important part of my heritage, but my parents were not religious and neither am I'.[56]

Ed is keen to tell friends and colleagues that his parents never told him what to believe or how to think, but that they did instruct him in the importance of having strong beliefs and thinking critically. This wasn't just a result of passively observing the meetings and discussions with Tariq Ali, Tony Benn and the rest; Ed's whole childhood was one long and intense lesson on the meaning of politics, the left and the Labour Party.

In one particularly revealing letter to Ed in November 1981 on the latest developments affecting the Labour left, Ralph wrote: 'If

anyone else read this and did not know the way we talk, you talk; they would think I was crazy to be writing this to a twelve year old boy: but I know better, and find it very nice.'[57]

When it came to Labour, Ralph was the odd one out in his family. Both David and Ed had joined the party as teenagers and Marion had been a long-standing member of the local Labour Party branch in Camden. Nonetheless, the author of *Parliamentary Socialism* was not averse to delivering leaflets for Labour during election campaigns – perhaps out of solidarity with the Labour left or driven by despair over Margaret Thatcher and the Tories. Aged thirteen, Ed remembers accompanying his father as the latter campaigned for the local Labour Party ahead of the 1983 general election.[58]

The 1980s, in fact, was a decade in which Ralph tried to reengage with the Labour Party through his friendship and collaboration with Tony Benn, who he considered to be 'a great resource for the [Labour] movement'[59] and a potential leader of a left-wing Labour Party open to socialist ideas and thinking. He saw his own role in helping prepare a practical, socialist programme of political and economic policies for the Bennites should they assume control of the Labour Party. He therefore pushed for the creation of the Independent Left Corresponding Society (ILCS) which met on Sunday evenings at Benn's house in Holland Park, and included Wainwright, Blackburn, the *New Left Review* editor, Perry Anderson; the economist Andrew Glyn; and other left-wing Labour MPs, including Jeremy Corbyn. But Bennism would fizzle out in the late 1980s, despite the Chesterfield conferences that Ralph helped to organise in Benn's constituency, and at which he spoke with his customary vigour and passion. Once again, the elder Miliband was left disillusioned by the Labour Party and, in particular, the failure of the Labour left to prevent a right-wing 'modernising drift': 'Miliband the pessimistic analyst proved more astute than Miliband the hopeful activist.'[60]

Ed, as we shall see, would part company from Ralph's Marxist analysis, and his dismissal of the Labour Party, in his teens. But he has never tried to distance himself from the values and principles – chief among them, the pursuit of equality and social justice – that he imbibed around the family dinner table in the basement of 29 Edis Street. Nor, for that matter, did his father (or mother) ever expect their young sons to fall into line, politically, socially or theologically. Asked during the Labour leadership campaign, what role Ralph had played in influencing his political career and his decision to stand, Ed replied: 'I'm doing it because of him but I'm not doing it for him.'[61]

His upbringing was stable and secure, happy and comfortable. But, despite the references to *Dallas*, bowling and backgammon that tend to feature in the various newspaper and magazine descriptions of Ed's childhood, it was far from a 'normal' household. Few party leaders in British political history, Labour or otherwise, were the offspring of Jewish refugees who had fled from the Nazis to resettle in the UK and start a new life in north London; few party leaders grew up in the home of 'the leading Marxist political scientist in the English-speaking world', as one tribute to Ralph described him after his death in 1994.[62] It was a home where the children were exposed at an early age to the value of ideas and the importance of politics as a force for change. When Ed says today he believes politics matters, he means it.

So it is difficult to overstate the importance of his family background when evaluating his life – and his career. As Ed himself confessed in his conference speech in Manchester, upon becoming Labour leader in September 2010, his belief in freedom and opportunity, in standing up to injustice and leaving behind a better world, 'is not something I chose. It's not something I learned from books, even from my Dad's books. It was something I was born into.'[63]

HAVERSTOCK

1981–1989

Haverstock School is situated in the heart of Camden, one of the most exclusive areas in London. A five-minute walk from Camden Market and the Roundhouse theatre, the comprehensive is also a stone's throw from Primrose Hill, the highly desirable – and beautiful – north London area where the Milibands grew up and went to primary school. Yet like all pockets of the capital, the London Borough of Camden is mixed, with a startling combination of rich and poor living side by side.

Though Haverstock School now has the highest Ofsted rating of any state school in the borough, only 38 per cent of its 1,250 pupils gain as many as five GCSEs with a grade C or above. And despite a £21 million refurbishment in 2006 when, under Labour, Haverstock became the first state school to benefit from the private finance initiative (PFI), the current headmaster, John Dowd, admits it is 'struggling to attract middle-class' parents and pupils.[1] The former cramped Victorian buildings have been replaced with modern glass blocks, but the school remains unchanged in its cross-section of pupils from very different social and ethnic backgrounds. In addition to David and Ed Miliband, its alumni include the footballers John Barnes and Joe Cole, the former Labour MP Oona King, the journalist and author Zoë Heller, and most recently the pop stars Fazer and Dappy from N-Dubz.

Nikki Haydon, who was head of English when the Milibands attended the school in the late 1970s and early 1980s, recalls that Haverstock had a large and distinct 'middle-class contingency' – far more so than today – including the children of people working in the media and politics. Haydon, who still works at Haverstock, also confirms that the school was even more multicultural then than it is now.[2] Ed often recalls this diversity with affection, even suggesting that it helped him develop his ability to connect with people of different cultures and persuasions. 'Haverstock was a school with more than sixty nationalities and people from all classes and backgrounds,' he has said. 'It gave me a fantastic education – not just in how to pass exams but also how to mix and make friends with people from all walks of life.' He has also applauded the quality of its teaching, saying, 'I was fortunate to be taught by some inspiring teachers, including in subjects where I was not naturally gifted: how else to explain being able to pass A-level physics, which I certainly wouldn't be able to do now?'[3]

Oona King, the former Labour MP, was in a class two years below David and two years above Ed. She agrees that Ed's ability to communicate with people owes much to Haverstock: 'If you were middle class, you had to learn pretty quickly how to be at ease with a wide range of people, because you wouldn't last very long otherwise.'[4] As Heller, a contemporary of David Miliband, has said: 'People who have been through the system know a bit more about the society they live in than those who have not.'[5]

Both brothers enjoyed their time at the school. David Miliband attended the school from 1978 to 1983, upon the family's return from Leeds, and obviously felt as indebted towards it as Ed. In January 2011, in one of his first announcements about his future, after losing the Labour leadership contest, David said that he would be returning to Haverstock to teach politics for a few hours each week.

Vivian Jacobs, who taught a number of subjects at the school when the Milibands were there, remembers them as 'lovely boys, great boys' and was aware of who their father was.[6]

Just as it struck their teachers at the time that the boys stood out as special, so it struck those who knew them later in life that they had been 'very well brought up by their parents', in the words of Andrew Turnbull, former head of the civil service and Cabinet Secretary between 2002 and 2006.[7] But were differences between the two brothers apparent even then? At least one teacher has commented that Ed was 'more outgoing'[8]. Both, however, appear to have been considered 'geeks'. Oscar Gregan, who taught mathematics at Haverstock, has said: 'When I joined in 1979 I remember meeting this tiny little kid called David. I heard his surname and I wondered if he had anything to do with the famous Ralph Miliband. I had met Ralph and his wife ... and realised I was teaching their sons. David was not a natural, geeky mathematician – Ed was more like that – but he was a lively, active student who developed a good mastery of maths. He was articulate and had a strong presence. He showed brilliant attention to detail, and a great sense of tenacity.' Haydon has joked about one claim put about by friends of Zoë Heller. 'I wasn't the teacher who wrote on one of David's essays, "Very good, but if you want to see how it should be done, take a look at Zoë's,"' she has said. 'I remember them as really nice kids… I guess David was the more bookish and Ed the more outgoing.'[9]

Others also remember David as the more studious of the two, and Jacobs, who kept in touch with him, recalls visiting David at Corpus Christi a few years later and finding him hard at work in his 'freezing cold' room with the window wide open and papers everywhere.[10]

The age gap – of four and a half years – meant that the two brothers, as children and teenagers, did not spend much time together at school or at home. 'I definitely looked up to him,' says Ed now, 'but he had different friends from me.'[11]

Though Ed admits to not thriving at physical education, he had already developed a strong interest in sport. Ed recalls arguing with his father over whether or not he could watch the world snooker final rather than do his art homework, and remembers going to watch Geoff Boycott play in his last innings at the Lords after completing his final O-level exam. At home, Ed loved playing computer games like Manic Miner, on his ZX81 home computer, when he was not studying.[12]

According to Rik Henderson, a fellow student: 'Ed used to hang around with a group of kids who were not the hardest kids but not the softest either. He used to make people laugh and kept out of trouble. He was sensible and while everyone was messing about at the back of class he used to sit at the front and listen to the teacher.'[13]

Another contemporary, Andy Adebowale, has said: 'Ed used to hang around with the geek crowd.' But he added: 'I remember David was not meek. He was quite a strong personality and Ed was the same. They could use their language skills as a shield against the bullies. It was the kids who were isolated who got bullied.'[14]

Says King: 'You needed a strong personality to thrive. I got beaten up by one girl for not saying "Please". That's what the playground was like: fight, fight, fight.' King says she 'laughs almost hysterically' when she hears the school being dubbed 'Labour's Eton', as it has been in the press. She describes it as a 'rough' school, emphasising that a large proportion of the children were from deprived backgrounds or broken homes, and revealing that one of her contemporaries was later jailed for murder.[15]

Whether the school can really be labelled 'rough' by the standards of London state schools, however, is debatable and contested by those who worked there. Ed Miliband himself has described it as 'tough' and has admitted to the occasional fight in the playground. One was described by a contemporary of Ed called Kevin Mustafa who, in a colourful account in the *Mail on Sunday* in February 2011, claimed that the future Labour leader had called him a 'Turkish bastard'. He has said that, 'School was about looking after yourself despite being weedy. You would have to take care not to get beaten up in the classroom.'

In the same *Mail on Sunday* report, contemporaries of Ed backed the idea of Haverstock as a tough school. Socratis Socratous, who studied A-level maths with Ed in the sixth form, said: 'Everybody would have been hit at school at some point. I used to have to walk around with my dinner money in my socks.' But he added: 'Both Ed and David were genuinely really good guys and were ultra-intelligent. If it were not for Ed I would not have passed my maths A-level. The teacher was crap. Ed used to give me his homework. From copying his homework I learned the process and passed my exams.'[16] Ed himself remembers enjoying maths, and still speaks highly of his maths teacher at the time, Steve Carlsson.[17]

Haydon insists that while there was some feuding between local comprehensive schools, Haverstock was relatively tame. 'We have always been concerned about making sure the students are safe. I would never say the school was an unsafe place. I wouldn't say it was ever any worse than other local schools.' She adds that, for middle-class parents in Islington, Haverstock was 'certainly the school that parents wanted to send their kids to'.[18] And – crucially – it was the school and not just the middle-class nature of pupils like the Miliband boys that aided their subsequent aspirations. 'We had some amazing teachers,' says King. 'And the school definitely contributed to our success.'[19]

As King explains, there were important lessons to be drawn over the decisively mixed make-up of the school. 'There were a lot of people from extremely deprived backgrounds that were at Haverstock. And I think to an extent it affected all of us who went there, the same in some ways for those of us who were on the left, we got to know these kids pretty well and it was clear those who were very intelligent. But no matter how intelligent they were, they didn't have a prayer of getting further than Budgens checkout.' Indeed, King goes even further, crediting the school with creating MPs out of herself, and Ed Miliband.

> I think Ed could see that Haverstock had virtues and he will probably know, like me, that the only reason we could become MPs and represent the constituencies that we, in my case did and in his case does, is because we went to Haverstock. I couldn't possibly have known how to interact with white, working class East-enders from Bethnal Green if I hadn't gone to Haverstock. There's just no way I could've done that and I know that Ed recognises that having gone to Haverstock gave us the necessary life skills along with an adequate level of academic achievement.[20]

The current headmaster, Dowd, says that aspiration is crucial to Haverstock's ethos. 'The key message we want to get across to our students is that they can achieve,' he has said:

> Nothing need be out of reach if you are prepared to work hard. And yes, it is harder to persuade pupils they can make a career in politics in a school where there are fewer middle-class children with parents encouraging them in that direction. But it is possible. One of our recent old boys is now a paid worker for the Labour Party in the south west. What makes all the difference is people such as Ed, David and Oona coming back here to engage with the students and to show them politics does make a difference.[21]

Overall, Ed was clearly at ease in the school, albeit happiest among the 'middle-class contingent'. He may have been bullied, as he confessed to a Treasury colleague two decades later but he certainly did not retreat into introspection. Indeed, Ed found time outside the classroom to make his debut in the media. As a teenager he appeared every fortnight for about three years as an unpaid 'Three O'Clock Reviewer' on LBC radio's *Young London* programme. Aired on Sunday afternoons, the programme discussed music, films and plays. The show's presenter, Clive Bull, remembers that Ed was 'really good at it, because normally teenagers have nothing to say. He was a dream, in that sense. He was up for it and always had something to say'. Not all the subject areas came naturally to young Ed, however. 'I think he was less able to comment on the new releases,' remembers Bull. 'But the truth is that none of the kids had something to say about the new releases – what can you say unless you're a real music fan? The bigger thing we talked about is what they went out to see. A film with a thought-provoking scene or a play at the National.' In style, Bull describes Ed as 'a radio producer's dream': calm and friendly. 'With a microphone on, he was definitely able to talk and very opinionated.'

Clearly, Ralph and Marion approved. 'I remember ringing him up during the week we were producing the programme and his parents would answer the phone and they were quite up for it. We had to ask his parents each time.' Bull does concede that 'people might have thought he was a little bit geeky at the time'.[22] It is a view reinforced by journalist Vincent Graff, who was a fellow reviewer. He recalls that Ed was 'very nasal, very serious, very focused, quite humourless and quite dull... There was never any laughter in the green room; it was almost like he was doing a job.'[23] Later, however, Ed would laughingly tell friends at Oxford that he could scarcely believe he had done the show, because 'I know nothing about music'.[24]

Instead, Ed Miliband may have been more at home working for Tony Benn, which Benn's friend Ralph arranged for him to do in the summer of 1985, just after completing his O-levels at Haverstock. 'Very helpful,' wrote Benn in his diaries. 'He has just taken his O-levels and is at a loose end.'[25]

Benn, a hero-figure on the left, took a number of young people under his wing. His interns were charmingly nicknamed 'The teabags', which stood for The Eminent Association of Benn Archive Graduates. The keen students – including Simon Fletcher, later Ken Livingstone's right-hand man, and Andrew Hood, who would go on to work for Robin Cook – formed a club, with its own headed note paper. Their task was to help at the Benn home in Holland Park, sorting through the vast collection of cuttings and archives that would make up the famous Benn diaries. Today, Benn remembers the boy Ed Miliband as down-to-earth, 'not at all grandiose' and not opposed to performing menial tasks. 'I just remember I liked the lad. He was very helpful, thoughtful, decent and I just liked him.'[26]

His assistant Ruth Winstone remembers how modest the young Ed was. He received his O-level grades while working for Benn in his basement office but wouldn't tell him or Winstone what grades he had received. 'I said to him, "I bet you got all A grades," and he smiled. So he obviously did.'[27]

Ed got eight A grades at O-level and two As and two Bs at A-level (beating David's three Bs and a D). At the end of his Haverstock years, Ed Miliband had experienced a fine education in a mixed school with students from different socio-economic and ethnic groups, and tasted politics as well as the media. By the time Ed was ready to follow in his brother's footsteps not just to the same university – Oxford – but even to the same college – Corpus Christi – he had developed two crucial skills that he would depend upon in later life: how to relate to and communicate with people from different backgrounds.

ooooo

Ed didn't go straight from Haverstock to university – he took a gap year and headed for the United States.

Between September 1988 and September 1989, Ed and his mother Marion joined his father in New York, where Ralph had moved in order to take up a new teaching post at City University (CUNY). David was in Boston, doing a postgraduate degree at the Massachusetts Institute of Technology.

The family lived on the Upper West Side of Manhattan and Ed secured an internship at the *The MacNeil-Lehrer Newshour*, the award-winning nightly newscast on the US public broadcasting television network, PBS. On his haphazard first day at PBS, Ed remembers being put in charge of the switchboard. 'I was sure I was going to be sacked: I was manning the phones but I kept cutting everyone off. By the end of the day, and with just half an hour until the show was on air, people were having to walk across the hall to talk to each other because there was this guy with a funny English accent on the phone who was cutting everybody off as he tried to put them through to each other.'[28]

His next New York internship was with the *Nation*, the oldest continuously published weekly magazine in the United States and the self-proclaimed 'flagship of the left'. Ed was paid $50 a week and, like the rest of the interns, helped fact-check the columns and features in the magazine each week. He worked closely with Andrew Kopkind, the renowned and radical journalist and commentator and a former student of Ralph's at the LSE, who would invite the young student interns from the *Nation* to his ninety-acre farm in southern Vermont 'for a weekend of planting, eating, and intense political discussion'.

'My recollection of Miliband is of a dark, intense young man of obvious intelligence who wore lightly whatever baggage came with being the son of a famous man,' wrote Don Guttenplan, who is now the *Nation*'s London bureau chief, in 2007, and first came across Ed at Kopkind's kitchen table in 1989.[29]

Guttenplan and his *Nation* colleagues remember Ed – or 'Eddie'[30] as they knew him – fondly. He was friendly, hard-working, and precocious. As the *Nation*'s copy editor Judith Long would later recall: 'Eddie charmed everyone in the office with his English manners, his modest mien and his boyish pink cheeks.'[31]

For Ed, aged just nineteen, living and working in New York was an eye-opening experience. 'It seemed like the centre of the world,' he later told a friend.[32] The ongoing battles for the soul of the Labour Party back in Britain suddenly seemed so parochial. The teenager threw himself into the various discussions dominating the *Nation*'s office – about the Soviet war in Afghanistan, the Contra rebels in Nicaragua and George Bush Senior's election as President (in November 1988).

By the time Ed returned to the UK in the autumn of 1989, his experiences richer and more rounded than many of his contemporaries, he was ready to make the most of the challenge of Oxford.

OXFORD

1989–1992

Founded in 1517, Corpus Christi is one of the smallest of Oxford University's thirty-eight constituent colleges. Tucked away on a side street near the city centre, between Merton and Oriel, it has around 200 undergraduates and 100 graduate students.

In the autumn of 1989, when Ed Miliband arrived at the college as an undergraduate, fresh from his gap year in the United States, its alumni included Isaiah Berlin, John Ruskin, C. P. Scott – and David Miliband.

David had graduated from Corpus Christi in the summer of 1987 with a first-class degree in Politics, Philosophy and Economics (PPE); Ed arrived to read the same degree at the same college just two years after the departure of his big brother. He would later confess to friends that it was indeed strange that he ended up at the same college as David, doing the same course.

On the first day of Michaelmas term, in October 1989, the younger Miliband bumped into Marc Stears in the college quad. 'We became friends straight away,' says Stears, a fellow PPE fresher and Labour Party supporter. 'He was very friendly and very serious at the same time; he was the same then as he is now. He could relax and talk to anyone.'

Inside the small college, Ed soon became part of a small, tight-knit group of friends who he had met for the first time. 'There was a group of us who were on the left, who wanted to do politics from day one,' says Stears, who now teaches politics at University College, Oxford. 'So we'd get together, do academic stuff and political stuff.'[1]

Another member of the group was Gautam Mody, a PPE student from India, three years Ed's senior, who now serves as secretary of the Delhi-based New Trade Union Initiative. 'He came as a breath of fresh air,' recalls Mody. Other first-year undergraduates at Corpus Christi had expressed surprise upon meeting the Indian student, three years their senior, and hearing him speak with his flawless Queen's English; in contrast, Ed's first question to Mody concerned 'the state of the Indian left'.[2]

Shortly after arriving in Oxford, Ed – known by his family and friends up to this point as 'Edward' – became 'Ted'. His contemporaries differ as to how and when this transformation occurred. Some point the finger at a fellow PPE student named Simon Stow, now a professor of government in the United States.

'It was Simon's thing to start calling him "Ted", because Ed was a kind of old fogey even then in a kind of amusing way, and he seemed to quite enjoy that. So everyone called him Ted and he called himself Ted,' says Catherine O'Rawe, who arrived at Corpus Christi from Belfast to study English and Modern Languages, and quickly befriended both Ed and Stow. (O'Rawe now teaches Italian at Bristol University and says she hasn't spoken to the Labour leader 'for a couple of years').[3] Says Mody: 'Simon was loud and brash and started calling him "Teddy".'[4]

Not everyone, however, agrees with this version of events. Stears says it was their philosophy tutor, Jennifer Hornsby, who mistakenly referred to Ed as 'Ted' in her very first class and the rest of his peers then 'just assumed that was his name.'[5] Ed, it seems, never corrected them.

ooooo

The reason that both Miliband brothers had decided to read PPE at Corpus Christi could be summed up in two words: Andrew Glyn. Glyn, an economist and member of Tony Benn and Ralph Miliband's Independent Left Corresponding Society and his wife Wendy Carlin, an economist at UCL, were friends of the Miliband family and had known David and Ed since they were children.

Glyn – who died in December 2007 – had been teaching economics at Corpus Christi since 1969; he was a left-wing scholar of global repute. A fellow tutor remembers him as a 'force of nature'[6]: he was friendly but intellectually intimidating; serious as well as charismatic.

In those days, according to Mody, if a student went to Corpus Christi to read PPE 'it was normally because of Andrew Glyn'.[7] More than two decades on, it is difficult to overstate Glyn's importance to the college and its students. 'Andrew was a giant – a real presence in such a small college,' says Stears. 'He was a fiery leftie and an inspiration to us all. He showed us that you could be in the heart of academe, teaching in Oxford University, but also be a fiery, passionate socialist.'[8]

In a college known for its left-wing politics, Glyn was the most renowned and respected of left-wing tutors. He was popular with the student population of Corpus Christi, and was often seen waving at undergraduates across the college's quad, smiling, laughing, stopping to chat with his charges, treating them as his equals – not the behaviour of your average Oxford University don.

'He wrote about left-wing politics and economics in a way which fed through into the student scene in Corpus,' says the political philosopher Adam Swift, who teaches at Balliol College, Oxford, and also taught Ed Miliband.[9]

'Generations of Oxford students have reason to be grateful for the combination of integrity, patience, open-mindedness and sense of fun that characterised Andrew Glyn,' Ed wrote in the wake of Glyn's death in December 2007. 'After college, he became a friend to me, as he did to many of his ex-students.'[10]

But Glyn became more than just a friend to Ed; he was a mentor, an adviser, a confidant. Stears argues that it would be difficult to exaggerate the impact that Glyn had on Ed's life:

'Andrew underscored and re-emphasised what Ed had got from his dad: intellectual seriousness. Much more important than the content of his classes was his style, his approach: that ideas are important and that controversial ideas that aren't in the mainstream are worth sticking with and investigating.'[11]

Glyn taught the classical economics course for first-year PPE students – Adam Smith, Karl Marx, David Ricardo and the rest. Stears and Ed had their economics tutorials together under Glyn, before Stears – taking advantage of the option available to Oxford undergraduates to make their PPE degrees bipartite, rather than tripartite – dropped economics at the end of the first year, to focus on politics and philosophy instead. Ed, however, dropped philosophy – he found it 'difficult'[12] says a friend – and stuck with economics, which he considered to be more serious and rigorous and for which he had a greater aptitude. Says Stears: 'Ed's economic thinking will have evolved over the past twenty years but his overall approach is something he picked up from Andrew at Corpus.'[13]

A former Marxist, Glyn's politics were to the left of Kinnock's Labour, but they were not of the Militant or Bennite variety. Formed in the Keynesian tradition, but much more sceptical of the emerging neoliberal order in the 1990s than most of his soft-Keynesian peers at Oxford, Glyn published his last book, *Capitalism Unleashed*, in 2006 – a socialist critique of the injustices and instability of market fundamentalism, in which he posed the question: 'Will the ever more complex financial system implode in a major financial crisis and bring prolonged recession?' (A year later he was dead; two years later his question was answered.)

'He was a major figure for us all,' remembers Stears. 'We all wanted to emulate Andrew's manner, his way of interacting with the world.'[14] Ed, in particular, was in awe of him. A friend recalls, on one occasion, seeing Ed emerge from a tutorial with Glyn, only to turn to Stears, and say: 'Oh my God, I can't believe I said that in front of him.'[15]

ooooo

'You are behaving like a student politician and frankly that's all you'll ever be,' said David Cameron, who read PPE at Brasenose College, Oxford, between 1985 and 1988, at Prime Minister's Questions in December 2010. But the Leader of the Opposition, on the receiving end of the premier's barbed comments, wasn't having any of it.

'I was a student politician,' Ed hit back, to jeers from the Tory backbenches. 'But I was not hanging around with people who were throwing bread rolls and wrecking restaurants.'[16]

Cameron joined the notorious Bullingdon Club during his Oxford days; Ed joined the Labour Club. It was the political scene which interested him at university, not the social scene. Ralph and Marion's son had been schooled from an early age to recognise the importance of politics; in Ed's 19-year-old mind, politics was about issues and ideas, not a game, hobby or pastime for bored students.

Despite the polarised state of national politics in the late 1980s, and the hatred of Margaret Thatcher's Conservative government among the nation's undergraduates, Ed discovered that the Oxford

University Labour Club (OULC) was in a pretty poor state upon his arrival in Oxford in 1989.

He and Stears joined the OULC in the first term of their first year and theirs was a remarkably rapid rise to the top. Stears was chair by the second term and Ed by the third term. (Again, he was following, consciously or unconsciously, in David's footsteps: his elder brother had been active in the Labour Club, becoming secretary during his undergraduate days at Oxford.)

For Ed, chairing the club offered an opportunity to foster intellectual debate and serious discussions among young Labour students in one of the country's most prestigious universities. He used his father's contact book to boost the quality of guest speakers – Stears remembers Ed organising an OULC event with Tony Benn that drew a crowd of more than 300 people: 'most meetings until then had had around ten or twelve people'[17].

These were tumultuous political times. 'The world was undergoing significant change,' recalls Mody. 'By the time we broke for Christmas, at the end of our first term, the Berlin Wall had collapsed. Those were phenomenal days.'[18] Ed, Stears, Stow, Mody and the rest of the group were keen to keep up-to-date with current affairs; his friends would come to his room to listen to *World at One* on Radio 4. Childhood habits die hard.

Like Ralph, Ed was a critic of Communism, from the perspective of a democratic socialist, and welcomed the fall of Soviet satellites across Eastern Europe. His more left-wing and radically-inclined peers were surprised. 'I came from a political tradition which was supportive of regimes in that part of the world and found the collapse of the Soviet bloc a struggle to deal with,' says Mody, 'but Ed was extremely persuasive about the need for liberty and social and economic rights in those countries.'[19]

The future Labour leader used his leadership of the Labour Club at Oxford in 1990 to prompt debates and discussions on individual liberty and the failure of illiberal, statist socialists across Eastern Europe. The Trotskyists, small in number but vocal and impassioned, were none too pleased. Meanwhile, other more mainstream Kinnockite members of the OULC complained that there were too many 'intellectual conversations' and too few 'practical campaigns' during Ed's period as chair.[20]

But that was all about to change.

ooooo

In the second term of his second year, Ed was elected president of Corpus Christi's Junior Common Room (JCR) – having run unopposed. (In most Oxford colleges, the JCR exists to provide representation for undergraduates in the organisational structures of the colleges and to oversee the provision of accommodation and other services.)

Here too, however, his brother David had 'done it first'. 'David had been a success as JCR president,' recalls Stears. 'There was still a "David aura" in the air.'[21]

Friends have remembered the way in which the elder Miliband had composed essays in the college bar, holding a Mars bar and a pint of orange juice. He was hugely popular in Corpus and, as JCR president, led an anti-apartheid campaign against the South African regime, winning the admiration of his peers and the respect of his tutors.[22]

Could Ed have a similar impact on Corpus, as JCR president? This was a period of increasing 'marketisation' in British higher education. In 1988, Margaret Thatcher's notorious white paper on education, written by Kenneth Baker, declared that the policy of the Conservative government was to 'bring higher education institutions closer to the world of business'.[23]

Oxford University was not immune to the financial and market pressures; colleges responded to cuts in budgets by letting out their rooms to private firms for meetings and conferences and, controversially, raising rents for undergraduates. 'They were small things that led to big changes in our lives,' says Stears. 'You could be thrown out of your room as soon as term finished just so that they could let it out to private companies.'[24]

The tension between undergraduates and university authorities was marked and growing – and the key issue for student politicians was to protect student interests from the fallout from marketisation: above all else, rent rises.

Ed's predecessor as JCR president of Corpus Christi College was Godfrey Binaisa, a PPE student in the year above him and the son of a Ugandan exile. 'Godfrey had been very left-wing but a little bit too loony for mainstream student opinion,' says a former

Corpus undergraduate. 'Ed was the sensible face of student Labour and of socialist politics. His platform was to carry on what Godfrey was doing but do it more moderately, calmly and intelligently.'[25]

Ed enjoyed doing so. It was as JCR president that he first discovered a zeal – and a knack – for campaigning that would serve him in good stead later in his political career. 'My best four weeks at university were when we had a rent dispute with the college,' he told a newspaper interviewer in 2008. 'I wasn't particularly bookish; what really got me going was student activism, and mobilising people.'[26]

The opportunity to mobilise came early on in his presidential term. Having initially been distracted by events in the Middle East – Saddam Hussein invaded Kuwait in August 1990 – Ed turned his attention to the key issue on the minds of Corpus's students: the cost of living. The college authorities had announced a near 40 per cent increase in rent for undergraduates living in Corpus's halls of residence, provoking fury and outrage among students.

'When the offer of a 39 per cent rent increase was announced … many thought simply that a decimal point had gone astray, and when it was confirmed that the proposal was 'for real' there was disbelief, and anger,' Ed later wrote in the Corpus Christi student newsletter, *The Pelican Record*.[27]

As JCR president, Ed drew up plans for a campaign of resistance and opposition to the rent rise – but not a 'strike', as it has since been misreported in the media. Stears describes Ed's campaign against the rent rise as 'an insurgency; we used guerrilla tactics'.[28] It wouldn't be the last time that Ed Miliband would be described as an insurgent.

The campaign was intense – 'absolutely relentless' in the words of Stears – and took place over six weeks – a substantial amount of time given the fact that Oxford University students have eight-week terms. Ed, with Stears's help, spent 'all day, all night' planning and campaigning; they would stay up until 5am in the college computer room writing their literature and designing their posters and flyers.[29]

Ed took the campaign very seriously. He had two tasks – to get the college's students on side and keep them on side, and to have a serious conversation with the college authorities.

He also proved to be the master choreographer and strategist, sitting in long and exhausting meetings with Stears and others to decide the step-by-step process by which the campaign would unfold over the six-week period. He organised protests and persuaded TV cameras from ITV Central News to come and cover them – on one occasion, the protesters happened to be heckling the President of Corpus Christi, Sir Keith Thomas, as he arrived at the college. 'Thomas was really pissed off,' says a friend of Ed's.[30] On another occasion, Ed organised for a reporter from ITV Central News to ring up Sir Keith Thomas for a comment on the campaign – in the middle of a meeting that he himself happened to be having with the college President! (Thomas refused to talk to us for this book – a fellow tutor of his at Oxford University suggests it is because he still feels 'humiliated' at how Ed 'got the better of him' over the rent-rise campaign.[31])

Contemporaries cite two other landmark events in the rent-rise campaign – again, both involving the President of Corpus Christi and both of an 'insurgency' nature. The first was the 'silent handclap' delivered to Thomas one morning as he walked from his home, diagonally opposite the college, on Merton Street, to his office inside the college. The entire student body quietly lined up from one end of the street to the other end of the college to clap him as he walked to work.

The second was the boycott of 'formal hall' – the traditional evening meal held at Oxford colleges at which students dress in formal attire, and often gowns, to dine with the tutors. 'I remember it being funny because we all pretended that we were going, and we got dressed up and stood out in the quad,' says O'Rawe. 'I remember we all had to mill about for ages, as if we were all about go into the hall for dinner, but when the bell rang for dinner, we all just vanished.'[32]

Mody agrees that it was a 'masterstroke' by Ed, who had persuaded the overwhelming majority of Corpus students to put their names down for formal hall that night. 'People turned out, including the toffs, dressed in suits and ties and gowns, ready to go to dinner but didn't go to dinner. And the President [Keith Thomas] had to lead his colleagues and guests into an empty hall for the evening meal.'[33]

When the Head Butler of Corpus Christi arrived in the quad to ask what had happened, he was told politely by the JCR president that the students were boycotting formal hall over the rent rise. It was another humiliation for the college authorities. Twenty-one-year-old Ed seemed to have perfected the art of guerrilla warfare.

Yet despite his undoubted irritation and frustration, the college President still viewed Ed as a student politician that he could do business with and engage in constructive dialogue. 'The rest of us were too extreme,' says O'Rawe.[34] Stears remembers how his friend left 'the door open to the university elite, heads of the college and dons, and they would be perfectly happy chatting away with Ed. He could also get down and dirty and make people's lives hell. He could walk between the two worlds of radicalism and real world.'[35]

Ed even managed to recruit the support of Bernard Williams, the legendary moral philosopher, who was then teaching at Corpus Christi and agreed to act as a liaison between students and the college authorities. Andrew Glyn, however, was sceptical of his protégé's guerrilla campaign: 'His attitude was "Come on guys, this isn't the class struggle, this isn't the biggest issue that you need to be caring about. Invest your energy somewhere else,"' says a friend of Ed's from Corpus. 'I don't think Andrew realised that it was a kind of training in politics as much as anything for Ed and for the rest of us, and that we were learning about politics as we went along. Andrew just saw it is a bit of a distraction.'[36]

But it was as JCR president that Ed proved himself as a coalition-builder and as a non-tribal politician. From the far left to the Tory right, he persuaded the students of Corpus Christi to back his campaign against the college's rent rise. 'It was noticeable because it brought together even those very Sloaney, posh people who wouldn't normally be seen dead participating in any kind of political action,' says a contemporary of Ed's.[37]

'There was no opposition to him,' recalls Stears. 'That was his magic: that he managed to keep all these different people onboard.'[38]

To this day, Ed recognises that his biggest achievement was not the result of the rent-rise campaign – which, ultimately, failed to stop rents from rising – but the pluralist and broad-based nature of the campaign itself. He had shown clear and coherent leadership and succeeded in uniting previously disunited and disparate factions, groupings and individuals. 'The biggest moment I remember was when we had to get a motion through to support Ed's actions so that he could go to the authorities and say, "The students are on our side,"' says Stears.[39] He and Ed printed off campaign posters and took them to the JCR room in college, unsure of whether they would win the vote or not. Ed lined up a range of speakers in support of the campaign, including Stears, and then concluded the evening programme with his own passionate 'this is why I want to do this' speech. The room was packed; posters were distributed to the audience of undergraduates.

The next day, 'the whole college was plastered in these "no to rent rise" posters'.[40] Other campaign posters featured a giant pelican – the symbol of Corpus Christi – feasting on a group of tiny human beings, with the tag line: 'The vampire pelican vulns its young to feed itself.'[41] There weren't just posters; T-shirts were printed too with similar anti-rent-rise slogans.

Says Stears: 'He managed to keep open relations with the authorities whilst campaigning for something he believed in and getting everyone on board and that was what he wanted to do really.' Plus, 'everyone had fun doing it'.[42]

In the end, however, the college authorities agreed to what Stears now calls a 'dodgy compromise'.[43] Fully aware that they could revisit the issue at a time of their choosing, once Ed and his supporters have moved on and graduated, Sir Keith Thomas and his fellow dons agreed to a partial rather than a full rent rise.

Ed wasn't happy with the result – but he knew how and when to do a deal. 'He was very conscious that you had to be willing to sit down and talk,' says a friend. 'There were people who then complained about Ed not having been willing to fight on but I think what was important was to recognise how far you could go and keep your unity.'[44]

In his heart, if not his head, Ed understood that the real achievement had been the building and mobilising of his non-tribal student coalition. He had failed in his campaign to halt the rent rise but had succeeded in proving himself as a leader and an insurgent – and a leader and insurgent who could unite people from all walks of life.

ooooo

Chair of the Labour Club in his first year, JCR president in his second, it would be difficult to come to any other conclusion than that Ed was a popular, as well as ambitious, student at Oxford University.

Inside the cramped environs of his college, he had no problems fitting in, 'right from the start we had a good group of friends,' says O'Rawe.[45] He was hugely popular in Corpus. 'He was just nice,' she says now. 'Everyone liked him. I can't really remember anyone saying a bad word about him – even people who were very cruel and would've thought that he was hopelessly untrendy and unfashionable in all sorts of ways. They thought he was a decent guy; he didn't piss people off.'

In particular, O'Rawe recalls her year abroad in Italy, as part of her Modern Languages course. 'I was staying in this awful place in Campania [near Naples], having a terrible time, on my own, and he went out of his way to try and stay in touch with me.' In an era before mobile phones and the internet, Ed took advantage of the landline in the JCR president's office to stay in touch with his lonely friend, despite the college's prohibition on personal calls. 'He called me several times, even trying to speak Italian to the landlady of the place where I was staying, and making this heroic effort to check on how I was doing, which was really nice of him.'

O'Rawe's relationship with Ed was strictly platonic and they didn't ever date; in fact, she says, 'He was just someone who always struck me as not being that bothered about that kind of stuff.'[46] Other friends say Ed did not have a single girlfriend during his three years at Oxford – nor did he go on many, if any, dates. 'I think maybe he was just focused on everything else.'[47]

One exception to Ed's seeming obsession with politics was his fondness for soap operas. Again, childhood habits die hard. His Oxford friends remember him slinking off to the college TV room to watch *Dallas*, *Neighbours* and, occasionally, *EastEnders*. But beyond his soft spot for soaps, contemporaries struggle to cite any specific cultural interests. 'He went to see what everyone else went to see in the cinema,' says O'Rawe. 'He would come to the bar, but he didn't drink very much. It just never seemed to interest him. He would have a few drinks, but he would always be very in control. I remember him dancing – but he was a terrible dancer.'[48]

'He didn't smoke or do drugs, and he drunk very little,' says a friend. 'But I do remember him agonising over which chocolate bars to buy from the machine in the graduate common room.'[49]

Some of Ed's contemporaries from his Oxford days have described him as a 'geek' – it is a charge that is denied by Gautam

Mody: 'Edward was serious but to say he was geeky – that wasn't him, because he didn't have his nose in a book.' Yet Mody also testifies to the fact that, unlike other undergraduates, Ed had no posters on the walls of his college room; he wasn't interested in movie stars or pop singers. He did, however, have a postcard of C. L. R. James on his side table.

'Our concerns were fundamentally political,' says Mody, defending his friend's seeming lack of a hinterland. 'Politics was at the centre of our lives.'[50] For Ed, this focus on 'politics' took several forms – the politics and political theory (from Marx to Rawls) that he was studying in tutorials with academics like Adam Swift, Andrew Glyn and others; the practical politics and campaigns of the Corpus Christi Junior Common Room and Oxford University Labour Club; and politics at a national (and, for that matter, inter-national) level – from the Poll Tax to the first Gulf War. Mody describes Ed's other, non-political interests, as 'by the way'.[51]

Other university friends are more open about Ed's geekiness and gaucheness as a student. 'He didn't have a great fashion sense back then – not that he's a fashion guru now,' laughs O'Rawe. 'He used to wear white trainers and these terrible jumpers.' She insisted he undergo a mini-makeover prior to launching his election campaign for JCR president: 'My big brainwave was that he needed to wear a buttoned-up cardigan with a shirt and tie and jeans and ordinary shoes.'

Ed didn't resist, agreeing to the changes suggested by his female friend. Says O'Rawe: 'He was very self-deprecating and ironic; his cluelessness didn't bother him, which was one of the reasons why I liked him.'[52]

Twenty years on, his friends from Oxford remember him fondly as someone who listened to their problems and looked out for them in times of trouble. In November 1991, shortly after the start of Ed's third year at Corpus, his friend Gautam Mody's father passed away, back home in India. 'I was in the Bodleian Library and Andrew [Glyn] and Ed came and pulled me out to tell me that this had happened,' recalls Mody. 'I went back to college with them and they helped me pack and got me a coach ticket to Heathrow Airport.' As a distraught and emotional Mody prepared to leave that evening, Ed said: 'Look, I think I'm going to come with you. You can't go to Heathrow on your own in this state.' Ed went all the way to the airport with Mody, returning alone, late at night. 'He probably said very little on the coach journey, but I think the fact that he was there just made an enormous amount of difference to me,' says Mody, who has maintained his friendship with Ed over the past two decades, despite living 4,000 miles away in India.[53]

○○○○○

In November 1990, in the first term of Ed's second year at Oxford, Margaret Thatcher stood down as Prime Minister, after eleven long years in office. Like so many Labour students, Ed couldn't contain his glee, referring in the JCR president's newsletter to the 'elation among many Corpus undergraduates'. 'He was ecstatic,' says a friend. 'All of us were. We didn't leave the college TV room for twenty-four hours. It was the biggest event of our lives.'[54]

Less than two years later, however, a much bigger political event would occur that had a profound effect on Ed and his approach to politics, the Labour Party and campaigning. On 9 April 1992, in one of the biggest surprises in modern British politics, the Conservatives were elected for the fourth consecutive time, with a majority of twenty-one for John Major's government. Kinnock had been defeated by Major as well as Thatcher. Thirteen years after Jim Callaghan had left Downing Street, Labour seemed destined to languish in opposition.

Ed's peers in Oxford remember him being distraught. 'I think that's the only time I've seen him deeply depressed,' says Mody. 'But I think that in a way it also made up his mind about where to go, and what to do with his life. He was deeply depressed about that outcome and, for a lot of people, at that age, at that stage of university, depression translates into disinterest, into a writing off of politics. That did not happen with him: it invigorated him.'[55]

There was a further and perhaps bigger disappointment for Ed in the summer of 1992. Despite working hard in his third and final year at Oxford, focusing on his studies and not student politics, he failed to get a first. It came as a blow to him. David had graduated from Corpus Christi with a first-class degree; so too did his friends, Marc Stears, Gautam Mody and Catherine O'Rawe.

By general consent, Ed was a bright student – several friends of

Ralph have told us that they believe Ed to be the brighter of the two Miliband brothers.

His tutors at Oxford agree that he seemed to be heading for a first in his PPE degree. Martin Conway taught Ed politics in his first year at Corpus Christi: 'Ted was one of the two strongest students in that year; the other was Marc Stears,' he says. 'Ted wasn't one of those first year students who you needed to teach how to write an essay.'

But the big surprise, says Conway, 'was that he didn't get a distinction in his Prelims'.[56] O'Rawe remembers Ed being disappointed in his first year 'because in his exams he did OK but not fabulously'.[57] Annoyed and frustrated, he went to see his tutor.

'The last time I met Ted was when he came to see me after Prelims to see why he hadn't got a distinction, but just a pass,' says Conway. 'He was rather upset. Perhaps in an exam environment he played safe and maybe wrote anonymous essays.'

In tutorials, as opposed to exams, Ed excelled; his tutors in politics and economics remember him as serious, conscientious and focused on his course. 'He didn't come across as a student hack – he wasn't dishevelled or chaotic, missing deadlines,' says Conway. 'He was not like that. He was a straightforward, committed undergraduate.'[58]

David Leopold, who teaches politics at Mansfield College, Oxford, and taught Ed's Marxism paper, remembers a 'clever, sharp student who could think, not only about arguments, but about objections and so on'. He agrees that Ed was efficient, well-organised and hard-working: 'Often when people are engaged in student politics they're not always engaged with their work, whereas Ed was actually very good at getting work done. That is relatively unusual.'

Despite taking a Marxism paper, and being the son of one of Britain's most famous Marxist theoreticians, Ed himself wasn't a Marxist. Says Leopold: 'He was critically interested in Marxism. He wasn't a believer; he was open-minded – and he was certainly capable of getting a first.'[59]

Adam Swift, a tutor at Balliol College and author of the popular textbook *Political Philosophy: A Beginner's Guide*, who taught Ed the 'Theory of Politics' course in his second and third years at Corpus Christi, agrees with Leopold: 'I thought he would get a first.'

Swift reveals that Ed had planned to do a postgraduate degree after Oxford – perhaps in order to follow in his father's distinguished footsteps and become an academic. (David, it is worth noting, had received his masters in political science from the Massachusetts Institute of Technology in the United States in 1990.)

'I wrote Ed a reference to go to Cambridge to do an MPhil in social and political theory,' says Swift. 'I thought it was a realistic option for him to become an academic, based on what I'd seen of him at that point. Four of his eight Finals papers were in political theory – he was very good at political theory even though he wasn't doing philosophy.'

His tutors remember him as a modest young man; in his tutorials, unlike the typical self-confident Oxford undergraduate, Ed held back from expressing instant views on the issues of the day. 'He was quite reluctant to offer his own opinions, compared to some students, but when he did they were always very well thought out,' recalls Swift. 'He was noticeably cautious – but then when he did end up arguing a position, it was very well-argued.' It is a useful character trait that the Oxford academic believes Ed has retained throughout his post-university political career. 'He was judicious and sensible. He may have been the son of a Marxist but he wasn't a ranter.'[60]

So what went wrong for Ed in his Finals? Some have suggested that he was distracted not so much by student politics as national politics. Friends remember the future Labour leader spending a large portion of his final year campaigning for Labour in the run-up to the 1992 general election – both in Oxford and back home in London. 'He failed to get a first because of me,' jokes Kinnock.[61]

Others put it down to poor time management in the exam hall. Swift remembers Ed telling him that 'it was down to bad time organisation; having to do four answers in three hours back then. You had to think of something to say, and just say it. It was quite common to run out of time – and Ed thought that's what had done him in.'[62]

But perhaps it was Ed's approach to examinations that was to blame. 'He worked too hard,' says another friend. 'He packed his stuff full of facts and details and didn't let it breathe. Examiners love to see a bit of creativity, students taking risks, strong arguments. But what Ed was probably writing in his exams was too much like a really detailed textbook or encyclopaedia entry.'[63]

'He was disappointed and like anyone else he aspired to a first,' says Mody, who remembers talking to him the day after the results were published. 'But he very much had this attitude: "What's happened has happened but so be it."'[64]

By all accounts, Ed was frustrated but calm, disappointed but composed; there was to be no personal crisis, no self-doubt. 'It can't be the end of the world,' Ed is said to have remarked to another friend. 'I can do better at the next stage of my life.'[65]

INTO OPPOSITION

1992–1997

As an undergraduate at Oxford in the 1950s, Michael Heseltine is said to have scribbled his life's ambitions on the back of an envelope, ending with his desire to be ensconced inside Number 10 Downing Street by the 1990s.

Twenty-two-year old Ed Miliband was without doubt ambitious, but he had no such plan. He had considered becoming an academic but, for now, it wasn't to be. He hadn't got a first at Oxford, so he wouldn't be heading for Cambridge.

'What am I going to do now?' he wondered. With spare time on his hands, and no postgraduate degree or job lined up, Ed headed back to New York in the summer of 1992 for a second, brief stint as an intern at the *Nation* magazine. Journalism had always interested and excited him. As a teenager he had thoroughly enjoyed himself, first on LBC's Young London show, then at the *Nation*, and then at the *MacNeil-Lehrer NewsHour*. He had watched, and been mesmerised by, Robert Redford and Dustin Hoffman in *All the President's Men*, the Oscar-winning Hollywood film in which they played Bob Woodward and Carl Bernstein, the two *Washington Post* journalists who broke the Watergate story in the 1970s.

Returning to the UK from the United States, Ed spotted an ad in a newspaper for a junior researcher's job at Channel 4's award-winning politics programme, *A Week in Politics*. He applied and was called in for an interview with Anne Lapping at Brooke Productions, which produced the programme for Channel 4.

Lapping – one of Britain's best-known documentary-makers, who went on to be awarded with a CBE in 2005 – was then the executive producer of *A Week in Politics*, which she had helped create in 1982. In fact, says *The Observer*'s Andrew Rawnsley, who co-presented the programme with the veteran Northern Irish broadcaster Vincent Hanna, until the latter's death in 1997,

Lapping 'was very good at collecting ferociously bright boys and girls as researchers and Ed Miliband was one of them'.[1]

It was a classic 'first job' for thrusting young political and media types in the early 1990s. Other alumni of the show included Tim Allan, who went on to work for Tony Blair before later moving into public relations, and Andrew Balls, younger brother of Labour's shadow Chancellor, Ed, who is now head of European investments for the world's biggest bond fund, PIMCO.

'Ed Miliband interviewed pretty well,' recalls Lapping, who offered the 22-year-old Oxford graduate a researcher's job on the show. Coincidentally, Lapping had been taught by Ralph Miliband at the LSE in the 1960s. 'He was a quite brilliant teacher,' she says. 'But I thought it might embarrass him to say, "Who's your father?" or "Is your father so and so?", so I waited till the end of the interview to raise the subject of his father and then asked Ed to send him my best wishes.'

Lapping remembers Ed as a good researcher; clever, collegiate, committed. 'But there was something a little shy about him, a little tentative,' she observes. 'That might sound odd now but I suppose it was his first job and also a new world for him.'[2]

Lapping took an instant liking to Ed, and so too did the presenters, Hanna and Rawnsley, who would often sing his praises to other members of the team. He may have been one of the more serious members of *A Week in Politics* but he was friendly, hard-working and, above all else, modest. 'Our young team regarded Ed affectionately but thought him a bit nerdy,' says Rawnsley. 'Some of the female researchers helped him to improve his dress sense.'[3] In an office full of ambitious young careerists, Ed did not push himself forward; he was quiet, demure and bashful – perhaps too much so. 'He was bright and good at what he did but there was a slight air of diffidence,' says Lapping. 'I just wonder if there is something that slightly holds him back.'[4]

Nonetheless, Ed thrived in the intellectually demanding environment, contributing to the robust and rigorous arguments about the direction of the programme and its political interviews. His job as a researcher involved thinking through the key political issues and stories of the week, booking guests for the programme from all three major parties and, crucially, crafting questions for the key interviews.

His questions were 'excellent',[5] says Lapping; in particular, Ed, the number-cruncher from Oxford, was a specialist in constructing interviews on economics and finance.

Little did he know that this skill would help transform his career – and his life. In the autumn of 1993, Harriet Harman, who had joined Labour's shadow Cabinet the previous year, as shadow chief secretary to the Treasury and number two to shadow Chancellor Gordon Brown, was booked as a guest by *A Week in Politics*.

The show's producers and the Labour Party press office had agreed in advance that the interview would be on the subject of the pound, and whether or not it was overvalued in relation to the major European currencies. Labour frontbenchers had been dancing around the issue; in the wake of Black Wednesday, Her Majesty's Opposition could not be seen to be talking down sterling.

'I was Gordon's deputy and it was a difficult time for the British economy,' recalls Harman. 'The interview was at the weekend, I had my daughter in the back of the car and we were singing nursery rhymes.'

Six-year-old Amy Harman may have enjoyed the journey but as her mother approached the TV studios she sensed that she might be under-prepared: 'I had this sinking feeling that the interview was going to be a car crash.'[6]

Harman's interviewer was Hanna, whose interview questions had been formulated and structured by Ed. 'Oh my God, what's our policy?' a panicked Harman asked Hanna, upon her arrival.[7]

She never stood a chance.

'It was a terrible interview,' admits Harman, eighteen years later.[8] Hanna, faithfully following Ed's script, destroyed the shadow chief secretary to the Treasury. 'She was a puddle on the studio floor,' says Rawnsley.[9]

A few weeks later, in an ironic twist, Harman rang Rawnsley, who was in the midst of writing his *Guardian* column. 'I need a new aide,' she said. 'Is Ed Miliband as good as people say he is? I believe he works for you.' Rawnsley told the Labour frontbencher that Ed was 'fantastic' and recommended him highly. What he deliberately didn't tell Harman, however, was that it was Ed who had constructed the Hanna interview that had left her a 'gibbering wreck'.[10]

Lapping was on holiday in France when Ed rang her out of the blue. 'I've had another job offer,' he said, informing her of the sudden approach from Harman. 'You can't possibly accept,' replied Lapping coolly. 'I think you can really do much better than working for Harriet Harman. I think you should stay in television.'[11]

But Ed decided to ignore the advice of the first boss he ever had and, turning his back on television less than a year after entering the industry, he made his leap into party politics, as a researcher for the shadow chief secretary to the Treasury – and future Cabinet minister and deputy leader of the Labour Party. 'He was set to be a high-flyer in television,' says Harman, 'but Ed realised that he could play an important role in getting Labour's economic arguments on the right track.'[12]

It had always been clear to his colleagues on the programme that he was on the left and that he was a Labour Party supporter. But, to Ed's credit, says Rawnsley, 'he could still do a journalistic job as he did with Harriet: constructing an interview from a different point of view, a point of view that wasn't friendly to Labour'.[13]

Could Ed have stayed on and prospered in television? Or was it always a means to an end? His colleagues on *A Week in Politics* remember him being no more or less interested in politics than the rest of them – he didn't give them the impression that working on the programme was a stepping stone into Parliament. 'He didn't in any way mislead me,' says Lapping. 'But he certainly didn't give the impression he wanted to go into politics.'[14]

The veteran producer and talent-spotter believes Ed could have had a promising career in television. But Ed's heart had never been committed to a career in the media, despite proving himself as an able and adept researcher on *A Week in Politics*. 'It wasn't something he was desperate to do,' says his university friend, Marc Stears. 'We were still trying to find our way and, when he got that job in TV, he took that to be his way.'[15] But, within a year, Harman had offered him a different 'way'. Given the chance, Ed decided that he wanted to be part of the political debate, at the heart of Westminster, rather than reporting on it from the sidelines.

ooooo

Ed joined HM Opposition, and Harriet's team, as a replacement for another Oxford economics graduate, Yvette Cooper, who was off sick with ME (and didn't return to work until the start of 1994). Cooper had read PPE at Balliol and then gone on to be a Kennedy scholar at Harvard University and a member of Bill Clinton's 1992 presidential campaign. Ed had been sharing a flat with Cooper in Belsize Park, in north London, when he replaced her on Harman's team. 'He probably did more washing up than I did,' Cooper has said about her ex-flatmate, 'But he never cooked.'[16]

Ed thrived under Harman. 'Harriet was very excited to have this very clever young man working for her and he did a fantastic job for her,' says a friend,[17] who noticed a transformation in Harman's performances at the despatch box; Ed wasn't just number-crunching but speechwriting too.

Within a month of joining Harman, however, Ed came close to losing his job – through no fault of his own. In the shadow Cabinet elections in October 1993, Harriet Harman was one of two shadow ministers voted off the frontbench (the other was Ann Clwyd). Harman rang her new researcher in a panic: 'Ed, I'm off, I've been knocked off the shadow Cabinet.'[18] Had the then Labour leader John Smith not decided to keep her on as shadow chief secretary to the Treasury, as he subsequently did, Ed would have been out of a job too.

Luck was on his side – and just three months later, Ed was to score his first direct hit on the Tory government and attract the attention of Brown himself – again, thanks to his love for numbers.

In January 1994, Ed, with the aid of a clerk in the House of Commons Library called Robert Twigger, discovered that the Tories were on the verge of taxing more than the last Labour government, under Jim Callaghan, had done – raising the tax burden for a married man with two children above the 1978–79 level in 1994–95. 'It was a big moment,' recalls Ed.[19] Stephen Dorrell, the financial secretary to the Treasury, was forced to confirm the numbers in a parliamentary written reply.[20]

Harman and Ed had instantly recognised the political significance of the figures. Major had been re-elected against the odds in 1992 promising 'year on year' tax cuts. The shadow chief secretary to the Treasury sent her researcher to show his figures to Brown, who didn't seem impressed. He told Harman and Ed that they could press-release their story but that he didn't think the media would be interested.

Brown was wrong. The figures dominated the Sunday newspapers on 23 January. It was yet another blow to the hapless Tories' economic credibility. The shadow Chancellor rang Ed on that Sunday to congratulate him and concede that he'd misjudged the story. 'Well, I was totally wrong, wasn't I?' Brown, not normally known for his humility, confessed to the young researcher, who was in the middle of a brunch at the home of his brother David, adding: 'Look, I just wanted to tell you that I was wrong and you were brilliant.'[21]

It was a proud moment for the 24-year-old. Here he was in the home of his brother being congratulated by the shadow Chancellor. David had been prospering at the Institute for Public Policy Research, where he was a research fellow and had served as secretary of John Smith's Social Justice Commission and impressed senior figures in the Labour Party. He had become a close confidant and adviser of Blair, who would appoint him as his head of policy upon becoming leader in July. Later that year, he would edit a book called *Reinventing the Left*, a collection of very New Labour essays – including one from Brown – that aimed 'to give modern relevance to old values'.

In the words of *The Times* columnist Daniel Finkelstein, David was 'on the up. It was all "I think David Miliband is coming to our seminar" and "Have you seen, David Miliband is here?"'[22]

Ed, meanwhile, was torn. He was enjoying himself on the frontline, getting down and dirty, lobbing grenades at the Conservative government, but didn't feel as politically or intellectually stretched as he would liked to have been as Harman's aide.

For a start, Ed was well aware of how junior his position was on the pecking order of aides, researchers and special advisers (or 'spads'). These days, both Harman and Ed enjoy telling the story of how, in his first week in the shadow chief secretary's office, Ed was sent off to look for her coat. It perhaps wasn't what the bright Oxford graduate, with a passion for political theory, had left the world of television for.

Sue Nye, a long-standing aide to Brown who followed him into the Treasury and then Number 10 as his 'gatekeeper', and who later went on to become a close friend and mentor of Ed's, remembers the first time she bumped into him, at a conference in 1993: 'I was working for Gordon, he was working for Harriet and he came over to ask me what Gordon's speech had been about. I said 'Pathways out of poverty' and then turned around and walked away. And he felt kind of dismissed.'[23]

But Ed need not have worried. Brown liked to surround himself with intellectually serious and mathematically-gifted aides and, having belatedly spotted the potential in Harman's new researcher, decided to make his move in February 1994. 'I recruited brilliant people, they shone working for me and then Gordon would start smiling at them in meetings,' jokes Harman. 'Gordon started praising Ed and then off Ed went to work for him.'[24] Or, in the memorable phrase of Brown's former spin doctor, Charlie Whelan: 'We needed a number-cruncher. We burgled him off Harriet.'[25]

Harman maintains that she wasn't bitter – 'It was right that he should be at the higher level. He could do more to help there'[26] – but a former Brown aide says the shadow chief secretary to the Treasury was (understandably) 'annoyed'[27] by the brazen act of daylight robbery carried out by her boss, the shadow Chancellor, in front of her eyes.

Less than a year after joining Harman and less than two years after graduating from Oxford, Ed was in the big league: Brown, along with the then shadow Home Secretary, Tony Blair, was one of the two undisputed stars of the Labour frontbench. Some in the party saw Brown as the natural heir to John Smith, who had succeeded Neil Kinnock as Labour leader in 1992.

The members of Labour's shadow Treasury team were on a mission: after the heart-wrenching defeat in 1992 their overriding, all-consuming aim was to change the public's perception of Labour as a high-tax, high-spend party and to rebuild the party's fiscal credibility and economic narrative. It was intense and hectic but enjoyable at the same time.

Ed brought youth and energy to the Brown operation. The 24-year-old still looked like a teenager: tall with dark hair, he had an earnest and fresh face and round glasses. Neal Lawson, who was working in the shadow Chancellor's office at the time and now runs the centre-left pressure group Compass, remembers Ed as 'a bit Harry Potter; nice, knowledgeable and clever'.[28]

It was hard work: Team Brown was a 24/7 operation. Ed and

his colleagues had to be on call at all times of the day and night. He became busier, losing touch with school and university friends – including Marc Stears and Gautam Mody – as the years passed by. As a key aide to the workaholic Brown, he had little time for socialising; friends and relatives would ring him and laugh out loud at the message on his answering machine: 'Hi, this is Ed. I'm not here right now. But if this is Gordon you can reach me on the following number...'[29]

His parents looked on bemused as their son's waking hours were consumed by his new career in the Labour Party. In fact, Ed had made clear to his father that politics was his passion prior to accepting the job offer from Harriet. 'I don't think I'm going to be an academic,' he told Ralph, 'because I'm drawn to politics and that's what motivates me.' 'I can see that's what you're drawn to, and if that's what you're drawn to then that's OK,' replied his father.[30] This was a significant moment for Ed; he had got the unlikely endorsement of his father to pursue a career in Westminster. It came as a relief.

Ed's growing political pragmatism, like David's, had not gone unnoticed by their Marxist father. In 1993, Tony Benn recorded in his diary, 'Ralph Miliband came for about an hour and a half today ... He was saying how his sons say to him, "Oh, Dad, how would you do that? Would it work? What are your positive proposals?" I said, "Well, it's the same with my sons." He was very relieved to hear that. I think he thought he was very out of date.'[31]

Ralph's health had been steadily deteriorating. In February 1991, he had a heart bypass operation which involved horrible complications and led to him spending four weeks in intensive care. During this fraught period, Ed would travel back from Oxford to see Ralph almost every weekend and occasionally missing tutorials during the weekdays too, in order to be at his bedside.

Ralph died on 21 May 1994 – he had turned seventy only four months earlier. Ed was not yet twenty-five. It was the saddest he had ever been; he still regards it as the day that his world was turned upside down.

Three years earlier, in Oxford, in 1991, Ed had broken the news of the death of Gautam Mody's father to his friend from India outside the Bodleian Library. Now, Mody was calling Ed from a pay phone 4,000 miles away to offer his condolences. Marion answered the phone and handed it to Ed. 'You've been through this already, Gautam,' he told his friend from university, his voice cracking. 'You've been dealing with this sorrow for three years.' Ed was 'deeply, deeply upset', recalls Mody.[32] Ralph could occasionally be a 'stern'[33] father, according to a close friend of Ed's. But there is no doubt Ed's father was his political 'lodestar'[34] too, and given how politics had dominated his family and life the hole left by Ralph's death was deep. Ed says now it did not affect him politically. 'I don't think it particularly affected my political direction,' he said, 'because I was already doing what I was doing for Labour.'[35] But given that it coincided with the rise of Tony Blair's leadership it is hard to imagine that the fundamental dilemma that has haunted Ed throughout his life – between the ideological politics of his father and the politics of his party-political masters – was not heightened at this time.

Meanwhile, the small Miliband family had suffered a devastating blow; the dominant figure in the household had gone. An anyway small and relatively unextended family had just lost its central member. Ed's eulogy at Ralph's funeral, on 27 May 1994, was as personal as it was poignant:

> There is sometimes a general presumption that intellectuals and academics, occupied with thinking, writing and teaching, do not have time for such mundane things as their children and that when they do, it is only to force-feed them with their latest ideas. In Ralph's case, nothing could be further from the truth... I never heard the words 'Not now, I'm too busy' pass from his lips... He might be up against a deadline, but our needs trumped all others... When we were young children, he was an absolutely amazing story-teller. We sometimes joked that he was passing up the chance of undreamt sales – undreamt of, at least, by a socialist academic – by not going into print with the stories he used to tell us about the adventures of Boo-Boo and Hee-Hee, two sheep on the Yorkshire Moors... Ralph relished our political views and encouraged them. Indeed, I remember on more than one occasion, him leaping to the defence of the 12-year-old in the corner, who was arguing with a rather surprised friend or academic who happened to come round to dinner... Ralph's respect for our point of view was unflinching.[36]

David, of course, also delivered a eulogy at Ralph's funeral - but some friends of the Marxist academic had long considered Ed to be the political heir to his father. Once both brothers had finished speaking, Wendy Carlin, wife of Andrew Glyn and close family friend of the Milibands, turned to her husband and said: 'Edward is the real believer in progressive politics.'

It was only after Ralph's death that David went on to be head of Tony Blair's Policy Unit in Downing Street and Ed became a special adviser to the Chancellor of the Exchequer in the Treasury. But, as Tony Benn's diary entry illustrates, their direction of travel inside the Labour Party was clear to Ralph and he never stood in their way. He was proud of his sons' achievements, even if he disagreed with a substantial number of policies that the 1990s Labour Party, even its pre-Blair avatar, was advocating.

Nine days after Ralph passed away, the Labour leader John Smith died from a heart attack. Two months later, Tony Blair would become leader of the party and New Labour would be born.

ooooo

Ed's journey away from his father's politics, and the critique of Labour's parliamentary approach articulated so forcefully by him in *Parliamentary Socialism*, had begun in his teens but crystallised when he read Ralph's last and unashamedly left-wing book, *Socialism for a Sceptical Age*, completed just a few months before the latter's death in 1994. Ralph had written the book with the intention of refuting the view that socialism had been dead and buried with the end of the Cold War, the fall of the Soviet Union and the rise of social democratic parties across Europe. The book began by criticising 'mild social democracy' as an 'adaptation' to capitalism, rather than an alternative to it. And Anthony Crosland's *The Future of Socialism*, perhaps the most important social-democratic text of the post-war era – which had a huge influence on, among others, his two sons – was dismissed by their father in a footnote as 'the bible of Labour "revisionism"'. For Ralph, socialism had to be a 'fundamental recasting of the social order', no less, no more.

His pragmatic, Croslandite sons weren't impressed. As Ralph admitted in the Acknowledgements to the book, 'It also gives me great pleasure to acknowledge the very helpful (and stringent) criticism and suggestions I have had from David and Edward Miliband.'[37] In fact, David put it rather bluntly to his father in his comments on a draft of the book in August 1993:

> This does not seem to... be sufficiently compelling... I think that defending longstanding socialist ideals as more flexible, less statist etc. than they have been in practice does not take us very far forward. Asking people not to give up... uncorrupted socialist visions are not enough.[38]

Ed too considered the book to be, at best, 'a blueprint for a world a long way off' and made his own criticisms clear. By the mid-1990s, he had come to the conclusion that his father was too 'dogmatic and sectarian' and the book was a reflection of Ralph's dogmatic approach.[39] Nonetheless, he has since identified the last two sentences of *Socialism for a Sceptical Age* as his favourite of any in Ralph's works. It reads:

> In all countries, there are people, in numbers large or small, who are moved by the vision of a new social order in which democracy, egalitarianism and co-operation – the essential values of socialism – would be the prevailing principles of social organisation. It is in the growth in their numbers and in the success of their struggles that lies the best hope for humankind.[40]

It was an unrepentantly optimistic sentiment that was articulated by the father – and shared, whatever their other differences, by the son.

ooooo

As a member of Team Brown, Ed may have been a card-carrying New Labour 'moderniser' but his left-wing inclinations were often on display. Phil Collins, who would go on to become a speech-writer for Tony Blair in Downing Street, remembers bumping into Ed at a party at the north London home of the economist David Soskice, whose daughter Juliet would later be involved in a brief relationship with Ed. Collins had finished his PhD and was working for an investment bank. He and Ed chatted for around half an hour, about Utopian political philosophy, before Collins revealed where he worked. 'A look of horror swept over Ed's face,' he recalls. 'Perhaps it was disgust or incomprehension. The overwhelming sense was that he just couldn't get it.'[41]

Like his boss, the shadow Chancellor, Ed was obsessed with policy. In the summer of 1995, Ed and his then girlfriend Liz Lloyd, who worked for Blair, went on holiday with Juliet Soskice and her then boyfriend Phil Collins to the Soskice holiday home in the south of France. The two couples went swimming – Ed enjoys doing laps – and played tennis together but the holiday was dominated by discussion of a national minimum wage, which had been reaffirmed as Labour Party policy by Tony Blair and Gordon Brown. 'We discussed it like we were in a Fabian Society seminar,' says Collins. 'I remember being in the kitchen and listening to Ed and David [Soskice] having a conversation about it in real detail. I, for my shame, had no real view.'[42]

The defining issue of this period, however, was not policy but politics. As Steve Richards notes in his overview of the period, *Whatever It Takes: The Real Story of Gordon Brown and New Labour*, '[Brown] was playing a much longer game [than Blair], assuming that when there was next a leadership contest he would be established as the senior figure who had transformed Labour's economic policy.'[43] Ed had this drummed into him from the moment he started working for Brown.

In July 1994, however, it was Blair and not Brown who succeeded John Smith, who had died two months earlier. As the third member of the New Labour triumvirate, Peter Mandelson, would later remark in a BBC radio interview in 2006, 'Within the party, or more strictly within the New Labour family, there has been a fissure really from the word go. And the reason for that is that Gordon thought that he could and should have been leader in 1994. He believed that he should have succeeded John Smith and he's never fully reconciled himself to not doing so.'[44]

Much ink has been spilled on the so-called 'Granita deal' between Blair and Brown in the summer of 1994 – a reference to the now defunct restaurant in Islington at which the shadow Chancellor and shadow Home Secretary met on 31 May 1994 to agree on which of them would run for leader in the wake of Smith's death. Hard-core

Brownites believe their man was persuaded to stand aside by Blair and give the younger man a clear run for the leadership on the basis that Blair would hand over power to him within a decade and, in the meantime, give him wide powers over domestic policy.

But the bigger question is whether Brown could have won in a head-to-head contest with Blair. In Brownite mythology, Gordon would have beaten Tony in 1994 had he stood. The facts suggest otherwise. Ed has told friends he was not one of those Brownite die-hards – like Charlie Whelan or the journalist and author Paul Routledge – who believed, or at least liked to claim, that Brown would have beaten Blair had he decided to run. Ed did, however, learn a lesson during this fraught period that would influence his own decision-making process in the future: deals are to be avoided, pacts are counter-productive and leadership contests are ultimately good for the Labour Party.

His colleagues, however, were bitter. 'Brown's small team, already introverted, became much more insular after the summer of 1994, almost as a collective act of defiance,' writes Richards. 'Together they had been through the trauma of betrayal as they irrationally saw it.'[45] Ed was in a minority in believing however, that Brown had not been 'robbed' of the leadership in 1994. It is a view he maintains today.[46]

ooooo

It was in opposition, and not government, that Brown began to build up and promote his inner circle, his 'court', as an alternative power base to Blair. The young Miliband found himself with much greater influence than he otherwise would have done – he had the ear of Labour's all-powerful shadow Chancellor.

But he had competition. When Ed joined Brown's team there was already another Ed with his feet under the table. Ed Balls was a gifted and ambitious Oxford and Harvard graduate, two years his senior, and he had joined the shadow Chancellor's team from the *Financial Times* in October 1993. A trained economist and a talented political strategist, Balls was Brown's most trusted adviser and closest confidant. It was Balls, for example, who began inserting the repeated references to 'boom and bust' into Brown's speeches and articles, as well as the infamous phrase 'neo-classical endogenous growth theory'.

'They were a pretty heavyweight team,' says Professor Paul Gregg of Bristol University, who advised Brown in opposition and later went on to work for him in the Treasury, as a member of the Chancellor's Council of Economic Advisers. 'I was impressed that they were, in a sense, running an opposition but also building a policy programme at the same time.'[47]

'Before 1997, the difference between us wasn't senior or junior, as some have tried to paint it,' maintains Balls, 'or "I decide and he does" – the broad division of work was that Ed focused on the vital task of opposition while I started to do some of the longer-term work on preparing for government. Each of us were doing absolutely essential tasks ahead of the 1997 election.'[48]

Others have vouched for the fact that Ed's primary responsibility in opposition was to handle the party relations and party politics aspects of Brown's role as shadow Chancellor; Balls, meanwhile, 'prepared for government', holding meetings with senior civil servants like Terry Burns (the permanent secretary at the Treasury) and Bank of England officials like Eddie George (the then governor of the Bank of England).[49]

Ed's other responsibility in opposition was working on Brown's speeches, providing Brown's words with 'presentational panache'.[50] It was Ed, joined by another young adviser, Douglas Alexander and Brown's old friend from Scotland, Dr Collin Currie, who was tasked with working on the final drafts of Brown's crucial party conference and Budget speeches.

But he had ambitions of being more than a speechwriter or a researcher, in a team in which intellectual credentials were highly valued. In an attempt to bolster his CV, and to do the postgraduate degree he had originally planned to do at Cambridge before the 2:1 in his PPE degree stopped him dead in his tracks, Ed applied to do a masters (MSc) in economics at the university where his father had taught politics: the London School of Economics. He confided to a family friend his worry that if he didn't obtain a postgraduate qualification of this sort 'he wouldn't be taken seriously as a policy person'.[51]

In January 1995, with Brown's encouragement, Ed left the shadow Chancellor's team to go off and do his masters 'in preparation for playing a leading part in the New Labour Treasury'.[52]

Upon his return, Ed did indeed start getting more involved in economic policy and, as was so often the case with Brown, the presentation of economic policy. It was the 1994–97 opposition period that saw the birth of the 'Two Eds' – a moniker which has stuck with the pair until the present day. According to Balls, the controversial and high-risk decision to stick to Tory spending plans – described by the then Tory Chancellor of the Exchequer, Kenneth Clarke, as 'eye-wateringly tight' – for the first two years of a Labour government, to prove the party's fiscal credibility, was the result of a 'joint effort'[53] of the two Eds, who spent months working on the idea.

In a speech to business leaders at Westminster's QEII centre on 20 January 1997, Brown declared:

> So our first Budget will not reopen overall spending allocations for the 1997/98 financial year... Each departmental minister will want to use their first year to work out with their departments and permanent secretaries how they can overhaul existing spending so that ... spending is reordered to meet Labour's priorities in the 1998/99 financial year...'[54]

Prior to the delivery of this key speech, Balls had been to brief the lobby journalists that public spending totals would be frozen for the first two years of a Labour government while Ed's task was to inform the party leader, Tony Blair. He nervously rang Blair at home but his wife answered. 'Why are you bothering us on a Sunday?' said an irate Cherie. 'We're having a birthday party for the children.' Ed patiently explained to the Labour leader's wife that he was in possession of the text of a rather important speech by the shadow Chancellor that he needed to pass on to her husband. Cherie asked him to fax it – but it is believed that she never passed it on to her husband, placing it in a drawer at home instead. The first Blair is said to have heard of Brown's radical plan to freeze spending levels was when he saw it on the television news bulletin later that evening. Ed was mortified.[55]

The Brown gang consisted of more than the two Eds, however. There was Cooper – who would marry Balls in 1998 – and Douglas Alexander, then a young solicitor and occasional speechwriter for the shadow Chancellor. The group was as driven as it was tight-knit – and ferociously loyal to Brown. Indeed, it was in opposition that the seeds were planted for what the Oxford academic David

Runciman would later call the 'family affair'[56] (Balls, Cooper, Miliband, Alexander) at 'the heart of the Brown government'. As we shall see, these four key members of the Brown inner circle – Ed Miliband, Ed Balls, Douglas Alexander and Yvette Cooper – would go on to occupy the top four party jobs: respectively leader, shadow Chancellor, shadow Foreign Secretary and shadow Home Secretary.

ooooo

Like every other member of the Labour Party, Ed was incredibly excited on the night of the 1997 general election. It was a landslide victory for Labour – a majority of 179 seats. That evening, Brown and his inner circle of aides and MPs 'huddled together in a corner of the Royal Festival Hall for an hour'.[57] As others at the venue danced into the early hours of the morning, to D:Ream's 'Things Can Only Get Better', the Brownites were preparing for a bitter struggle over the ideological and strategic direction of the new government.

Ed may well have been aware that he would be bloodied in the impending Blair–Brown wars – but little did he know that he would soon have battles to fight closer to home.

TREASURY

1997–2002

Ed Balls was in full flow. 'If you're going to make immigration politically sustainable then you've got to understand the economic issues.'

Balls was speaking at the first Labour leadership hustings, on 9 June 2009, along with his four fellow candidates – Ed Miliband, David Miliband, Andy Burnham and Diane Abbott.

'Ed, you've got to let your fellow candidate speak,' said the chair, *New Statesman* editor Jason Cowley, trying, for a third time, to interrupt Balls and bring Ed Miliband into the discussion.

'Feels like being back at the Treasury,' observed Ed Miliband, prompting laughter from the 600-strong audience at the Church House conference centre in Westminster. The laughs morphed into a gasp-like 'ooh' as Balls, expressionless and unblinking, fixed a stare on Ed, who added with a smile: 'But only occasionally.'

His lips curling into a sardonic smile, Balls hit back: 'Tell us the answer, Ed, like you normally do.'

'Two Eds are better than one,' replied Ed, grinning, trying to take the sting out of the awkward exchange.[1]

ooooo

At 4pm on 2 May 1997, hundreds of civil service staff lined the hallway, stairs and balcony of the Treasury, to cheer as Gordon Brown entered the building. Labour's first Chancellor of the Exchequer for eighteen years was flanked by his closest advisers – Sue Nye, Charlie Whelan, Ed Balls and Ed Miliband – to whom he later described the whole experience as the best of his political career.

Ed was just as exhilarated as his boss – if not more so. 'They clapped Gordon into the building,' he excitedly told a friend on the phone, later that evening. 'It was incredible. Just amazing.'[2] Here he was, twenty-seven years of age, a trusted aide to the second most powerful man in the new government – and, that too, a Labour government with a landslide majority and a clear mandate for 'change'.

As the Brown biographers Hugh Pym and Nick Kochan note in their definitive account of the Chancellor's first year in office, 'Not since Ramsay MacDonald and his Labour colleagues arrived in Downing Street in 1924 had the great offices of state been taken up by politicians with no experience of government.'[3]

These were heady days. Brown and his team hit the ground running. On 6 May, four days after arriving at the Treasury, the Chancellor stunned the financial markets and the Westminster village with his decision to set the Bank of England free from political control – perhaps the most radical shake-up in the central bank's 300-year history.

It was a typically New Labour move – sowing disarray in Conservative ranks while impressing business leaders. Addressing a press conference on the Tuesday after the election, Brown said: 'I want to set in place a long-term framework for economic prosperity... I want to break from the boom bust economics of previous years.' It was not the last time he would refer to ending 'boom bust economics' – words that he, and the Labour Party, would come to regret in future years.

Meanwhile, behind the scenes, Brown's special advisers – led by Balls, who had been the intellectual and political brain behind Brown's bold plan to make the Bank of England operationally independent – settled into their new roles in government. Previous Chancellors had brought external advisers with them into the Treasury – indeed, a young David Cameron had performed the role for Norman Lamont during the ERM debacle in 1992 – but, as has been documented in countless books and articles over the past decade, the election of New Labour in 1997 marked the first time that these advisers were allowed to exercise greater power and influence inside their departments than the senior civil servants themselves.

'I was amazed at how self-sufficient Brown's team of advisers were,' says a former permanent secretary at the Treasury. 'They would involve civil service officials only when they thought they needed to.'[4]

Their confidence – or was it overconfidence? – was on full display in the 1997 ITV documentary, *We are the Treasury*, a fly on the wall account of Brown's first few months in office. As the cameras followed them around, Brown's chief aides 'could scarcely contain their excitement at the prospect of running the economy: there were whispered asides to the cameras, ostentatious phone calls, a great deal of striding between meetings'.[5]

A former member of the Brown inner circle now describes the documentary as 'a disaster'.[6] Much of the film revolved around the gregarious if self-promoting Whelan and the more intellectual and serious Balls; Ed, in a reflection perhaps of his status as well as his modesty, had only a supporting role in the film.

In 2000, Geoffrey Robinson, the former Treasury minister who, like Charlie Whelan, was eventually forced to resign during the row over the notorious home loan he had given to Peter Mandelson, published his book, *The Unconventional Minister: My Life Inside New Labour*, in which he provided a telling description of the Brown inner circle, inspired by a football analogy:

> We all had our roles. Gordon was chairman of the club, its coach and captain, and main striker. Ed Balls was his deputy in all roles, and in charge of policy and tactics in his own right. Charlie Whelan was Nobby Stiles: he would take out an opponent – press or political – as soon as look at them. My own modest role might best be described as sweeper-cum-attacking midfield... There were several other crucial players, notably Sue Nye and Ed Miliband. Sue's advice and influence were pervasive in the whole strategy and Ed was vital in writing speeches and coordinating with Millbank.[7]

Robinson is a close ally of Ed Balls and, as we shall see, would later give David Miliband, and not Ed, his second preference in the Labour leadership election, but it would be a mistake to dismiss his description of Balls as Brown's 'deputy' as partisan. Few would dispute the fact that it was Ed Balls, and not Ed Miliband, who was the supremely dominant figure in Brown's Treasury between 1997 and 2004 (when he left to secure his seat in Parliament). Senior civil servants referred to Balls as the 'deputy Chancellor'[8] while journalists called him Brown's 'brain' and 'the most powerful unelected person in Britain'. 'Ed [Balls] is like an extension of Brown. You bolt on an extra server and increase the capacity,' Andrew Turnbull, the then permanent secretary at the Treasury, remarked in 1999.[9]

Such was Balls's seniority that, of 'the two Eds', he was the one referred to inside the Treasury as 'Ed', without the qualifier of a surname. Ed Miliband was referred to as 'Ed M' or 'Ed Mili' – and later took self-deprecatingly to calling himself the 'other Ed'. (Balls, however, would occasionally, and jokingly, call Ed 'Teddy').[10]

By 1999, Brown had promoted Balls to 'Chief Economic Adviser to the Treasury'. He was no longer, informally, first among equals but, formally, a cut above the rest of Brown's advisers. He also had the corner office, which was bigger and with a nicer view than the rest of the advisers' offices. Ed's office, marooned between Brown's and Balls's, became a corridor for the latter; occasionally, Ed would shut the door and force Balls to walk around. 'Of such things are splits made of,' jokes a senior Brownite.[11]

And splits there were in the Brown gang, despite denials from the two Eds more than a decade later. Former Treasury insiders say that Brown's team of advisers divided into two rival factions, 'the boys and the girls',[12] perhaps reflecting the two sides of the Chancellor's personality: the more blokey, aggressive, hot-headed types – Balls, Whelan, Ian Austin and Damian McBride – and the more personable, sensitive, emotive types – Nye, Alexander, Spencer Livermore (who would join the Treasury in 1998) and, of course, Ed. The two groups of Brownites have also been described, more bluntly, as the 'bad guys and the good guys' (albeit, by a self-appointed member of the good guys).[13]

Ed became very close to Sue Nye. He would go on vacation with Nye and her husband, the then Goldman Sachs banker (and later BBC chairman) Gavyn Davies, and join them at their holiday home in the south of France, where he would methodically swim his lengths in the pool.

He also became good friends with Spencer Livermore, who moved over to the Treasury from the Labour Party's Economic Secretariat. Aged twenty-three, Livermore saw Ed almost as a mentor and has maintained a close friendship with him over the years.

As for Douglas Alexander, with whom Ed shared an office until the latter was elected to Parliament in a by-election in November 1997, he and Ed would holiday together in Scotland, Ireland, France and the United States.

But Ed never considered Balls to be a friend, or treated him as such. They might have gone out for a drink together after work, as colleagues, or spent their weekends side by side in Brown's flat preparing speeches or policy statements for the Chancellor till the early hours of the morning; they might have even gone out for the odd dinner with their partners, Liz Lloyd and Yvette Cooper. But they weren't friends.

For a start, Ed was well aware of the fact that Balls jealously guarded his status as Brown's number two and therefore saw the younger man as a rival, as a threat. 'Ed Miliband's career from the moment he joined Gordon to the moment he emerged as more likely to win the leadership than Ed Balls has been a battle to remain relevant and stop Balls from squashing him,' says a former member of the Brown inner circle, who worked with both men.[14]

Then there were the two advisers' very different personalities and styles. 'I think Ed Balls is a supremely confident person; I think Ed Miliband understands doubt and so they are different personalities,' says a former senior Treasury official who observed the two Eds closely in the late nineties and early noughties. 'Ed Balls has a different way of operating than Ed Miliband has.'[15] Balls was confident, aggressive, and confrontational; Ed was shyer, more modest, and less prone to rows or fights. 'There wasn't a fear factor with Ed Miliband, as there was with Ed Balls,' says another ex-Treasury official. 'You'd often come out of a meeting with Ed Balls with the fear of God put into you.'[16]

Ed and Alexander could often be overheard in their shared office 'slagging off' Balls, using colourful language. Their dislike for the elder Ed was an open secret inside the building.[17] (These days, Ed will only say, diplomatically, that he and Balls had 'a remarkably good working relationship'[18] at the Treasury.) But the resentment that Ed (and Alexander) had for the other, more senior, Ed related to issues of personality and process – hierarchy, meetings, access to Brown, perceived snubs and the rest – rather than issues of substance. Inside the Brown team there were rarely disagreements on substantive, policy issues. 'We were united in our opposition to a common enemy – Number 10 – and that forced us to be quite unified. Once we'd lost that enemy, and Blair departed the scene, the team became a lot less cohesive.'[19]

Ed was, indisputably, the more junior figure; he was 'little' Ed. 'Until he became Labour leader, he was always little Ed – little Ed to David, little Ed to the other Ed,' says a family friend of Ed.[20]

It bothered Ed and, on occasion, he would vent his frustrations in front of others. A senior and friendly lobby journalist remembers Ed mentioning to him how, while his brother David was running Number 10's Policy Unit, and on his way towards getting a seat in Parliament, and various other friends and acquaintances were advancing through the ranks of the media and academia, he was still stuck in his 'lowly' position. There was a sense that while others were moving on rather rapidly with their lives and careers, his own may have stalled at the Treasury. 'You'll be fine,' the journalist reassured him.[21]

Nonetheless Balls remained, through the two Eds' period in the Treasury, the dominant and senior partner in their relationship. He made deals on Brown's behalf and pushed the Chancellor into adopting positions the latter may not originally have wanted to adopt. 'If Gordon was going to move an inch, Ed Balls would move the inch,' says a close ally of Blair who had dealings with the Treasury during the late 1990s.[22]

But just as it would be wrong to overstate Ed's role in the Treasury, it would be equally wrong to understate his role. He was no longer just Brown's speechwriter and researcher, as he largely had been in opposition. He had real power and authority inside the department as well as his own areas of influence: welfare to work, low pay, and childcare. These may have been micro-issues of social policy, rather than macro-issues of economic policy like spending or borrowing, which were the responsibility of Balls, but they were solidly social-democratic issues.

Ed was also respected by Brown, who would often ask for his opinion or view on a particular policy or approach. As a *Guardian* profile of the Treasury team noted in 1999: 'The two Eds, in particular, know how the Chancellor thinks and can tell staff almost immediately whether their ideas will find favour or be rejected out of hand.'[23]

And Ed was trusted by the Chancellor to carry out important, ultra-discreet missions on his behalf, to act as his envoy and representative. In opposition, for example, Brown, like Blair, had become a fan of focus groups and other market-research techniques. Focus groups enabled New Labour to tailor its policies to be as voter-friendly as possible in the key marginal seats of 'Middle England'. In government, the Chancellor tasked his chief adviser on opinion polling and focus-group research, Deborah Mattinson, to take charge of the first pre-Budget focus group. But he was nervous about anyone finding out about the exercise.

As Pym and Kochan write:

> Miliband slipped out of the Treasury, armed with sheaves of documents. Travelling down to Norwood [south London], he felt as if he was part of a cloak-and-dagger operation... The exercise served its purpose and the secret was not rumbled. Miliband returned to [the] Treasury relieved and able to brief Brown with some interesting conclusions. The group had been impressed with the idea of new funds for hospitals and schools. They warmed to the figures expressed as thousands of pounds per school rather than the overall total in billions.[24]

The 1997 Budget would announce £3.5 billion extra for health and education. It was the beginning of Labour's record investment in public services.

For the rest of Labour's first term in office, between 1997 and 2001, Ed accompanied Mattinson to almost all of her focus-group meetings around the country. It was a useful training exercise for the young special adviser, taking him away from the rarefied atmosphere of the Treasury, Westminster and north London, and offering him an insight into the lives and views of ordinary voters from all walks of life. 'He was savvy in his observations,' says Mattinson, who would later back Ed's candidacy for the Labour leadership. 'He and I would run through what we'd learned from the focus group on the way back to London and I was always struck by how insightful his observations and opinions were.'[25]

Few of his colleagues questioned his lack of experience, his youth or his abilities. Ed was hugely popular with Treasury staff, many of whom admired him for not exploiting his position and his relationship with the Chancellor. 'He didn't shout at people or look down on them,' says Andrew Turnbull, the chief civil servant at the Treasury between 1998 and 2002. 'Ed never threw his weight around.'[26] Again, the instant comparison would be made with the other Ed, Balls, who was seen, in the words of one former colleague, as 'burlier, tougher, rougher'.[27]

'I never remember Ed Miliband being angry,' says Charles

Falconer, a loyal ally and former flatmate of Tony Blair. 'He was always empathetic and easy to deal with.' Falconer remembers meeting Ed for the first time in a cross-departmental meeting on a 'complex issue of welfare reform' involving ministerial and civil-service representatives from the then Department for Social Security, the Cabinet Office and the Treasury. Ed arrived, accompanied by a civil servant, and convinced everyone in the room to fall into line with the Treasury position. 'He was very persuasive.'[28]

Overall, of course, as has been much discussed and documented, including by Blair himself in his 2010 memoir, relations between the Blair and Brown camps were poor – and had been since Granita. 'From day one, it was terrible,' Jonathan Powell, Blair's former chief of staff, has said.[29] Brown behaved as if he was a co-equal to the Prime Minister, dominating the Whitehall machine and, through his control of the purse strings, controlling almost every aspect of domestic policy. The New Labour government was a dual premiership; in the words of Brown's former permanent secretary Andrew Turnbull: 'There were Tony's subjects and there were Gordon's subjects. Tony did foreign affairs, Northern Ireland and education. Gordon did overseas development and welfare.'[30] The tensions between the two camps weren't eased when, in January 1998, a senior member of the Blair entourage – widely alleged at the time to be Blair's director of communications Alastair Campbell – described the Chancellor as having 'psychological flaws'[31] in a conversation with *The Observer*'s Andrew Rawnsley, who would anatomise the Blair–Brown wars – or 'the TB–GBs', as insiders referred to it – in his books, *Servants of the People* and *The End of the Party*.

Nonetheless, Blair's own relationship with Ed, if not with Brown, was a relatively friendly one. A close ally of the former PM says that 'Tony always liked Ed Miliband, and found him easy to get on with. He respected Ed's intellect and, during that whole period with Gordon in the Treasury, he considered Ed Miliband to be a man you could do business with.'[31]

Balls, on the other hand, is accused by one of Blair's closest officials of showing 'complete contempt for Tony. He would just lay into Tony at meetings.'[33] (It is a charge that Balls has flatly denied.)

Blair's positive view of Ed was shared by the leading Blairites – including Peter Mandelson who 'rated' the Brownite, younger

Miliband brother from very early on. In Blairite circles, Ed was known as the 'emissary from Planet Fuck'. He was the Brownite who didn't tell supporters of the Prime Minister to 'fuck off'.

It helped, of course, that he was dating Liz Lloyd during much of this period. Lloyd had worked for Blair since his days as shadow Home Secretary in 1993 and followed him into Number 10 in 1997, where she worked in the Prime Minister's Policy Unit as his home-affairs adviser (and would later go on to serve as deputy chief of staff). She sat in a cramped office in Number 10, next to Ed's brother David, who started off as the acting head of the Unit before becoming the permanent head (until his election to Parliament in 2001). By going out with Lloyd, wrote Alice Miles (*The Times* journalist who herself later dated Ed), the younger Miliband 'put himself firmly among the Blairite troika of Lloyd, Tim Allan and James Purnell, inseparable Islington flatmates and former schoolmates, originally from Surrey and known as the "Guildford three"' (Lloyd, Allan and Purnell all went to the Royal Grammar School in Guildford).[34] Purnell worked with David and Lloyd in the Policy Unit and would later join Ed and Douglas Alexander on a holiday in Ireland in 2000; Allan was Alastair Campbell's deputy in the Downing Street press office. Few Brownites, with the exception perhaps of Sue Nye, who had a close friendship with Anji Hunter, Blair's own gatekeeper and director of government relations in Number 10, could claim a better relationship with the Blair court than Ed.

ooooo

In the late 1990s, Ed was working in the Treasury; David was working in Number 10, as head of the Prime Minister's Policy Unit (until he left Downing Street to stand for Parliament in South Shields in 2001).

In their respective roles in the Treasury and Number 10, they had little direct interaction. But Ed did, literally, live on top of David, in a house in Chalcot Square, in Primrose Hill, that their mother had originally bought for their late grandmother in 1981. David turned the ground and first-floor flats into one home while Ed moved into the second floor flat and reportedly acquired the leasehold for around £100,000[35]. Friends remember the doors always being open between the two flats – with Ed bounding down the stairs to chat to David and, after they married in 1998, David's wife Louise. A fellow member of the Brown team remembers faxing messages intended for Ed to David's fax machine, as Ed didn't own one. She would then ring Ed to tell him she had sent the fax and he would go down and collect it from David.[36]

The brothers would also spend time together with their mother, as a family, every Sunday. They would talk, debate and reminisce around the dining table. But, by now, visitors to Edis Street were mildly amused to see the adult sons of the late Ralph Miliband in their new avatars as advisers to, and defenders of, the New Labour government. In December 2000, Tony Benn wrote in his diary: 'Went to Marion Miliband's for dinner with David and Edward… I was keen not to be provocative in any way, and it wouldn't have been possible anyway. The boys live entirely in the world of the Prime Minister's advisers… I was treated as a sort of kindly old gentleman.'[37]

Marion herself, an unashamed socialist and Old Labour to her core, had issues with the policies and direction of the government her sons worked for. 'Why oh why,' she would say to David and Ed, 'why oh why has New Labour done this?' 'W.O.W.' is how her sons nicknamed the plaintive cry from their left-wing mother.[38]

The conversations about the limits and inadequacies of New Labour's triangulating, centrist approach to governance would, occasionally, become heated. Marion would rail against Blair, who she could not stand. A visitor to the family home soon after David was appointed by Blair as a junior schools minister, remembers a dinner hosted by Marion at which he and Marion were joined by David and Louise. David, having come straight to dinner from his department, had his red ministerial box with him. Spotting the box, an indignant Marion said to her son, in a shrill voice: 'How can you be doing things like that?' – referring to the Blairite education reform of 'city academies'. David let his mother's remark roll over him; he did not reply or respond, instead changing the subject and trying to charm his fellow guests.[39]

Ed, on the other hand, say friends of Ralph and Marion, was always more open to the criticisms. 'Unlike David, he still saw himself as a man of the left,' says one.[40] 'He was always more curious about what was going on outside of New Labour,' says another.[41] As a result, Ed adopted a more plural approach, refusing to dismiss voices from the left, or from the green or anti-globalisation movements, in the way in which some of his New Labour peers seemed to revel in doing. It is difficult to imagine any other special adviser, Blairite or Brownite, enthusiastically attending the anti-globalisation World Social Forum in Porto Alegre, as Ed did in 2003 (from where he wrote, in the *New Statesman*, that 'whether or not you agree with the forum's ideas, Porto Alegre convinces people that, in a world of big forces that are often beyond their control, they can make a difference... For those of us who try to enthuse people about our politics, that is a lesson we would do well to remember'[42]).

Ed's pluralism may have been a reaction to the dogmatism he experienced as a child. Ed loved and admired Ralph but he had long ago rejected what he believed to be the sectarianism inherent in his father's approach to politics. He now believed that he had identified a similar sectarianism, a narrowness of approach and vision, a fixed and unchanging view of the world, in New Labour.

Privately, Ed had little sympathy for Blairism and New Labour's reverence for markets. He felt he was still a man of the centre-left and that he had to retain a healthy scepticism for the private-sector, non-state solutions so beloved of Blair and his acolytes. From foundation hospitals to city academies to tuition fees, Ed, like his boss, the Chancellor, had few qualms in expressing outright opposition to these policies in the various discussions between Number 10 and the Treasury. He reserved his own strongest criticisms for tuition fees where, like Brown, Ed viewed fees as a deterrent to children from poorer families attending university and feared the creation of a marketplace in higher education. His preferred option was a graduate tax – under which students would essentially pay their tuition costs through general taxation once they began work – and he was 'pretty uncompromising', according to a former Blair aide who debated the issue with Ed at the time.[43]

Ed still saw himself as a pragmatist – he recognised the failures of Old Labour and had thrown in his lot with New Labour. But, at the same time, he prided himself on being a self-consciously distinctive and different creature to the ambitious, thrusting, non-ideological types who filled the ranks of the New Labour government's special advisers. 'Even then,' says a family friend,

'Ed had a more radical sensibility than his brother or the other New Labour spads.'[44]

He would later tell friends that he 'had always had a critical distance' from the Blair–Brown project. Labour, he argues, tried to run a better welfare state and well-funded public services without reforming capitalism and its excesses. In the wake of the financial crisis of 2008, Ed told friends that he felt vindicated to have been so sceptical of the neoliberal direction adopted by Blair, Brown and Balls from the 1997 election onwards.[45]

But why didn't he speak out? Ever the pragmatist, modest about his own power and influence, he did not dissent from the Blair–Brown strategy of deregulating and then taxing the banks in order to invest in health and education. There is no evidence that he made his concerns clear to his superiors. Challenged by a journalist a few years later as to why he did not speak his mind, Ed responded: 'This was their show, the Blair–Brown show. Advisers just advise.'[46]

There is also a sense that Ed was in awe of Brown – his intellect, his grasp of economics, his political savvy, his ambition and self-confidence. He would praise and defend Brown to friends who were not Labour members or supporters. He was genuinely proud of the progress he believed that the government – and, in particular, the Treasury of which he was part – was making on poverty, welfare reform and investment in public services.

Ed has been heard telling colleagues that his two proudest personal achievements in the Treasury were securing extra funding for the NHS, out of general taxation, and instituting a tax credits regime that put more money in the pockets of the poorest workers while encouraging those on benefits to get paid jobs.

Sitting on David Frost's studio sofa in January 2000, Blair had pledged to increase UK health spending up to the European Union average within five years – prompting the now infamous response from his irate Chancellor: 'You've stolen my fucking Budget.'[47]

Brown had wanted to make the announcement on health spending. His team, led by the two Eds, had already been discussing the need to increase spending on the NHS, funded by increases in direct taxation, and preparing the ground for such a policy. Before the 2001 general election, Balls and Ed, on Brown's behalf, approached first Adair Turner, the former director general of the CBI, and then Derek Wanless, the former chief executive of NatWest Bank, to ask whether either of them would agree to chair a review of NHS funding. It was Wanless who said yes.

Up until 2002, Brown had been a practitioner of 'stealth' taxation, furtively raising taxes for the purposes of redistribution and investment in public services. But Wanless helped him build the case for an explicit tax rise to fund extra spending on a cash-starved health service.

In November 2001, ahead of Brown's Pre-Budget Report, Wanless published an interim report which made the case for greater NHS expenditure and dismissed 'any alternative financing method'[48] to general taxation. It was a turning point. The night before the interim report was published, a tired Ed joined an equally-exhausted Balls and his wife Yvette Cooper for dinner at a Japanese restaurant. As they waited for their sushi to arrive, the trio agreed that the impending tax rise would be the 'most significant decision' of Brown's chancellorship so far.[49]

On 17 April 2002, the day of the Budget, Wanless published his final report, setting out projections of how much it would cost in future decades to deliver high quality services throughout the NHS. As was expected, he recommended that 'over the next twenty years, the UK will need to devote a substantially larger share of national income to health care', with the percentage of total health spending rising from 7.7 per cent of GDP in 2002/03 to between 9.4 per cent and 9.5 per cent in 2007/08 (and between 10.6 per cent and 12.5 per cent in 2022/23).[50]

In his Budget statement a few hours later, using the Wanless Report as cover, the Chancellor announced real terms increases in funding for the NHS of 7.4 per cent annually over the next five years – to be partly paid for by a 1 per cent increase in National Insurance contributions (NIC) for employers and employees. Brown described it as a 'Budget to make our NHS the best insurance policy in the world'.[51]

It was a risky strategy, which went against one of the fundamental tenets of New Labour – that is, not raising taxes on income. Blair privately worried that it 'could cost me the next election'.[52] Brown, meanwhile, feared the verdict of a right-wing media and fretted, in Steve Richards's words, 'that it could destroy his reputation as a New Labour Chancellor'.[53] But it was the two

Eds, together, who had steadied his nerve ahead of the Budget, adamant that they could not back down now and promising him that he would be rewarded by the voters.

'It was a big leap,' says Ed now. 'No other social democratic government in Europe was willing to stick its neck out and say "We think this investment should take place"'.[54]

At the first Prime Minister's Questions after the announcement of the NIC rise in Brown's Budget, 'not a single Conservative MP stood up to attack the National Insurance increase'.[55] Meanwhile, the opinion polls were extraordinarily positive for Brown and his Budget. An ICM survey commissioned for *The Guardian* found 72 per cent of the public approved of the Chancellor's decision to raise National Insurance contributions, including a majority – 54 per cent – of Tory voters.[56] One government adviser subsequently described it as 'the most popular tax rise in the Western world'.[57]

It was an indication that, belatedly, after five years of New Labour holding the reins of power, the party was beginning to shift the political consensus on tax-and-spend from right to left.

The two Eds had been proved right. 'If it hadn't been for the joint work we did on that policy over the preceding three years, we would not have got to that point and to such a popular tax rise,' says Balls now.[58] In the words of another member of the Brown team, 'The two Eds were, in a way, like Blair and Brown. They had their problems but together they were greater than the sum of their parts. That showed when it came to the National Insurance increase.'[59]

But it wasn't just the NIC rise for the NHS that Ed can help take credit for. There was also the introduction of tax credits. 'Ed basically owned the tax credit agenda,' says a former member of Tony Blair's Policy Unit. 'It was a massive deal for Gordon, and Ed delivered for him.'[60]

Tax credits, often described as Labour's flagship welfare policy, were aimed at integrating benefits into the tax system, rather than offering straightforward handouts, and were designed to reward people who were in work – thereby making work pay.

Ed was a prime mover in the Treasury behind the Working Families Tax Credit (WFTC), introduced in 1999 to replace the Tories' Family Credit. With WFTC, 'families where one adult worked now saw a huge rise in their incomes – up to £50 more a week, with an average rise of £24 over the old Family Credit system... As WFTC paid so much more than Family Credit it brought more families into its net, and one million households received it.'[61] The introduction of WFTC also included a direct childcare subsidy for parents for the first time and was administered by the Inland Revenue, rather than the Benefits Agency.

Referring to the introduction of tax credits like WFFC, the civil servant in charge of welfare reform, Nick Macpherson, who has since become permanent secretary at the Treasury, described Ed in 1999 as 'the great unsung hero'[62] of Brown's kitchen cabinet.

Tax credits ended up costing the equivalent of around 4p to 5p on the basic rate of income tax over Labour's thirteen years in office and turned the Treasury, in the words of the former Cabinet Secretary, Richard Wilson, into 'the largest spending department in Whitehall'.[63] It was a vitally important policy for which, at the age of just twenty-nine, Ed oversaw both the introduction and implementation.

In recent years, tax credits have been subjected to a barrage of criticisms, from right and left. Some on the right say they are a perfect example of Brown's statist, top-down, meddling approach to welfare reform and poverty reduction. They believe tax credits disempower and infantilise the poor. Others on the left say they are a subsidy to employers who pay poverty wages to their workers; they believe that the introduction of tax credits encouraged Labour to turn a blind eye to the injustice of low pay. Most agree that they are, at a minimum, fiendishly complicated and an 'administrative nightmare for HM Revenue & Customs'.[64]

Despite all this, however, Brownites can legitimately argue that the introduction of tax credits was an example of a successful and worthwhile New Labour social policy – and it was deeply progressive. The steep rise in tax credit payments boosted the incomes of the lowest-paid members of the workforce between 1997 and 2010. In fact, according to the Institute for Fiscal Studies (IFS), in a long-term study published ahead of the 2010 general election, the tax credit strategy as a whole resulted in the poorest 10 per cent of households seeing their incomes rise by 13 per cent.[65]

ooooo

For Ed, working for Brown in the Treasury was both a pleasure and a pain. A pleasure because Ed, young, ambitious, politically-motivated, had a privileged position inside of government, an opportunity to make a difference and shape policy on the issues he cared about – from poverty and welfare reform to public services and, in particular, the NHS.

A pain because Brown was an intense and all-consuming employer, a workaholic who expected his young spads to be available around the clock. The Chancellor would call Ed at all times of the day and night, with requests, instructions, and complaints or, often, just to chat and talk strategy or tactics. 'You don't work for Gordon and stop at six o'clock on a Friday night,' says a frustrated former girlfriend of Ed's. 'He is in your life 24/7. Fridays, Saturdays, Sundays.'[66]

On Sunday mornings, Ed would unplug his landline at home to avoid having to receive the dreaded call from his boss at 8 o'clock. It has even been reported that Ed once deleted his number from Brown's mobile phone 'because he was so fed up with being rung at all hours'.[67] But the truth is that the Chancellor had asked Ed to enter his number into his phone and Ed, conveniently, forgot to do so. 'It was a sin of omission rather than commission,' says a friend.[68]

By 2002, Ed had begun to wonder whether or not it was time to take a break from his hectic life as a Treasury special adviser. He was thirty-two years old and had spent the majority of his adult life – nine years – as a political adviser. He was intellectually, as well as physically, exhausted and felt he needed some time to himself, to think for himself. Such was the dominance of Brown in his life, that Ed often felt he was thinking for Brown – 'What does Gordon think?' rather than 'What do I think?' He wanted to think through his emerging doubts about the New Labour project and explore his 'critical distance' from the government. Stewart Wood, on secondment to the Treasury from his day job as a politics tutor at Magdalen College, Oxford, remembers Ed telling him on more than one occasion: 'I'm envious of you because you get time to think and time to write.'[69]

A friend of Ed told him during this period: 'You're not going to lie on your deathbed and think to yourself: "I wish I'd spent more time working for Gordon."'[70] It was painfully true.

The 2001 general election, in which Ed had helped another Brown protégé, Douglas Alexander, run Labour's campaign and honed his political skills, was out of the way. So too was the Treasury's three-year spending review, which had been completed and published. It was the ideal opportunity to take a sabbatical from government – and Ed had received an offer to study at Harvard for a year.

Above all else, he was delighted to discover that the Chancellor was not going to stand in his way. 'Gordon took the view that it would be better for Ed to go for a year, get it out of his system and then come back to the Treasury – than stop him from going and have him quit altogether,' says a former aide to Brown.[71]

The press reaction to Ed's departure illustrates how integral he had become not just to the Brown team but to New Labour as a whole. 'It will deprive Labour of one of its strongest assets,' wrote a Tory-supporting journalist in the summer of 2002.[72]

Was he making a mistake in leaving the Westminster scene? Prior to making his decision to take a sabbatical from Team Brown, he had consulted with his closest friends and colleagues, including Spencer Livermore, Sue Nye and Wood. The latter encouraged him to go; Nye, on the other hand, was less keen and worried that his departure would harm his budding political career.[73]

But did Ed definitely want a career in politics? A year at Harvard would give him the space and time to explore other options – chief among them, academe. Friends of his father had often told him that he had the ability and the potential to follow in Ralph's footsteps. This was an exciting chance to put the proposition to the test.

HARVARD

2002-2004

Harvard University's Busch Hall, located at 27 Kirkland Street in the heart of Cambridge, Massachusetts, was built in 1917 and opened to the public in 1921. It is named after the German-born brewer and philanthropist Adolphus Busch, who contributed $265,000 to its building fund before his death in 1913, but is perhaps best remembered as the creator of Budweiser beer. Originally intended to house the university's Germanic museum, it has since become the home of Harvard's Centre for European Studies (CES). The CES was founded in 1969 to bring students and scholars together to discuss and debate modern European affairs – or, in the words of its website, 'to fostering the study of European history, politics, culture, and society at Harvard'.

Every year the CES admits around thirty visiting scholars from across Europe and the United States. The majority of these visiting scholars tend to be academics or postgraduate students but the CES takes great pride in also admitting a small number of ministers, civil servants and journalists on sabbatical.

In the autumn of 2002, Ed Miliband arrived at Busch Hall to begin his year as a visiting scholar at the CES. Once again, he was following in the footsteps of his brother David, who had attended the Massachusetts Institute of Technology – also located in Cambridge, Massachusetts – as a Kennedy Scholar, between 1988 and 1989, and received a master's degree in political science.

Ed had been invited to Harvard by the then director of the CES, Professor Peter Hall. The bearded and scholarly Hall was familiar to Ed: two years earlier, in 2001, he had co-authored a book called *Varieties of Capitalism* with the economist David Soskice – father of Ed's ex-girlfriend, Juliet.

Hall remembers Ed telling him that he wanted to take a break from the daily grind of the policy world to think with more time and detachment about issues of social justice and what Labour, in particular, should be doing about them. The professor's own sense was that Ed also wanted to use his spell at Harvard to think about his own future in the Labour Party and what kind of role he wanted to play within it.[1]

Other Harvard contemporaries agree. 'I think this was the time where he could think about what he wanted to do,' says Trisha Craig, the executive director of the CES, who became close friends with Ed. 'Did he want to go on in politics or take a different route? It was a crossroads in his life.'[2]

Martin O'Neill, who was completing a PhD in the university's philosophy department at the time, and became friends with Ed, remembers asking the young spad why he had come to Harvard. 'His answer was that he wanted to take a step back from day-to-day politics and he wanted to maybe write a book about progressive thought and the future of the left,' recalls O'Neill, who now teaches political philosophy at the University of York. 'I got the sense at that time that this was a guy who had been very involved in day-to-day politics but maybe wasn't going to stay in it. He seemed to have some dissatisfaction with the lack of thinking space that he had in the day job he was doing.'[3]

If Ed was going to take time out from the Treasury to explore his political beliefs and expand his intellectual horizons, where better to do so than at one of the world's most prestigious universities? The opportunity offered by Peter Hall and the CES had been almost irresistible. Established in 1636, Harvard is the oldest institution of higher education in the United States and is often ranked first in the various national lists of university rankings. Eight US Presidents have graduated from Harvard and seventy-five Nobel Laureates have been affiliated with the university as students, faculty, or staff.

As a visiting scholar, Ed had the opportunity to make contact with some of the West's leading progressive thinkers, including the Harvard political scientist Robert Putnam, famous for his work on social capital, and the Harvard political philosopher, Michael Sandel, who has taught the celebrated 'Justice' course at the university for the past two decades. 'He was looking for people who had ideas,' says George Ross, a former director of the CES, a friend of Ed's and a former student of Ralph's.[4]

There was also a sense that he was returning 'home'. Ed had

been an Americanophile since childhood, having lived and gone to school in Boston while Ralph taught at Boston and Brandeis Universities – one of the happiest periods of his peripatetic childhood. Ed has always been in awe of America, its sense of excitement, opportunity, optimism and unique culture.

He became a baseball fan. Despite his father describing the sport as 'two and a half hours of mind-destroying boredom',[5] living in Boston as a child made Ed, in his own words, 'a fanatic' for the Boston Red Sox (which helped make going to Harvard, in nearby Cambridge, so appealing). He later told an interviewer: 'The Boston Red Sox have this amazing story because in some ways they bear some resemblance to the Labour Party because they won the World Series in 1918 ... and they didn't win it again until 2004. And what's even more extraordinary about them is that they came very close to winning on a whole number of occasions in that 86-year period. So it's an amazing story of disaster and then redemption.'[6]

ooooo

Friends remember Ed as ruminative and reflective during his Harvard days. He was keen to absorb and explore the thoughts and ideas of others; he would go out of his way to find out what projects or reports other academics or visiting scholars were working on. If he did end up returning to politics at the end of it all, Ed told a colleague at the CES, this was going to be his last opportunity 'to be free'.[7]

Martin O'Neill bumped into Ed at one of those seminars. As is so often the case, the British students gravitated towards one another; Ed and O'Neill went out for dinner and a drink after the seminar was over. 'I knew the name "Miliband" but not much more and I remember at the time this vague sense of regret that there were two semi-famous people from England visiting Harvard – Ed and the novelist Zadie Smith [who was a Radcliffe fellow from 2002 to 2003] – and I had the misfortune of meeting the less interesting of the two,' jokes O'Neill.[8]

Ed made contacts all over campus. As in Corpus Christi, his easy charm and self-deprecating humour made him immensely popular: 'If Cambridge, Massachusetts could vote in British elections, he would have this constituency sewn up,' says Hall. 'He was a charming man and we were charmed.'[9]

One of the friendships Ed struck up was with a young academic working in Harvard's John F. Kennedy School of Government, named Archon Fung, an expert on civic participation and public deliberation, whose insights into empowering neighbourhoods and local communities would later inform David Cameron's 'Big Society' project.

The two men bonded intellectually and ideologically, spending hours locked in conversations on the role of the state and its interaction with society, the future of progressive politics in the West and in particular – in a period prior to the rise of Barack Obama – the failure of progressive politicians in the United States.

Fung remembers Ed bemoaning the weakness of the American left on more than one occasion. 'The phrase that resonated from Ed is that the Republicans are "preference-transforming" and the Democrats are "preference-adapting,"' recalls Fung. 'So the Democrats are tacking to where they think public opinion lies while the Republicans are happy to change opinion, on principle, as Margaret Thatcher did in the UK and Ronald Reagan did here in the US.' Fung got the impression from Ed that progressives should learn a lesson from conservatives: leading opinion rather than following it. Seven years before Ed stood for the leadership of the Labour Party, Fung had spotted his potential: 'What I walked away thinking is that Ed has a sense of leadership, of making a set of arguments and trying to swing people over to what he views as right and principled, even if they don't happen to feel that way when they're eating their breakfast cereal at 8 o'clock that morning.'[10]

Ed lived very near to Fung in the quiet, residential neighbourhood of Cambridgeport. The Harvard professor remembers Ed coming round to visit him and sinking into the couch in Fung's apartment as the pair watched episodes of *The West Wing* while munching on slices of pizza.

Ed's own Cambridgeport apartment was part of a 'triple-decker': the three-story building common to the New England region of the United States, where each floor typically consists of a single apartment. It was minimally furnished and always neat and tidy. 'I remember thinking that this was a man who lived a life of the mind,' observes Fung. 'I don't know whether it was a condition of the scholarship but he spent most of his time reading and think-ing and going to seminars and so on.'

It is worth noting that, as in Oxford, Ed did not embark upon any serious relationships while at Harvard. Romance was not his priority. He knew why he was there: to read, study, think and reflect. 'He seemed to be completely focused on developing his politics for twelve or thirteen hours a day, which I found quite amazing,' says Fung.[11]

ooooo

Ed's year as a visiting scholar at Harvard came to a close in the summer of 2003, but he decided to extend his stay in Cambridge by a single term in order to teach for the first time in his life. The son was following in the footsteps of the father. 'He was finding the environment very stimulating, he was interested in teaching so he decided to see if he could stay on,' says Hall, who helped his transition from a visiting scholar to a visiting lecturer.[12]

Ed returned to Harvard in the autumn of 2003 but this time to the university's government department rather than the Centre for European Studies. His background as an adviser to Gordon Brown helped him obtain such a prestigious post. 'Given his role at the Treasury, he was a middle-level important person and Harvard people love to have such people as lecturers,' says a former CES staffer. 'Harvard people love power.'[13]

The course that Ed taught was entitled, provocatively, 'What's left? The politics of social justice.' The course description on the Harvard University website read:

> What does it mean to be on the Left today? How can we organise our societies to achieve social justice? The course debates these questions and compares recent experience of left-of-center governments in different European nations and the US. It examines policy dilemmas confronting politicians seeking social justice amidst trends like globalisation, economic insecurity and multiculturalism. And it explores innovative, feasible ideas in welfare, economy and society which can define a future for progressive politics.

Ed was 'very conscientious',[14] says a friend, in preparing for the course and had spent the summer poring over a vast array of books on social democracy, welfare capitalism and equality, as well as political philosophy journals and academic articles. 'To prepare a class from scratch you need to do a lot of background reading that doesn't even make it onto the final syllabus or reading lists,' says Craig. 'Ed wanted to ensure he taught a really good class and appealed to his students.'[15]

But there was a small problem. In Harvard, students are allowed to sample as many (or as few) classes as they like during the so-called 'Shopping Week', at the start of each academic year. The university's Q Guide (or CUE Guide, as it was known back in 2003) is an important student resource during this particular period as it provides students with feedback from their peers about courses and lecturers based on their experiences in previous terms.

Since Ed's course was new, it didn't appear in the Q Guide. He was at a comparative disadvantage. A few days before his first class, Ed panicked. 'People don't know who I am,' he told Craig. 'What if no one comes?' Craig and Ed decided to go into publicity overdrive: in an echo of his Corpus Christi days, they made posters for his class and wandered around the Harvard campus taping them to walls and bulletin boards. Craig recruited undergraduates from the CES to take posters and literature promoting Ed's class back to their dormitories each night.[16]

On 14 September 2003, around 200 students crowded into Harvard's red-brick Sever Hall to hear the adviser from the British government speak for the first time. It was 'standing room only', says O'Neill, who went along to the first class to offer his friend some moral support.[17]

'I wasn't expecting such a large turnout,' Ed truthfully told the Harvard Crimson newspaper the next day, before adding: 'But there's a thirst to hear about something new.'

So why did so many students turn up for his classes? Craig offers three reasons. The first relates to his popularity and his status – the modest Miliband had undersold himself. He was not just well-liked but well-known across campus. His reputation preceded him and students at Harvard tend to prefer to hear from people who can offer practical, as well as theoretical insights; people who have first-hand experience of the issues and have 'been in the trenches', in Craig's words.[18] Second, the advertising blitz across Harvard dorms in the days leading up to his first class helped boost attendance. And then there was his teaching style: once in his class, students responded positively to the engaging and challenging lecturer and his conversational approach. He also made himself accessible after class to students who had questions; once again, his listening skills were put to good use. 'I met several students who told me it was their favourite class,' says Hall.[19] Ed himself admits today that he was good at 'the performance' of public speaking then as now.[20]

Aside from the Q Guide, Harvard offers students an opportunity, via anonymous forms, to evaluate their lecturers. The forms are collated and lecturers are offered scores out of five – by the end of his course, Ed had obtained a score of 4.9. 'It was a phenomenally good score and he was rightly proud of himself,' recalls Craig.[21]

One of Ed's closest friends describes the class as a 'watershed moment' for Ed; the 33-year-old special adviser from north London standing up in front of undergraduates in one of the world's top universities; making speeches, giving lectures, holding seminars. Far away from Gordon Brown, Ed Balls and the Treasury, says the friend, 'Ed was coming out of his shell, proving to himself that he could do it, that he was important in his own right.'

Ed used his course to ask questions about a subject that he cared deeply about: inequality. Does it matter? Should it matter? How should it be defined? 'He didn't preach to the students,' says O'Neill, 'but given what they were reading the one thing the course would do is give the students reasons for why inequality mattered.'[22]

In the very first class of his course, Ed played a video to his students of the famous BBC *Newsnight* interview with Tony Blair in the run-up to the 2001 general election. Presenter Jeremy Paxman had asked the then Prime Minister six times whether the gap between rich and poor mattered – but, each time, to no avail. Blair's response was typically evasive: 'It's not a burning ambition for me to make sure that David Beckham earns less money.'[23]

For Blair, reducing poverty, and not inequality, was the goal; for Ed, however, the two went hand in hand. In fact, the failure of the government that he was part of to tackle the gap between the wealthy and the rest was, in the words of a friend, 'a key source of his dissatisfaction with Blair and New Labour'.[24]

Despite being 3,000 miles away from the UK, Ed never succeeded in cutting himself off totally from the British politic scene – nor, perhaps, did he want to. Members of the Brown gang – including his friends Douglas Alexander, Stewart Wood and Spencer Livermore – came out to visit him in Cambridge. Brown himself would call regularly, at all hours of the day and night, interrupting Ed in the midst of a class or a conversation. Neither the Atlantic Ocean nor the time difference were barriers to the Chancellor of the Exchequer.

Ed, however, was loyal to his boss throughout his period at Harvard – friends cannot recollect a single occasion on which he criticised or even poked fun at his mentor. 'He was discrete and guarded,' says a former Harvard colleague. 'He only ever talked about Brown admiringly and positively; he had enormous respect for Brown's intellect.'[25] David Blackbourn, the current director of the CES, adds: 'Ed had some good stories about Gordon Brown that painted the then Chancellor as a much warmer and funnier private person than the public image of the dour Scot.'[26]

Nonetheless, says O'Neill, 'he was clearly someone who was frustrated with the limitations of New Labour as a whole. There he was, as a special adviser, close to the levers of power, but with a real awareness of the limitations.'[27] Both in his role as a visiting scholar and then as a visiting lecturer, Ed was keen to use his time in Harvard to explore the possibility of Labour doing much more to be a party and a government focused on equality and social justice.

ooooo

It would be a mistake, however, to assume that Ed went to Harvard and became lost in highbrow intellectual discussions and obscure academic literature. He may have had a limited hinterland, but it was a hinterland nonetheless. Outside of his studies and seminars, he would play tennis and go to watch his beloved Boston Red Sox play. 'If you wanted to be his friend, you had to go watch a Red Sox game with him,' says Trisha Craig. Ed, the Red Sox fan, left Harvard and returned to the UK in January 2004; in October of that year, his team won the World Series for the first time since 1918. Craig remembers Ed calling her up from London on the night the team triumphed, his voice filled with elation: 'Are you listening to this?'[28]

His interests weren't limited to baseball. On one memorable occasion, Ed surprised his friends at Harvard by securing tickets for a rare Bruce Springsteen concert, to be held at Fenway Park, home of the Red Sox, in September 2003.

He also used his year-and-a-half at Harvard to learn to ski for the first time. 'I remember him turning up to ski wearing a goofy hat and a long coat,' recalls Craig. She would often join Ed and the British journalist Kirsty Milne, who was then a visiting fellow at Harvard's Nieman Foundation, on the ski slopes in nearby New Hampshire. 'I don't think he is going to be vying for a spot on the British national team anytime soon but he liked the idea of trying something new and athletic, as an adult, and finding that he was quite good at it.'[29]

Then there was Ed's childhood love for bowling, which was rekindled during this period. Annoyed by the fact that Cambridge lacked a 'decent' bowling alley, he rounded up a group of five friends one evening and took the subway, known locally as the T, to a bowling alley in the suburbs of south Boston. 'For the first time, I saw how competitive he was,' says O'Neill, who joined Ed on the excursion. 'And he won.'[30]

Whenever he got a chance, O'Neill would drag Ed to various pubs and bars in the area, from a noisy Irish pub called The Burren in Davis Square to John Harvard's Brewhouse in the main Harvard Square. But Ed's boyish looks were often a problem. On one occasion, towards the start of his sabbatical in Harvard, 32-year-old Ed went with a friend to a bar in Boston where he was asked to produce ID, in order to prove he was over twenty-one. 'He wasn't remotely thrown by it,' recalls the friend. 'Ed just laughed and said "Look, I've got a Harvard card. Would that be alright?"' The sheepish doorman then let them into the bar.[31]

Like his Oxford friends, Ed's Harvard friends cannot recall Ed having a girlfriend, or going on dates, during his time in Cambridge. But he was happy. Spencer Livermore, who went out from London to visit Ed in Cambridge, in January 2003, remembers his friend being much more relaxed as a Harvard fellow than he had been back in Britain as an employee of the intense and stress-filled Treasury under Gordon Brown.[32]

So why did he come back? His Harvard friends and colleagues – Archon Fung, Trisha Craig and Martin O'Neill – believe Ed could have pursued the path of an intellectual or a scholar, rather than the path of a politician. His intellectual abilities were beyond doubt. Despite having overseen dozens of visiting scholars from all walks of life, and all corners of Europe and North America, Hall says: 'Ed was the most successful of those visitors.'[33]

His Treasury colleagues differ as to whether or not Ed was on the verge of quitting politics for academia or even the world of think tanks. 'There was no sense that he was not coming back,' says Livermore.[34] Wood disagrees: 'There was a period where I didn't think he was going to come back to politics. He probably didn't know if he was going to come back either. It wasn't an easy decision to make and he wrestled with it.'[35]

It is worth noting that the academic route wouldn't have been easy: Ed had no published papers nor did he have a PhD. But above all else, the political itch in Ed was just too strong.

As if to prove the point, towards the end of his time at Harvard, Ed (who had always been interested in US politics and political history) became obsessed with following the ins and outs of the 2004 US presidential campaign – and not in an academic or impartial manner. He would go on regular trips to the neighbouring state of New Hampshire, which has held the first presidential primary in the nation since 1920, to weigh up the merits and demerits of the various Democratic candidates. 'He wanted to talk to Democratic primary voters,' says Craig. 'He was interested in people's stories, in their hopes and fears, even though he wasn't campaigning for himself or for a particular Democratic candidate.'[36] He was, however, fascinated by Howard Dean's primary campaign: the left-populism, the use of the internet to organise and fundraise, the young and enthusiastic volunteer base. It was a model that some say would partly inspire his own bid for the Labour leadership six years later.

His passion for American politics was mirrored by his ongoing love affair with British politics. Ed had gone to Harvard to find time to think and reflect, to find some breathing space from the daily stresses and strains of life in the Treasury. He came very close to becoming an academic, before realising towards the end of his stay in Harvard that his future was in Westminster. He was not someone who could sit on the sidelines. At a crossroads in his life, he turned his back on the career path of his father, instead choosing to follow in the footsteps of his brother: he chose politics over academia.

'I did have this sense when he was at the CES that he was somewhat temped by the academic life because he had a fine mind and an appreciation for ideas that one does not always find in politicians,' says Hall. 'But he is, ultimately, a doer and I think that became clear to him while he was at Harvard.'[37]

IRAQ

2003

The single defining event of the New Labour years, if not of British politics since the Second World War, occurred while Ed was away at Harvard – the decision to invade Iraq.

In the autumn of 2002, the drumbeat for war was growing louder by the day. On 12 September, President George W. Bush addressed the United Nations General Assembly, warning world leaders to confront the 'grave and gathering danger' of Iraq – or witness the UN become 'irrelevant'.[1] On 24 September, the British government published its now notorious intelligence dossier outlining the threat posed by Iraq's weapons of mass destruction (WMD). 'The document discloses that his military planning allows for some of the WMD to be ready within forty-five minutes of an order to use them,' claimed Tony Blair hyperbolically in the dossier's foreword.[2]

Sceptics questioned not just the motives for the impending invasion, but the timing too. What had Saddam Hussein done to warrant such urgent and global attention? And why wasn't his decision to allow UN weapons inspectors to roam freely through his country enough to reduce the supposed threat from his WMD? As even the most loyal and devoted of the Blairites, Alastair Campbell, wrote in his diary on 3 September 2002: 'Why Iraq, why now?'[3]

Inside the Treasury, Ed had been one of those asking a similar question of his colleagues prior to his departure for Harvard in September. 'How can we justify attacking Iraq?' an exasperated Ed asked, on more than one occasion. 'How do we even know he has weapons of mass destruction?'[4]

Richard Sennett, the renowned LSE sociologist, is a family friend of the Milibands. Towards the beginning of 2003, he and his wife Saskia Sassen invited Ed around for dinner; the latter was back at home in London on a brief return trip from Harvard. Sitting at Sennett's dining table, Ed, unhappy and angst-ridden, told his hosts that he was opposed to the forthcoming military action against Saddam Hussein and said he believed it was 'going to split the Labour Party'.⁵ He may have been a 33-year-old special adviser, but he showed prescient judgement.

He was also angry, says his university friend Gautam Mody. Why were alternatives not being considered? Why were the sceptics being dismissed or ignored? Mody recalls Ed's concerns as being two-fold: first, it was completely unethical to invade Iraq without provocation and without allowing the UN inspectors to finish their work; second, it went against the grain of the Labour Party's traditions of internationalism and multilateralism to join a right-wing Republican President's unilateral action against Saddam Hussein.⁶ As the years passed by, Ed didn't let the Iraq issue drop; as evidence of Blair and Bush's premeditation emerged from the various inquiries into the war – Lord Hutton's, Lord Butler's and the rest – he felt vindicated.

ooooo

At Harvard, friends remember Ed being quietly 'appalled'⁷ by the British government's decision to ally with the Bush administration. The US President was not a popular figure among the anti-war liberals who dominated the Harvard campus. The veteran Harvard political scientist, Stanley Hoffmann, the founder of the Centre for European Studies, was one of US academia's most outspoken opponents of Bush and the war in Iraq.

'Ed was very much against the war,' recalls Trisha Craig, 'but he wasn't the type to go around criticising his own government in public.'⁸ A few weeks before the start of the war, George Ross, an academic then based at the CES and a friend of Ralph and Marion's from their Boston days, confronted Ed in the foyer of Busch Hall. 'This is a disaster for Blair,' Ross told him. 'It is going to be a catastrophe.' Ed, says Ross, 'looked aghast and didn't really respond. He was really worried about Iraq but he was internalising his reaction.'⁹

Spencer Livermore remembers going to visit Ed in Harvard in January 2003. Tony Blair was meeting George Bush in Washington around the same time – a leaked memo would later reveal that this was the trip on which the British Prime Minister told the

US President he was 'solidly' behind US plans to invade Iraq and 'ready to do whatever it took to disarm Saddam'.

Livermore says he had been 'agnostic' on the issue of Iraq. 'Before I went out to see Ed, I didn't understand the rush to war but I was told by colleagues in government that it was the right thing to do and I was relaxed about it.'[10] Treasury officials like Livermore, Balls and Ed were not privy to the various intelligence reports on Saddam Hussein's alleged weapons of mass destruction (WMD) doing the rounds of Whitehall. They had to trust their colleagues in Number 10, the Foreign Office and the Ministry of Defence.

Upon arriving in Cambridge, however, Livermore realised that 'the Americans were going to war on a completely different basis to the one we were going to war on back home in the UK'. It became obvious to him, as it had become to Ed, that the United States had a single, explicit goal in Iraq: regime change. 'For Bush, it was about unfinished business with his daddy.' It was a view shared by his friend. Ed was 'horrified', recalls Livermore.[11]

The two men spent a great deal of time sitting on Ed's couch in his apartment discussing the prospect of war against Iraq and debating the possible political fallout. 'We read the papers together, we watched the Sunday-morning talk shows,' recalls Livermore, who says his visit to America was a 'tipping point' for his view on Iraq.

According to Livermore, Ed, ever the Labour loyalist, considered action against Iraq to be the 'wrong thing to do' not only for geopolitical and moral reasons but for party-political reasons too. Won't this be a disaster for the party? Why is Gordon not opposing it? How much will Labour be damaged by joining with Bush and the Republicans? These were just some of the questions Ed raised with his house guest in January 2003.[12]

Livermore arrived at Ed's home in Cambridge as an agnostic on Iraq; he returned to London as a fully-fledged dove. Brown, however, remained on the side of the hawks. One of the great myths that attached itself to Gordon Brown in 2003 was that he was secretly opposed to the invasion of Iraq and critical of his Downing Street neighbour's alliance with George W. Bush as well as the intelligence on WMD. The left wanted to believe that the Chancellor, unlike the Prime Minister, was a dove.

But Brown, like Blair, was an ardent Atlanticist who believed the bond between Number 10 and the White House transcended all others. And Brown, like Blair, had a huge respect for, and tended to defer to, the opinion of the intelligence agencies – one of New Labour's ugliest tics. 'Perhaps he decided to deceive himself [on WMD],' says a former Brown aide.[13]

Brown's silence on Iraq in private and in public had little to do with ideology or principle; he feared the consequences of forcing Blair out over Iraq and inheriting a weak party and divided government. And he was worried about the reaction of the Americans and the pro-war, right-wing press.

At the beginning of March, just weeks before Blair would order UK forces into combat in Iraq, Brown received a transatlantic phone call from Ed in his study at the Treasury. The Chancellor, sitting at his desk, could be heard remonstrating with his adviser on the phone: 'Ed, you've got to understand that we cannot break with the Americans.'

The call went on for several minutes. Ed urged Brown to give Hans Blix and the UN weapons inspectors more time to finish their work. Use your influence with Blair, he urged. Try and delay the military action. If you resign, suggested Ed to Brown, 'it's over'.[14]

Ed understood, as did, ironically, the Blairites in Number 10, that Blair was in a weak position and Brown in a strong one. He sensed an opportunity. 'I can imagine Ed thinking he had to call Gordon for the sake of his conscience,' says a friend. 'Despite being far away, he will have wanted to put his view forward and make the case.'

Such was the seriousness with which Brown took his young spad's views that, upon putting down the phone, he immediately summoned his closest aides to discuss whether or not to follow Ed's advice. Sue Nye, Ed Balls, Bob Shrum and Spencer Livermore trooped into the Chancellor's study. 'This is what Ed Miliband thinks,' began Brown, as he shared Ed's concerns about Iraq with the rest of the team. Ed is urging caution, Brown told his colleagues.

Balls, always keen to safeguard his position as the dominant figure in Brown's court, was keen to belittle Ed's views, says a participant at the meeting. 'He told Gordon that it was easy for Ed Miliband, swanning off to America, but the rest of us have to deal with this here and now.'[15] (Balls would later claim that he too had been opposed to the Iraq war in 2003 but also admitted that he would have voted in favour of military action had he, like his wife, been a Member of Parliament at the time.)

The 'deputy Chancellor' may have been the 'driving force' behind dismissing Ed's advice in that crucial meeting, says the Brown aide, but Shrum too was pushing Brown to maintain his pro-Atlanticist position. Shrum, a US political consultant and long-time Democratic strategist, who had befriended Brown and hosted him at Cape Cod, put pressure on the Chancellor to back Blair and Bush on Iraq. Brown, argued Shrum, couldn't afford to look anti-American if he wanted to be the next Prime Minister of the United Kingdom. Perhaps Shrum's political advice should have been taken with a pinch of salt – he has worked on eight Democratic presidential campaigns, all of which have ended in defeat. Six months earlier, Shrum had persuaded a 'sceptical' John Edwards, the US senator who would become the Democrats' 2004 vice-presidential candidate, to vote for the congressional resolution authorising US military action against Iraq in order 'to be taken seriously' – a vote that Edwards would later describe as a 'mistake'.[16]

Had Ed been back in the UK, physically present and able to argue his case, perhaps the result would have been different and Brown's stance on Iraq might have shifted. But being in Harvard severely limited his role and influence as a member of the Chancellor's inner circle.

On 11 March, the Chancellor met Blair and John Prescott, the deputy Prime Minister, for a private dinner to discuss the thorny issue of Iraq. Brown complained that there were no alternatives being offered to the party other than staying shoulder to shoulder with the Americans but, crucially, at the same time, made it clear to a relieved Blair that he would not oppose the impending invasion. Two days later, he persuaded his close ally Clare Short, the anti-war International Development Secretary, not to quit the Cabinet over Iraq and then arrived at a Cabinet meeting and delivered a detailed and impassioned statement in support of the Prime Minister's approach. By 18 March, Brown was personally lobbying sceptical Labour backbenchers to back military action in the all-important vote in the House of Commons.[17]

Ed's advice had been well and truly ignored by his boss.

As political historian Anthony Seldon observed: 'If Brown was negative, Blair's strategy was finished, and there would be no British troops in Iraq.' But the Chancellor 'chose not to strike at the vulnerable PM'.[18]

Brown didn't resign – or even threaten to resign – over Iraq. His enduring presence in the Cabinet helped Blair steady the Labour ship and retain a veneer of unity at the top of government. In the end, just three Labour ministers quit over the decision to invade: Robin Cook, the Leader of the House of Commons and the sole Cabinet resignee, John Denham, a junior Home Office minister, and Lord Hunt, a junior health minister.

Ed was full of admiration for the trio. In March 2003, Paul Gregg, the Bristol University academic and adviser to the Treasury, went out for a meal with Ed to the Cinnamon Club, a popular and very expensive Indian restaurant a stone's throw from the House of Commons. Spotting Denham at the bar, Ed went over and shook his hand. The academic says Ed was 'immensely impressed' with Denham for having stood up for his beliefs but adds: 'I took it to be more than that; that Ed agreed with his decision to resign over Iraq.'[19]

ooooo

The question of whether or not Ed opposed the invasion of Iraq would come to dominate the Labour leadership campaign seven years later. His chief rivals – brother David and ex-Treasury colleague Balls – were keen to cast aspersions on his claim to have been anti-war. They and their supporters claimed to have no recollection or specific memories of Ed's opposition.

Friends of the younger Miliband offer three explanations on his behalf.

The first is that Ed was 'out in America, stuck in Harvard and no one was talking to him'. He stayed in touch with Brown and a handful of Treasury colleagues but he wasn't in touch with lobby journalists or Labour backbenchers or the Blairite hawks in and around Number 10. 'No one from the British press was ringing up asking Ed Miliband for his views on Iraq,' says Trisha Craig. 'No one challenged him on campus and no one saw him as a repre-sentative of the British government.'[20]

The second is that Ed is a ferociously loyal individual. He may have disagreed with Brown (and Balls) on Iraq and their strategy of supporting Blair and Bush but he wasn't willing to disown, or even criticise, them in public. 'He isn't the kind of guy to go wandering around the bars of Westminster saying how shit his boss is.'[21]

The third is that his opponents in 2010 were deliberately and knowingly rewriting the history of 2003. As we shall see, they saw an opportunity to make mischief and raise questions about Ed's integrity and honesty.

Not only were David and his supporters fully aware in 2010 of Ed's anti-war views, says a friend of the younger Miliband, but they had been on the receiving end of those views in 2002 and 2003. 'There was a discussion between Douglas [Alexander], David and Ed where Ed was pushing the other two, who were both ministers, to say something critical about the rush to war. They both told Ed that they couldn't do it because it would be the end of their careers. Ed could have revealed that conversation during the leadership campaign, and exposed them both, but he didn't.'[22]

So was Ed opposed to the invasion of Iraq? The answer, conclu-sively, is yes. Various friends and former colleagues – Richard Sennett, Paul Gregg and Spencer Livermore in the UK; Archon Fung, Trisha Craig and George Ross, in the United States, have vouched for the fact that Ed was privately opposed to the war.

The question then becomes: why 'privately' opposed? Why not publicly?

It is a legitimate criticism. He could have resigned from his post as special adviser to the Chancellor in protest. He didn't. Given the doubts he had been having in Harvard about whether or not to continue with his political career, this was the perfect chance to put principle ahead of pragmatism. That he did not resign, and voiced his concerns only in private, suggest Ed understood the impor-tance of discretion and not rocking the boat. Here was a young politician who may have exercised good judgement on matters of war and peace but who also understood how and when to fall into line; who viewed the interests of his party and his political masters as paramount. Here was a man with clear political ambition.

COUNCIL OF ECONOMIC
ADVISERS

2004–2005

In February 2004, Ed returned from Harvard to the Treasury after eighteen months away, to take up a new post as chairman of the Council of Economic Advisers.

The 'council' was not in fact a proper council: its members met formally as a group on only a couple of occasions. 'It was a deal that Gordon struck with Tony in order to increase the number of special advisers inside the Treasury,' says a former aide to the Chancellor.[1] (The council would later attract the attention of the right-wing press: 'Brown's kitchen cabinet costs £1m a year,' proclaimed a headline in the *Daily Telegraph* in 2007.[2])

'Part of Ed's deal with Gordon was that he would come back to do more medium-term and long-term policy,' says a friend.[3] Another part of the deal was that Ed would be senior player in Brown's circle during a final, major push for Blair to make way for Brown in Number 10. Ed made it clear to the Chancellor that he had no desire to return to the relentless daily grind of special-advising. Brown agreed, giving him a new role instead.

'It was a title,' says a former senior civil servant in the Treasury. 'Gordon liked titles.'[4]

It was also an opportunity for a refreshed, re-energised, post-Harvard Ed to do some medium and long-term thinking, outside of the day-to-day pressures now faced by the likes of his friend Spencer Livermore, who had taken over much of Ed's special-advising responsibilities and policy areas while he had been away in the United States. As Brown prepared to replace Blair in Downing Street, a decade on from Granita, Ed had returned to be at his side and join him in his moment of glory. The lure of working for the Prime-Minister-in-waiting proved irresistible.

Ed had enjoyed himself at Harvard, where he had, in a sense, been a free man. But he now knew he had to reapply himself to the British political scene. 'He felt that this was a job that had to be done,' says a Treasury colleague. 'It might not be fun but it was big-cheese stuff.'⁵

'I got the sense that Ed's job at that time was more about the beginning of the manifesto,' says Paul Gregg, who was a member of the Council of Economic Advisers. 'Gordon Brown was beginning to think that he might become Prime Minister soon and he wanted to start thinking about the next election.'⁶

Gregg's 'sense' was correct: Brown, the impatient Chancellor with prime ministerial ambitions, wanted to be politically prepared for all aspects of the top job that he believed would shortly be coming his way. Despite its title, the members of the Council of Economic Advisers tended not to focus on strictly economic issues but ranged across domestic policy. Michael Jacobs, a former general secretary of the Fabian Society, had responsibility for issues related to climate change and the environment. Stewart Wood, the politics tutor from Oxford University, handled education, local government and European Union policy.

Ed had met Wood nine years earlier, in 1995, when Ed went out to visit his old friend David Soskice in Germany. Soskice ran a research institute in Berlin, and Wood happened to be one of his PhD students. 'We clicked straight away and stayed in touch,' says Wood, who would later become one of Ed's closest friends, confidants and political advisers. Despite his academic background, Wood had long been keen to move from teaching political theory to his undergraduates to practising politics in Westminster; he wanted a job in government as a special adviser. In 1996, he had co-founded Nexus, a network of academics, commentators and policy experts, which fed new policy ideas into the New Labour government after 1997.

When James Purnell quit his job as the culture adviser in the Downing Street Policy Unit in 2000, in order to run for Parliament, Wood wrote to David Miliband and put his name forward for the vacancy. David didn't think he was right for the role but later mentioned Wood's application to Ed, who was then still living in a flat above David and Louise in Chalcot Square. Ed rang Wood: 'Why didn't you tell me you wanted to work in government? You should come and work for Gordon.'⁷ Wood had two interviews with Brown who gave him the 'thumbs up'.[8] He secured a five-year break from his teaching post at Oxford University and started full-time as a member of the Council of Economic Advisers at the Treasury in June 2001, after the general election.

Wood, says a former Treasury colleague, was 'very clever and quite self-deprecating; not cocky at all'.[9] He and Ed bonded not just over their politics and their view of the world, but also in their approach to dealing with people and building relationships and friendships across ideological and factional lines.

Their approach was in contrast to Shriti Vadera, another member of the Council of Economic Advisers and 'an incredibly in your face sort of person',[10] who seemed to be overly self-assertive, a view widely reported in the press at the time. Vadera was one of Brown's favoured advisers, a former banker at the City firm Warburg, who shared the Chancellor's interest in Africa and international development. She was nicknamed 'Shriti the Shriek' by her colleagues. 'Shriti was like Marmite – people either loved her or hated her,' says an ex-Treasury official.[11]

A new face at the Treasury for Ed, upon his return, was Nicholas Stern, who had joined the department in 2003 from the World Bank as second permanent secretary, initially with responsibility for public finances. As the new chairman of the Council of Economic Advisers, Ed was given a spacious adjoining office to Stern, and the two men became good friends. Stern, who had been a professor of economics at the LSE and then chief economist of the World Bank, was impressed by Ed's intellect and his passion for ideas. He also echoes the common refrain from former colleagues of Ed: 'Ed is a great person to talk to. He listens to you. And he doesn't fall out with people – I never heard anyone say a bad word about him.'[12]

Ed's personal touch stood out among the spads. In early 2005, at a party to celebrate the launch of the government's childcare strategy, Ed bumped into Naomi Eisenstadt, the civil servant in charge of the Sure Start Unit. Eisenstadt's father had just passed away. 'He asked me where my father had come from, how he had "got out", which is such a Jewish question,' recalls Eisenstadt, whose Jewish father had fled Austria during the Second World War. 'It was a very personal conversation and not the kind of conversation you expect to have with a special adviser.'[13]

Ed mentioned to Eisenstadt his own father's experience of flee-ing Belgium during the Nazi invasion of the country in 1940. It had been more than a decade since Ralph's death, but his name would crop up in conversation from time to time. Stern remembers teasing Ed about the stark differences between his approach and the view of the economy espoused by his late father: 'If only your dad could see you now, Ed.' Ed would just grin, says Stern. 'He didn't mind being teased about that.'[14]

∞∞∞

What was Ed's long-term career plan upon returning to the UK from the United States? Becoming an MP was the natural and logical next step for an articulate, intelligent and likeable special adviser with political ambitions.

But others have suggested he planned to pursue a career in policy. Ed has admitted to friends that he considered going for the (then vacant) job of director of the Institute for Public Policy Research (IPPR), the Labour-leaning think tank. Some say he wanted to (again) emulate David and become head of the Number 10 Policy Unit under a Brown premiership. Brown, obsessed with making a smooth move from Number 11 to Number 10 Downing Street, had asked the two Eds to start planning his programme for government.

But the big question remained whether or not Brown was on the verge of succeeding Blair? Or, as some Brownites suspected, were Blair's latest series of quasi-promises to his Chancellor as vague and conditional as his previous statements on the subject?

In the words of John Prescott: 'Tony's technique was to persuade him [Gordon] to back him on certain matters ... and in return Tony would come out with the same old promise. He was definitely going in, six months, perhaps a year, certainly before the election. When it never happened, Gordon was furious – and the whole cycle began again.'[15]

Prescott saw himself as the only figure with the weight and authority to put an end to the TB–GBs; he would regularly invite Blair and Brown for 'marriage counselling dinners'.[16] Perhaps the most significant such dinner occurred in November 2003, when the deputy Prime Minister hosted Blair and Brown for a steak and kidney pudding dinner at his grace-and-favour apartment in Admiralty House, in the hope that he could try and reconcile the Prime Minister and his Chancellor. The various accounts of the Blair–Brown wars suggest that it was at this dinner that Blair promised to hand over to Brown in the summer of 2004, if, that is, Brown were to help him get 'through the next six months'. The next day, a jubilant Brown told his team that 'Tony has said he is going to go. We should start preparing.'[17]

Balls, Livermore and Nye were sceptical – and they were right to have been. By the following April, Brown himself had become suspicious that Blair would renege on his 'promise'. Under pressure to stay on from loyal Cabinet colleagues like Tessa Jowell, John Reid, Charles Falconer and Charles Clarke, and old friends and aides like Alastair Campbell, Peter Mandelson and Anji Hunter, as well as his wife Cherie, by the Easter break Blair was leaning towards staying on in Downing Street and fighting an unprecedented third general election in 2005. The turning point is believed to have been the local and European elections in June 2004, where the results for Labour may have been poor but the predicted 'meltdown' was avoided and the Tories, under Michael Howard, failed to reach an all-important 40 per cent of the vote mark. Philip Gould, Blair's chief pollster, told the PM that victory for Labour at the next election beckoned – and the Blairites immediately began briefing the press that their man would be staying on for a third term.

Once again, Brown and his advisers felt they had been misled by Blair. At one stage, the Chancellor arrived at Number 10 in a rage, for a meeting with the Prime Minister. 'When are you going to fuck off and give me a date?' he is said to have shouted at Blair. 'I want the job now.'[18]

Every member of the Chancellor's inner circle was livid at this latest 'betrayal', not just the traditionally confrontational Ed Balls but the normally polite and placid Ed Miliband too. And it was Sally Morgan, the Blair aide who had replaced Anji Hunter as the Prime Minister's gatekeeper, who was to be on the receiving end of a rare explosion from Ed. One afternoon, he stormed into her office in Number 10 demanding to know when Blair was planning to quit. 'Why haven't you packed up yet to go? There's a deal and he's got to go.' Morgan denied all knowledge of such a deal – 'I don't know anything of the sort' – prompting an enraged Ed to cite the Prescott dinner from the previous November. It was a new and tougher side to the emissary from Planet Fuck. A stunned Morgan later relayed the incident to Blair: 'You're not going to believe this. I've had Ed Miliband round telling me to pack up.' An irritated Blair then told Prescott who 'went mad' and called Brown to complain. But that wasn't the end of the matter. Ed is said to have then rung Morgan and yelled: 'That was supposed to be a private conversation.'[19]

'I was surprised because Ed was unpleasant and aggressive [towards Morgan],' recalls a former adviser to Blair. 'It was all extremely tense and tetchy.' Friends say Ed was genuinely angry and upset on Brown's behalf; he felt his boss had been led down the garden path by his Downing Street neighbour. There may have been an element of personal frustration too: he had returned from Harvard to serve in a Brown administration. But Blair wasn't budging from Number 10.

Prior to the Sally Morgan row, observes a close friend of Ed's, 'people might have been seduced into thinking that Ed was some sort of pushover or softie but he actually has strongly held beliefs that he will argue and fight for'. One of those (Brownite) beliefs was that the Chancellor had every right to insist the Prime Minister stand aside. 'I thought it was time for Tony to go,' Ed later admitted to a close friend.[20]

Ed's aides now say they do not 'recognise'[21] the description of Ed as being angry and rude in the incident with Morgan. But a friend of Ed who worked with him in the Treasury says that the account of his confrontation with Blair's gatekeeper is 'absolutely accurate'.[21] It is consistent with other flashes of ruthlessness shown by Ed in subsequent years.

ooooo

To those who knew him best, Ed was now a changed man. His US break had done him a world of good – away from Brown, Balls and the Treasury. He was a more assured and self-consciously senior figure. 'He came back from Harvard calm, confident, comfortable in his own skin,' says a former senior civil servant.[22]

Geoffrey Robinson, the former Treasury minister, recalls seeing Ed briefing the press on Brown's behalf upon his return from

Harvard. 'When the time came to wrap up, he just raised his hand and said "That's enough" and walked off', says Robinson, a close ally of Ed Balls. 'He was a different person. So confident.'[23]

'For the first time,' says a former Treasury colleague, 'Ed Miliband had emerged from Ed Balls's shadow.'[24]

But there was awkwardness too. Ed's relationship with Livermore changed in the wake of the former's sabbatical in the United States. 'The low point in our friendship was when he came back from Harvard because I had grown into, and secured, the role he had used to do. He came back more self-confident than ever but I had his job.'[25] A sense of rivalry emerged between Livermore and Ed, with the latter feeling the need to exert the seniority over the former. 'It was an uncomfortable period,' recalls Livermore, 'but it didn't last longer than six months or so.'

The two men's friendship, forged in the hothouse of the Treasury, in the combative world of the Brown gang, endured the temporary blip. In fact, Ed came to respect his friend's newfound seniority. On one occasion, says a former Treasury adviser, 'I tried to go around Spencer and go to Ed to air my frustration with some of our policies but Ed told me I shouldn't go behind Spencer's back.'[26]

There was no sense that Ed had been out of the Treasury loop while out in Massachusetts. He used to join Brown on the latter's official trips to America and made sure his presence was felt. On one occasion, in 2003, Ed had joined Brown, Balls and Damian McBride, who had recently been appointed as the Chancellor's press secretary, for a dinner with Bob Shrum. At the time, the well-known US political consultant was working on John Kerry's presidential campaign and the centrist Kerry was in the midst of a bitter primary battle with liberal Vermont governor Howard Dean. As they sat around the table eating, a smiling Ed announced to Shrum that 'this guy here, Damian, he's really into Howard Dean' (omitting to mention that he himself was a Dean sympathiser too). An irritated Shrum responded: 'We've got this idiot guy Dean running in the primaries and we don't know what to do with him because he's got a fan club of idiots who support him.' There was silence around the table, as the Brown team waited to see whether McBride would stick up for himself. The new press secretary turned to Shrum and said: 'Well, he's even impressed some people in the UK. I happen to be a member of his fan club'. Brown guffawed, as Ed patted McBride on the back and said: 'Well done, you've passed the test.' At this point, it was clear that Ed got on well with McBride. That would dramatically change.

But Brown's relationship with Ed was stronger than ever before. Ed was the man who could lighten the Chancellor's mood, cheer him up, motivate him and, on occasion, persuade him to adopt a different path.

On 30 September 2004, at the end of the Labour Party conference in Brighton and as Brown and a team of Treasury aides flew across the Atlantic to a meeting of the IMF in Washington DC, Blair announced that he would not only be staying on as Labour leader for a third general election but that he intended to serve a full third term as Prime Minister. Brown had not been warned in advance. As he stepped off the plane in America, the news came as a bitter blow to the Chancellor, whose hopes of a pre-election handover of power had already been dashed in the summer of 2004.

His aides erupted in fury and the briefings began. *The Guardian*'s Larry Elliott wrote a story containing a colourful quote from a member of the Brown camp referring to the Blair announcement as being akin to 'an African coup'.[27]

It was a provocative remark. Balls is said to have later told friends that the phrase 'African coup' was not his but that 'it was an accurate summary of what we all felt'. Meanwhile, out in the States, denying to colleagues that he was the source of the leak, McBride went on the war path: 'Who the fuck said this?'[28]

Brown sat in his hotel bar in Washington watching the first fifteen minutes of the first George Bush–John Kerry presidential debate. 'Gordon was depressed,' says a former aide to the Chancellor. 'Kerry looked like he was going to lose to Bush while Gordon was wondering to himself whether he would ever be Prime Minister.'[29]

A sombre Brown needed comforting and reassuring. The call went out: 'Get Ed Miliband over here.' Ed arrived in Washington to try and reassure Brown and gee him up. 'He was good at getting Gordon out of the funk.'[30]

Upon his arrival in Washington DC, however, Ed was told that he had to conduct an internal mole hunt, with suspicions centring on Shriti Vadera.[31]

Later, Ed looked tormented, say onlookers, as he prepared to confront the tough-talking Vadera out on the sidewalk. McBride and Michael Ellam, another Treasury official, were walking fifteen yards ahead of Ed and Vadera, when they heard the former suddenly shout at the latter: 'Did you tell Larry Elliott that it was an African coup?' 'No!' replied a startled Vadera. 'Right,' said Ed, and he hurriedly walked over to join McBride and Ellam. 'It wasn't Shriti,' he told them, looking off into the distance.[32]

Harvard may have emboldened Ed, but he still wasn't yet as ruthless or confrontational as the other Brownites. That would come later.

ooooo

The return from Harvard heralded not just a change in his career path but in his private life too. Two months after moving back to the UK in March 2004, Ed went to a dinner party in London where he struck up a conversation with a clever young lawyer from Nottingham named Justine Thornton.

Though she was struck by his eyes – wide and brown and fixed on their subject - a friend remembers Justine's undoubted excitement after meeting Ed as 'gosh how fascinating, he's really clever' rather than 'gosh how handsome'.[33] It wasn't love at first sight and it was several months before the pair started formally dating.

Justine was born in 1970, and attended the prestigious Nottingham Girls' High School where fees are now around £10,000 a year. (Former pupils include the ex-director general of MI5 Stella Rimmington and the children's author Helen Cresswell.)

She first came to public notice as a teenage actress, appearing in 1987 as a rebellious schoolgirl who refers to Geoffrey Howe, the then Tory Foreign Secretary, as a 'fascist' in the pilot episode of *Hardwicke House*, a Central Television drama made in Nottingham, near where she grew up. The programme, however, was swiftly cancelled after only two episodes in response to a public outcry over its provocative storylines and unsavoury characters – in the words of the *Daily Telegraph*: 'The drama's irreverence, comic violence and portrayal of dysfunctional pupils and incompetent teachers in a city comprehensive prompted a backlash that led ITV chiefs to pull the plug.'

Justine would go onto to appear in another children's programme, the award-winning *Dramarama*, but her flirtation with acting was brief. In 1989, she was admitted to Cambridge University to study law, graduating in 1992 with a 2:1. Called to the Bar in 1994, she became a specialist in environmental law and was working as a senior associate at Allen and Overy Solicitors when she met Ed in 2004. (She has since moved to 39 Essex Street and has been variously described in legal directories as 'intelligent, thorough and pleasant', 'charming and highly committed' and 'switched on'.)

She and Ed had much in common: their intellectual curiosity, their interest in the environment, and many of their political beliefs. Already a member of the Labour Party when they met, Justine has been described by one friend as belonging to the 'more moderate wing' and by another as a 'traditional, liberal, moderate centre-leftist'.[34]

But she herself wasn't political. She offered Ed a glimpse of life outside Downing Street, the Treasury and the Brown gang; of non-political activities and a much-needed hinterland. For Ed, who had dated several women from the worlds of politics and the media – Liz Lloyd, Alice Miles and (the current BBC economics editor) Stephanie Flanders, with whom Ed split up not long before he started dating Justine – his new girlfriend in 2004 came as a breath of fresh air. Nonetheless, his very next career move would confirm that his focus was still very much on Westminster.

DONCASTER

2005

Tony Blair has a reputation for having let down most of his advisers and allies who wanted parliamentary seats, agonising over losing their full-time private support to the trials of public life. Gordon Brown, in contrast, did all he could to secure safe seats for his people, who could then be added to his growing power base on the green benches. And by 2005, Ed Miliband had decided his future was inside the Commons, where, once again, he would follow in his brother's footsteps. Before he went to Harvard, Ed had discussions about whether or not to become an MP, including with Ed Balls, who was always open about his ambitions to enter the Commons. Ed preferred to portray himself as a different kind of figure, outside the conventional mould of politician. Yet having gone to Oxford and become a special adviser now looking for a seat, he was not only following David – not for the first or last time – but also a very traditional British political route up Gladstone's 'greasy poll'.

A junior Cabinet Office minister at the time, David Miliband had not yet gained a place at Blair's Cabinet table; that would come a year later, when he would be appointed Environment Secretary and dubbed by Blair as the 'Wayne Rooney' of his Cabinet. But he had been a rising star since leaving his job as head of the Number 10 Policy Unit in 2001 to contest the seat of South Shields. It is said that when David left Downing Street, Blair – unusually – had encouraged him to go for a seat, partly because he was too 'wonkish' and even too 'left-wing'[1]. Five years later however, David was already being talked about in Westminster as a future party leader.

Now it was time for Ed to get elected. Along with other key Brown aides including Ed Balls, Yvette Cooper and, later, Ian Austin, Ed would receive all the assistance he needed to secure the sort of increasingly rare 'safe' Labour seat that guarantees entry into Parliament under the niceties of the first-past-the-post electoral system. But that is not to say it would be an easy ride. Selection had to be plotted carefully, with safe seats – especially for men in the age of all-women shortlists – few and far between.

Throughout the spring of 2005, Ed discussed seats with a number of friends who insist his motivations included genuine idealism as well as ambition and pragmatism. He had thought long and hard about whether he wanted to commit to a parliamentary career. For Ed, there was a tension between taking the cool, detached position of the analytical political observer and getting stuck in as a pragmatic, hands-on political participant. Among the people he consulted during this period were Andrew Glyn and his wife Wendy Carlin. Ed told them that he felt he had to try and become an MP if he was ever going to be in a position to bring about a more egalitarian and just society – despite all the downsides and moral compromises associated with practical, parliamentary poli- tics. Glyn said he admired Ed's willingness 'to do something'.[2]

On one occasion during this period while Ed was consider- ing going for a seat, he went to a dinner party held by Douglas Alexander and his wife Jackie. Alexander had first met Ed in the London kitchen of David Miliband in 1990, but was close to both brothers. During the evening, most of the talk was of Ed's future despite the hectic work of government. One of those present was David Muir, later to be a senior adviser to Brown. Muir remembers that Ed, arriving at the dinner party, had a haunted look on his face. 'He was very keen to get a seat.' But this ambition was not, Muir says, for its own sake: 'You get special advisers who always say: "I want a seat", and you always say, "For what, and for what purpose?" He struck me as an incredibly nice guy and at that time most of the conversation was about him getting a seat.' At that stage, Muir says, 'it looked like Ed was going to get Michael Foot's old seat [in Plymouth].'[3]

Jonathan Ashworth, the current MP for Leicester South, was at the time a fellow special adviser in the Brown Treasury and the Chancellor's link-man with the trade unions. He recalls doing 'a lot' of research into the Plymouth Moor View seat – the succes- sor to Foot's Plymouth Devonport seat – for Ed: 'I remember we looked into Plymouth and I got involved in finding out about it and talking to regional players and that kind of thing and putting them in touch with Ed.' And Ashworth confirms that Brown –

surely now with the leadership in mind – personally 'took great pride' in getting safe seats for 'his people'.[4] (Brown was, an insider remembers, 'particularly chuffed' that Ed would eventually be selected in the same week as another of the Chancellor's aides, Ian Austin, in Dudley.[5])

In the event, the Plymouth seat became one of those with an all-women shortlist, going to Alison Seabeck who holds it today. The next seat that came up was Doncaster North, after its MP, Kevin Hughes, became seriously ill. The south Yorkshire constituency, held by Labour since it was first contested in 1983, was created out of the old seats of Don Valley and Goole. It has a population of 100,000, around 98 per cent of which is white, with some 40 per cent without any official qualifications according to the Census. Overall, Doncaster has suffered considerably higher unemployment than the national average in modern times, reaching up to 20 per cent under the Tories in 1990. In 2009/2010, full-time male wages were 'a fifth below the national average and the total number of benefit claimants a third above'.[6]

Hughes, a Yorkshire-born former miner who went on to be a pro-war 'Blairite', held the seat from 1992 until he was cruelly diagnosed with motor neurone disease in 2005. He would tragically die the following year at the age of fifty-three.

The seat, which became available relatively late in a parliamentary cycle in which normally a candidate would track an MP for several years, subsequently escaped a mandatory all-women shortlist, with two high profile men contesting it. One was Ed, and it is claimed by at least one senior party figure who knows the area that the NEC deliberately – and very unusually – 'kept the seat' open instead of making it all-women because of Ed's interest.[7] The anomaly clearly shows the strength of support Ed had at the centre and top of the party. The other, by awkward coincidence, happened to be a close friend of Ashworth: Michael Dugher, at the time a special adviser to the then Defence Secretary Geoff Hoon, and later a Brown spokesman in the run-up to the 2010 general election. After it became clear Hughes was standing down, Dugher, a dryly witty, old-right Labour bruiser who was born in Doncaster, appeared to be a shoo-in while Ed appeared to be an establishment outsider.

Ed would gain nominations from both Brown and Blair, but

this would initially only serve to underline how far this north London boy was from being local. Though he did spend early years in Leeds, Ed had returned to London at the age of seven. As is pointed out by Trickett, a former leader of Leeds City Council whose parliamentary seat of Hemsworth neighbours Doncaster North: 'Every previous holder of Doncaster North had been a miner. I think Ed was the first non-miner in that seat, and non-local too. I only moved twelve miles; he moved 200. For both of us there was much work to do in understanding the culture which we were to represent.'[8]

The question of whether a candidate is 'local', ever-important to constituency parties if less so to voters, was certainly an issue in Doncaster North, where only three of the six shortlisted were from the area. In March the *Doncaster Free Press* reported the 'row', with one Adwick ward councillor, Ted Kitchen, declaring: 'I am disgusted and a lot of people are unhappy. There were two Doncaster North councillors on the long list – why haven't we got the right to have someone on the shortlist?'[9]

Yet despite this, and despite his help from down south, Ed would, crucially and cleverly, turn a disadvantage on its head. He would use a strategy that he also relied on at Corpus Christi as well as in the leadership contest five years later. Remarkably, he managed in Doncaster to play the role of insurgent against party establishment, despite the fact that he was being helped by party HQ and nominated for the seat by the Prime Minister and Chancellor.

At the time, Ed's decision to run in Doncaster understandably caused tension with Dugher who – though he was not a miner and from the south, not north, of the town – was considerably more 'local' than Ed. Now however, Dugher – who would be part of the pivotal group of Ed Balls supporters who cast their second-preference votes for Ed Miliband in the leadership contest to come five years later – looks back on Ed's ascent with warmth. And he admits he had a problem: 'It was less than two years after the Iraq war and Iraq was a massive issue in the run-up to the 2005 election,' he says. As adviser to the Defence Secretary, who had been singled out during the Hutton Inquiry into the death of the weapons inspector Dr David Kelly, Dugher's chances were damaged by the fallout from the conflict.

Iraq, Dugher says, 'was incredibly divisive and lost us loads of

support. The operation itself had turned bad and had become difficult and we had all the controversy about the handling of it, Alastair
Campbell and sexing-up and all that.' Nonetheless, Dugher went
for it and gained the support, albeit late in the campaign, of Kevin
Hughes. 'Kevin sort of tacitly helped me and that was going round
and picking up some – particularly some of Kevin's very strong
supporters,' he says.

Dugher used what he calls the 'usual selection pitch', of having
strong local roots but national experience and now 'coming home'.
However, it became apparent that Dugher's perfectly admirable
links to and endorsement from Hughes was a mixed blessing.
'Kevin was a great guy but did have a number of enemies. Although
he was a good constituency MP, his CLP was dominated by the
local councillors. Kevin had come from the NUM and a different
era really and he was selected in the late 1980s.'[10]

Brown, at the same time, went into classic fixer mode for Ed.
He contacted Rodney Bickerstaffe, the ex-UNISON general
secretary who is from Doncaster. A senior party source says that
'Rodney was able to deliver for Gordon and Ed Miliband the sort
of UNISON and local councillor set... [In] most wards it would
be the councillors, the councillors' kids and those seeking reselec-
tion for the council nomination. They were basically the activists
of the CLP.'[11] Bickerstaffe contacted Chris Taylor, an activist for
UNISON, which would later back Ed Miliband for the leadership. Between them, Taylor and Bickerstaffe made sure Ed gained
steady support from the party councillor set. Chris Taylor's organisational help was critical and Ed would go on to employ him to
run his constituency office.[12]

Meanwhile, Ed Miliband was receiving regular advice from
Ed Balls, who was also issuing words of wisdom to Ian Austin in
Dudley. Balls was himself fighting what Dugher called a 'tenacious selection campaign ... visiting every member three times'[13]
in Normanton, the seat he would win. It is incidentally notable
that at this time, though Ed Miliband surely spoke regularly to
his brother, who doubtless encouraged his entry into Parliament,
his 'main adviser' in getting elected was Balls rather than David
Miliband. That they were not close friends was irrelevant; they
were both members of Team Brown. Another key helper was
Rosie Winterton, the MP for Doncaster Central since 1997, who

passed on useful intelligence she was picking up from party figures in the town and would replace Nick Brown as chief whip in one of Ed's first acts as Labour leader in 2010. 'Rosie did a lot for Ed and was really important,' says a friend of Ed's.[14]

Ed also gained subtle, behind-the-scenes support from another key local figure, Nan Sloane, who was Regional Director of the Labour Party and the returning officer. Sloane was also close to Balls. According to a source who knows both Eds, 'Ed Balls sort of delivered Nan Sloane for him. Nan was very keen to help Gordon – she was one of Gordon's people. So she gave a lot of bureaucratic support. There's no suggestion that any rules were broken at all – but she told him about the process and how the hustings would work, what he needed to do, all of that kind of stuff.'[15]

Despite all this, until at least a week before the selection the result looked uncertain, so much so that Ed was apparently convinced he would lose. According to a source close to Brown, Ed relayed this directly to his mentor. 'A week before, Ed basically tells Gordon that it can't be won. He says "Look, the local thing is just too important".'[16] It appears that a plan B was at this stage afoot should Doncaster not work out, in which Ed would go for the selection in Wolverhampton, which would have played host to another Blairite-Brownite fight, with Ed taking on the senior Blair aide Pat McFadden.

Instead, Brown went into overdrive. In London, he called a meeting with the Mayor of Doncaster, Martin Winter, a regular at local Labour Party meetings. 'Gordon got him down and it was one of the classic things where Martin Winter left the room thinking he was on the promise for something very nice in the future as agreed to help Ed,' says a source.[17] Ed now based himself in the Doncaster flat belonging to Winter, who advised him and even fed him in the evenings. Winter would eventually fall out with the Labour hierarchy and leave the party, and friends say he is bitter that his support for Ed during the selection was not rewarded.[18]

Brown had an even more lethal weapon up his sleeve: his own personal charm, which despite his public reputation counted for a great deal among the Labour grassroots. Local party figures were surprised to find Brown regularly on the other end of their telephones as the Chancellor tried to persuade them of Ed's merits – and the personal importance he attached to this selection. The

Chancellor even set up a phone bank in the penthouse apartment of his ally Geoffrey Robinson.[19] An aide to Brown describes the conversations: 'It was Gordon who was ringing round individual members in Doncaster North saying "He's brilliant. He's worked really hard for me. He's going to work really hard for you. He'll be great." So, he rang round members.'[20]

According to sources working for Brown at the time, he was 'obsessed' with whether Ed would get selected. On the night of the selection result in Doncaster, he happened to be flying on a trip back to the UK from Brussels on an RAF flight. Frustrated that he could not use his mobile phone, Brown stomped down to the pilot's cockpit and demanded a phone call be made to Doncaster to find out the result. A senior civil servant had to persuade him that this would be a waste of taxpayers' money, so Brown eventually padded back to his cramped seat on the plane. As soon as the plane landed but before it came to a stop, Brown uncharacteristically ignored the rules and switched his phone on. A message came through that Ed had won. Brown was seen in a rare moment of real joy, punching the air as if his local football team had just won the FA Cup, and punching it so hard that his hand hit the luggage compartment above his head with a crunch.[21]

To be fair however, even party figures not backing Ed in Doncaster do not claim that Brown's intervention was the deciding factor. 'It wasn't the reason he won,' says one such local party official, 'but I think in the few days in the run-up to selection and conference that was quite important because people loved Gordon's traditional Labour emphasis and they were very anti-Blair and Iraq.'[22]

Meanwhile – and despite the fact that Brown, perhaps the most ardent Atlanticist in the Labour Party, had himself backed the Iraq invasion – there were alleged attempts by some close to Brown in London to portray Dugher as a pro-war, gung-ho Blairite, a tactic which held an irony not lost on Dugher himself now, given his later job working for Brown. Dugher says: 'I became the sort of Blairite aide to the Secretary of State for Defence, the sort of pro-war candidate. [And Brown's] endorsement was obviously hugely important.' But Dugher acknowledges: 'Ed ran a great campaign because he had UNISON, the local councillors, the next leader of the Labour Party Gordon Brown and Ed Balls on his side.'[23]

John Healey, MP for neighbouring Wentworth since 1997 and a Balls ally who would later become a senior shadow Cabinet member, also hosted Ed Miliband in his house, providing late suppers, a glass of wine and conversation after 10pm in the evenings when Ed would return from campaigning. (Healey remembers that when discussing Iraq, Ed sided with Healey's wife, Jackie, who had been opposed to the war.)[24]

Yet despite this, there was clearly a calculated 'insurgent' strategy in play. As Dugher says, Ed 'managed to portray himself again as the sort of insurgent outsider against the establishment Blairite.'

On the night of the selection on 26 March 2005, Ed had one last trick up his sleeve, one that would be invoked again as he prepared for the leadership in the run-up to 2010: his oratory. On the night of his selection, as the contest with Dugher was still going down to the wire, Ed Miliband gave a brilliant and passionate speech, according to those who were there. Under the headline 'Oh brother, a star in the making,' a gushing account from local journalist Simon McGee in the *Yorkshire Post*, described how 'he preached, he conquered – and he landed'.[25] In front of some 150 members of Doncaster North Labour, Ed removed his jacket and spoke without notes, as he would do in later years at Labour Party conferences, meetings about climate change and, of course, as part of his leadership campaign. Setting the microphone aside, he paced the room, looking members in the eyes and telling them to trust him. Sources who were in the room agree that the somewhat 'evangelical' pitch alienated a tiny minority of Labour traditionalists, including some of Hughes's friends. But overall it was a success.[26] The *Post* report acknowledged that Ed's support from Brown and Blair had helped but said it was the speech that had won it and concluded with the words, 'Watch this space.'[27]

Dugher's memory of the night concurs. 'On the night of the selection conference, he basically turned up and blew people away,' he says. 'Now, I had a slightly off night. I was probably a bit below par, a bit nervous and feared that it was all running away from me. He came on and did his usual; took his jacket off, stood in the middle of the room and gave without notes a brilliant, an evangelical performance about "put your trust in me".'[28]

Ed looked individual members in the eyes, mentioned their names and the names of their children and even grandchildren, and said that his mission would be to change and improve their life chances. The majority of people in the room leapt to their feet. Ed's oratory and personal skills had worked. 'Whatever advantages he'd had throughout the selection,' Dugher concludes gracefully, 'I actually think the thing that sealed it was his performance on the night – it was just brilliant, and he thoroughly deserved to win.'

Ed, Dugher adds, 'was very good to me after the selection. I learned a lot from him and was a much better candidate for the experience when I went for the neighbouring Barnsley East seat [which Dugher won] five years later.'[29]

After winning the nomination, Ed's first phone call was to Marion in London. His mother was in the middle of dinner with an old friend, George Ross. 'Marion was clearly elated,' recalls Ross. 'It was such a loving conversation and she was so happy for him.'[30]

In the end, the Labour folk of Doncaster North had put aside their concerns about locality in order to plump for a touch of stardust. As a friend of Ed explains, 'Labour Party members will always say they want a local candidate, but they always like to have a superstar to put their constituency on the map.'[31] McGee echoed this at the time in his reporting: 'After all, party members love to pick someone they think can go all the way to the top, and there is no doubt that Miliband has the potential to do so.'[32]

The herograms and predictions were prophetic. After just five years in the House of Commons, Ed Miliband would become the first leader of the Labour Party with a Yorkshire seat since Hugh Gaitskell. Some of those who had helped him gain the seat – such as Winterton – would gain key positions under him. And there would be a shift in the shadow Cabinet from north east – a Blairite stronghold – to north west representatives, as if to underline the change in the centre of gravity in the party from the likes of Blair, Peter Mandelson and Alan Milburn to Balls, Cooper and Trickett.

On 5 May 2005, Ed was elected to Parliament as the Member for Doncaster North, securing a majority of 12,656 over the second-placed Conservative candidate, Martin Drake. It was a momentous night for him, professionally and personally. He had invited Justine Thornton, who he had started dating a few months earlier, to join him at the count. Justine, says a friend, was 'pretty keen on him by the 2005 general election'.[33] When Ed asked her to come up to Doncaster, the young lawyer was thrilled; her mother told her that the invite was 'significant'.[34] She was right.

Years later, Ed would express his mindfulness that 'it was the people of Doncaster who put me in Parliament and made this journey possible and I will never forget that.'[35] And there is no doubt that this north London liberal was to be heavily influenced by the local politics of his new northern base. He later remarked, 'It's the discussions I have had on Doncaster doorsteps that have guided my vision for the changes Labour needs to make to win back power.'[36] But in 2005, a leadership bid was a long way off, and despite his considerable success in Doncaster, Ed Miliband still had a political – and personal – mountain to climb.

INTO PARLIAMENT

2005–2007

Early in his first parliamentary term Ed attended what was for him a very unlikely party. The venue was the Westminster flat rented by three of the new intake of MPs elected in May 2005, Lyn Brown, Sarah McCarthy-Fry and Lynda Waltho. And the entertainment was karaoke.

Members of a group calling themselves '555' – MPs elected on 5 May 2005 – were escorted by their three hostesses across Westminster Bridge to the flat in what was the old County Hall building on the South Bank. There from 7pm onwards, they tucked into curry take-away washed down with the 'many' bottles of wine and cold beers in the kitchen. In the sitting room, a karaoke set borrowed from the MP Tom Harris was hooked up to a TV and a number of MPs took to the microphone. Karaoke was by now well established as a regular, if bizarre, after hours pastime among certain Labour MPs, including Tom Watson, who organised a number of sessions at bars in Whitehall and Covent Garden. Late into the evening, guests at this very informal gathering were surprised to see Ed Miliband walk through the door. Some felt he was 'a little buttoned up', but were grateful he was there at all. Ed arrived proclaiming he definitely wouldn't be singing, but to cheers – at around 1.30am – he finally did perform what is described as a 'crap' rendition of the Neil Diamond track, 'Sweet Caroline'. He left shortly afterwards, just as some of the night's more risqué 'party games' were getting under way.[1]

To any outsider, the Palace of Westminster can seem a very strange place. Famous for its 'corridors of power', the sprawling gothic complex has all the alcoves, courtyards – and gossip – of a village. The Commons is effectively a debating chamber surrounded by offices, cafés and bars. Riddled with men in tights, pomp and ceremony, it is in many ways a dysfunctional workplace in the modern sense, one where you can buy a bottle of whiskey but not a packet of printer paper.

Above all it is hierarchical. So when the fifty-six new Labour MPs arrived for induction in May 2005, they did not expect to see a lot of Ed Miliband. After all Pat McFadden, one of the few former Blair aides to be elected that year (in Wolverhampton East), did not hang out much with the new intake. And like Ed Balls and to a lesser extent Ian Austin, Ed Miliband was still acting as a key adviser to Gordon Brown as Chancellor. Just as before the election, he would be called in to Brown's chaotic office at the Treasury while the big man sat hunched at his desk, smashing away at a keyboard. And he would often be on the phone, advising his mentor at all times of the day and night.

Nonetheless Ed Miliband stood out among the newcomers. He mucked in where other 'famous' new MPs did not, taking time to talk to and socialise with them.

Soon after being elected to Parliament, the chatter about Ed's leadership potential began. On one occasion in mid-2005, Jon Trickett bumped into Ed outside his Commons office and told him that he should start seeing himself as a future party leader. Instead of laughing off the suggestion, Ed invited Trickett into his office and asked him to elaborate.[2] This was the first of a series of such conversations he would have over the course of the parliament. Yet, despite being a much-discussed 'star' of the new intake, his fellow MPs still saw him as one of their own.

Early on in the parliamentary term, Tony Blair and Brown would invite the new MPs for receptions at Numbers 10 or 11 Downing Street. Those MPs knew Ed had a pass to get in round the back, through the Cabinet Office, or straight through the black iron gates, and so were surprised to see him queuing up and chatting with the rest of them. Ed quickly became a regular at a series of informal dinners organised by the '555' group. The dinners took place every Monday evening at 7–10pm, over wine and the boarding-school-dinners style Commons food, and were organised by the three women who lived at County Hall. They made sure that each Monday one of them, or one of two other women MPs, Barbara Keeley and Diana Johnson, had booked a table. 'On a crap night we had about six people turn up,' admits Lyn Brown. 'But on a good night it could be thirty and we would be adding new tables to the one big one.'[3] Lyn Brown, who later would support Balls for the leadership, says that both Eds would attend the gatherings regularly, but there was a difference: Balls wanted to discuss football and gossip while Ed Miliband used them as opportunities for serious policy discussions. The '555' gatherings continued until June 2010, when the last was held at Brown's home in her constituency of West Ham. Balls was up for going, but was told he couldn't because the group wanted to discuss the imminent party leadership contest. Both Eds, however, have remained close to 'the 555'.

Looking back, some might ascribe cynical motives for their presence on this scene: was Ed using his natural charm to work a crucial part of the electorate of a future leadership election? However most MPs think that certainly in 2005, Ed Miliband was not acting out part of a plan for the leadership; he genuinely wanted to be sociable and make friends. MPs recall that at one '555' dinner to celebrate the two Eds and McFadden becoming ministers in 2006, McFadden didn't turn up at all, Balls turned up late but Ed Miliband was there throughout.

Sadiq Khan MP, who would eventually act as Ed's agent during the 2010 leadership campaign, explains how his own friendship with the younger Miliband began: 'The first time I met Ed was when there was an induction for new MPs. Some of us weren't yet politicians or weren't inside or didn't know anybody. I mean, I was a clean-skin, I knew nobody in politics really. We knew of people, we knew who Ed Miliband, Ed Balls, Pat McFadden and Ian Austin were. What was remarkable about Ed Miliband, bearing in mind how powerful he was supposed to be, was that he was the most down-to-earth. He was a normal new boy, like the first day at school like the rest of us which I found quite remarkable.'[4] Lyn Brown says that 'When I got to Parliament, as with a number of others, I realised we hadn't been part of the spad network and hadn't been acquainted with the main players at all. So we wanted to get to know them.'[5] Ed had, of course, had spent years working in and around Parliament and understood the internal dynamics – and politics – of the Parliamentary Labour Party (PLP). But he was always quick to share his knowledge of the inner-workings of the Westminster political system with his new parliamentary colleagues.

On 24 May 2005 there was a contest for the role of chair of the PLP. MPs were divided between the incumbent, the loyal Blairite Ann Clwyd, and her challenger and later successor, Tony Lloyd. Disgruntled leftists such as Clare Short had attacked Clwyd, portraying her as a dictator. Sadiq Khan, who at one point was talking 'quite loudly' in favour of Lloyd at a PLP meeting, recalls that 'Ed said, "Look, I think you probably shouldn't speak so loudly."' 'It was the advice he gave. It wasn't, "You should keep quiet" but more like "Look Sadiq, be a bit careful in this place; it's full of people who will hold it against you." Once again, it was advice he didn't need to give me but I appreciated the fact that he did.'[6]

Such incidents serve to illustrate Ed Miliband's complicated politics during this period. He was near the heart of New Labour leadership, but he was also a backbench MP. He was a member of Brown's inner circle, but very unusually he was open in private about that circle's 'dark side'. It was a side to Brown's own character and operation that produced negative briefings from, first, Charlie Whelan and later Damian McBride. It wasn't Miliband's style, and in that sense he was not a classic 'Brownite'. He also admired Blair as Labour's most successful leader, as well as his ultimate boss, and never engaged in the most poisonous gossip about him that so many around Brown did. Ed retained, of course, a crucial link to the Blair circle: his brother David. Though they had distinct identities and were by now socialising in different circles – and the party conference of 2005 saw the emergence for the first time of badges with the words 'My favourite Miliband is Ed' – they still spoke regularly, with the proud older brother offering Ed advice just as Ed offered advice to those newer than him to the Westminster world. At the end of a parliamentary day, Ed would even often share a lift back to Primrose Hill in David's ministerial car.[7]

However, Ed had a number of private misgivings over Blair's policies at this time, including the Prime Minister's authoritarian stance on security and counter-terrorism, and his seeming disregard for civil liberties. In the wake of the terrorist attacks on the London transport network on 7 July 2005, Blair was trying to push through enhanced powers for the police to be able to hold terrorist suspects for up to ninety days without trial. Amid major unrest on the Labour backbenches, Ed told Brown directly: 'This is mad.'[8] The vote, set for 9 November, was so tight that Brown was ordered back from Israel literally minutes after landing there and Jack Straw was called back from EU–Russia talks in Moscow. The proposal was defeated by 322 votes to 291.

Khan, one of those who voted against despite dire warnings not to, confirms that he discussed the issue with Ed before the vote. Ed did not object to Khan voting against the government.

Ed Miliband's own name was not among the forty-nine Labour MPs who had voted against, despite his private doubts. Setting aside his principles, he had backed the government on one of its most controversial and harsh measures.

But as Khan points out, 'Ed carried on being a mate. The obvious thing for him to do was to keep a distance. Yet he was not embarrassed to be seen with me in public, he wasn't embarrassed to have a meal with me. I mean, you don't forget that sort of stuff.'[9] Yet Khan and his fellow rebels could be forgiven for feeling let down by Ed. Cynics would argue that no one who voted against such a heavily-whipped measure could have hoped to join the government in the near future. Yet it is surely inconceivable that on becoming Prime Minister, Brown would not have appointed Ed a minister. There are examples of several ministers, including Khan himself, promoted by Brown after being snubbed under Blair. Not for the first or last time, Ed was torn between loyalty to his party's leadership, and his feelings of increasing detachment from the New Labour agenda. As usual however, whether through loyalty or ambition, he jumped in with the party line. The 'ninety days' drama was not Ed's finest hour.

ooooo

It had been a busy start to his parliamentary career. But Ed managed to find time to make progress in his fledgling relationship with Justine.

Samantha Cameron has said, about her husband David, 'When we started going out seriously he was very up front and said "I want to be an MP. If you think you would hate it, you have to say so."'[10] Did Ed ask the same question of Justine? Did he tell her he might one day consider running for leader of his party? 'She was interested in the man not the politics,' says a friend. 'They would have discussed his political career, but I'd be surprised if they had a discussion about him being leader.'[11]

Justine brought a sense of fun and adventure into his serious, political life. She may have been a lawyer but she wasn't dull. Those who know her best describe her as not just sociable and outgoing but adventurous too. In June 2005, not long after she started dating Ed, Justine and her close friend and fellow barrister Quincy Whitaker climbed the 4,167 metres of Mount Toubkal in Morocco – the highest peak in the Atlas Mountains. The duo daringly started off their trek up the mountain wearing just T-shirts and shorts but, as they reached the top, and the temperature dropped, they were forced to ask their Berber guides to unwrap their turbans and use them as makeshift shawls to keep warm.

Justine's sense of adventure wasn't diminished. Later, when Whitaker planned a trip for the two of them to India, Justine proposed they go 'via Afghanistan'. Whitaker had to talk her out of it.

A few months after the Morocco trip, backbencher Ed joined Justine and Whitaker on another of their foreign holidays – this time to Libya, where they were virtually the only Western tourists inspecting scenic Roman ruins. The trip was 'dry' – non-alcoholic – but nonetheless the conversation flowed, from Roman history to Haverstock – where, coincidentally, both Ed and Whitaker had gone to school – to British politics and the failings of New Labour, about which Ed was 'in no way aggressive or defensive' in the face of what Whitaker admits now were her 'rants' on Iraq and civil liberties.[12]

Back home in the UK, the Liberal Democrat leader, Charles Kennedy, was labelling Blair a 'lame duck'. But the Prime Minister was insisting he would not resign, amid yet more audible shouting matches in Downing Street between Blair and Brown.

Though, as usual, Ed was caught up in the middle of the fights, as the 'nice Brownite' and 'emissary from Planet Fuck', and was regularly ushered into the Treasury for crisis meetings with the Chancellor, he remained loyal to his constituency base in Doncaster North throughout this period, holding regular surgeries once a fortnight and staying in a rented, three-bedroom house that would stand him in good stead during the expenses scandal to come.

In his maiden Commons speech of 23 May 2005, Ed had made no secret of the fact that 'my roots do not lie in Doncaster'.

> I am the son of two immigrants who met in London after the war, who had strong political beliefs, to which I refer because it helps to explain why I am here today. Ours was a socialist household, in which we were brought up not just to think that the injustices of society were wrong, but to believe that through political change, something could be done about them. Of course, as we grow up all of us make our own way. But it is right to recognise that it is this upbringing and that belief which brings me to this House to represent Doncaster North.

But he lavished praise on the town: 'Our advantage is that Doncaster, led by an elected Labour mayor, is a town – in fact, a city in all but name – on the up, experiencing the economic prosperity that is returning to the north of England...'

As his elder brother proudly watched from a nearby Commons bench, Ed joked:

> I want to end by referring to my right hon. Friend the Minister of Communities and Local Government, who is winding up the debate tonight. It is daunting, on such occasions, to have members of one's family watching in the Public Gallery – but worse, I feel, to have them sitting in the Chamber. As the House will know, he and I are now the only brothers in this place, although there are two sets of distinguished Labour sisters. I quickly offer this reassurance to the House: there are no more Miliband brothers to come. I am sure that hon. Members will agree that two is more than enough.

He then concluded more seriously:

> I also want to put on the record, however, how much my family owes to this country. Our father left Belgium in 1940 on the last boat to Britain, the evening before the Nazis arrived, and would have perished without the welcoming arms of a country that recognised its duty to help those fleeing from terror. I hope that I and my brother, in the service that we give in the

House, can in some small way help to repay the debt that we owe to this country. In my contributions in this House, I will strive to reflect not only the voices of the constituents who put me here this month, but the humanity and solidarity shown to my family more than sixty years ago, which led my family out of the dark times of despair to a place of hope, and me to the Floor of this House today.[13]

ooooo

Ed's first campaign as an MP in his Yorkshire constituency came in the local elections of May 2006.

Nationally, Labour did badly, losing some 300 councillors and polling 26 per cent of the share of the vote compared to 40 per cent for the Tories and 27 per cent for the Lib Dems. Ed went to bed very late that night, tired and dejected. But there was joy in the morning. Ed was sitting with his team in the Doncaster North constituency office when he received a call on his mobile. It was Blair. Ed went into a different room where he could hear the embattled Prime Minister, who was trying to reassert his authority with a heavily criticised reshuffle that saw a stunned Margaret Beckett replacing Jack Straw as Foreign Secretary and John Reid replacing a furious Charles Clarke as Home Secretary. Clarke, thrown to the wolves of the right-wing press by Blair over the 'foreign prisoners' affair, was offered several other roles including that of Defence Secretary but refused them and resigned to the backbenches.

Appointing – and congratulating – Ed as minister for the 'third sector' in the Cabinet Office was a relatively straightforward task for Blair, who liked and respected the younger Miliband. Ed was told he would work under Hilary Armstrong, the Chancellor of the Duchy of Lancaster, and told to enjoy the role. As a first job, responsible for coordinating charities and pressure groups and outside interests with politics and public services, he could have done a lot worse. Grinning broadly, Ed returned to his staff and delighted them with the words: 'I'm a minister!'[14]

Re-energised, Ed headed back to London to explore his new role. On the train, he spoke to his brother David, who had been promoted to Environment Secretary. Both men were delighted and congratulated one another.

When Ed arrived in the capital it was Friday evening, and his hard-working parliamentary assistant Simon Alcock headed home for a well-deserved rest. Ed, though, headed straight to Whitehall, to meet civil servants, collect briefings and get stuck into a new job he relished.

He was ideally suited to working with charities and voluntary groups, and became one of the first New Labour figures to appreciate the importance of wooing, and working with, the third sector and forging an early, progressive version of what David Cameron would later claim as his trademark mission for a 'Big Society'. At this point Ed first became attracted by 'mutualism', the best-known modern example of which is John Lewis, the company where every employee holds a stake. A few years later, Ed would put mutualism at the heart of his party's manifesto, in an attempt to counter Tory claims of a 'broken Britain'. In doing so, he was drawing on 200 years of history stretching back to the Co-operative movement and the labour exchanges founded by the eighteenth-century social reformer Robert Owen, which in turn paved the way for credit unions and savings banks.

'My upbringing was about the state making a difference to injustice,' Ed said while explaining his approach as third sector minister. 'Now, I continue to believe the state can make a big difference to tackling injustice, but I also think social entrepreneurs are finding ways of saying that capitalism can produce just or unjust results, depending on the nature of a company and the way it behaves.'[15]

Practically, the crowning achievement of Ed Miliband's time as third sector minister was pushing through the Charities Act, which after some delays gained Royal Assent in August 2006. Billed as the biggest reforms to aid the charity sector in 400 years, it reduced regulation of smaller charities, defined charities as needing a public benefit, and increased the accountability of the Charity Commission.

In other reforms, Ed helped oversee the establishment of a £125 million 'Future Builder's Fund', allowing support organisations to bid for public service contracts from April 2008. He launched a £30 million Community Assets Fund to assist the transferring of assets from councils to third sector bodies and he ushered in a £2 million training plan to encourage 2,000 commissioners from across the public sector to contract more services from the third sector. Ed wanted to 'catalyse the market; to set an example' as he put it at the time.[16] 'Before long,' wrote the Tory commentator Peter Oborne, 'he had the charity sector eating out of his hand.'[17]

Ed was getting on well in his debut role in Whitehall, but adjacent to the Cabinet Office in Downing Street, all was far from happy.

The final, fatal area of contention for Blair was, perhaps appropriately given the discontent over Iraq, another conflict in the Middle East. Through the summer of 2006, Israel bombarded Lebanon from the air and on the ground in an asymmetrical war amid Hezbollah rocket attacks aimed at the north of the country. Blair refused to call for an Israeli ceasefire, despite criticism of the war from the Foreign Office minister Kim Howells; for many in the PLP this was the last straw. David Miliband distinguished himself by speaking out against Blair's position in Cabinet. Ed, who one friend says was 'really pissed off'[18] over the issue too, was proud of his older brother's stance. But again the younger Miliband brother did not show the courage to speak out publicly. David, as a so-called 'Blairite', could be forgiven by rebels for not resigning. But Ed showed once again that – despite later attacks on the 'New Labour establishment' – he was often as much a part of it as his brother.

MPs now agree that the Lebanon fiasco did more than any other single episode to lead to the eventual removal of Blair, who further riled the PLP by indicating in a defiant interview with *The Times* that he would stay on to fight another full term. Needless to say, Brown was infuriated. With his tacit support, some in the 2001 intake, led by Blairite-turned-Brownite Tom Watson, organised a letter calling for Blair to stand down. Ed Miliband made clear to his parliamentary colleagues, including to the rebels themselves, that he did not support such a move and was among many who refused to sign the letter.[19] But in July, a plan B was hatched in which eight parliamentary private secretaries – the rung on the government ladder below a junior minister – resigned at the same time. Again Ed Miliband was disturbed by the 'coup' attempt, and refused to associate with it. But Blair was forced into an unedifying statement making it clear that the coming annual party conference would be his last as Labour leader and Prime Minister, meaning he would leave office in 2007. 'I would have preferred to do this my own way,' he said on a visit to a London school with Alan Johnson. Brown, responding in Scotland, said in his typically guarded fashion: 'It is for him to make the decision.' And in a reference to the debate over Brown's legitimacy that was to come, he added: 'This cannot and should not be about private arrangements but of what is in the best interests of our party ... and the best interests of our country.' But the balance of power had shifted; Brown was at last on his way to Number 10.

Belatedly, the Brownites had forced Blair to begin the slow-motion process of leaving office. Though Ed himself had no blood on his hands, the prospect of a Brown premiership – the thought of which had helped persuade Ed to return from Harvard and become an MP – was at last in view.

Meanwhile. his own profile was growing. An appearance on BBC One's *Question Time* in his role as third sector minister on 19 April 2007, led to Ed being propositioned by an attractive young audience member with whom he had debated during the recording of the show. The day after the broadcast she sent a note to his office asking him out on a date. Ed, now living with Justine, politely declined. But – as the 'My favourite Miliband is Ed' badges show – his star was on the rise. With his patron Brown in Number 10, Ed would soon be at the centre of power.

INTO CABINET

2007–2008

The much-publicised photograph of the Miliband brothers as they left their first Cabinet meeting together in June 2007 was, in a classic piece of New Labour media management, carefully choreographed.[1] But that didn't take away from the occasion's significance. It was the first time two siblings had faced each other across the Cabinet table since 1938, when the Stanley brothers – sons of the seventh Earl of Derby – both served in the Cabinet under Neville Chamberlain.

In Gordon Brown's first reshuffle, in June 2007, he shrewdly appointed David Miliband as Foreign Secretary, both as a reward for David's refusal to stand against Brown for the leadership and in an attempt to lock him into loyalty. David could hardly say no to one of the greatest offices of state, a job he would come to relish as he forged a post-Blair foreign policy emphasising political as well as military progress in the Middle East and Afghanistan. Ed became Cabinet Office minister and Chancellor of the Duchy of Lancaster. He would often be far from happy in the Cabinet Office, having been denied a portfolio of his own. But he had at least reached the same ministerial status as his brother. He was also made responsible for the manifesto, which gave him the opportunity to connect with Labour members and activists.

It is strange now to recall the mood during the first, heady weeks of Brown's premiership. Labour's poll ratings had soared leaving the party with a double-digit lead over the Tories, an unusual development for a mid-term count, brought about by a sense of freshness following Blair's ten-year reign. Amid praise in the media for a new 'moral' direction, Brown pulled off a series of popular U-turns on Blairite policies such as 'super-casinos' and ID cards. He also navigated successfully through a number of testing events. Within days of his entering office in June 2007, there were terrorist attacks in both London and Glasgow; Brown acted swiftly in calling an emergency meeting of Cobra, the government emergencies committee, to review plans for protecting the public. He also made a televised address to the nation from Downing Street, calling for vigilance and saying: 'I know that the British people will stand together, united, resolute and strong.' That same summer, Brown's resolute handling of widespread flooding in the north of England, as well as outbreaks of foot and mouth disease, only added to the sense of momentum leading Labour into the autumn party conference season.

Sadly for Brown, his fortunes were about to be dramatically reversed with the infamous 'election that never was'. This would be the most significant turning point in Brown's troubled, three-year premiership. From this point on, he would be portrayed by gleeful Tories and their media allies as the man who 'bottled out' of gaining a mandate of his own from the country. To this day, his critics wrongly claim that Brown had been clamouring to go to the country and then changed his mind at the last minute on inspection of private polling. The truth is more complicated and nuanced. Brown was in fact sceptical throughout. He wanted to continue his political honeymoon and hold an election some time in 2009, after rolling out a policy agenda distinct from that of the Blair government. Ed Miliband, never one to rush to judgement, and always preferring analysis and deliberation to rushes of blood to the head, broadly shared this view. Ed Balls, however, did not. The combative Children's Secretary thought it was the perfect opportunity to smash the Tories and gain a new term in office. Brown was persuaded to keep the option open – publicly at least – during the Tory conference, to unsettle the opposition.

So while nudges and hints were being dealt out to the media about the prospect of an early election, shambolic last-minute plans were under way to prepare Labour for the event should Brown decide to make the call.

It was a chaotic period that would test old friendships. Douglas Alexander suddenly found himself having to organise and produce election material and work out a strategy for the campaign, while Ed was put in charge of the manifesto. According to Peter Watt, then the general secretary of the Labour Party, Alexander expressed amazement at the lack of policy progress by Ed and his manifesto team: 'You'd imagine that after ten years of waiting, and ten years complaining about Tony, we would have some idea of what we are going to do, but we don't seem to have any policies.'[2]

On 1 October, in the middle of the Tory conference, George Osborne announced his own hastily formulated – and distinctly regressive – plan to raise the threshold of inheritance tax for estates worth £1 million. If the plan was an attempt to frighten Brown, it worked, largely because it was almost universally welcomed by senior media figures, most of whom were wealthy enough to benefit from it.

News leaked out that Brown had recorded an interview for BBC One's Sunday *Andrew Marr Show* on Saturday 6 October, at the end of Tory conference, confirming that he was calling off plans for an early election so he could pursue his 'vision for change' for the country. By the following day the Sunday papers were full of the fallout, including claims that Ed Miliband and Douglas Alexander were to blame for 'dithering' and 'bottling out' of the plan to go early. The truth is that, from the outset, Ed had been highly ambivalent about an early election. He saw it, perhaps wrongly in retrospect, as a stunt which would not help Brown in the long term. But Ed was not only sceptical – he was woefully unprepared. As well as being against the idea of Brown going to the polls in the same year as he took office, he had not seen the crisis coming, had not expected it, and had therefore not got working early enough on the manifesto.

According to one insider, Miliband found himself 'caught in the crossfire' of the extensive briefings and counter-briefings about who was to blame for the fiasco that followed. The real target, say some senior Brownites, was Douglas Alexander, who was seen as having moved over to the Blair wing of the party since his elevation to the Cabinet in 2006.[3] Alexander would acknowledge in July 2009 that 'there was clearly briefing against me'.[4] It is widely assumed that the chief culprit was Damian McBride, Brown's press secretary and a close ally of Ed Balls.

Indeed Spencer Livermore would later claim in a Radio 4 documentary that Ed told Alexander: 'I bet within twenty minutes we find we're going to get the blame for this.' According to Livermore: 'Twenty minutes turned out to be slightly longer than it took... Damian told me he had been instructed to blame certain individuals.' Livermore says McBride told him that the order had come from Balls.[5] Today, both Balls and McBride deny being responsible for the briefings.[6]

But Ed, who these days claims not to 'care'[7] about the affair, certainly did at the time; he and Alexander pored over newspaper websites, totting up the number of pieces in which their names were mentioned. They were convinced that the blame for the briefings against them lay with McBride, a figure whom Ed would become increasingly mistrustful of.[8]

On the morning of Sunday 7 October there was an extraordinary telephone conversation between Ed and McBride, which McBride would later tell friends showed Ed's 'hard' streak for the first time in his experience. McBride rang Ed on his mobile, saying: 'Ed, there's this real problem. I'm having this stuff chucked at me.'

Ed was cool: 'Damian, where does all this stuff in the papers today come from?'

But McBride insisted: 'Ed, I'm telling you, I am not responsible for any of this stuff in the papers today about you or Douglas or anyone else.' At this point, Ed said bluntly, 'Damian, I don't believe you'. After yet another impassioned denial from McBride, Ed repeated that he would like to believe the spin doctor but he just didn't.

McBride appealed: 'Ed, don't call me a liar – you cannot call me a liar. I cannot be in a position where you're calling me a liar.'

Ed, however, did not budge: 'But you are lying, Damian, I don't believe a word of what you're saying.'

McBride explained that for a minister to make clear he did not believe the word of the Prime Minister's press secretary would provoke a serious breakdown in relations: 'Ed, you realise that we can't have a relationship if you're telling me you think I'm a liar?'

But Ed just said: 'Well there we go then.'

McBride pleaded for one last time: 'Ed, don't do this to me – please.'

Ed hung up. Whether or not McBride was lying, Ed showed his steely side; he was not afraid of confrontation. This was not the Ed Miliband who had avoided dressing down Shriti Vadera in Washington three years earlier.

But it was also a demonstration of how bad feelings were between Ed – and indeed Alexander – on one side, and McBride and Balls on the other. The co-operation, the banter and easy familiarity between the three Brownite MPs would be strained from that moment onwards. As Livermore has said: 'It never, never went back to the way it was. And that was of huge cost to Gordon because he didn't have a small team unified in purpose and totally committed to him, which he so desperately needed at that point. When he was at his most vulnerable, people had retreated to their own departments or their own priorities, rather than rallying around.'[9]

Disheartened by the row, Ed was increasingly frustrated by his own Cabinet Office job. Before Brown appointed him he had offered the position to Balls, who was strong and assertive enough to turn it down and demand a proper department of his own – which turned out to be Education (or 'Children, Schools and Families' as it became known under Brown). But Ed had accepted the job and had become, in the words of a close friend, 'a glorified special adviser'[10] without a proper department or portfolio of his own. Despite now being a member of the Cabinet, he was still expected to be at the Prime Minister's beck and call twenty-four hours a day, seven days a week. On one occasion, in the summer of 2007, according to a former Downing Street official, Brown demanded Ed join a meeting via conference call as the latter was preparing to go on holiday to the United States with Justine. Offiicals sitting in Number 10 could hear Ed zipping up his suitcase at home and carrying on the conversation with Brown as he got into a cab and then joined the check-in queue at Heathrow Airport. As he boarded the flight to California, an oblivious Brown asked Ed to call him back once he had landed.[11]

The irony was that Brown had wanted to keep one of the two Eds close to him because they were among the handful of Labour figures whose judgement he trusted. Ed, in particular, had impressed the new Prime Minister since his election to Parliament in 2005. He had begun to see Ed as a future leader.

In fact, at the 2007 party conference, Brown surprised Damian McBride by singling Ed out as a future contender for the top job. McBride had asked the PM which Cabinet ministers he should 'build up' in briefings to the media. Despite his troubles with David Miliband, Brown replied: 'Miliband, Purnell, Balls, Cooper, Burnham, Miliband…' McBride interrupted: 'You already said Miliband'. Brown: 'No, Ed. You've got to watch Ed Miliband.' Like everyone else, McBride had assumed up to this point that

Brown wanted Balls to succeed him as party leader. But the Prime Minister added, in reference to the two Eds: 'After me, Damian, you've got a big choice to make … after me you're going to have to make a choice.'[12]

ooooo

On 2 March 2008, Ed wowed the Labour faithful in his first major speech given without notes at the party's spring conference. It was a trick first used by David Cameron during the Tory leadership contest that he won in 2005 – and repeated again in the Tory conference of 2007. The only difference between the Conservative Party leader's approach and that of the future Labour leader was that Cameron would, as far as he could, memorise the speeches in advance, word for word, while Ed would try and remember the broad thrust and a few jokes but would also aim to improvise.

Over the years, Ed had often described himself as 'the other Ed' or 'the other Miliband', in a reference to Balls and his brother respectively. The apparently modest formula impressed those who didn't know him as much as it began to annoy those who did, who wanted him to emerge from the shadows of both David Miliband and Ed Balls. In his speech to that year's spring conference, outlining the 'road to the manifesto', Ed opened with a light-hearted passage about his brother that, at closer reading, was telling. Outwardly, at least, it was self-deprecating:

> Of course it's always a bit odd to be a Miliband at party conference, and that's because of my famous older brother David. We often get confused with each other actually, and I suppose my low moment was at party conference last year. Sky News produced a Top Trumps pack comparing different politicians and I have to say I was pretty upset when I saw the Top Trumps pack, because there was David and he beat me on parliamentary skills and I thought, OK, he's been there longer than me. He beat me on charisma, and I thought, well OK, that's a fair enough judgement. But then I really thought these guys were biased because he beat me on looks as well. But then I knew it was a Tory conspiracy, because George Osborne beat us on all three counts and that's simply not credible.[13]

Modest or defensive, at this stage Ed was still joking about the presence of his 'famous older brother' and even relished the emerging comparisons between the two. Over the course of perhaps the most difficult year for Labour since it came to office, however, that would change.

On 1 May 2008, Labour received its worst local election results in forty years, with a share of the vote of just 24 per cent, putting it in third place behind the Lib Dems. To add insult to injury, Boris Johnson beat Ken Livingstone to become Mayor of London.

Worse was still to come. On the night of 25 July the SNP unexpectedly pulled off a stunning by-election victory in Glasgow East against Labour, which saw its majority of 13,507 overturned, leading to an SNP win with a swing of 22.54 per cent. The result was far more significant than the traditional battle between Labour and the Scottish Nationalists: it was disastrous for Brown personally. The Cabinet was in despair and leadership speculation was rising to fever pitch.

For Ed Miliband, however, it was a time to be loyal to the leader who by all accounts 'adored' him like a son.[14] Ed agreed to defend Brown on *Newsnight*, which he did as best he could. The following day, the party was due to meet at Warwick University for a policy forum. The mood was palpably dire. Previously loyal Cabinet ministers and special advisers were refusing to rule out an impending change to the leadership. Brown arrived and gave a technocratic, jargon-filled speech about globalisation that showed him to be in denial of the urgent political need for him to connect with ordinary – and disillusioned – voters. But dutifully, Ed gave Brown's awful oration a standing ovation from the back of the hall.

His brother, meanwhile, was less intent on propping up Brown. Over the weekend David and his advisers had decided that he needed to make a significant intervention. To this day, David denies that what followed was a leadership challenge, and technically it is hard to dispute this. But the effect was devastating, first for Brown, then for the brothers, and ultimately for David himself.

On the evening of Monday 28 July political editors in the corridors of the Commons' press gallery were contacted by Sarah Schaefer, one of David's two special advisers. She was giving the 'heads up' on a piece David had written for the following day's *Guardian*.[15] She told at least one of the journalists, in reference to recurrent criticism that the Foreign Secretary had done nothing to challenge Brown: 'You think David hasn't got balls? See tomorrow's *Guardian*.'[16] On the face of it, David's article was a rather anodyne and worthy piece about how Labour could get the better of the Tories on a range of policy areas, from the environment to Europe. Significantly, however, it contained not a single reference to Gordon Brown. And it was almost entirely about domestic policy, which lay outside David's brief in the Foreign Office. It concluded cryptically:

> [In] government, unless you choose sides, you get found out. New Labour won three elections by offering real change, not just in policy but in the way we do politics. We must do so again. So let's stop feeling sorry for ourselves, enjoy a break, and then find the confidence to make our case afresh.

Looking back, David Miliband's move, such as it was, perhaps fell between two stools – it was neither a clear challenge to Brown nor a show of loyalty. Instead it appears to have been an attempt on David's part to start building momentum around himself as the party headed into a critical conference season.

Gordon Brown, who was about to take a few days' holiday with Sarah, hit the phones. One of the first people he spoke to was an agonised Ed Miliband, caught between his boss and his brother. Ed had not been warned by his brother about the provocative article. He relayed this to a livid Brown, who bluntly – and perhaps unfairly – asked Ed what was going on. Crucially, Ed also spoke to David, who assured his brother that this was not a leadership challenge and that he was entitled to speak out – surely the whole Cabinet should be coming up with ideas and plans? 'What else could I have done?' he asked, defensively. 'Well, you could have done it differently,' replied an exasperated Ed.[17]

At this stage Ed could rebuke his brother privately, but understandably did not feel he could attack him publicly, unlike Ed Balls, who used a series of broadcast interviews to say that he had known David for a long time and was sure he would do the right thing and remain loyal to Brown. But the significance of this episode in terms of the brothers' relationship should not be underestimated. Ed Miliband had a choice to make, between loyalty to his brother and loyalty to Brown. He chose the latter. As he told close friends at the time, 'I am not my brother's keeper.'[18]

ooooo

By late summer the personal strain of his dilemma was taking its toll, and not for the first time in his life he wanted to get away from it all, so in August, Ed and Justine took a holiday in California. Conveniently, the ever-political Ed made sure the trip coincided with the Democratic convention in Denver, Colorado, where Barack Obama, who had beaten Hillary Clinton to be the party's presidential candidate, would be giving the keynote address. Such was Ed's unusually despondent mood, however, he almost didn't attend the conference. He and Justine decided to drive part of the length of the stunning west coast, from San Francisco and through Big Sur, with its astonishing views, flora and fauna. For the first time he could remember, Ed felt free, independent; he was having innocent, non-political fun. A friend who dined with him in London soon after their return remembers Ed talking with 'sweet' wonderment about the trip.[19] He had been on a real holiday for once, one that almost caused him to miss the big moment for the Democratic Party which – alongside other Labour figures – he followed obsessionally. Friends agree that for Ed to have even considered not going to the convention showed the affection he now felt for Justine.[20]

Soon, though, Ed had to face an altogether more fractious gathering closer to home. The stage was set for a political arm-wrestle between David Miliband and Gordon Brown at Labour's annual party conference in Manchester. Brown had to salvage his teetering leadership, which – despite months of decisiveness on the part of the Prime Minister and his Chancellor, Alistair Darling, in responding to the financial crisis – was fragile at best. David could not afford to make any mistakes. In the end, Brown, the greater survivor of the two, would prevail, to the benefit of his protégé Ed Miliband.

The party was divided over the question of whether or not David had shown disloyalty by his *Guardian* article in July, but the media were gunning for him. So when he was overheard by a BBC employee in a lift at the Manchester conference, allegedly making a reference to Michael Heseltine's failed leadership ambitions, the press pounced. David's every move was monitored, so that even an image of him limply holding a banana became – absurdly – the main image of the week.

Ed, meanwhile, was helping Brown compose the speech of his life. On Ed's advice, the final draft was unusually humble; Brown knew it was 'now or never' and, after Sarah Brown introduced 'my husband, my hero', the normally reserved Prime Minister started by saying that he had learned much about himself and had taken criticisms on board. A line now attributed to Ed Balls – who picked it up from the then *Sun* editor, Rebekah Wade – was the memorable put-down, 'This is no time for a novice', officially aimed at David Cameron but widely taken to refer to David Miliband too. And it was Ed Miliband who added the precursor: 'I'm all in favour of apprenticeships, but…'[21]

It is impossible to know who, if anyone, told the TV cameras to switch to David Miliband just after the line was delivered, but the effect was to seal a terrible week for the Foreign Secretary. Brown, in contrast, had reasserted his authority as leader and Prime Minister – for now at least – by conceding some of his faults but reminding the party faithful that he was best placed to handle the economic crash. 'If people say I'm too serious, quite honestly there's a lot to be serious about,' roared an unashamedly dour Brown as the Labour rank and file – always sympathetic towards a troubled leader – went wild.

ooooo

The combination of Brown's 'rehabilitation' and the sudden decline in David's fortunes, proved to be of huge benefit to Ed Miliband. For the first time there was talk on the fringes of the conference about Ed, not David, being the Miliband best placed to lead Labour after Brown. And as became apparent, Ed was not unreceptive to the notion.

But more important than the gossip that comes with any conference, Ed pulled off another of his speeches without notes, seen by now as a mandatory skill in any aspiring leader. The speech was similar to that at the spring conference but on a bigger scale, though less than twenty minutes long given his limited brief in the Cabinet Office. Taking off his jacket he paced the stage, thanking the conference for the privilege of masterminding the upcoming manifesto, and acknowledged the scale of the task ahead. These had been 'tough times for our country and tough times for our party,' he said. He went on to a personal passage: 'You know my dad came to this conference forty years ago, and he said that being in the Labour Party was part of a big adventure. He was right then, and it's right now.' Raising his voice and gesticulating wildly, Ed got into his stride:

> We are the idealists in politics today. We are the people who believe that every child can realise their dream... [So] despite the tough times, let it be said of us, the Labour Party, that we saw through the darkness, that we set out the big causes we want to fight for, that we showed we had the stomach for the fight, that we showed we could fight for fairness, and that we resolved to stand up to fight and win for the people of this country.

At the end of the conference, Brown had survived once again. David had faltered. And Ed, caught in the middle, was slowly on the up. But the drama was far from over.

ooooo

Contrary to conventional wisdom, Peter Mandelson had no idea as he watched from the sidelines in Manchester that Brown was about to bring him back from Brussels, where he was serving as European Commissioner, to the heart of the Cabinet as Business Secretary. He sometimes spoke to the Prime Minister, but if Brown had formulated such a plan, he had kept it to himself. During an interview in his hotel room with the *New Statesman*, Mandelson spoke for the first time about wanting to return in some way, but when pressed on what his future held he was uncharacteristically hesitant, and had to ring his loyal adviser Peter Power in Brussels for advice on what he could or should say. But significantly, he chose to back Brown's leadership in the interview, albeit with the proviso that he stick to a 'New Labour' course. Ed, who unlike

Balls had always admired Mandelson despite the bitterness of the Blair–Brown wars, was delighted when he heard that Mandelson was about to endorse Brown – and not David – and relayed the information to the Prime Minister himself.[22]

He also took the opportunity to warn Brown that Damian McBride was becoming a major problem. McBride – always keen on late-night socialising with political journalists – had been seen briefing members of the lobby about the impending reshuffle, and the possible departure of various Cabinet ministers; this included Ruth Kelly – and came several hours prior to her official resignation. McBride had a unique relationship with the right-wing press, but it was clear that he was getting out of control. Ed, whose own approach was so different, was appalled and wanted McBride out.[23]

It was on 3 October, when the interview was published, that Mandelson was sensationally recalled by Brown, who effectively ended a fifteen-year feud by declaring that 'serious times call for serious people'. Ed Balls called the move a 'risk'. Ed Miliband was thrilled, privately referring to Mandelson as a 'benevolent uncle' figure who could help restore the party's – and Brown's – fortunes. As it happens, Mandelson also told Brown that, as a condition of his return, McBride should be removed from his role as special adviser at the earliest opportunity.[24]

Suddenly the shape, feel and direction of the government had changed in a way that encouraged Ed – there was a new sense of unity and self-confidence. Crucially, the so-called Blairite threat, from his brother David – and others – had been neutralised by Mandelson's surprise return to the Cabinet.

During the course of 2007 and 2008, Ed Miliband had learned that he could not always trust his own brother or his former ally Ed Balls. By the end of the year, he had emerged from the shadows of both. To cap it all, he was about to be elevated into a fresh job which would be the making of him. At last, Ed Miliband was a senior and respected politician in his own right, no longer 'the other Ed' – or 'the other Miliband'.

CLIMATE CHANGE

2008–2010

One of the many consequences of Peter Mandelson's dramatic return to the Cabinet in the reshuffle on 3 October 2008 was that Ed Miliband was not required as much in Downing Street to advise Gordon Brown. Mandelson got on with and respected Ed, but Brown's obsessive focus switched to his old enemy-turned-confidant. This suited Ed fine. He had finally got a department of his own – Energy and Climate Change (DECC) – to run and a brief close to his heart. 'Gordon asked me what department I'd like and what I was interested in, and I said climate change,' says Ed now[1], and he is believed to have lobbied hard to merge energy policy and climate policy in one ministry, with the aid of the Prime Minister's environment adviser, Michael Jacobs. But it was a deeply strategic and political move too. As a former Brown aide points out: 'Ed has got a good antennae for popular movements, and the DECC job was a good job for engaging with popular movements.'[2]

That said, Ed had always cared about green issues: when his brother David was appointed Environment Secretary by Tony Blair, in May 2006, Ed told him it was one of the most important causes of all.[3] David may have subsequently introduced the Climate Change Bill, which passed into law in 2008, and made it the duty of the Secretary of State to ensure that carbon emissions in the year 2050 were at least 60 per cent lower than in 1990 but his brother faced an even bigger challenge: the road to Copenhagen.

Just thirteen days after he was appointed, on 16 October, Ed announced that the government would up its target from 60 to 80 per cent carbon emissions cuts by 2050.[4] Right from the start, he sought to lead the world by example in the run-up to what he was already learning was a 'make or break' conference on climate change the following year. The first challenge he faced was managing and organising a brand new department with limited basic resources. The Department for Energy and Climate Change (DECC) was made up of the old Department for the Environment, Food and Rural Affairs (DEFRA) and Business, Enterprise and Regulatory Reform (BERR). Civil servants from both former departments found themselves in sparse new offices at 3 Whitehall Place. The new DECC headquarters were in an old, vacated DEFRA building; it was no longer set up for work and had no ministerial suites. For the first few weeks, Ed lacked a proper office of his own and, in the early days, officials sat around with him in hastily partitioned sections rather than meeting rooms. One civil servant remembers working with Ed around a table of drying sandwich crusts from a previous meeting in the same area. 'I sensed Ed rather enjoyed himself because it was all about rolling up your sleeves and working out policy,' says the civil servant who warmed to Ed while working for him, 'rather than the grand side of being a Secretary of State'.[5] Eventually the Whitehall accommodation system went into gear and gave Ed a proper office on the ground floor, which later moved to the fifth floor because of the perceived security risk of overlooking the street. Now formally installed, Ed 'disappeared' into his brief, according to departmental observers.[6]

He re-emerged in spectacular style in January 2009 for what a former government insider calls an 'epic'[7] row with Brown – the first of many – on the proposed third runway at Heathrow. Four months before Ed's appointment as Climate Change Secretary, in June 2008, David Cameron – trying to emphasise his 'vote blue, go green' message – had ruled out a third runway under a Conservative government. Cameron's pledge only hardened Brown's own instinctive support for the runway – always keen on his 'dividing lines', the Prime Minister saw it as an opportunity to portray Labour, and not the Tories, as the party of business.

Much has been written about Ed's stance on the Heathrow runway, including plenty of speculation that he almost resigned over the matter. David Muir and Douglas Alexander were alarmed to find themselves, on a trip to Washington, bombarded with calls from anxious Number 10 officials believing Ed would 'walk' in January 2009.[8] 'It was interesting for us all to watch,' says one former Downing Street insider. 'Ed pushed Gordon fucking hard.'[9] Advisers to both Ed and Brown say they never heard him use the word 'resignation', but he did tell Gavin Kelly, the Brown aide who was handling the runway issue, 'I will not do this deal unless I get much more', that is, policy concessions.[10] Ed's view throughout the negotiating process was that the expansion of Heathrow would make it near-impossible for the government to implement its pledge to reduce carbon emissions by 80 per cent by 2050. Another Downing Street aide says Ed's strategy was 'to really dig in and make some big demands. At each stage, he would demand more. And each time you thought he would cave, he wouldn't.'[11] Ed's obdurate approach came as a shock to Number 10's permanent secretary, Jeremy Heywood, who told Brown the matter needed to be resolved. 'Why is this new minister holding up the wheels of government like this?' Heywood was overheard asking a colleague. Meanwhile, on one occasion, the Prime Minister was 'livid', according to an aide. He shouted of Ed, 'Get him on the phone. This is a total betrayal.'[12]

Kelly says today: 'Ed and I had a very difficult, acrimonious row over Heathrow when I was dealing with him at Number 10. We really took it to the limit on that; I didn't know how that was going to end up to be honest but he played hard, very aggressively... We were right up against the deadline and he didn't blink. It was probably the most difficult negotiation that I can remember having with a Cabinet minister. He got a lot more than anyone thought he was going to get.'[13]

The reality is that although the thought had crossed Ed's mind, he never came anywhere close to going through with resignation – or even threatening to do so. 'It would have been ludicrous to resign after just three months in the job,' he told friends later.[14] Instead, while his special adviser Polly Billington briefed the press, especially *The Guardian*, that Ed was unhappy,[15] he took the only route he believed was open to him: Ed 'talked truth to power' as his aides put it now, but in a private and not a public setting. 'There were blazing rows,' says a former Cabinet minister.[16] Ed's stubbornness in meetings – both one-to-one and Cabinet – shocked Brown. It also infuriated Ed Balls and Peter Mandelson, both of whom sided with the business community and argued that the move would create jobs – with the latter reportedly having banged his head on the Cabinet table in frustration (a claim he has since denied to friends[17]). Mandelson did, however, lend his considerable weight to support the position of Geoff Hoon, the Transport Secretary, who took it upon himself to push the case for the runway inside government and voice considerable frustration with Ed's blocking tactics on behalf of other pro-business Cabinet ministers. Anonymous quotes started appearing in the press accusing Ed of having 'gone native'.

But Ed wasn't on his own in his opposition to the runway. He set about building a coalition inside Cabinet to challenge the Hoon-Mandelson-Balls axis, and drew on the support of John Denham, the Skills Secretary, Baroness Royall, the Leader of the Lords and his old boss Harriet Harman, the Leader of the Commons. At the crucial Cabinet meeting in January 2009 at which the policy was decided, Ed's brother David, the Foreign Secretary, and Douglas Alexander, the International Development Secretary, were abroad on official trips but sent 'messages of support'. The Climate Change Secretary's chief ally, however, was Hilary Benn, the Environment Secretary. Journalists and MPs spoke of a 'Milibenn' tendency in Cabinet.[18] At one meeting of ministers, Benn repeatedly and loudly interrupted Hoon's defence of the government's position. 'Stop heckling me,' Hoon barked back.[19]

A senior official describes another tense meeting with Hoon, Heywood and Ed. 'Jeremy clearly felt Geoff had given enough. But Ed refused to leave the room until he had a meeting with Gordon. He had gone red, almost like a child. He was clearly very emotional. Jeremy thought he was being unreasonable and puerile. But then I don't think Ed gave a toss. He wanted concessions – and he won.'[20]

Supporters of Ed see the row over Heathrow as his coming of age in the Cabinet. He did not resign, but in the end did win a series of concessions out of his rows with Brown. Aviation's contribution to carbon emissions was to decline and airlines using the new runway would be required to use the newest, least-polluting aircraft. When Hoon announced the go-ahead on 15 January, he said the government was satisfied environmental targets could be met (as it would put an initial cap on additional flights from the new runway of 125,000 a year), would ensure new slots were 'green slots' used by only the 'cleanest planes' and would set a new target on aircraft emission. 'Taken together', Hoon said, 'this gives us the toughest climate change regime for aviation of any country in the world.'[21]

Above and below, a young Ed with his father Ralph, who could be playful as well as intensely political, 1982. 'A fantastic father,' says Ed, pictured alone below left.
© Miliband family archive

Ed at university with his close friend Marc Stears. Stears would later remark of Ed's first speech as leader how little his mannerisms and appearance had changed since his university days. © A. Grant

Ed, the Treasury insider, with Ed Balls, late 1990s. Their relationship would be tested by rivalry but now their fortunes are tied as leader and shadow Chancellor. The new Blair and Brown?
© Guardian News & Media Ltd 2010

Ed with Gordon Brown, a mentor and sponsor who 'adored' his younger protegé. Brown's leadership would become the crucial dividing issue between Ed and his brother, David.

The calm before the storm: Ed the Cabinet minister, emerging from Number 10 with David in June 2007. They were the first brothers in Cabinet together since 1938.

First off the block: scarred by accusations of 'bottling out' of challenging Brown, David declares he is running for the leadership the day after Brown resigns as Prime Minister, 12 May 2010.

'David is my best friend in the whole world,' says Ed. 'I love him dearly and I think it is absolutely possible and necessary for this party to have a civilised contest.' Ed declares four days after his brother, at a Fabian Society conference, 17 May 2010.

Above, the five candidates: Diane Abbott, David Miliband, Andy Burnham, Ed Balls and Ed Miliband at one of dozens of hustings where tensions would build between the two brothers.

Left, the result: After an agonisingly long announcement in Manchester, Ed is embraced by his defeated elder brother in front of the cameras, 25 September 2010.

Ed accepts the leadership. 'I first joined the party aged seventeen,' he said. 'Never in my wildest imagination did I believe I would one day lead this party'.

Right, Ed the Leader of the Opposition, facing David Cameron across the despatch box at Prime Minister's Questions. Ed has had a slow start but is improving.

Below, Ed with his shadow Cabinet.

Ed and Justine wed in Nottinghamshire, on 27 May 2011.
'You are the most beautiful, generous and kind person
that I've ever met in my life,' said Ed of a tearful Justine.
David attended the wedding – but not the reception.

Right, Ed and
Justine with their
two sons, Daniel
and Samuel.

More crucially still for Ed, in return for agreeing to the compromise on Heathrow, he persuaded Brown to agree to commit to working extra hard for a positive outcome at the Copenhagen summit later that year. Ed had learned how to negotiate with Brown while working with him at close quarters at the Treasury; he knew how to extract concessions from his old boss. Heywood had never seen anything like it and at one point told colleagues in Number 10: 'This just isn't supposed to happen.'[22]

Nonetheless, on 28 January 2009, Brown's government narrowly won a vote on the third runway forced by the Opposition, although its majority was cut by two-thirds to just nineteen after twenty-eight Labour MPs rebelled. Ed, ever the loyalist in public, and having won his concessions, was spotted ushering Labour MPs through the government lobby.

ooooo

Ed was keen to persuade the left in general, and the Labour Party in particular, that despite the complicatedly disparate nature of the left, the struggle against climate change should be motivated by traditional, social-democratic principles of solidarity, social justice and equality. He was well aware of the empirical evidence suggesting that rising temperatures would impact disproportionately and negatively on the world's poorest communities.

In his Ralph Miliband Memorial Lecture at the LSE, entitled 'The Politics of Climate Change', and delivered in November 2009, a month before the Copenhagen summit, Ed proclaimed:[23]

The... most important aspect of a climate politics of the common good is about idealism.

Even after we have done all we can to build public support through candour and fairness, institutionalised intergenerational equity and spoken to people's self-interest, there will still be work to do.

It is in that space, after the work of self-interest is done, that we cannot live without ideals.

We need a politics of climate change that speaks to people's idealism as well as their wallets. It must chime with the ideal of the good society.

For me, the most important ideal is social justice.

We do not just need to preserve our world for future generations; we need to hand over a fairer world.

So we need to show people how action on climate change can reduce inequality and help build a stronger more cohesive society.

That includes the elements I talked about before: on energy bills, on keeping costs down, on ensuring fair access to the new jobs and opportunities.

But it is also something bigger. I said we are a transition economy. We are. And it is at moments of transition that we have the greatest ability to shape society for the better.

The central challenge is to incorporate climate change into everything we do: so it is an intrinsic part of our economic policy, our energy policy, our approach to social justice.

It was a passionate address – described by one of his aides as 'the best speech he has ever given'. Ed concluded the lecture, named in honour of his late father, by quoting his favourite lines from Ralph's writings:

[T]he green movement has already moved opinion in so many countries.

That movement will face big challenges in the years ahead as it reaches out to a wider constituency but it is a vital part of winning the battle to create a wider consensus on climate change.

And in that context, I want to leave the last words for my father, in a passage from the end of his last book.

'In all countries, there are people, in numbers large and small, who are moved by the vision of a new social order... It is in the growth in their numbers and in the success of their struggles that lies the best hope for humankind.'

Brown's approach to tackling climate change during this period was to delegate the issue, almost in its entirety, to Ed and his new department. 'Gordon could see that someone he trusted, someone with good political judgement, had prioritised climate change and he let him run with it,' says a former Labour government adviser.[24]

Ed's special adviser Polly Billington, a tough-talking former

BBC radio journalist who had come to work for him in October 2007, came up with the idea of 'Ed's Pledge' – a website hosted by the Labour Party that allowed members of the public to show their support for efforts to get a climate change deal at the Copenhagen climate change summit in December. It displayed a prominent photo of Ed on the front page and a message from the Climate Change Secretary:

> I'll be pushing for clear action to get a global climate deal that's ambitious, effective and fair. This means ambitious cuts in greenhouse gas emissions, keeping countries to their word and supporting poorer countries in adapting to climate change.

Personalising the campaign around Ed was a risky move. A modest man, Ed resisted the idea at first, asking for his name to be removed from the pledge until, finally, he was overruled by a determined Billington. She was right to do so: in the end, 'Ed's Pledge' proved to be hugely popular and, for the first time, gave Ed a name recognition, and popularity, outside of the Westminster village. As a former senior adviser on climate change to the Brown government has since noted: 'I thought it was rather remarkable to have people sign up to something under a politician's name and I think this is where the first wind of his leadership bid comes from. How many other Cabinet ministers could have done that and made it a success?'[25]

Ed's profile was growing – and thanks to his warm manner, persuasiveness and listening skills, the Climate Change Secretary managed to achieve what so many other frontline politicians had failed to do: he became a popular and trusted figure among campaigners, activists and NGOs, just as he had as minister for the third sector. 'He charmed the pants off of all the green groups,' says the environmental journalist and activist Mark Lynas.[26]

He also impressed them. Touring the country, addressing conferences, seminars and rallies, Ed bonded with the young and idealistic members of the green movement with his distinctive approach. 'He's charismatic in small groups,' says a friend who watched him woo the greens. 'He had those guys eating out of the palm of his hand – with that very soft style, quite disarming and self-deprecating, but with a real sense of passion behind his politics and his position.'[27]

As Lynas points out: 'He spoke to those audiences as if he was talking to people on a one-to-one level. He didn't come across as arrogant or as if he was pontificating. He actually sounded genuine.'[28]

This was not Red Ed, as he would later be derided; this was Green Ed. Climate change and the road to Copenhagen took over his life in 2009 – and won him hundreds of new friends and admirers who would flock to his side less than two years later during the Labour leadership contest. In the words of one of his former Cabinet colleagues: 'His brother had started it all but Ed turned it into a really big thing and he became a kind of cult figure in the green movement. To become a cult figure for greens in a government that was regarded by most of the liberal left as so toxic that they were all decamping en masse to the Lib Dems was quite an achievement.'[29]

ooooo

The climate change portfolio gave Ed the opportunity to travel abroad, to interact with foreign governments and participate in high-level diplomatic negotiations. It was in the summer of 2009 that officials from DECC and the Department for International Development (DFID) worked together to organise a joint trip, the first of its kind, with the respective Secretaries of States Ed and Douglas Alexander, to Bangladesh and India.

The purpose of the visit was two-fold: to raise the stakes in the run-up to the Copenhagen summit by highlighting the effect of climate change in one of the poorest parts of the world, Bangladesh, where the UK was the single biggest bilateral donor with £125m in 2009 and £150m in 2010; and then, more testingly, somehow to persuade India – which had resisted greenhouse gas reductions – to agree to cut carbon emissions at the same time as pursuing development.

NGOs were arguing that in order to prevent a global temperature rise of 2 degrees or more, the West had to cut emissions by at least 40 per cent by 2020. The previous December, the independent UK Committee on Climate Change had argued that this pledge should be strengthened to 42 per cent for a 50–50 chance of preventing the rise. Miliband's promise of a 34 per cent reduction had pleased campaigners but there was a huge amount more to do to secure a deal in December.

Ed and Alexander arrived in Dhaka, the Bangladeshi capital, with a handful of officials. One of them, Richard Darlington, Alexander's special adviser and a key figure behind the project, explains the context:

'The idea behind the trip was to give Ed, as the UK's lead negotiator at the Copenhagen climate summit in December, first hand experience of the way the developing world was already on the frontline of experiencing dangerous climate change.'[30]

While Secretaries of State often accompanied the PM on overseas trips, it was very rare for them to do joint visits to foreign countries. But Ed and Alexander were old friends and close Cabinet allies and both were convinced that the public would not support cutting emissions and tackling global poverty unless they could see that one could not be achieved without the other.

During their trip, the two men laughed regularly and were entirely happy in each other's company. 'They were constantly stealing each other's best lines in speeches, press conferences and media interviews. On the flights and in the cars the two would banter constantly,' Darlington says.[31] There was little sign of the tensions to come between the two men.

On his tour through muddy Bangladeshi villages, in the intense 40-degree heat, Ed met families who had benefited from British government funding – the Chars Livelihoods programme was providing a one-off asset worth up to £150, plus a small monthly stipend for eighteen months to households whose wooden huts stood raised above flooding levels on plinths. Inside one hut, he met a woman named Rehena and, through a translator, discovered that that she and Ed had babies born within a month of one another. Ed found the discovery poignant, he would say on the flight back, because it highlighted the interconnected nature of the problem and of the world.

Back at the residence, Ed seemed at once naturally comfortable and awkwardly dismayed, occasionally frowning or grimacing at the formality of meals or diplomatic rituals. But in the afternoon, after a little self-conscious hesitation Ed went for a swim in an outside, oasis-like pool typical of the overly-luxurious conditions of British official residences abroad. Ed was feeling better about politics now, after the unhappy period of the year before. On this trip, Ed was asked about a report in the *Mail on Sunday* claiming he had considered 'quitting' British politics, and he dismissed it as 'rubbish'.[32] He had, of course, been unhappy at the Cabinet Office and was unsure of the direction of the Brown government. There is no doubt, however, that above all at this time Ed was preoccupied with Copenhagen, which he described on the trip as 'one of the most important things I'll ever to do in my life'. Perhaps because of that, Ed took a conscious decision, perhaps mistakenly in retrospect, to play up the 'make or break' nature of Copenhagen, saying more than once that there was 'no plan B'.

The trip to India and Bangladesh was an eye-opener for Ed – he went from talking with the world's poorest people to, for the first time, meeting and negotiating with senior members of foreign governments, including the Prime Minister of Bangladesh, Sheikh Hasina, and India's influential environment minister, Jairam Ramesh. A former official who accompanied Ed on the trip recalls:

> In Delhi, it was clear that Ed was itching to get to the global stage and to make a difference. He was constantly running scenarios with the DECC officials to see if he could come up with numbers on emissions reductions and mitigation financing that could unlock a deal. When he returned from meeting his opposite number in the Indian government he was fizzing with excitement and optimistic about getting India's support for a deal... Ed hardly slept: talking constantly about what we'd seen, who we'd met and how the negotiations might play out. We all returned feeling that India could be brought on side and that the US and China were the two remaining obstacles.[33]

ooooo

Ed prepared meticulously for Copenhagen. Offices in DECC were set up like election-campaign 'war rooms', with diagrams and charts, facts and figures, instant rebuttals. There was a real buzz among civil servants, some of the more passionate ones on secondment from other departments, in T-shirts and jeans, inspired by the prospect of an international summit that could change history. A memo from Moira Wallace, DECC's permanent secretary, read out to staff and leaked to the press described DECC's role as that of a 'campaigning department'.

Some civil servants inside the department reportedly worried that the Wallace memo was 'a tacit admission that DECC did not have the influence to deliver policies, only to campaign for them'.[34] But as Ed had shown in his first few weeks in the job, when he raised the 2050 emissions reduction target from 60 per cent to 80 per cent, he could deliver. In April 2009, a month after he had been ambushed by the award-winning actor Pete Postlethwaite at the London premiere of the climate change movie, *The Age of Stupid*, who told Ed he planned to hand back his OBE if the government gave the go-ahead to the controversial Kingsnorth coal-fired power station in Kent, the Climate Change Secretary won plaudits from green groups when he announced a new 'clean coal' policy. No new coal-fired power stations would be allowed to be built in Britain unless they captured and buried at least 25 per cent of greenhouse gases immediately and 100 per cent by 2025.[35] 'Bravo Ed Miliband,' was the response of John Sauven, the executive director of Greenpeace UK.[36]

The issue of coal-fired power stations, however, did cause Ed some personal problems. The month before his announcement on 'clean coal', in March 2009, the *Daily Telegraph* zeroed in on a 'potential conflict of interest' involving his girlfriend Justine:

> In his declaration for the register of ministers' interests, released this week, Ed Miliband kept the identity of his girlfriend a secret from the media, although his department is aware who she is.
>
> But the *Daily Telegraph* can disclose the woman is Justine Thornton, an energy and planning expert whose work includes representing major companies. She is described in the barristers' bible, Chambers and Partners, as the 'preferred counsel of E.On'.
>
> The German company is awaiting the go-ahead from Mr Miliband's department to build four nuclear plants in Britain.
>
> The revelation has raised questions about a potential conflict of interest and aides to Mr Miliband last night confirmed that he had not excused himself from any decisions taken at the department.[37]

But, as the *Telegraph* conceded, Ed had told officials in his department of the nature of Justine's work when he was appointed as Climate Change and Energy Secretary in October 2008. A spokesman for DECC would later state that Ed had abided by all the relevant rules – but also make clear that Justine had not 'acted for or against the department and will not receive or accept any such work in the future'. Quincy Whitaker, Justine's friend and fellow lawyer, says the story was 'absurd': 'She represents a whole range of interests and she operates, like all barristers, on a cab-rank principle.'[38]

Minor personal controversies aside, DECC was the perfect department for Ed. It enabled him to blend his various strengths: creative-thinking, number-crunching, policy-making and, of course, campaigning. He was able to bring passion to the job and, as a former adviser to Brown notes: 'If he'd been Health Secretary or Work and Pensions Secretary, it would have been much harder to be as passionate and inspiring as he ended up being at DECC.'[39]

A source close to Chris Huhne, Ed's Lib Dem successor as Climate Change and Energy Secretary, says: 'Ed begun the process of turning round Labour's very poor legacy on energy and climate change domestic policy... but he really wasn't there long enough to make a substantial difference.'[40] But a senior adviser on climate change to the Conservative–Liberal Democrat coalition says Huhne privately acknowledges that 'he inherited a department that had succeeded in integrating staff from business and environmental backgrounds, which is pretty impressive given how ingrained and conservative civil service culture can be.'[41]

In fact, in a mock 'report card' on Brown's government, published in *The Guardian* in the summer of 2009, DECC was the only department to receive an A grade.

Meanwhile, Ed had thrown himself into the Copenhagen process in the run-up to the summit in December, impressing negotiators from EU countries in the various informal meetings that were held in European capitals throughout 2009. Back home in the UK, he gave dozens of speeches and interviews on the importance of tackling climate change, and took the fight to the sceptics. He declared a 'battle' against the 'siren voices'[42] who denied global warming was real or caused by humans, and publicly debated with Nigel Lawson, the former Conservative Chancellor and climate sceptic who he referred to as a 'saboteur'.[43] He called opposition to wind farms – and other sources of renewable energy – as 'socially unacceptable' as failing to wear seatbelts in cars.[44] Day after day, week after week, he and his department constantly made 'the UK government's case for an ambitious international agreement on climate change'.

But the cause Ed was championing received a major blow before the various international delegations even flew to Denmark. In the run-up to the conference, attended by ministers and representatives from 193 countries, China declared that the EU's proposal to set a target for developed nations to cut emissions by 80 per cent by 2050 was unacceptable. Both China and India rejected amendments proposed by Brown and Ed to legally binding 50 per cent reductions in emissions by 2050. Ed would not achieve the much-heralded agreement on 50 per cent reductions in global emissions by 2050, or 80 per cent reductions by developed countries, both of which were vetoed by China. Those who saw him in action during that week, and in the days afterwards, say that he broke a taboo of international diplomacy: he stood up to the Chinese.

In the run-up to the Copenhagen summit, he also put pressure on the Americans, urging the Obama administration to back legally binding reductions. 'He pushed the Americans fucking hard,' says a former Downing Street adviser to Brown. 'The administration complained about him to us.'[45] (A leaked US State Department cable published by Wikileaks in December 2010 showed that the United States and China had secretly joined forces 'to stymie every attempt by European nations to reach agreement [at Copenhagen]'.[46])

Copenhagen itself didn't live up to the hype – and failed to produce the desired outcome. Some in the Labour Party have suggested that Ed himself 'failed to bring home the bacon'[47] but it would be absurd to pin the blame on Ed rather than the Chinese or the Americans or the rest – in fact, as we shall see, there is a case to be made for saying that Ed may have saved Copenhagen from total collapse.

Ed's mistake in the run-up to the summit may have been his deliberate raising of expectations as part of his headline-grabbing, populist campaigning throughout 2009. There was much talk of a 'countdown' to 'saving the world'. A fortnight before Copenhagen he used an interview in *The Observer* to warn that the consequence of failure would be 'scary' in terms of the effect on the environment. Yet today, he says he has no regrets about ramping up the stakes.[48]

In fact, Ed had known the summit would be a nightmare before he even touched down in Copenhagen. As he told *The Guardian* writer John Harris on the flight to Denmark, 'Imagine if you knew 189 people, and you got them all together and said, "Here's how we want you to run a significant part of your lives in the next thirty or forty years – and by the way, you have to unanimously agree that that's how you want to do it."'

Halfway through the conference, after endless rounds of bilateral meetings, Ed anticipated what was to come, telling Harris, who was shadowing him: 'I remain frustrated. How do I put this? There's a calculated repositioning of aspirations, where it's being agreed that we're not going to do anything that's binding, we're not going to do anything substantive, and a lot of people blame everybody else for everything going too slow. And for small island states like ours, that's very disconcerting.'[49]

The activist Mark Lynas, who was in Copenhagen in an official capacity as an adviser to the Maldives government says 'negativity and bitterness and polarisation', overtook the negotiations at Copenhagen; the mood was one of suspicion and distrust among the delegates from developing-world countries. Lynas highlights the damage done by the 'Danish text', a document prepared by the Danish government on 27 November and leaked to *The Guardian* newspaper[50] on only the second day of the Copenhagen summit, which suggested that rich countries had been involved in a parallel track, outside the main United Nations negotiating process. 'After *The Guardian* published this supposed leaked "Danish text", it was used as a pretext by some developing countries to stir up ill-feeling,' he says. 'That was probably the single event which destroyed any chance of a positive outcome.'

Ed was enraged by *The Guardian* story. Spotting John Vidal, the newspaper's environment correspondent, at a press conference during the summit, the Climate Change Secretary pulled him to one side and began berating him. 'What the fuck have you done?' yelled Ed. 'You have wrecked everything.'[51] Veterans of the negotiating circuit say Ed's public outburst was a sign of his political immaturity. 'That he expected *The Guardian*, or the British press, not to print the leak was touchingly naïve,' says one.[52]

Ed, however, has since put much of the blame for the conference's overall failure to achieve a legally binding deal on 'process'. Petty rows, he would later tell MPs in the Commons, 'meant that it was not until 3am on Friday, the last day of a two-week conference, that substantive negotiations began on what became the Copenhagen accord. By then, there was simply too little time to bridge some of the differences that existed.'

Ed described 'a chaotic process dogged by procedural games. Thirty leaders left their negotiators at 3am on Friday, the last night to haggle over the short Danish text that became the accord.'[53]

Despite all the intense difficulties and inevitable eccentricities involved in negotiating at an international conference, an agreement was brokered by US President Barack Obama with representatives from China, India, Brazil and South Africa. The 'Copenhagen accord' was based on a commitment 'to reduce global emissions so as to hold the increase in global temperature below 2C' and to achieve 'the peaking of global and national emissions as soon as possible'.

On the night of 18 December President Barack Obama went on television to announce what he called a 'meaningful deal' prior to some developing countries seeing the text of the supposed deal. 'We're going to have to build on the momentum that we've established here in Copenhagen to ensure that international action to significantly reduce emissions is sustained and sufficient over time,' Obama told a televised press conference. 'We've come a long way but we have much further to go.'[54]

Representatives from a small number of developing countries reacted with astonishing fury, producing a series of posturing and hyperbolic outbursts at the final plenary session in the early hours of Saturday 19 December. Venezuela's hysterical representative, Claudia Salerno, cut her hand and waved it in the air before asking:

'Do I have to bleed to grab your attention? International agreements cannot be imposed by a small exclusive group. You are endorsing a coup d'état against the United Nations.'[55]

Ed Miliband had gone to bed in his hotel room believing an agreement of sorts had been reached before the outbursts, only to be woken at 3am by aides and told of this latest diplomatic crisis. He rushed to the hall, arriving as Lumumba Di-Aping, the Sudanese chair of the G77-China bloc, invoked the memory of the Holocaust:

> [This] is asking Africa to sign a suicide pact, an incineration pact in order to maintain the economic dependence of a few countries. It's a solution based on values that funnelled six million people in Europe into furnaces.[56]

Ed knew he had to intervene. Tired, unshaven, pale, in an open neck white shirt, Ed, speaking off the cuff and without notes, did not mince his words:

> The work we have done faces a moment of profound crisis at this meeting here in the early hours of the morning. I think we have a choice of two roads … there is a road of a document that has been produced with a process that has been done in good faith by you under very difficult circumstances. It is a document which is by no means perfect… But most importantly it is a document that in substantive ways will make the lives of people round this planet better … it does a limited number of things but it does very important things. So we have one choice before us to accept this document and go forward and start the money flowing and start implementing the decisions under it. And then we face a choice that Ambassador Lumumba offers us. It is a choice of disgusting comparisons to the Holocaust which should offend people across this conference from whatever background they come from. And frankly it a choice of wrecking this conference.

Ed concluded his impromptu remarks with an impassioned plea to the delegates not to wreck the possibility of an agreement, and the funding associated with such an agreement – prompting a standing ovation from the majority of delegates inside the hall.[57]

'It was an extraordinary performance and he pulled the conference back from the brink of disaster,' says Jacobs. 'The agreement was "noted", not accepted, but if Ed hadn't spoken, arguably it would have been defeated.'[58]

Others agree with Jacobs. 'Did Ed Miliband save the

Copenhagen summit from complete failure?' asked the respected British science writer, Fred Pearce, in an article for *The Guardian* four days after the end of the summit, suggesting that the answer was yes.[59] Pearce points to a second but equally important intervention by Ed at 7am on the Saturday, with the conference fourteen hours into overtime and an exhausted, frustrated and confused chairman of the summit, Danish Prime Minister Lars Lokke Rasmussen, about to give up. After listening to more than forty speeches from the floor and with dozens more delegates waiting to be heard, Rasmussen said there was no consensus on adopting the draft agreement produced by US President Obama and twenty-five other heads of state the previous day. 'Therefore I propose that we...'

According to Pearce: 'Almost certainly his next words would have been a recommendation to drop or delete the text... Then up spoke Ed Miliband, younger brother of the more famous British Foreign Secretary, David Miliband. "Point of order", he called from the floor, and asked for an adjournment of the meeting. Rasmussen looked like a drowning man saved.'

A new chairman took over from Rasmussen when the meeting resumed three hours later, and a compromise was reached in which the accord was 'taken note of' by the conference as a whole, rather than agreed or voted down. 'The gavel fell. The accord was saved. Wild applause broke out.'

Outside the hall, however, green campaigners refused to hide their disappointment and frustration at the lack of a binding accord. 'The city of Copenhagen is a crime scene tonight, with the guilty men and women fleeing to the airport,' said an angry John Sauven. 'There are no targets for carbon cuts and no agreement on a legally binding treaty.'[60]

According to one British official who worked very closely with Ed during the intensive negotiations, the Secretary of State's mood was one of 'exhaustion more than anything; intense disappointment that two years of work had come to an unsatisfactory agreement'.[61] Ed arrived at the airport for his flight back to London tired and dejected. Having been awake and in meetings for the previous three nights, he collapsed into his seat on the plane and fell asleep.

But, as is his wont, Ed would now work hard to turn a seeming failure into a political opportunity and, even, a semi-triumph. In a series of media interviews he emphasised the upsides. And, in *The Guardian* under the headline 'The Road from Copenhagen', he wrote:[62]

> Countries signing the accord have endorsed the science that says we must prevent warming of more than 2C. For the first time developing countries, including China, as well as developed countries, have agreed emissions commitments for the next decade. If countries deliver on the most ambitious targets, we will be within striking distance of what is needed to prevent warming of more than 2C. These commitments will also for the first time be listed and independently scrutinised, with reports to the UN required every two years.
>
> We have also established an unprecedented commitment among rich countries to finance the response to climate change: $10bn a year over the next three years – starting to flow now – rising to $100bn a year by 2020, the goal first set out by the Prime Minister in June.
>
> In the months ahead, these concrete achievements must be secured and extended... Today many people will be feeling gloomy about the results of their efforts. But no campaign ever wholly succeeds at the first time of asking. We should take heart from the achievements and step up our efforts. The road from Copenhagen will have as many obstacles as the road to it. But this year has proved what can be done, as well as the scale of the challenge we face.

Whatever the small successes and bigger failures of Copenhagen, there is no doubt that Ed himself emerged from it with his reputation enhanced – as he had over the Heathrow runway. He had earned respect in fighting his corner and, as at Oxford, he had snatched a victory of sorts from the jaws of defeat.

Between October 2008 and the general election of May 2010, as Secretary of State for Energy and Climate Change, Ed underwent a transformation: from thoughtful, intelligent, up-and-coming junior Cabinet minister to charismatic, empathetic and focused campaigner and one of Labour's big-hitters. 'I just saw him grow' says a friend who worked with him in the Treasury and Downing

Street. 'He didn't grow as a politician in the Cabinet Office. He really didn't.'[63] One of Ed's former Cabinet colleagues, who would later back David's leadership bid, remarks, begrudgingly: 'DECC was the making of Ed as a politician.'[64]

Looking back at 2009, Ed himself realised that his appeal was in his ability to lead and campaign, to inspire civil servants and activists alike, to attract otherwise disillusioned people to a political and moral cause. 'He helped the Labour Party engage with a new generation who had basically written us off, post-Iraq,' says another former Cabinet colleague. 'We were not getting through to them but Ed, as Climate Change Secretary, did get through to them.'[65] 'We were trying to get a mood of insurgency as a government after twelve years by using Energy and Climate Change to try and get people motivated,' says the Labour frontbencher Sadiq Khan, who would later help run Ed's leadership campaign.[66] It was a campaign, as we shall see, that was self-consciously insurgent.

But it was a campaign that couldn't have happened without Ed's work on climate change and the Copenhagen process. 'I think he learned in the DECC job more about decisiveness', says Nick Pearce, the head of the Number 10 Policy Unit under Brown. 'He couldn't have just gone from the Cabinet Office to standing for the Labour leadership.'[67]

Another former Downing Street official, who went on to advise the younger Miliband's leadership campaign, says Ed 'started looking like he could carry the [leadership] torch when he took over at DECC. Something changed visibly in his stature.'[68]

But something also changed inside of him. For the first time, as he has since confirmed to friends, Ed began to see himself as a future Labour leader.[69]

GENERAL ELECTION

2010

Though now widely forgotten, Gordon Brown delivered the best public performance of his life just four days after his description of Gillian Duffy as a 'bigoted woman' rocked Labour's general election campaign. So powerful and moving was his speech to London Citizens at Westminster's Methodist Central Hall on 3 May, that those present felt he may even have recovered from the unmitigated disaster of the previous week.

Brown, David Cameron and Nick Clegg all spoke at the event, which fleetingly electrified the general election campaign. Before that, however, the hundreds of community workers and activists heard from 14-year-old Thiare Sanchez. Fighting back tears, she told the story of her mother, Sandra Sanchez, who struggled to bring up her three children on her own by travelling on a night bus in the early hours of each morning from Hounslow to the Treasury, where she worked as a cleaner. As a Treasury cleaner, she earned £6.95 an hour – £278 for a 40-hour week – leaving the single mother trying to feed her kids below the poverty line.

Brown, at his rarely-seen best, embraced the child and then spoke angrily, passionately, about the need for a 'living wage'. Ed Miliband was not only responsible for the Prime Minister sign-ing up to the concept; he was the man behind putting Brown and Sanchez together on that podium. Two months earlier he had been introduced to Sandra Sanchez by Maurice Glasman, then a lead organiser in London Citizens and now appointed by Ed to the House of Lords. Glasman had held several meet-ings with Ed from February in the DECC offices as Ed sought to bring the living wage campaign, along with mutualism and community-based activism that would later become branded 'blue Labour' into his campaign. When Ed met Sandra, he was totally absorbed. He questioned her closely on her family story, and decided to help her. As the woman left Ed's office, she told

Glasman that this had been the first time any politician had taken such detailed interest in her plight. She could not believe how much he seemed to care.

It was Ed who persuaded Brown, at the very last minute, to attend the London Citizens rally held forty-eight hours before the general election, and convinced the Prime Minister to deliver a speech largely written by Glasman. 'There has been no better testimony for a living wage, no better case for fairness for all of us, than the case made by Thiare this afternoon, and I want you to thank her for what she said and the way she said it,' Brown boomed. 'When people say that politics can't make a difference, when people say that people are apathetic and indifferent, when people say there are no great causes left, let them come here.' For the first and perhaps last time in the campaign, Brown was on fire and – showing his compassion for ordinary people – easily got the better of the other two party leaders who also attended, and spoke at, the rally. It was a rare success – before a crushing electoral defeat.

ooooo

Ed had first been assigned the job of overseeing the party's manifesto when Brown took office in June 2007. In the run-up to the 'election that never was' that autumn, he was unprepared. The second time round, he had done the legwork.

Throughout 2009 and 2010, Ed hosted a series of meetings to go through drafts. Because he was also busy with the DECC day job, several of these had to take place at weekends. Over Hobnob biscuits, fruit and orange juice, Ed and Douglas Alexander, the party's election coordinator, sat side by side in Ed's sitting room on Saturday afternoons, hashing out drafts of the manifesto with their key advisers.

Inside Downing Street, Ed had help writing the manifesto from Patrick Diamond, a former adviser to Peter Mandelson. Nick Pearce and Gavin Kelly were the two other key members of the manifesto-writing team.

There is no doubt that there were disagreements between Ed and Number 10 on the one hand, and departmental ministers on the other. One source close to Ed at this time says it was clear the ministers were 'running out of steam' and not engaging fully on future policy. Others say that the conservatism of Brown himself stopped Ed from being as 'radical' as he wanted to be, for example on the issue of Trident renewal. Others still say that Peter Mandelson was an obstacle, as his primary concern was to defend the interests of business.[1] As Diamond has said:

> After thirteen years inside government [our] task was to break out of the insider mindset. We met literally hundreds of NGOs and voluntary sector organisations. We knew we wanted a new industrial policy for growth and the business community, we knew we wanted a new emphasis on public services and something on immigration for the bulk of middle income earners, and after the economic downturn, there [was] an appetite for a new approach to the governance model for both the private and public sector which we thought a return to mutualism could help us with. Early on we knew the idea of a people's bank was the right one. Other than that, we listened.[2]

Officials representing the Australian Prime Minister Kevin Rudd and the Spanish Prime Minister José Luis Rodríguez Zapatero attended Downing Street seminars on how to 'sell' climate change to voters and in what way to develop the minimum wage. The Venezuelan academic Carlota Perez influenced one of Ed's set-piece ideas, reforming credit cards and rethinking personal debt in general.

Ed outlined many of these ideas at the autumn 2009 party conference where he addressed the hall, once again without notes, not as DECC Secretary of State but in his role as manifesto coordinator. Behind the scenes, however, he had a near-impossible balancing act to perform, somehow pleasing both the likes of Peter Mandelson on the right of the party and the Compass pressure group on the left.

Strange as it may seem now, Mandelson is said at this stage to have warmed to Ed so much that he started to rethink his view that David should be the next leader in the event Labour lost the general election. Mandelson denies it, but it is claimed by some senior Labour figures that he began to see Ed as the better option.[3] The two men were certainly talking a lot, sometimes in private, around September and October 2009. At one point during the 2009 party conference, Mandelson was sitting in Brown's hotel room watching the proceedings in the chamber on television when he spotted the younger Miliband. 'There's Eddie!' he cried out, extravagantly, a smile across his face. Witnessing the scene, David Muir, Gavin Kelly and Sue Nye all glanced at each other.[4] Clearly however, 'something went wrong', in the words of one senior party source[5], as Mandelson would later back David and issue a full-frontal attack on Ed during the leadership campaign.

At the turn of the year, Ed was still working closely with Douglas Alexander, who was looking ahead to the general election campaign. Two days before Christmas, Alexander passed to Brown a plan which proposed the campaign strap-line 'A Future Fair for All' and outlined main themes. The top priority was to attack the Tories on the economy, and the plan included a 150-page dossier adding up the costs of Conservative spending plans, which Alistair Darling subsequently launched in January.

Ed was also ready by Christmas with a first draft of the manifesto, but there was more work to do.

First, however, Brown had to overcome his final – and most serious – coup attempt. A column in *The Independent* published on New Year's Day was the first to give a hint of the plotting that had taken place over the festive period. Under the headline, 'Will they, won't they launch a coup', the piece outlined the arguments of several senior Labour figures who wanted one, concluding: '[It] does look as if the next fortnight will be critical. It appears that Tory support is wide but shallow and that another Labour leader could reduce it. But if the Prime Minister survives January – and past experience suggests he will – then Labour will probably have to take its chances with Mr Brown.'[6]

Exactly a week later, during Prime Minister's Questions on 6 January, a letter circulated round Labour MPs calling for a confidence vote in Brown. The letter was coordinated by Geoff Hoon and Patricia Hewitt, though Charles Clarke had pulled many of the strings to launch what became known as – after the weather of the time – 'the snow plot'. The document said:

Many colleagues have expressed their frustration at the way in which this question is affecting our political performance. We have therefore come to the conclusion that the only way to resolve this issue would be to allow every member to express their view in a secret ballot... There is a risk otherwise that the persistent background briefing and grumbling could continue up to and possibly through the election campaign, affecting our ability to concentrate all of our energies on getting our real message across. In what will inevitably be a difficult and demanding election campaign, we must have a determined and united parliamentary party... It is our job to lead the fight against our political opponents. We can only do that if we resolve these distractions. We hope that you will support this proposal.[7]

It was strangely unclear, in that it fell back on the need to clear the air, stopping short of calling for Brown to go. It failed to fly. David Miliband, who as we have seen had tried, and failed, privately to recruit Ed to the anti-Brown cause the previous month, was reported to have 'dithered' in his office for hours before eventually saying he was getting on with the job during a brief 'doorstep' to the cameras as he entered the Foreign Office in the early evening. In fact, he told one friend later, he was simply waiting to see what would happen.[8] Ed, in contrast, was telling anyone who would listen that Brown had to stay on, and went on the airwaves to make his case. The last truly loyal Cabinet minister, with the possible exception of Ed Balls, Ed had summed up his views on the prospect of a coup in the previous months when he told fellow Brownite Douglas Alexander that 'it would be like killing our father'.[9] This vivid phrase – which one observer points out is 'very Ed'[10] – again signifies Ed's loyalty to his political 'father', Brown, not his real-life brother, David.

Meanwhile, the manifesto process dragged on. During long afternoons inside Downing Street, Diamond took notes as Ed chaired meetings of voluntary groups that he had cultivated as minister for the third sector, representatives from co-op groups, nurses and teachers. The concept of 'mutualism' was to be one of the manifesto's big ideas.

On 8 February, Ed hosted a meeting in 11 Downing Street with some thirty entrepreneurs with experience of building social enterprises along co-operative lines. The theme was enlightened self-interest; as one businesswoman told the seminar, the value for mutual bodies is 'low staff turnover, low sickness and increased commitment' from employees whose morale is high.

Also present was Tessa Jowell, long an advocate of mutualism. She pointed out that some two million Britons used 'mutuals', including the 1.3 million members of the 122 NHS foundation trusts across England, through parents and teachers working together at co-op trust schools, and those in housing co-ops.

Strategically, the plan to lay heavy emphasis on mutualism was aimed at reclaiming this territory from the Tories. In 2008, Cameron had launched the 'Conservative Co-operative Movement'. It soon fizzled out. Days after a report of the Downing Street seminar on mutualism appeared, the Tories attempted to relaunch the plan, aimed at 'Conservative minded' community-based activists. For the first time in months, there was a brief sense that Labour had the Tories on the back-foot.

ooooo

On Tuesday 6 April 2010, Ed Miliband filed out of Number 10 into Downing Street behind Gordon Brown, who had just confirmed to the Cabinet he was about to kick off the general election campaign. Standing with other ministers, Ed watched from the sidelines as Brown told the political world what it all already knew. 'It's probably the least well-kept secret of recent years but the Queen has kindly agreed to the dissolution of Parliament and a general election will take place on 6 May', the Prime Minister said.

After the announcement, Brown headed – not for the last time – to a supermarket, in Rochester, Kent, to meet voters, while David Cameron went to a hospital in Edgbaston, Birmingham. With Labour almost ten points behind in the polls, the race was on. Labour's challenge was to defy political gravity by achieving an unprecedented fourth continuous term in office amid the worst economic crash in modern times.

On 12 April, after a series of last-minute meetings between Ed and Brown, the Cabinet and a stream of MPs and advisers headed for Birmingham, with media following, to launch the manifesto. The 'Soviet-style' front cover of the document itself was criticised by the press – and not totally without justification. It showed a family staring towards a sun with the words 'A Future Fair for All', and contrasted sharply with the Tory manifesto, which was published as a hardbound book, navy blue and in the form of a personal 'contract' with Britain signed by David Cameron.

On the way up to Birmingham, the headline themes being briefed to journalists were the need to fix the economy and fix politics. On the former, the sub-headings were Labour's plans for 'securing the recovery' and boosting manufacturing. Also leaked was the idea of a 'toddler tax credit', which would provide families with one- and two-year-olds with £4 extra per week from 2012.

'The future will be progressive or Conservative but it will not be both,' Brown declared at the manifesto launch. 'We are in the future business; we are building a future fair for all.' All appeared to be going smoothly – until, that is, the message became mixed when Mandelson summed up the theme of the manifesto in a television interview as 'Blair-plus'. In fact, a single, overarching theme was hard to define. Looking back, many of Ed's allies concede there was no overall 'narrative', no compelling 'story' that Labour was telling about what it wanted to do in a fourth term.[11]

Understandably given the fiscal climate, there were no major spending promises, though there was a pledge not to raise income tax, as there had been in 2005 – only to be broken. There were similar commitments not to extend VAT to food, children's clothes, books, newspapers and public transport fares. Ed had pushed through his living wage commitment, which Labour said would be set in government at £7.60 – higher than the minimum wage. And there would be a global bank levy.

But the centrepiece of the economy section was the plan, devised by Alistair Darling, to halve the deficit by 2014, so controversial because it would later be disowned by Ed Balls in the leadership election and become the heart of a fiscal debate at the top of Labour.

On education, there were moves to give parents more power to change the leadership of schools, perhaps in anticipation of similar moves by the Tories. Nursery places would be extended for two-year-olds, with more flexible hours of teaching for three- and four-year-olds. There were pledges of £4 extra for family tax credits, 70,000 advanced apprenticeships, and a doubling of paid paternity leave (later to be taken by Ed himself). The set-piece health pledge, that the Tories failed to match, was the guarantee of cancer test results within a week. Elsewhere, Labour politicians highlighted supposedly-radical pledges on constitutional reform. At the 2009 annual conference, Brown had been persuaded at the very last minute to commit to a referendum on the Alternative Vote electoral system, a break from the New Labour leadership's hitherto total failure to embrace electoral reform (although as would later repeatedly be pointed out, during the 2011 referendum campaign, AV is not proportional). Added to the AV pledge was a package including a second chamber elected by proportional representation, and the right to 'recall' MPs found guilty of gross misconduct, a response to the expenses scandal. But, for many inside the party, the manifesto proposals were 'too little, too late'.

During the campaign itself, Ed kept a relatively low profile. He had been based much of the time in Labour's Victoria Street headquarters coordinating the manifesto. And though he spoke to Brown ahead of the televised debates that took place for the first time between the party leaders, he was not part of the key briefing team that included David Muir, Douglas Alexander and Alastair Campbell.

The biggest campaign event that Ed played a prominent role in was the first and perhaps last joint-appearance of its kind with his brother David. It was not an unmitigated success. On Saturday 3 April, at a comprehensive school in Basildon, Essex, David unveiled the winning entry for a 'people's poster' competition, adopted by Labour, portraying the *Ashes to Ashes* character Gene Hunt as David Cameron. Under the photo-shopped picture of 'Cameron' sitting on the bonnet of a car was the slogan, 'Don't let him take Britain back to the 1980s.' At the event, vaguely aimed at winning over young people, David contrasted how Cameron had joined the Tories in the 1980s because he 'so loved' what Margaret Thatcher was doing, while he and Ed had joined Labour in the same decade because they 'hated' what Thatcher was doing. He made a strong case for 'a Labour Party that is reaching out', providing a real 'alternative' of the sort not presented to the electorate in the 1980s. He also paid tribute to Ed's 'amazing leadership' on climate change. Ed, after looking on at David admiringly, quipped that his brother had been 'older than me in the 1980s' but echoed the theme, describing the 'big choices on the ballot'. But the event – and the poster launch – was to fall flat. Within hours of the Miliband brothers' launch, the Tories had released online an alternative, embracing the image – with a slightly better picture of Cameron's face – with the line, 'Fire up the Quattro. It's time for change.' Cameron claimed he was 'flattered' to have been linked to the star.

After a final round of canvassing on polling day, Ed spent the night of the general election at his constituency home in Doncaster, with Justine. Personally, he was happy to have beaten his Tory rival Sophie Brodie, securing 47.3 per cent of the vote, if a little alarmed by a 3.8 swing against him. But with the national result still in doubt, and no clear national winner having yet emerged, Ed returned from Doncaster to London on the night of 6 May. Immediately he was told by Brown that he was to be a member of the team of Labour figures tasked with negotiating a 'progressive alliance' with the Liberal Democrats, should the third party's talks with the Tories break down or end in deadlock.

ooooo

On the morning of Tuesday 11 May, after the Lib Dems had met with the Tories William Hague, Oliver Letwin, Ed Llewellyn and George Osborne, the Labour delegation sat down, in secret, with Nick Clegg's negotiating team in room 319 of Portcullis House. Ed, in his role as manifesto chief, took his seat alongside Andrew Adonis, Peter Mandelson, Ed Balls and Harriet Harman. On the other side of the table sat Danny Alexander, David Laws, Chris Huhne and Andrew Stunell.

Soon after the meeting started Alexander, Clegg's chief of staff, surprised those present by announcing that a planned meeting that was to have taken place simultaneously between Vince Cable and Alistair Darling, to discuss how the parties might work together on the economy, had been cancelled. This was the moment when it became clear to the Labour negotiators that the Lib Dems were not serious about doing a deal with them. Labour's team had only been granted three hours with the Lib Dems, compared with the twenty hours of talks that the Lib Dems had conducted with the Conservatives' negotiating team.

Adonis, Mandelson and, to a lesser extent, Ed have subsequently made it clear they believe the Lib Dems had already decided to go in with the Tories as early as the day after the election, if not before. They note that Clegg helped prepare the ground by implying that he would side with the greatest 'mandate' in terms of votes cast and seats won in the event of a hung parliament, and that he would not allow Gordon Brown to 'squat' in Downing Street. Clegg reiterated this in his statement outside the Cowley Street Lib Dem headquarters in Westminster on the morning of Friday 7 May. Hours later, Cameron had made his 'big, open and comprehensive offer' to the Lib Dems.

Adonis, particularly, maintained that the Lib Dems' main 'alibi' – that the 'numbers' would not add up – was false. He briefed an eager Brown, who told the Cabinet at 5pm on 10 May that the Queen's Speech could be passed under a Labour–Liberal coalition with a '20-plus' majority. The Scottish Nationalists and Plaid Cymru had made it clear they would not side with the Tories, while the Democratic Unionist Party would abstain, Brown pointed out. Meanwhile the Independent and Green MPs, Sylvia Hermon and Caroline Lucas respectively, could also be brought on side. At the same meeting, Brown told the Cabinet that he intended to step down in the autumn if his attempt at a 'progressive alliance' could be pulled off. Suddenly, those who still wanted a Labour–Liberal coalition – unlike tribal senior party figures such as John Reid and David Blunkett – had reason for renewed optimism.

That night, there was palpable excitement in the more progressive Labour circles, as the prospect of the party staying in power with the aid of the Liberal Democrats was – fleetingly – revived.

The following morning, Paddy Ashdown told BBC Radio 4's *Today* programme that Labour and the Lib Dems could form a de facto minority government and 'dare' the smaller parties to vote them down. However, a combination of pressure from senior Labour refuseniks and Cameron's clever offer of an AV referendum, following a brief panic in Tory high command, meant the dream of a Lib–Lab coalition was dead by the end of the day. After several attempts by Vince Cable and Clegg to delay Brown's final decision, he left Downing Street before sundown.

The key question about Ed Miliband in these crucial days is whether – like Adonis – he was 100 per cent committed to securing a deal with the Lib Dems to stay in power. Lib Dem negotiators have alleged that in fact, he was half-hearted, his eye already on the prize of the Labour leadership to come.

In his account of the talks, *22 Days in May*, for example, David

Laws questions Ed's commitment to the cause of a Labour–Liberal alliance. Laws claims:

> I held out the hope that Ed Miliband might be an ally in the event that a Lib–Lab partnership ever proved viable... But, over time, I became a little more sceptical of the chances of this happening. Firstly, though Ed would often say in passing things like: 'We really must meet to discuss things', nothing ever seemed to come of these negotiations... Ed Miliband ... notably failed to follow up on his occasional suggestions that we should meet to talk about our 'common interests'... I had expected Ed Miliband to be far more constructive ... he gave the impression of being at best indifferent to the success of the talks.

While it is undoubtedly true that Ed Miliband was thinking about the leadership by now, having first considered it seriously in 2008 and decided he was minded to go for it as early as January 2010, Laws's claims are emphatically denied by both Ed and his colleagues. As one fellow member of the negotiating team says, 'Ed played a completely straight bat about the coalition negotiations. He wanted them to succeed, he was constructive in the three sessions we had with the Lib Dems and ... the Lib Dem stuff about body language of the two Eds being negative is completely wrong: they were constructive throughout.'[12]

Another who was in the room says: 'Ed Balls, in typical Ed Balls style, got into big arguments with the Lib Dems about deficit reduction and things like that ... but Ed Miliband didn't even do that: he was going out of his way to be positive and constructive at every level... Insofar as Ed was thinking about a potential leadership election, it wasn't in any way cutting across what we're all seeking to achieve.'[13]

This is easy to believe. After all, Ed was the Cabinet minister most devoted to Brown's leadership. He had fought for Brown to stay when other former 'Brownites' had wanted the Prime Minister out. In those powerful words, he had told his former fellow Brown protégé that ousting Brown would be 'like killing our father'. And, in typical Ed style, the Climate Change Secretary had been the most charming Labour representative involved in the negotiations, disarmingly presenting the Lib Dem team with cappuccinos at their second meeting 'as a token of my great affection'. Indeed, Ed began that session, on Tuesday 11 May, saying: 'I want to be absolutely clear that our aim is for these negotiations to succeed. We want to see a Lab–Lib government and we're doing all we can to make it possible.'[14]

According to a Labour insider, Ed Miliband left Ed Balls to confront the Lib Dems over their U-turn on the timing of deficit reduction and spending cuts. 'Ed Miliband wasn't even engaged in that discussion,' says the insider.[15]

Instead, Ed had what one Labour negotiator says was a 'very long exchange with Chris Huhne about nuclear power. It was a perfectly constructive one. Huhne had some totally unrealistic policies on renewable power. He was trying to shift his stance without it looking like he was. Ed knew what he was talking about, there were toing and frowing. Ed dealt with it all very constructively.'[16]

Naturally, Huhne emphatically denies that his suggestions were in any way 'unrealistic'.[17] What there is less doubt about, however, is that by the time Gordon Brown resigned as Prime Minister, Ed Miliband could not have done much more to halt the surreal but unstoppable alliance between Cameron's Conservatives and Clegg's Liberal Democrats. But that is not to say he had his doubts. And in preparation for the breakdown of Labour–Liberal talks, Ed, ever the pragmatist, by now had one eye on the Labour leadership contest to come.

DECISION TO RUN

MAY 2010

On the morning of Tuesday 11 May, there was a mood of renewed energy inside 10 Downing Street. The previous evening, Gordon Brown had played the final card in his last-ditch bid to forge the way for a Labour–Liberal Democrat 'progressive' alliance. When he finally sacrificed himself as party leader, Brown met the condition insisted on by many Lib Dems, including Nick Clegg. A combative Alastair Campbell had taken to the airwaves alongside Andrew Adonis to talk up a deal. Now, Ed Miliband, Campbell, Adonis, Ed Balls and a handful of resident Downing Street advisers were discussing how to keep up the momentum, having apparently pulled the rug from under the Tories' feet.

Yet in the middle of these talks, Ed Miliband asked one of Brown's advisers, Greg Beales, for a private word. The two walked through to the adjoining Number 11, home of the Chancellor. Ed proposed they get a cup of tea, and they sat down opposite one another in Alistair Darling's empty study. 'It doesn't appear that this is going to be successful,' Ed said. Taken aback, Beales protested that things were surely looking up for a Labour–Lib Dem alliance. Ed then dropped a bombshell. 'I know, I know. But it doesn't look like it's going to be successful. And if it's not successful I'm going to run for the leadership of the party and I'd like you to be involved.' In the months leading up to the general election, Beales had hinted to Ed that he, rather than David, was best placed to lead the party after Brown and make the much-needed break from New Labour. But until now Ed had refused to respond, out of loyalty to the Prime Minister. Beales, perhaps aware that this was a watershed moment, pressed Ed on why he had decided to stand to lead the party. 'I have to run in this race. David will be a good leader, and the others will be good leaders, but I am the only person who can decisively move the Labour Party on from the Blair–Brown era'. Ed added that Beales, were he to lend his support, would 'make a difference'. The latter pledged his allegiance to the younger Miliband on the spot.[1]

Ed had recruited his first campaign helper before the Labour–Liberal talks had broken down and – crucially – well before the point at which he now publicly claims to have made his decision to run. Given that he was confident all along of winning, his decision to run in the first place was arguably the point of 'fratricide', not the moment the result was announced. In fact, the moment Ed made clear to friends and colleagues that he planned to stand against David was the point of rupture between the two Miliband brothers.

Steps to gather support on Ed's behalf had been well under way several days earlier. The evening after the general election, Ed's old friend Marc Stears texted, urging Ed to run. The reply was a non-committal 'thanks', though as ever Ed did not rule it out.[2] But on Saturday 8 May, Peter Hain took a call on his mobile from Hilary Benn, who had become a close Cabinet ally of Ed when the pair worked together on climate change. Benn, who had clearly spoken to Ed, asked Hain if he would join him in supporting the younger Miliband for the leadership. Hain said he was interested but would appreciate a call from Ed himself. The following day, Hain had just returned to his London flat from his general election count in Neath, when he got a call from Ed. 'We are going to fight an insurgent campaign,' Ed said. Hain replied that he liked what he was hearing, but added: 'I'm not interested in fighting a campaign for its own sake, simply to float a lot of ideas. I've been through too many campaigns like that, including my own [for the deputy leadership in 2007]. And I'm not interested in a campaign that isn't serious about winning.' Back came the reply: 'No, no, no – I'm serious about winning.' With Hain still wavering, Ed now revealed that he had other senior figures on side, including John Denham and Sadiq Khan, both liberals within Labour whose politics were close to Hain's. Hain was reassured, and by the end of the call he had agreed to back Ed.[3]

At 5pm on the day of Ed's Downing Street conversation with Beales, 11 May, Gordon Brown resigned as Prime Minister after it became clear that Nick Clegg had made his mind up to side with the Tories. Like many of the party's elite, Ed made his way to Labour's headquarters on Victoria Street for an emotional gathering to mark the end of New Labour in office. Then, in the pouring rain, he walked round the corner with Alastair Campbell to the pub where party workers were coming together to drown their sorrows. That evening, Oona King rang Ed on his mobile and spoke to him about the leadership. She started by saying 'You've got to run'. King detected he had 'probably made up his mind', though Ed claimed to be merely taking soundings. 'I think the only thing holding him back was the fact that David was running. And I'm certain that if David hadn't been running there wouldn't even have been an issue.' King ended the call with, 'I can't imagine how hard this is for you.' Ed replied, 'Yes, it's really hard', but, says King, he didn't say anything more than that.[4]

The following morning the focus had completely shifted to the leadership. Ed woke on 12 May to hear Alan Johnson, long seen as a possible contender, offering his support for David on the *Today* programme. An undoubted heavyweight, Johnson said David was 'the best person for the job', emphasising that the former Foreign Secretary's 'experience, clarity, intellect and ability to relate to people make him an excellent candidate'.[5] Whether this reference to David's ability to relate was designed to pre-empt Ed's own appeal is debatable: at this stage neither David nor his team were certain whether Ed would run. But that possibility, plus the bruising effect of months of accusations of dithering and being a 'bottler', surely contributed to David's decision to be first off the blocks later that morning.

It is claimed by some that while Brown was still Prime Minister, David had proposed that he be allowed to announce his candidacy outside Number 10, and that this was roundly dismissed by Brown, who banged his fist on his desk and said: 'That can't happen.'[6] True or not, David settled on making his announcement in the traditional spot for political statements: outside St Stephen's entrance to the House of Commons. Surrounded by fifteen MPs already signed up to support him, David swept into the sunshine and did what many of his supporters wished he had done as much as three years previously. Keen for a quick election in which he would be presented as the obvious candidate, David declared that – in the light of the new coalition – 'We live in a new political world, and the responsibility of office may return sooner than people think.'[7] It was a key part of his pitch that Labour could neither afford months of introspection during a drawn-out contest over the summer, nor assume that the revival of the Labour Party should be a 'slow burn' affair over the course of a full term. Instead, David insisted privately, the party had to be 'ready' sooner rather than later. And only he had the authority and experience to project himself immediately as an alternative Prime Minister. Finally, in a clear attempt to portray himself as the man who could win over Liberal Democrat voters disaffected over the alliance with the Tories, he said that Labour could be the 'great unifying force of all shades of centre and centre-left opinion'.

Ed watched his brother's declaration on television, from the sitting room of his home, where he had by now been joined by two supportive former Brown advisers, his right-hand man Stewart Wood, and Gavin Kelly. Despite Ed's conversation with Beales more than twenty-four hours earlier, not to mention his calls to Benn and Hain, he insists today that he had not yet decided to run at the time of David's statement. Be that as it may, he now became locked into forty-eight hours of intense talks at home with his closest aides and his partner Justine. A prolific user of text messages, Ed was also engaged in an endless round of text exchanges and calls to MPs, allies and friends. There were three main issues in Ed's mind as he mulled over the final decision: first, did he have something distinct to say; secondly did he have enough support; and thirdly was it the right thing to do.

Beales, Wood and Kelly had all made it clear to him that he had to be emphatically 'in it to win it' – with absolutely no doubts in his mind. He was getting a similar message from MPs. One of the few tricky conversations he had was with Andy Burnham, who had helped bury the prospect of a Labour–Liberal alliance by coming out against it on the Tuesday before Brown's resignation. Burnham took a call on his mobile to find Ed asking for his support. 'What are you thinking? What are you going to do?' asked Ed. But almost before Burnham could answer, Ed said: 'Well, I'm going to stand and we're good friends; I was wondering if we could sit down and talk about a role in my campaign.' Burnham politely said no, he was thinking of standing himself. Realising that Ed was serious about running, Burnham became immediately doubtful of his own chances, knowing that Ed could 'come through the middle' of a fight between David Miliband and

Ed Balls, who declared relatively late on 19 May, in the way that Burnham had hoped to do.[8]

Some of the groundwork having been laid among MPs, and with clearly enough support to gain the thirty-three nominations needed for a bid, Ed, Wood and Kelly had a last round of painstaking discussions about the pros and cons of Ed running. The fact that Ed would be standing against his own brother was 'the biggest obstacle', Ed says now.[9] While outwardly giving the impression of being relaxed about it to enquiring MPs – he told Hain he would 'never forgive'[10] himself for not running just because his brother was – Ed was acutely aware of the problem. He thought about the personal implications. He knew David would, at best, be bitterly disappointed. But he wouldn't let his elder brother's disappointment prevent him from standing. Ed wanted it too much – and he believed he had every right to stand. Since he was a young boy, he had been encouraged by his parents and, in particular, his father, to be cool, dispassionate and analytical. There is no reason to believe David, brought up in the same way, would have behaved any differently had the roles been reversed.

Though Ed did agonise out loud to confidants about 'the David issue', he took a rational and intellectual, as opposed to an emotional or sentimental, approach. On the basis that he had 'something different to offer' and was the only candidate able to break from Blair and Brown, represented in his eyes by David and Ed Balls respectively, he decided to imagine a scenario in which David was not running. Would he then be running? He and his aides quickly concluded that he would be. They also firmly believed he was the best candidate, regardless of whether David was in the race or not. Ed told close friends, in a franker version of his campaign pitch later, that David was too 'managerial', too 'technocratic', while he, Ed, had a different and superior model of leadership in mind, based on listening, empathising and inspiring.[11]

Today, Ed Miliband claims that the fundamental reason he decided to stand was the need to break from New Labour, as he had told Beales and others. But there is one other factor that was certainly in his mind: the belief that this would be his only chance; that he would never be able to succeed his brother as leader. At one point during the campaign, a friend of Ed asked him why he was challenging his own brother. 'I assume it's because you can't have two Milibands in a row,' said the friend. 'Yes, that's exactly it,' replied Ed without hesitation.[12] Accurately or not, Ed believed that the media would never have allowed two Miliband brothers to be leader or Prime Minister, despite the existence of political dynasties like the Kennedys, Bushes and Clintons in the United States.

Eventually, Ed turned to the question of how to tell David. The brothers had, extraordinarily, hardly discussed the issue of the Labour leadership in the preceding months. Ed knew the right thing to do was to go and see David face to face. He was extremely apprehensive – but he had the support of Justine. 'Life's an adventure,' she told him. 'And you've got to seize the day.'[13]

Finally, just after 10pm on Wednesday 12 May, say friends of Ed, the younger Miliband drove to David's house where he had a civilised forty-minute conversation in which, Ed claims, David said he did not want to be the reason Ed didn't stand. Privately, David denies any such meeting took place that week.

It may appear a minor discrepancy on the face of it, but the disagreement over whether and when this crucial conversation took place goes to the heart of the perhaps inevitably dysfunctional relationship that now exists between the brothers. It is evidence of the deep mistrust and increasing distance between them. Why would the Leader of the Opposition or his aides concoct such an elaborate and detailed story, as outlined in the prologue of this book? Then again, why would David deny such a meeting, if it did indeed take place? Ed's aides may have been unsure of the date of the meeting to begin with, but they have never budged on the fundamentals: Ed, they say, met David in his home to do the right thing and tell his brother he was also planning to challenge for the leadership. Except David continues to tell friends that his younger brother did no such thing. More than a year later, there is no agreed 'line' between the Ed and David camps on this crucial issue; bizarrely and inexplicably, the brothers have not sought to square the circle. It is a mystery unresolved. And it does not bode well for the future.

ooooo

Ed spent much of the week speaking to and texting close friends, finally telling them the news. To one confidant who had been urging him to run for several years, he texted: 'You took a position on this long before I did – thanks.'[14] Now all he had to do was prepare his announcement.

Sunder Katwala, the Fabians' general secretary, had first approached Ed's team before the general election to invite him to address the conference. It was of course in Katwala's mind that there would be a 'buzz' around Ed as a potential candidate, but it looked at least as likely that Ed would swing behind David. At a meeting at DECC on 8 March, Katwala and Fatima Hassan, the Fabians' events director made it clear to Ed and Polly Billington they wanted him to speak whatever the circumstances, including whether Labour was in power or not. Ed agreed he would be able to give the talk, subject to final confirmation, and the Fabian organisers knew that, whether a candidate or not, Ed Miliband would be an interesting speaker. The Fabians learned straight after the election that Ed was definitely speaking, through contacts in Ed's office. Then, on the Tuesday of Brown's resignation, the day Ed had asked Beales to work for him, Katwala received a call from Polly Billington, Ed's press officer. She broached the question of whether it would be 'appropriate' to announce that he was running for leader at the event. Ed's team were willing to organise their own launch elsewhere if it was taking a liberty to use the Fabian talk to announce Ed was running. Katwala agreed to host the announcement, absorbed the news and told no one but a few of his closest colleagues at the Fabians in absolute confidence. He then wrote a heavily coded blogpost in which he repeated a case he had made before, for both Miliband brothers standing.[15]

Meanwhile, there were concerns in the Ed camp that the Fabian conference was too 'wonky' a venue at which to break the news, and that there needed to be more of a grassroots feel to the announcement. Handily, Ed had arranged to travel up to Doncaster on the Friday and inform his local party. One of the activists used the social networking website Twitter to reveal that evening Ed's announcement to her few followers. This was immediately picked up by the website Labour List, which blogged on Ed's news under the headline 'I'm in the race'. This move, from the tweet to the blog, was carefully coordinated by Ed's team.

It was therefore amid an increasing assumption in the party that he was in the race that Ed Miliband was driven to the Fabian conference on the morning of Saturday 15 May to deliver his speech, accompanied by a very nervous Justine. Billington and Ed both communicated to the Fabian organisers that they were particularly concerned that Justine should be protected from the press pack and the crowd of interested students who had gathered outside the university hall in which Ed was speaking. The 300-strong audience that warmly welcomed Ed on arrival was largely made up not of hand-picked Ed supporters but of paying, ticketed Fabians. However, the conference also saw the first appearance of a noisy group of youthful 'activists' who – apparently on a freelance basis – were supporting Ed's candidacy.

The controversial 'Ed speaks human' placards that did so much to infuriate David's supporters also made their first appearance at this event. Ed's team has repeatedly denied any knowledge of these, but supporters of David have long argued that these placards were designed and distributed by the Ed campaign. Questions have also been raised about the independence of the 'unofficial' website – edmilibandforleader.com – which made a remarkably similar case for the younger Miliband's candidacy as the campaign proper would later do, and a Facebook page entitled 'Run, Ed, Run!' that had already accumulated some 800 signatures.

Nonetheless, the applause was spontaneous when Ed rather casually confirmed near the beginning of his speech that he would indeed be a leadership candidate. 'We have to use this leadership campaign as the first step on the road back to power because that is where we should be as a political party,' he said. 'It involves facing up to uncomfortable truths... We lost that radical edge ... we let being in government constrain our willingness to be as radical again.'

Turning to the issue he must have known would dominate the headlines, Ed said: 'David is my best friend in the world. I love him dearly and I think it is absolutely possible and necessary for this party to have a civilised contest. There is no way I'm going to take lumps out of him either on the record, off the record or behind the scenes. It is not my way of doing politics, and I'm certainly not going to do it to my brother and nor is he. I'm in it to win it, but win or lose we will remain the best of friends and I will still love him dearly.'[16]

These were warm words, and demonstrated the extent to which Ed had been thinking about his brother over the past forty-eight hours. But there was no getting away from the fact that Ed was now out in the open as a serious and committed challenger to his brother, having made the first step towards what David's supporters would later claim was 'fratricide'.[17]

ooooo

Pinning down the exact moment Ed Miliband decided to run for the leadership is, as Lloyd George said of negotiating with Eamon de Velara, like trying 'to pick up mercury with a fork', not least because Ed himself is strangely reluctant to identify a single moment, preferring to describe it to friends as more of a slow, almost subconscious, process. 'Perhaps this is how decisions are made,' Ed has said.[18] He claims today that he had not fully made up his mind by Wednesday 12 May, the day David declared. Yet he tells friends that he informed David of his intention to stand that same day.[19]

In fact, as we have seen, there is plenty of evidence that Ed had taken a firm decision before Brown quit as premier at 5pm on Tuesday 11 May. Earlier that day, he recruited Greg Beales at a meeting in Number 11, at the height of Labour excitement over the possibility of a pact with the Lib Dems. Ed's aides make out they were frustrated with him during the coalition negotiations because they wanted to discuss the leadership and he was too busy. The Beales conversation suggests otherwise, though we must add that there is no suggestion that Ed did anything less than he could to work for a Labour–Liberal deal. On the same day, his special adviser checked with the Fabian Society whether he could use his speech the coming Saturday to announce his candidacy. On the Sunday before – 9 May – he persuaded Peter Hain to back him, described the nature of his forthcoming 'insurgency' campaign and even informed Hain he was in it to win it. And the previous day, on Saturday 8 May, Hilary Benn had begun ringing round and canvassing ministerial colleagues on Ed's behalf. In short, it is clear that Ed had put serious thought into running for leader by the May 2010 general election and, on the basis of the available evidence, it is more likely than not that he had made up his mind to run long before he says he told David on the night of 12 May.

It may be true that Ed did not himself raise the issue of the leadership with friends and colleagues in the previous months or years – but when the subject was raised by others, he was often keen to hear more. And he certainly failed to rule it out in private conversations between 2005 and 2010.

Though he emphatically denies that his ascent to the job of leader was pre-planned, a close family friend says Ed told him that he had dreamed of being Prime Minister 'as a teenager'.[20] This could of course be dismissed as the common fantasy of a politically minded youth. But most youths eventually abandon such ambitions; Ed – for better or worse – did not.

His speeches without notes at the 2008 and 2009 annual conferences, which did so much to win over the party faithful, and give him a high profile, could be interpreted by the more cynically minded as Ed capitalising on his rhetorical skills and testing the water. Friends of Ed went out of their way to tell political journalists at the 2008 conference that they should not miss the younger Miliband's speech.[21] During his stint at the Cabinet Office, between 2007 and 2008, Sue Nye is believed to have raised the subject of the leadership with him on more than one occasion. Nye has told friends that she first spotted Ed's leadership potential when he was a special adviser in the Treasury in the late 1990s.[22]

By the end of 2009 Ed had begun seriously considering running for the leadership, buoyed by his undeniable campaigning success – whatever the failures of Copenhagen – as Climate Change Secretary over the previous year.

Was David aware of any of this? Friends of the elder Miliband say they were surprised at how indifferent and relaxed he was about the rise and rise of his younger brother. 'He didn't see him as a threat,' says one. 'Until it was too late.'[23]

As with so much to do with the Miliband brothers, there are two opposing accounts of one of the few direct conversations they admit to having had about the leadership, at the start of December 2009. Ed claims that it was about whether David should take the job of EU High Representative for Foreign Affairs. He tells friends that he felt it was right to indicate during this brief chat with his brother that he 'might' run for the leadership. And he claims that David's reaction was merely: 'Fine, what do you think about the Europe job?'[24]

But the timeline suggests otherwise; after all, David had already publicly declined the job on 11 November and, by 19 November,

Catherine Ashton had been appointed as the new EU High Rep. Instead, a close friend of David's says he discussed with Ed the idea of moving against Brown, and that it was only after Ed showed resistance to such an idea that David became suspicious his little brother might be considering a leadership bid himself. Perhaps it was naïvety, or perhaps it was arrogance, but up until this point, David did not seem to see Ed as a threat to his own leadership ambitions.

One of the most explosive claims surrounding Ed's ambitions, however, is that Ed persuaded David not to stand against Brown in the summer of 2009. The charge is that this was not out of loyalty to Brown, but because he was already planning a leadership challenge himself, and needed a full-blown Labour leadership contest in opposition in order to have a chance of beating his better-known brother.

Indeed, it is said that one of the specific reasons today for the resentment felt by David's wife Louise towards Ed is over an incident that apparently occurred in June 2009. After polls closed for the European elections at 10pm on the night of 4 June, James Purnell resigned from the Cabinet as Work and Pensions Secretary. To this day, many of David's supporters deeply regret that the elder Miliband did not follow his close friend Purnell out of government, resigning as Foreign Secretary and almost certainly ending the Brown premiership. According to some claims, Ed rang his brother to urge him not to quit, on the grounds that the leadership was his after Brown. Yet this specific claim has been flatly denied by David as well as Ed.[25] There is no evidence to suggest that Ed's reluctance to back a challenge against the Prime Minister by his brother was motivated by anything other than a deep-rooted if perhaps misplaced loyalty towards, and admiration for, Brown.

ooooo

By the start of 2010, however, the leadership issue was at the forefront of Ed's mind. One senior MP who played an important role in Ed's campaign says he was alerted as early as January that Ed was thinking of running.[26]

But it was in in the last week of February 2010, less than three months before the general election, that one of the most influential and important discussions concerning Ed's leadership was to take place. The former Labour leader, Neil Kinnock, had walked from the House of Lords to DECC for a meeting with Ed. Kinnock had requested a 'short political chat', ostensibly about the manifesto. He was shown into Ed's office by Billington, who shut the door and left the two men to talk. Kinnock began the meeting with a challenge: make the document as concise as possible. It could not be an essay. Kinnock explains:

'You can only do that if you're George Orwell or Michael Foot. It's important because for the first time since the 1940s we can show real and tangible progress of a Labour government. I did that as a warm up. That might be why he thought I came in, to act as a backseat driver giving him a blast.'

Then Kinnock surprised Ed by revealing the main reason for his visit:

I told him if we lose, given the condition we are in, he should run for leader. He did one of his Ed double-takes. He told me he had thought about it a lot. The basic question for him was 'When David runs, will I?' He told me he couldn't give me the answer. I replied by imploring him to do it for the party. Think of the party, not David… He told me 'Because it's you who has raised it I'll have to give it more thought.'[27]

In the end, Ed put party before family – or, as his critics would say, he put himself before his brother. Did he think through the implications of his decision? Did he underestimate the risks to his family relations? The day after Ed stood it so happened that Sue Nye was holding a post-election party at her London home for Brown supporters. Ed Balls and Yvette Cooper were scheduled to arrive but pulled out at the last minute, choosing to stay at home. Douglas Alexander was there, and though he had yet to declare for David, it was assumed by some at the party he would. On Ed's arrival Nye pointed out to him that plenty of people in the room would be willing to work for him, 'Therefore, you know, could you go and talk to them please?' So off Ed went to work the room. In the midst of this, Anji Hunter, the loyal Blair aide but a friend of Nye's, approached Ed. She told him to look out for his family, especially his mother, because the press, she said, would be all over that element to the contest. According to one guest, Ed appeared taken aback, as if he had not thought through how damaging the contest would be for Marion – and the family as a whole. 'Good point,' he said pensively.[28]

That is not to say that Ed did not think long and hard about 'the David issue' but, as he himself now admits to friends, he 'underestimated how difficult' it would be to go up against his own flesh and blood.[29]

Some David supporters claim that Ed had always been covertly plotting against his elder brother. Friends of Ed argue that it would be naïve to expect their man only to have made up his mind in the forty-eight hours after David stood. Either way, the truth is that Ed Miliband, who doesn't like the word 'ruthless', let nothing, including his immediate family, get in the way of his exceptional determination to be leader of the Labour Party.

LEADERSHIP CAMPAIGN

MAY–SEPTEMBER 2010

Chaos. That is the word used by members of Ed Miliband's campaign team to describe the state of confusion and disorder that they found themselves in during the first few weeks of the Labour leadership contest. 'It was chaotic, disorganised, lacking a grip,' says a close ally of Ed.[1] 'Frankly, it was a nightmare,' says another.[2] The campaign began from a 'standing start', admits Peter Hain.[3] Ed had no money, no organisation and no strategy. David had been preparing for months.

To begin with, the team didn't even have that elementary requirement: a base. Having flitted between the offices of various supportive MPs, Ed and his staff eventually moved to a new headquarters: 10 Greycoat Place in Victoria, a walk away from Westminster. The offices were tiny, and such was the candidate's lack of resources that, in the first few days, the phones would ring out – there just weren't enough staffers or volunteers to answer all the calls.[4]

The two policy brains of Brown's Downing Street operation, Nick Pearce and Gavin Kelly, exhausted from their three years in the prime ministerial bunker, and then the five intense days of coalition negotiations, had already made their decisions to move on from party politics. Having stuck around to help him launch his campaign, Kelly, whom Ed is said to have wanted to appoint as his chief of staff, had promised his partner that they would go away on holiday after the general election. He left the country the week after Ed declared he was standing for leader.

Polly Billington and Stewart Wood aside, Greg Beales was the first to come on board Ed's ship, joining the campaign as head of policy. Beales, a former special adviser to Blair and Brown, considered to be a dyed-in-the-wool Blairite for his championing of foundation hospitals, was a shrewd appointment by a candidate worried about being defined by his opponents as a left-wing

Brownite. But, almost immediately after starting on the campaign, Beales disappeared off to California with his girlfriend Katie Myler, daughter of the *News of the World* editor Colin Myler and a former special adviser to Andy Burnham, on his own long-arranged vacation. Initially, the couple had gone to stay for a fortnight in Myler's parents' holiday home in California but ended up staying nearly a month because Myler's grandfather fell ill. An impatient Ed rang his new head of policy several times during this period to ask: 'Where the fuck are you?'[5]

Ed was lucky. The lack of staff and money could have destroyed his campaign before it got off the ground. One of the key challenges faced by his team from the get-go was that it had no sense of those MPs who were supporting the younger Miliband, those who might support him and those who had already declared for his brother, Balls and the other two candidates – Andy Burnham and Diane Abbott. Embarrassingly, at the start of the contest, Ed and his aides struggled to put together a spreadsheet or grid containing the all-important information on MPs' preferences.

'There were three or four days in those first few weeks where I thought, "We could be out of it by the end of today,"' recalls a former adviser to Ed.[6] 'What we had was the ambition of David, but the resources of Ed Balls,' says Stewart Wood.[7]

Billington, Beales and Wood had a mixture of policy, strategy and communications skills but none of them had experience as campaign managers. They were making it up as they went along, playing catch-up, reacting to events. Lucy Powell, Labour's defeated parliamentary candidate in Manchester Withington and a former director of the pro-European campaign group, Britain in Europe, joined Team Ed as campaign chief. Her impact was instant. 'Lucy was a Godsend,' says Wood. 'We needed someone who could both run an office and run a political campaign.'[8]

Up until then, the former Oxford don had been juggling strategy, communications, logistics and the rest. 'Is this just a one-man campaign?' the *Financial Times*'s political editor, George Parker, asked him. 'Are you doing everything?'

There were other key signings. James Morris, a pollster who had worked for Deborah Mattinson, and was in the process of setting up a London office for US pollster Stan Greenberg, came on board to hone Ed's message, run the campaign website and help on speeches and strategy. Marcus Roberts, who had worked on the Kerry and Obama campaigns as a volunteer organiser, was recruited as the campaign's field director. Roberts was a natural number-cruncher who would spend hours poring over spreadsheets and tables. His first task was to design the statistical model around which the Ed team could organise its leadership campaign and strategy.

From the outset, these officials were conscious of the David campaign's financial and organisational superiority; in their eyes, the latter was running the equivalent of a national election campaign, backed by a large infrastructure. In the short-term, the priority for Ed was to win some high-profile endorsements. David had 'started hoovering up everyone'.[9] Alastair Campbell, Alistair Darling, Jack Straw, Alan Johnson, Andrew Adonis, Tessa Jowell – all lined up behind the man once described by Tony Blair as the 'Wayne Rooney' of his Cabinet. 'The New Labour establishment,' as Ed privately referred to David's base, unable to resist mocking his brother's big-name supporters.[10]

There was, however, a downside for the David campaign in attracting and then promoting these high-profile endorsements. In a leadership contest which, as we shall see, became focused on the importance of 'change', they tied the elder Miliband to the past, not the future. Having secured the backing of the former Chancellor Alistair Darling, for example, David was then locked into the so-called Darling plan – of halving the deficit over four years through a 2:1 ratio of spending cuts to tax rises – that had been rejected by the voters at the general election. Meanwhile, another of his key supporters, the former Home Secretary Alan Johnson, defiantly proclaimed that he couldn't think 'of a single issue on which Labour got the balance wrong on civil liberties.' The reality was that David was to the left of Tony Blair. But he would become trapped as the 'Blairite' candidate and he would not do enough to shake it off.

Ed, on the other hand, had much more space to manoeuvre, to be flexible – and distance himself from the negative and unpopular aspects (and personnel) – of New Labour's thirteen-year period in office. For the first time since Harvard, he was free to be his own man again, liberated from the shackles of having to defer to Blair, Brown or collective Cabinet responsibility. 'I told Ed that he would win because he was nobody's project,' says a senior Labour strategist who worked for Brown. 'He was not the project or crea-ture of anyone else; he was his own man.'[11] Ed didn't need those 'old men', adds another of the younger Miliband's allies, referring dismissively to figures like Darling, Johnson and Straw.[12]

But Ed also knew that he couldn't afford to let his brother 'shock and awe' the Labour frontbench; in the end, he persuaded five members of the shadow Cabinet – Sadiq Khan, Peter Hain, John Denham, Hilary Benn and Rosie Winterton – to endorse his candidacy. 'It wasn't a lot, but it was enough to keep Ed in the game,' says one of his aides.[13]

He was also keen to recruit support from some of the newer, younger MPs, elected to the House for the first time in 2010. Ed, the second youngest of the five Labour leadership candidates, picked up the first preferences of 28-year old Luciana Berger, 30-year-old Lisa Nandy, 31-year-old Rachel Reeves and 31-year-old Chuka Umunna. Not all of Ed's supporters in the PLP, however, were members of what he would later describe as Labour's 'new genera-tion'. The veteran Labour MP, former minister and ex-Bennite Michael Meacher told Sadiq Khan, who had joined Team Ed as the candidate's election agent: 'Sadiq, I'm going to back Ed Miliband. But you should know that I've never backed a winning candidate in a Labour leadership election before.' Khan replied: 'Michael, please don't tell anybody that.'[14]

Meacher wasn't the only so-called 'Old Labour' figure to come out for the younger Miliband. Former leader Neil Kinnock and former deputy leader Roy Hattersley were outspoken support-ers. 'Ed had a lot of losers like Neil Kinnock and Roy Hattersley running around on his behalf,' says a close ally of Tony Blair, who backed David.[15]

But Kinnock played a key role in the Ed campaign and other members of David's team have since recognised the significance of the former Labour leader's support for the younger Miliband. 'Neil Kinnock is a very popular and persuasive figure inside the Labour Party,' says a Blairite ex-Cabinet minister. 'When Neil spoke to people of influence in the party and said "Why don't you vote for Ed?" that was a very important tool in Ed's locker.'[16]

Strategists on the Ed campaign believe Kinnock, aided and abetted by his wife Glenys, the Labour peer and ex-Foreign

Office minister, was crucial in getting Ed close to within 'striking distance' of David among party members.[17] Neil's wife Glenys – the only former Foreign Office minister who didn't back David, the ex-Foreign Secretary – even persuaded Elizabeth Smith, widow of the late Labour leader, John Smith, to throw her support behind Ed after bumping into her on the Tube. On 18 July, Smith announced that she was backing Ed Miliband 'because I identify with Ed's values and principles, and I know that John would have done so too. Ed is also the candidate who I know has the ability to unify the party going forward.'

While Ed enthusiastically embraced Kinnock, Hattersley and the memory of John Smith, he was equally keen to distance himself from another Labour grandee: Peter Mandelson.

After Mandelson returned to the Cabinet in 2008, and after he gave an extremely well-received speech to conference in 2009, the Labour Party's rank and file did look as if it had met Tony Blair's famous test of the durability of New Labour by 'learning to love Peter Mandelson'. This highly tribal figure has never been as hated by the rank and file as his enemies claim. And his post-return relations with Labour MPs as well as the press were much better than before. Nonetheless, some activists and trade unionists saw Mandelson as a symbol of New Labour's flaws – the spin, the triangulation, the indifference to growing inequality and the relaxed attitude towards the 'filthy rich'. Ed decided to use the first hustings of the contest, hosted by the GMB in Southport on 7 June, before even the nominations for leader had closed, to take a swipe at Mandelson – who he had two years earlier described as a 'benevolent uncle'[18] – and boost his own fledgling campaign in the process.

He had some help. Tom Watson, the backbench Labour MP and Balls ally had bumped into Ed before the hustings. 'Paul Kenny [the GMB general secretary] says they're going to ask all the candidates whether or not they plan to bring back Peter Mandelson,' he warned Ed. 'What should I say?' asked the younger Miliband. 'Say you believe in dignity in retirement,' replied Watson with a chuckle.[19]

A few minutes later, the hustings kicked off in the main hall and, as expected, the chair Mary Turner opened proceedings by asking each of the candidates: 'As Labour leader, would you invite Peter Mandelson to join your shadow Cabinet?'

'All of us believe in dignity in retirement,' replied a cool and pre-prepared Ed Miliband. It was a stinging and public put-down of the former Business Secretary. Watson, sitting in the audience, couldn't hide the grin on his face.[20]

Mandelson would later remark that he felt 'hurt' and 'denigrated' by Ed's remarks: 'I felt as if I was being unfairly treated and packed off rather prematurely to an old folks' home' he told *Total Politics* magazine.[21]

But Ed's remark served its purpose. Right at the beginning of the campaign, he had put rhetorical distance between himself and New Labour – using one of its key architects, Peter Mandelson. David however struggled to disown the so-called Prince of Darkness. In an interview for the *New Statesman* magazine, in July, David would only go as far as to say that he was not worrying about 'whether or not Peter Mandelson is going to be in the next Cabinet'.[22] An explicit repudiation it wasn't.

Mandelson, meanwhile, wouldn't go quietly. Having annoyed the Labour leadership candidates by publishing his controversial and gossipy memoir, *The Third Man*, which raked up all the Blair/Brown rows of the previous two decades, in the midst of the first Labour leadership campaign for sixteen years, the arch-Blairite then used an interview in *The Times* to attack Ed's candidacy: 'I think that if he or anyone else wants to create a pre-New Labour future for the party, then he and the rest of them will quickly find that is an electoral cul-de-sac.'

Up until that point, Ed's aides had been unhappy that their candidate seemed to be restraining them from publicly hitting back against David's more aggressive supporters. 'My frustration was the "rope a dope" – Muhammad Ali took a beating on the ropes for seven, eight rounds because he knew he'd come back and counter-attack,' says Khan. 'My nervousness was that our opponents were attacking us and we weren't counter-attacking.' Volunteering for the role of campaign 'attack dog', Khan had told Ed early on in the campaign: 'Look, we're getting killed here. You've got to let me hit back.' His candidate replied: 'Listen, we're not going to do that.'

But when Mandelson intervened in the campaign again, with his 'cul-de-sac' comments, Ed, annoyed and frustrated by the constant sniping from the Blairite 'ultras', gave his campaign agent the 'green light' to counter-attack.[23]

'Party members and the public will not be convinced by hearing the same old messages from the New Labour attack machine being used against one of our leadership candidates,' Khan told reporters as he dismissed 'figures from Labour's past'.[24]

Neil Kinnock joined in the coordinated counter-attack on Mandelson, referring to his old friend's remarks as 'bilious rubbish': 'It's reviving the old factionalism and I thought we were over that. Sadly, Peter is the exception.'

But the public anger from Team Ed masked their inner delight; as Ed's fellow leadership candidate, Diane Abbott, pointed out, Mandelson's comments did not help his elder brother: 'If I was David Miliband I would want a period of silence from Peter Mandelson, because the impression that Peter Mandelson, Alastair Campbell, and the rest of the old crew, are pulling his strings will not be helpful in this election.'[25]

Tellingly, Khan addressed a rally of Ed supporters a fortnight before the result, and referred with a smile to the campaign's 'secret weapon': 'Three words to say to you: "Lord Peter Mandelson". There was a round of applause from the crowd.[26]

'The Mandelson intervention really hurt David Miliband,' says a member of Team Ed now. 'I used to joke to Ed: "Is Peter your sleeper agent?"'[27]

Another Ed ally says Mandelson's role 'was as decisive in the 2010 leadership campaign, as he was when he was called "Bobby" on Tony Blair's campaign [in 1994].'[28] Ed's benevolent uncle turned out to be a help, not a hindrance.

ooooo

The Labour leadership contest officially kicked off on 9 June 2010, when nominations closed, and continued till 22 September 2010, when voting officially ended. The so-called 'long contest' appealed to party officials as it offered a means of recruiting new, paying members, who were offered the opportunity of voting in the leadership election. It also appealed to Harriet Harman, the acting leader, as she had four months to stay on in her role.

By the time the contest was over, and the new leader elected, the five candidates had taken part in an astonishing fifty-six hustings, across the country, in which they were asked near-identical questions and offered near-identical (and time-limited) answers.

In his opening remarks at the first leadership hustings, organised and hosted by the *New Statesman* at Church House in Westminster on 9 June, the day the nominations closed, Ed presented himself as the candidate of 'change' and 'values':

> It's time to move on from the era of Blair and Brown and I believe I'm the best candidate to do that for this party and for the country. I'm proud of our record in government over thirteen years but the truth is that where we went wrong, we became managers and technocrats. We saw it over issues such as civil liberties, around Iraq, around housing and rights at work. I am the candidate who will put values at the centre of our mission and will win, not despite our values, but because of them. If we care about those values then they have to be at the centre of our party as well. Our party has to be a community organisation reaching out to the millions of people in this country who we can convert and party members need a proper voice in this party and that's why I'm running to be leader of the Labour Party.[29]

Four of the five contenders were white, forty-something, Oxbridge graduates who had worked their way up from being special advisers to Cabinet ministers. The hustings process may have been gruelling but it provided an opportunity for the candidates to differentiate themselves from one another and engage directly with their electorate. 'The hustings were a great opportunity for harvesting undecided voters,' says Kinnock now. 'And Ed won a lot of them.'

David had wanted a short contest – which most Westminster insiders agree he would have won with ease. The long campaign agreed by the party's National Executive Committee (NEC) and by Harman gave Ed time and space to narrow the considerable gap between his campaign and his brother's. The hustings also gave the younger Miliband a higher profile, while playing to his strengths. One of the Miliband brothers' leadership rivals says: 'I think David mishandled the situation in terms of the dynamics of the group, of the five of us, and mishandled the audience too. He seemed irritated that he was having to stand there listening to the rest of us and the members of the audience. His body language suggested that he didn't want to be there.'

The same rival says: 'Ed has much greater emotional intelligence than David. He understands people and is much more conscious of how people are thinking and feeling. That's what won him the leadership, in my view.'[30]

A friend of the Miliband family agrees: 'One of Ed's great qualities is his ability to talk to people in public, to get his point across, to listen and engage, to be honest and direct – and funny too.'[31] He, therefore, felt much more at home in a hustings format that seemed to stifle and frustrate some of his rivals.

The hustings also provided a public platform on which the brothers clashed, in a polite and grown-up manner. But there were other, more private and childish clashes between the two men.

On 13 July, the Milibands squared up at the TUC summer reception at Church House, in Westminster. David arrived with his entourage; onlookers remember him looking like the leader-in-waiting. 'David's team seemed to be in military mode,' says a union leader who was present.[32] David's allies – his campaign co-chair Jim Murphy, and Alan Johnson – were ruthless in delivering face time for their candidate with the various union general secretaries assembled in the room – and at the expense of his brother, too.

When Ed would start talking with a union leader, Johnson, Murphy or another David supporter would quickly walk over and start hovering nearby – or even begin interrupting the conversation. They made it impossible for Ed to have a private chat with a union leader. But when David started up a conversation with a union general secretary, his team would form a Praetorian Guard around him.[33]

'It might have been a coincidence,' recalls a Balls supporter who witnessed Team David's antics. 'But I've never seen so many coincidences in the space of twenty-five minutes.'[34]

'It was fucking outrageous,' says a senior member of Ed's campaign team. 'David's people behaved like a tag team.'[35]

Such childish antics only heightened tensions between the two camps. Prior to the leadership campaign, the brothers had had deep and intimate political conversations; they had discussed their careers, the direction of the party, the stances they planned to take on this or that issue. They used to speak with one another at least once every two or three days. But it had all changed on 15 May when Ed declared his candidacy at the Fabians – despite both David and Ed incessantly claiming in interviews, and at the various hustings, that they would not allow the contest to affect their love for one another.

How bad did relations get between the brothers? Looking back, Ed insists that relations were cordial.[36] But it was harder than he had assumed it would be. David may have decided not to try to block Ed from standing, but, deep down, he surely resented the fact that his own younger brother had decided to challenge him for the leadership of the party. A close family friend recalls speaking to Ed during the campaign and asking, bluntly: 'Are you guys still talking to one another?' Ed told the friend that David was 'trying very hard to be nice to him but he felt it was forced – David's smiles and politeness were forced'.[37]

Towards the end of June, less than a month after the campaign had officially kicked off, Ed joined the great and the good for a party to celebrate the sixtieth birthday of New Labour's pollster-in-chief, Philip Gould, at Shoreditch House. The next morning, he arrived at the campaign office, sombre and dejected, telling friends and colleagues that he had been 'blanked' and 'ignored' by David's supporters at the party. He sat alone in the corner of the office, pondering on how difficult the coming months would be.[38]

Both the David and Ed camps maintain that their candidate issued a diktat at the start of the campaign banning negative or personal attacks on each other. But the reality was that they could not control their people. Moments of tension peppered the summer-long campaign. 'He's too junior and inexperienced for the job,' said some David supporters.[39] 'He just tickles the tummy of the party,' said others.[40] Alastair Campbell waded into the campaign to declare that victory for Ed would make the party 'feel OK about losing'. Ed, he added, was not up to 'taking difficult decisions'.[41] By August, the sniping at the younger Miliband brother from support-ers of the elder Miliband brother had become deeply personal and bitter. Ed was taken aback at the constant, anonymous, negative briefings – he was called a 'Bennite', 'Red Ed', 'Forrest Gump', 'Wallace' from the animated short films, *Wallace and Gromit*, and 'Labour's Iain Duncan Smith'.[42] An aide says the regular attacks on Ed in the press from unnamed David supporters unsettled and upset the younger Miliband: 'I'd be lying if I said it didn't bother him.'[43]

Friends of David maintain today that their man wasn't behind these briefings and Ed himself has told friends that he believes his brother wasn't personally responsible for the actions of his allies. A friend of David remembers receiving a phone call from him in August: 'If you find out where this is coming from, please stop it. Let me be clear: I'm not having any of this.'[44] But it didn't stop – and further poisoned the relationship between the two camps.

Then there was the pressure applied to members of Ed's team by outriders for the elder Miliband. In August, for example, Stewart Wood was forced to take a break from the campaign to take care of his young son, who had fallen ill. Beales suggested to Ed that the team hire his girlfriend, Katie Myler, to replace Wood and handle the media operation. Ed agreed – but within hours of her appointment becoming public knowledge, Myler received a call from a high-profile MP and David supporter telling her that her career in Labour politics was over. 'Do you realise that if David wins he is never going to forget that you worked against him?'

Myler put the phone down in tears. 'What the fuck have I done?' Beales later told a friend. 'This was my girlfriend and I had put her in a horrible position.'[45]

Ed was shocked when he was told what had happened but, again, his first reaction was to defend his brother: 'David will not know anything about this and I'm going to raise it with him.' He was convinced that his elder brother was oblivious to the negative tactics being deployed by some of his supporters. Ed turned to Beales, with a quizzical look on his face: 'We haven't got anything going on like that, have we?'[46]

Ed had told friends that one of the reasons he decided to run for the Labour leadership was to show the party and the public that there was a way of conducting politics that wasn't nasty, brutal, annihilatory or machine-like. He wanted to prove that he wasn't a Brownite, in the ruthless and destructive sense of that word. But his leadership campaign wasn't averse to embracing some dark arts of its own. In early July, for example, stories began to appear in the papers suggesting Andy Burnham might drop out from the leadership race. Burnham 'nearly fell off his chair' when he read the claims in the papers, according to a report. The finger was pointed at Ed Balls, struggling to stay in third place, but sources suggest that both Burnham and Balls agreed that 'it was the other Ed's camp' that was to blame for the speculation.[47]

Burnham, of course, was a distraction. Over the course of the summer, Team Ed had its sights trained firmly on the frontrunner. Off the record, Ed's aides issued thinly-veiled attacks on David. Some supporters of the elder Miliband pointed the finger at the brusque Polly Billington.[48] The battle was constantly presented as 'David and Goliath,' with Ed cast confusingly as his brother's namesake, and his spin doctors making a point of emphasising their lack of resources against the 'establishment candidate'.

From the very beginning, they also had no qualms about highlighting what they perceived to be the elder Miliband's gaucheness and robotic style of speech. The 'Ed speaks human' placards at the launch of the younger Miliband's leadership campaign were perhaps the most obvious example of this tactic. 'Only the most politically illiterate or tin-eared would fail to spot what is really being said... Ed speaks human – unlike David,' wrote the columnist Matthew D'Ancona in the *Sunday Telegraph*.

Ed's campaign was 'really unprincipled and completely ruthless', says a close friend of Tony Blair's, who also advised the David campaign.[49] The elder Miliband told his team that he was hurt and offended by the 'Ed speaks human' line.[50]

A senior official on the Ed campaign maintains that the 'Ed speaks human' placards were not authorised or approved by them – but, he admits, 'Of course the line was an attack on David.' And a close friend of Ed's admits: 'It was hardball.'[51] In addition, a key ally of David claims supporters of Ed – including the former MP and mayoral candidate Oona King – used the 'Ed speaks human' line in their attempts to coax and cajole undecided MPs off the fence.[52]

Anonymous briefings from their outriders aside, on occasion, the tensions between the two brothers also erupted in public – most notably, towards the end of the summer. In a speech at the King Solomon academy school in north London on 25 August, David said: 'There is no future for Labour in the comfortable but deadening policies of the past. And there is no future in a politics based on a tactical, patchwork approach to building electoral support.' He continued: 'Opposition is necessary but insufficient.

At worse it can take us back into our comfort zone – and our pantomime role in politics.'[53]

In an article in *The Times* to coincide with the speech, the elder Miliband went further, describing the party's comfort zone, dismissively, as 'big in heart but essentially naïve, well-meaning but behind the times'.

Ed's name was not mentioned in either the speech or the article. Yet privately, the younger Miliband was furious. He rang a friendly journalist that afternoon. 'What do people think of this "comfort zone" stuff?' The journalist equivocated, suggesting it might not be an attack on him. 'It is an attack,' Ed replied coldly. 'It is an attack.'[54]

Ed was genuinely angry with his brother, say friends. That same afternoon, Ed hit back with a statement released to journalists attacking what he called the 'New Labour comfort zone'. 'It was a rare public intervention,' says a key Ed ally. 'Usually, we'd deflate Ed's annoyance in private and in public he'd be a lot more measured.'[55]

Not this time. As David claimed it was 'nonsense' to say that he had been personally criticising his younger brother, Ed went on the offensive, telling the BBC that it was 'insulting' to suggest he was relying on a 'core vote' strategy.

Finally, the frustrations that had built up between the brothers had exploded.

ooooo

There are hotly contested claims that David had an unfair advantage throughout the contest, as the party hierarchy and machine were secretly backing him. Some have accused the elder Miliband of using the general election campaign as an opportunity to kick-start his own leadership campaign. 'I was told that events were being organised in the general election campaign to boost David,' says one of David's rivals for the Labour leadership. 'I was told that our members were ringing head office asking, "Why are we not out on the doorstep? Why are we sitting here listening to David Miliband talk about foreign policy?"'[56]

Friends of Ed allege that in the first few weeks after the general election, David, the shadow Foreign Secretary, seemed to have become the Labour Party's public face, as he was doing interviews on a wide range of issues unrelated to his frontbench brief, from the economy to the environment. 'The Labour Party press office was working for David,' says a former senior official on the Ed team. He points the finger at the then head of press Roger Baker and his deputy Tom Price, both of whom were alleged to be privately backing the elder Miliband. The official says that Sadiq Khan rang to complain to the party's press office. 'This is bang out of order. You can't do this,' Khan told Labour officials.[57]

Then there is the issue of access to party membership lists. The five candidates' agents agreed with the party high command that a set number of emails would be sent out by party high command on their behalf to the mass membership. But friends of Ed believe his brother's team had unfair access to the Labour Party membership lists. Ordinary party members were getting unsolicited emails direct from the David campaign – 'I've got a private Hotmail account on which I was getting emails from David Miliband,' says an Ed ally. 'How is that possible without access to the lists?'[58]

Neil Kinnock, the former Labour leader and one of Ed's most senior allies, supports the thesis that the party high command, its infrastructure and resources were behind the David campaign. Key Labour Party officials didn't want to upset the candidate they assumed would be in charge of their party come September. 'The reason Ray Collins [Labour's general secretary] didn't call anyone on the membership lists was because he thought David was going to win,' says Kinnock.[59]

Other leadership candidates were equally frustrated at the undue advantage that David seemed to possess – especially the all-important access to membership lists. Andy Burnham's press secretary, Jo Tanner, asked her partner to join the Labour Party so that he would then be eligible to vote in the leadership contest – for her boss. Less than forty-eight hours after he received his party membership card, however, he received a call from a volunteer on the David campaign urging him to back their man. 'For us, this was clear evidence that information was being passed to David,' says a friend of Burnham's.[60] The latter, frustrated and in debt, asked his team: 'How can we compete against David Miliband's resources?'[61]

Another claim made by friends of Ed is that towards the end of the campaign, the David camp had access to supposedly confidential information, from Labour Party officials, about which MPs had voted and which hadn't. David's people were therefore able to contact those who had yet to cast their vote and apply direct, last-minute pressure. Tom Watson, the Balls-supporting MP and former minister, left his vote until the last day and received a call from a member of David's team, at the very last minute, trying to persuade him to give his second preference to David. As we shall see, he opted for Ed instead.

Marsha Singh, the MP for Bradford West who had nominated Ed Balls for the leadership, was seen as a swing voter by both Miliband camps. Singh received a text from David Miliband reminding him to vote. Then, Singh received another text from Keith Vaz MP, a prominent David backer: 'Marsha, I know you haven't voted. Please vote.' According to a third party, Singh was 'so pissed off that David's people had a mole inside Labour HQ that he voted for Ed Miliband'.[62]

Securing the support of as many Labour MPs as possible was, of course, the main goal of each of the five Labour leadership candidates, throughout the four-month contest. The party's electoral college is split three ways between MPs and MEPs, all party members (around 165,000) and members of affiliated trade unions and socialist societies. This means that the PLP wields disproportionate power: the vote of each Labour MP is equivalent to the votes of nearly 608 party members and 12,915 affiliated members.[63]

The candidate who had the backing of the most MPs would have a huge advantage over his rivals; as Sunder Katwala, general secretary of the Fabians, pointed out on his blog in July: 'A candidate with a lead of fifty MPs would win with a score draw among party members, or squeak home to win the college with tens of thousands less votes.'[64]

The first few weeks of the campaign saw Labour MPs flocking to David's side. The elder Miliband's strategy was clear: build up an unstoppable momentum by loudly and publicly revealing large numbers of MPs as supporters, as soon as possible. It was the classic 'inevitability' strategy.

Towards the start of the summer, the strategy seemed to be working – and several different factors played a role. First, David had a head start. He had been planning a leadership bid ever since deciding not to challenge Brown for the vacancy in May 2007 and had tapped up potential staff and donors in the run-up to the May 2010 general election. During the election campaign, David's distance from Brown meant he had more time to ponder and plan his next steps; Ed, meanwhile, was in charge of the manifesto and at the constant beck and call of a flustered Brown. David was also the first of the five Labour leadership candidates to declare – three days before his younger brother, although as we have seen Ed was planning a bid in the immediate days after the general election.

This head start should not be underestimated, says a key Ed ally: 'Politics is not complicated. If I ask you to back me first, you'll say yes to me just because I asked you first – not because we're similar or I agree with you. If I asked you second, you feel bad that you let me down but it's too late. It's often as simple as that.'[65]

Second, the elder Miliband was the undisputed frontrunner, the favourite. He had national and international name recognition and, within a few weeks of declaring, the bookies William Hill had him as odds-on favourite at 2/5. 'The first rule in politics is to back the winner.'[66]

Third, the Ed camp controversially claims that David's team used implicit threats about future jobs, or lack thereof, to secure the support of backbenchers – in the words of a senior Ed ally, David's strategy boiled down to a single line: 'You'd better vote for me because I'm going to win. Get on board.'[67]

There was a sense of power and grandeur associated with the super-confident ex-Foreign Secretary that his younger brother couldn't match. 'If you're a Labour MP and you didn't back David Miliband, you knew he'd kill you if he won,' says a frustrated former member of the Ed campaign. 'But you knew that there were no real consequences to not backing Ed Miliband – because he's a nice bloke.'[68]

Fourth, as we have seen, David had the support of the party's biggest names – from the majority of the shadow Cabinet and ex-Cabinet heavyweights like Charles Falconer and Andrew Adonis to the likes of Campbell and Mandelson. He even secured the endorsement of Gillian Duffy, Gordon Brown's nemesis and a member of the Unite union. (Upon hearing the news, Ed rolled his eyes and joked to a group of journalists that he intended to go and find Sharron Storer and ask for her support.[69])

Fifth, MPs were following the money. David had deep-pocketed donors like the supermarket billionaire, Lord Sainsbury and the film-maker and Labour peer, David Puttnam. In July, the Electoral Commission revealed that David Miliband had received £185,000 from donors since the start of the contest, Ed Balls had received £28,419 and Ed Miliband just £15,000.

Sixth, there was the Douglas Alexander factor. The shrewd Scottish frontbencher had surprised his former Brownite allies when he went to work for David – but he had been psychologically, if not politically, detached from the Brownites since 'the election that never was' fiasco in 2007 and had begun to take a more Blairite line on public service reform and the need to restrain spending. Alexander, it is often forgotten, was appointed to the Cabinet by Blair, not Brown, and, in his memoir, *A Journey*, published in the midst of the Labour leadership campaign, Blair tipped Alexander as a potential future Labour leader.

Alexander's contacts across the PLP were invaluable to David – the former International Development Secretary had also been Labour's election coordinator. Every single one of the sixty-six new Labour MPs elected to the Commons the previous month had been helped in some shape or form by Alexander. 'Where do you think their loyalties were?' asked an irritated friend of Ed's.[70]

The decision of Alexander to not just join David's campaign, but chair it too, came as a blow to the younger Miliband. He was one of Ed's oldest political friends; the two of them had gone on joint holidays together. Since 2000, they had vacationed together in Scotland, France and the United States. In recent years, their partners – Justine and Douglas's wife Jackie – had also become close. But from the moment Douglas went to work for David, he and his wife are said to have cut off ties with Ed and Justine.[71]

Ed's desire to be leader meant his personal relationships were taking a battering. One or two allies of Ed have yet fully to forgive Alexander for his alleged betrayal: 'Douglas used to slag off David to Ed. Justine was particularly pissed off when he went off to chair David's campaign.'[72]

In an article on the Labour Uncut website on 4 June, Alexander explained why he had decided to back the elder Miliband: 'I believe that David Miliband has good Labour values, can unite our party, and can lead us back to power at the next election. That is why I will be voting for him to be our next leader.'

But Ed privately told friends that he believed Alexander had defected to David's camp for two main reasons: a combination of annoyance and envy that a younger man than him was standing for leader (Alexander is talented and ambitious himself – and two years older than Ed); and a belief that a younger brother should not challenge his elder brother.[73] Alexander, for his part, was said to have privately believed that Ed's decision to challenge David had its roots in a long-established sibling rivalry and told a friend that while brotherly rivalry was fine, the Labour leadership should not be 'sacrificed' at the altar of Ed's desire to beat his brother.[74] The point is a highly powerful one. If it is true that Ed's challenge – with all the grief and ongoing fallout that it entailed – was the result more of sibling jostling or resentment than political vision then Labour will have paid a very high price for the strange dynamic between the Miliband brothers. Some David supporters suspect Ed's motives to be more personal than political. Ed and his followers maintain the challenge was purely because of an important difference in politics.

Even with the help of Alexander, David failed to sweep up as many MPs' first and second preferences as he should have done, given his status as the undisputed favourite and frontrunner (at one stage, towards the beginning of the campaign, the bookies had Ed as the 33:1 outsider).

David had a range of impressive strengths – intelligence, eloquence, self-confidence, experience. He had a sense of gravitas lacking in the other four candidates for the leadership; he looked and sounded prime ministerial in a way that his rivals, Ed included, didn't. But his strengths were also weaknesses. His experience was a reminder of his intimate association with the New Labour years and, in particular, with Tony Blair and Iraq. His self-confidence often seemed like arrogance. Labour MPs had long complained that he didn't make an effort to court them in the Commons tearooms. 'David has always had a problem of looking over your shoulder for the next, more important person to talk to,' says a shadow Cabinet minister who backed Ed.[75]

It was to cost him dearly. 'If David had won the backing of another half a dozen MPs, he would have won,' says a well-connected Labour strategist. 'But he didn't because he's rude to people; he's dismissive and patronising.'[76]

A former minister who worked closely with David at the Foreign Office, and backed him for the leadership, claims: 'When the time came to run for leader, David had been spoiled by his years at the FCO.'[77] As a result, he took MPs for granted. One Labour backbencher who gave his first preference to Balls and his second preference to Ed remembers being rung up by an irritated David: 'I thought you'd promised your second preference to me.' The MP hadn't – but David had just assumed he had.[78]

While Ed put huge effort into ingratiating himself with the PLP, David not only didn't struggle – he didn't bother. 'Ed is not a Stranger's regular,' says a senior Labour MP, referring to the MPs' bar overlooking the House of Commons terrace, 'but he became one throughout the leadership campaign.'[79] David, on the other hand, was the one candidate who noticeably didn't – despite having a lot of personal ground to make up with ordinary backbench MPs. 'Aside from David Miliband, there are 257 members of the PLP,' says the MP, who backed Balls. 'And each of those 257 MPs has a "David Miliband has been rude to me" story.'[80]

One such story which has done the rounds on Labour's backbenches is of a junior Labour MP who had hoped to befriend David when he spotted the Foreign Secretary outside a conference, standing in the rain, and offered him a lift in his car. David, so the story goes, was deep in conversation on his mobile phone throughout the drive and barely acknowledged his parliamentary colleague. He allegedly then left the car without even a word of thanks.[81]

The Ed campaign knew their candidate's friendliness, humility and self-effacing charm was a huge asset – especially compared to his brother's aloofness and perceived arrogance. 'David was incredibly rude,' says a senior Labour source. 'He hung up on people whose votes he needed.'[82] Ed, in contrast, did the exact opposite, wooing and flattering even those MPs who had already spurned him. He spent half an hour trying – and failing – to convince the prickly ex-minister John Spellar to switch over to him from David's camp. He rang another former minister, David Lammy, also a supporter of David, to try and persuade him to defect to his team. Again, he failed – but it was indicative of Ed's scrappy, insurgent, pull-out-all-the-stops mindset.[83]

The younger Miliband understood the rules of the game – he recognised the importance of not just first but second preferences and ruthlessly went after them. Some had assumed, for example, that the second preferences of the more Blairite Andy Burnham's supporters would go to David by default, but most of them went to Ed. So too, as we shall see, did Balls's and Abbott's supporters' second preferences. (Ed's aide, Anna Yearly, a former Downing Street staffer, was tasked with liasing with the PLP and put an immense effort into securing first- and second-preference votes for her candidate.)

Team Ed also understood the importance of building their own momentum and kicking sand in the wheels of David's bandwagon. Two crucial decisions were made in the first few weeks, say insiders. First, it was decided that the campaign should amass and then declare the thirty-three nominations required by Labour Party rules for a leadership bid as soon as possible: on 24 May, Ed's team disclosed that he had received thirty-five nominations from MPs, two more than required. 'We had to show we were credible,' says an adviser to Ed. 'We did it before David and we took him and his people by surprise.'

Second, there was a period in mid-June when the PLP, says the adviser, 'started drifting away from us and so we cleared Ed's diary for a week and a half and made sure he had enough time to go round meeting undecided MPs, in their offices, pressing the flesh. One-to-one meetings are what Ed is best at. He changed a lot of minds in those meetings.'[84]

Several MPs were persuaded by Ed to alter their plans and give him their first or second preference. But others proved immune to Ed's charms. Some MPs were unquestioning believers in primogeniture – they believed Ed had no right to be challenging his elder brother and nothing he said or did would change their minds. For Jon Cruddas, the influential Dagenham MP and former deputy leadership candidate, and a man of Irish, Roman Catholic and working-class roots, the sibling issue was 'visceral'. 'I just didn't get it,' he says. 'If you accept the new currency of politics revolves around issues of identity, nationhood, belonging and family, as I do, then the brother thing was always going to be a problem.'

Try as he might, Cruddas simply couldn't comprehend why Ed 'went against his brother'.[85] He was annoyed and angry on David's behalf, saying to the latter in the midst of the leadership campaign: 'Why don't you fucking punch him? That's what I'd do.' Startled, the elder Miliband said nothing in response.[86]

Cruddas had come under pressure from those in and around the popular, centre-left pressure group, Compass, to stand himself. 'I think the views I have would make Labour unelectable,' admits Cruddas bluntly. 'And I had no desire to lead the Parliamentary Labour Party. So the two questions for me were: who's the most electable of the five? And which of them are interested in the scale of the problems facing Labour?'[87] For Cruddas, David fitted the bill – especially after the latter delivered the Keir Hardie Memorial Lecture on 9 July, in which he stressed the values of solidarity, mutuality and reciprocity, and the need to tackle the hollowing out of the party. It was a speech written by Cruddas's fellow traveller on the so-called Blue Labour, communitarian left, Maurice Glasman, and was described by Cruddas himself at the time as 'the most important speech by a Labour politician for many years'.[88]

On 26 August, Cruddas endorsed David in an article in the *New Statesman* and an interview in the *Daily Mirror*. 'David is not just going down a checklist of policies; he seems to me to be echoing a more fundamental sentiment, in terms of what Labour needs to do,' he wrote. 'I'm much more interested in that, rather than in just reciting some policy options, because the scale of the defeat was so great. It's a much more fundamental question of identity that we need to return to.'[89]

There was another reason, however, why Cruddas swung behind David. Relations between Ed and Cruddas had broken down ahead of the general election. The two men met in secret at Ed's office at DECC, organised by Compass chair, Neal Lawson, in the spring of 2010. Cruddas had asked Ed to watch the award-winning 2009 film, *Fish Tank*, which offers a bleak glimpse of working-class life on a scruffy Essex housing estate, ahead of their meeting, but Ed had to admit in the meeting that he'd switched it off halfway through because he found it 'too depressing'. 'That pissed me off,' admits Cruddas. 'It was symptomatic of a problem inside of Labour – what's in that film is exactly what we as a party need to be discussing.'[90]

The half-an-hour meeting went downhill from there. Cruddas was sullen and belligerent to the point of rudeness; Ed was quiet, reserved and unwilling to engage. 'It was an unmitigated disaster,' says Lawson.[91]

Cruddas may have ended up opting for David over Ed, but other Compass luminaries had come out in support of Ed over David: Helena Kennedy, the human-rights lawyer and Labour peer; Chuka Umunna, the new MP for Streatham; and Jon Trickett, Cruddas's campaign manager during his 2007 deputy leadership campaign.

Ed had been cultivating Compass for several years: speaking at conferences and seminars, contributing to pamphlets and publications, reaching out to the likes of chair Neal Lawson and ex-chair Jon Trickett. The issues he championed during the leadership contest – a graduate tax, a living wage, a High Pay Commission, making the windfall tax on bankers' bonuses permanent, reforming the party through community organising and movement-building – were issues that Compass had highlighted over the previous five years.

On 3 September, Compass announced the result of its internal ballot of its members; they voted overwhelmingly in favour of Ed: 55 per cent to third-placed David's 12 per cent (Balls came fifth with 3 per cent of the vote).

'It became apparent to me as the contest went on,' says Lawson now, 'that David would be the continuation of Blairism while Ed was more likely to go beyond New Labour.'[92]

The Blairite tag haunted David throughout the leadership campaign – yet the not-so-unsubtle message that emerges from the memoirs of Peter Mandelson, Alastair Campbell and Blair himself is that David had never been fully committed to the Blair 'project' for public service reform – and is said to have dismissed Blair's cherished Third Way approach as 'wanky'. 'Tony always thought that David was 80 per cent Blairite,' remarked a former Blair aide in a *Guardian* profile of the Milibands published in January 2010.

Yet David didn't do enough during the leadership contest to distance himself from the unpopular Blair. On the contrary, he surrounded himself with Blair's friends and even accepted a donation from the former Prime Minister. 'I have a high regard for David and he's been a friend for many years, but it seemed to me in the way he conducted his campaign that he was the Blair mark II candidate,' says a senior shadow Cabinet minister. 'I suspect that if he hadn't allowed that to happen, he would have won.'[93]

The one issue that had tainted Blair's legacy beyond all others was, of course, the 2003 invasion of Iraq. Indeed, it was the one issue on which sections of the Labour Party and the wider left were unwilling to forgive David. He may have been a junior schools minister at the time but, in his role as Foreign Secretary, between June 2007 and May 2010, he passed up several opportunities to distance himself from Blair's decision to invade. Asked on BBC radio in November 2007, for example, whether the Iraq war would have occurred under a Brown premiership, David replied: 'Absolutely right.' He admitted that decisions taken since the invasion 'could have been done better' but insisted: 'No one is resiling from the original decision.'

During the leadership campaign, David's advisers struggled to articulate a convincing position for him on Iraq beyond the line that he had supported it in 'good faith'. Indeed, David himself seemed to believe that his refusal to budge on Iraq bolstered his credentials as a man of principle and integrity: 'I think that people will have to make up their mind if they can trust someone who sticks to their position as clearly as I have.' Yet his unwillingness to disown Iraq did more to tie him to the Blair years than any other decision, statement or policy proposal. Ed, however, had decided from the moment that he declared his candidacy that Iraq would be one of those issues on which he differentiated himself from Blair – and from David. In the very first Labour leadership hustings there were sharp intakes of breath from audience members as Ed and David repeatedly clashed on Iraq. Ed said that he felt at the time of the invasion in 2003, when he was not yet an MP, that Hans Blix, the chief UN weapons inspector, should have been given 'more time'. His elder brother appeared to raise his eyebrows at this point, as he did when Ed implied there had been a lack of 'values' in foreign policy under Labour.

Nonetheless, Ed was able to exploit David's stubborn and perhaps self-sabotaging refusal to distance himself from the Iraq debacle. 'I think it has been profoundly damaging to Britain, David, and I disagree with you on that,' said Ed at the hustings. 'Ed says there is a difference on this panel over whether war is the last resort. That's wrong,' said an irritated David. But Ed's differentiation strategy was clear to see – and, judging by the applause from the audience, it seemed to be working. 'What's important about this is not somehow claiming moral superiority about the past because I'm not trying to do that,' concluded Ed. 'What is important about this is the lessons that you draw for the future. And we draw different lessons about the future. In particular, David and myself draw different lessons about the future.'

David admitted that 'of course' he would not have voted for the war had he known there were no WMDs, and described George W. Bush as 'the worst thing that ever happened to Tony Blair', but he was on the defensive – where Ed wanted him.[94] After the hustings finished, David authorised a supporter to tell journalists on his behalf that 'we cannot fight this contest pandering on Iraq and Trident or we'll be like the Tories on Europe'. He himself told aides: 'I am not going to get bogged down in Iraq.'[95]

But bogged down he would become, thanks to his younger brother. The following week, in a leadership debate on BBC Two's *Newsnight*, Ed Miliband told a studio audience of former Labour voters that the lesson he had drawn from the invasion of Iraq was that war should always be a last resort. Visibly annoyed, eyes rolling, David was quick to challenge his brother's position: 'The idea that anyone on this panel doesn't think that war is the last resort doesn't do justice to the substance of this issue.'[96]

The exchanges over Iraq were even more heated during a debate on BBC Radio 5 Live on 29 July. By now David and Balls – who had revealed that he had privately been sceptical of the case for war but said he would have voted for the invasion had he been an MP at the time – were united in denying that Ed had opposed military action in 2003.

It was Ed, as usual, who raised the provocative subject of Iraq. 'One of the differences between David and myself is I think I am more critical of some of the things we did in government, and more willing to move on from some of the mistakes that we made, not just on foreign policy like Iraq, but on the economy and the fact that we have left lots of people on low wages. Unless you are willing to say we made mistakes and you are willing to move on from them we will have the same result at the next election.'

David hit back: 'I do not believe we lost the 2010 election because of Iraq and we fool ourselves if we think [we lost] places like Stevenage – that we won in 2005 – because of Iraq. We have all said that if we had known in 2003 there were no weapons of mass destruction then of course we would not have voted for the war... Diane Abbott is the only candidate that can say she was against the war at the time, and if that is the sole criterion, she is in a different position to every other candidate. She did not just think she was against it, she said she was against it, and she marched against it.'

It was a deliberate dig at Ed, a not-so-coded attack on his honesty – despite the fact that friends of Ed say the younger Miliband had personally told David himself of his concerns over the Iraq war in 2003 and David had shared many of them.[97]

Balls then weighed in to the discussion: 'I do not think Ed or any of the rest of us can claim with any credibility that in 2003 we thought the war was wrong but we just forgot to tell anyone, because that would make us look ridiculous.'

Yet Ed was adamant, telling the 5 Live audience (truthfully): 'I did tell people at the time that asked me, that I was against the war.' His rivals, however, would not let up. 'You did not tell people...' Balls said under his breath.[98]

By August and September, Ed and his advisers were much less keen to raise the issue of Iraq – they had belatedly recognised the importance of not antagonising the large group of Labour MPs who had grudgingly voted for the war in 2003 and whose first or second preferences Team Ed were chasing. But the damage to David had been done: his judgement had been questioned by his younger brother and his link to Blair's most catastrophic decision as Prime Minister had been revived in the minds of the Labour Party electorate. The elder Miliband had told former Labour voters during the general election campaign that they had 'punished us enough about Iraq'. But his strategic error as a leadership candidate was to fail to recognise how some Labour voters still wanted to punish him personally for his support for that war.

ooooo

Ed knew from the start that if he couldn't secure the endorsements of the big trade unions, he had no chance of cancelling out David's lead in the MPs' section and, possibly, the members' section too. He did, however, have a huge advantage over his brother. Boxed in as a Blairite, David struggled to win endorsements from the Labour-affiliated trade unions.

Could David have put more effort into trying to win the union vote? Despite his hardball tactics at the TUC summer reception, overall, and on the subject of trade union endorsements, there was a sense of complacency inside the frontrunner's camp. One shadow Cabinet supporter of the elder Miliband remembers telling his advisers that they were being too casual in their approach to the union movement: 'This is a tripartite electoral college. You can't just focus on two bits of the college.' The shadow Cabinet minister was told to relax.[99]

In fact, David's spokesman, Lisa Tremble, proudly briefed journalists that her man had the backing of the steelworkers' union, Community, and the shop workers' union, USDAW. 'Blair got Community's backing too when he ran for leader,' she said.

But it was 2010, not 1994. In a world of Labour-affiliated 'super unions' like Unite (1.2 million members) and UNISON (900,000 members), USDAW (380,000 members) and Community (23,000 members) were relative minnows.

The previous September, on the eve of the 2009 TUC conference, Derek Simpson, joint general secretary of Britain's biggest union Unite, said in public what many union members had begun to say privately when he anointed Ed as a possible successor to Gordon Brown. 'If I had to name one for the future I pick Ed Miliband. He has potential to be a lot more progressive,' he told the *Daily Mirror*.[100]

In March 2010, two months before the general election, Simpson again tipped Miliband as a future leader in an interview with the *New Statesman* – a line that the Labour-supporting magazine chose to flag up on its cover. Interviewer Mark Seddon wrote:

It has often been said that another aspirant Labour leader, Ed Balls, would have Unite's support. But clearly it is Ed Miliband, and not Balls, who is now the chosen one, Labour's leader-in-waiting, if Simpson and his friends have their way.[101]

By the time the Labour leadership contest had kicked off, however, Simpson's view had shifted. Under pressure from Unite's pugnacious political director, the former Brown spin doctor Charlie Whelan, he had started leaning towards Ed Balls – Whelan's old friend and ally from his Treasury days. The lazy assumption in Westminster circles was that Whelan would deliver Unite's 1.2 million members for Balls.

There were, however, other key players involved. Tony Woodley, the joint general secretary of Unite, was firmly in the Ed Miliband camp and had never been happy about Whelan's control of the union's political operation. 'Tony was unwavering in his support for Ed M,' says a well-placed Unite source.[102] Then there was Clare Moody, the well-connected political officer of the union and daughter of Tory political activists, who had been seconded to the Downing Street Policy Unit in the run-up to the general election. Moody had been impressed by Ed, in his role as manifesto coordinator, and had helped him push – unsuccessfully – for universal free school meals to be included in the party's 2010 manifesto. She began lobbying for Ed inside Unite.[103]

On 14 July, the day after the TUC's summer reception, the five general secretaries of the 'big four' unions, Unite's Simpson and Woodley (accompanied by Whelan), the CWU's Billy Hayes, the GMB's Paul Kenny and UNISON's Dave Prentis, met in secret at London's Commonwealth Club, off the Strand, to plot their anti-David strategy.

The meeting started late, as Unite's Simpson had been watching the Australia–Pakistan cricket match at Lord's. Whelan didn't say much – but he didn't need to, given his well-known closeness to Ed Balls. 'His silence was loud,' says one of the union leaders at the meeting.[104]

Of the five general secretaries, Kenny was 'out in front'[105] for Ed. The GMB leader had been heavily influenced by Peter Hain, one of Ed's five shadow Cabinet backers, and a member of the GMB. On 15 July, the GMB became the first of the 'big four' trade unions to endorse Ed.

Some have suggested that a 'deal' was done at the Commonwealth Club but a general secretary who attended the meeting flatly denies this: 'None of us were going to tell the rest of the group what to do. But there was a growing recognition at that stage that Ed Miliband was the only candidate who could beat David Miliband.'[106]

The mood at the meeting was 'very anti-David', says another participant. 'Once it was decided that he was the Blairite continuity candidate, he was dead in the water.'[107]

Whelan came out of the Commonwealth Club meeting realising that Balls had little chance of rounding up the bulk of the 'big four' endorsements. The best he could hope for was a coordinated split – with two unions backing Ed Balls and two unions backing Ed Miliband. Simpson started telling friends and colleagues that 'two Eds are better than one'.[108]

On 21 July, UNISON announced its endorsement – for Ed. The Balls camp was distraught. 'UNISON had been telling Ed [Balls] in private that they would go for him,' says an ally of Balls.[109]

But the real blow to Balls would come a few days later.

It was a sunny morning on Saturday 24 July when Unite's national policy committee, composed of rank-and-file members from across the country, met at the union's central London HQ in Holborn to decide which candidate to back. It was a lively meeting, with several delegates who had begun the morning favouring Ed Balls switching over to Ed Miliband by the end. The latter received the committee's overwhelming endorsement, with twenty-four votes. Trailing far behind were Balls and Andy Burnham with four votes each. David and Diane Abbott won only one each.

'If you want to stop David Miliband, then Ed [Miliband] is the only show in town,' a senior Unite official told one of us after the vote. 'Plus, we have to move beyond Blair and Brown, and David Miliband is the Blairite and Ed Balls is the Brownite.'

But how did Ed Miliband win the vote so emphatically? Few would have imagined Balls would do so badly – least of all Balls himself, who was left shaken by the result, and considered quitting the race. Woodley's influence was significant, of course, counterbalancing the Simpson/Whelan axis, but it was Ed's own efforts that helped him clinch the Unite endorsement. In the days running up to the vote of the national policy committee, Ed rang several undecideds on the committee to personally convince them to back him, having obtained their phone numbers from a friendly source inside the union. As is so often the case, Ed, affable, charming, persuasive, was able to swing those committee members behind him in one-to-one conversations. What promises he may have made to them, we do not know – but the brusque Balls never stood a chance. It was a secret yet crucial intervention by Ed in Unite's nomination process.[110]

On the afternoon of the vote, a group of Unite officials retreated to a pub on Kingsway to mull over the result. Whelan was at one end of the pub feeding back the bad news to the Balls camp on his mobile; Moody, on the other end, was telling Team Ed the good news.[111]

'Charlie was mortified with embarrassment that he over-promised and failed to deliver,' says a key Balls ally. 'The irony is that one of the reasons Ed [Balls] lost so much support inside Unite is because he was so closely associated with Charlie.'[112]

With Unite, UNISON and GMB behind Ed Miliband, Ed Balls knew that 'it was game over'.[113] So too did the bookies. The day after the Unite vote, Ladbrokes cut the odds on Ed Miliband winning the leadership battle from 7/4 to 6/4. The union endorsements meant there was now no doubt whatsoever that it was a two-horse race. The next leader of the Labour Party would be called Miliband – and there was a clear sense of momentum building behind the younger of the two brothers.

ooooo

So what would Balls do? Some have suggested that the two Eds had been in secret discussions with each other in the run-up to the general election, as to which of the two would be the 'stop David' candidate – but both camps have denied this claim.

In an interview in March 2011, Balls claimed that he had never entered the Labour leadership contest planning to win – but only in order 'to be part of the future of shaping the Labour Party and making the arguments that matter to me'. This isn't, however, strictly true. Balls, the hammer of the Tories and the self-styled heir of Keynes, had hoped to attract the support of the soft left of the party and defeat David Miliband in a one-on-one battle. He had been planning his own leadership campaign for several months. At a dinner with the former Mayor of London, Ken Livingstone, for example, towards the end of 2009, the two men discussed Balls's leadership prospects. During his eight years at City Hall, Livingstone had been impressed by Balls's mastery of machine politics at the Treasury and his ability to deliver on complex projects like Crossrail.

Balls and Livingstone agreed at the dinner that whoever got to the final round against David Miliband had a good chance of defeating him, given the role of second preferences and the latter's Blairite past. Livingstone told Balls that he would try and line up the support of the Labour left and the big trade unions. But the two men were to be disappointed.[114]

The day after the general election, on Friday 7 May, left-wing Labour MPs and union leaders held a secret meeting at the terraced house of Ken Livingstone in Cricklewood, in north-west London. Those present at the meeting included Livingstone, his long-standing adviser Simon Fletcher, Labour MP Jon Trickett, CWU leader Billy Hayes, *Guardian* columnist Seumas Milne and Steve Hart, the London regional secretary of the Unite union. Livingstone argued in favour of Balls, but others in the room began to discuss whether or not Ed Miliband would run. 'At this stage, less than twenty-four hours after the general election, we weren't sure if Ed would stand against his brother or not,' says one of the participants, who says he was leaning towards the younger Miliband.[115]

'I think at the end of the meeting, people were broadly sceptical about my case for Ed Balls,' admits Livingstone now.[116]

Such has been the intensity of focus on the fraternal nature of the contest, few have noted how difficult it must have been for Ed to also take on Ed Balls. 'In terms of family, he may have deferred to David, but in terms of career he deferred to Balls,' says a former Downing Street official who worked with both Balls and the Miliband brothers. 'But he took them both on.'[117]

It is worth remembering the words of the Miliband family friend: 'Until he became Labour leader, he was always little Ed – little Ed to David, little Ed to the other Ed.' The leadership campaign saw Ed shed both of these monikers. Meanwhile, over the course of the campaign and especially during the endless hustings around the country, both David and Balls made their disdain for Ed's candidacy clear. Balls, in particular, was furious that Ed had blocked him from taking on David, one on one, from the left. And, having persuaded his wife Yvette Cooper to stand aside so he could run for the leadership, he now frustratingly found himself taking on two brothers, whose personal and Shakespearean battle dominated the contest – and, of course, the media coverage of it. In a deliberate dig at the Milibands, Balls told one of us during the campaign that he and Cooper had decided they would not both stand for the leadership because it would be 'weird' to run against one another. A few weeks later, an irritated Balls denounced the 'daily soap opera' surrounding the Miliband brothers and their supporters.

Balls's comments didn't go unnoticed. Ed told a friend that he believed the other Ed, like David, was playing 'mind games' with him during the leadership contest.[118]

Meanwhile, in July and August, overexcited members of Team David began to brief lobby journalists that Balls's supporters' second preferences would end up with their candidate; some suggested Balls himself would pull out and swing behind David.

'Will Balls drop out to back David Mili?' asked the well-connected political correspondent, Paul Waugh, on his *Evening Standard* blog, on 23 July. '[T]he scenario painted to me is this: by dropping out and backing David M, his chances of becoming shadow Chancellor are greatly enhanced.'[119] The assumption was that Ed Miliband would be unable to appoint his fellow former Brownite, the other Ed, as his shadow Chancellor. (This, of course, has since been proved false.)

To add fuel to the fire, the following month, Phil Collins, the former Blair speechwriter and friend of David, used his column in *The Times* to reveal that, 'in 1999 Mr Balls and David Miliband used to meet regularly in Churchill's, a café opposite the Treasury on Whitehall, in a forlorn attempt to join up the government. It left Mr Balls with a basic respect for the elder Miliband that he does not have for the younger.'

The Balls camp denied that their man was on the verge of pulling out and swinging behind David – or Ed, for that matter. But rumours continued to spread, fuelled by a provocative intervention, on 1 September, from Geoffrey Robinson, the former Treasury minister, arch-Brownite and close ally and confidant of Balls. In an article in *The Independent*, the millionaire MP endorsed David Miliband as his second choice, behind Balls, arguing that the latter had 'the strength of character for the job' – and implying that the younger Miliband did not. It was an article that Robinson had run past Balls in advance of publication.[120]

Some senior members of Team Ed began to panic. Ed himself

approached his former Treasury colleague to 'have a discussion about second preferences'. But Balls told Ed that he had decided not to give a second preference nor would he instruct his supporters to swing behind another candidate with their own second preferences. An ever-complacent David, however, didn't even bother to make a formal approach to Balls. 'It was the biggest strategic blunder of the campaign by David,' says a close friend and ally of the elder Ed.[121]

Balls's close allies, meanwhile, were torn between the Miliband brothers. Tom Watson, who had served under Ed in the Cabinet Office, wanted Ed; Ian Austin, a former press officer for Brown and a leading Brownite, wanted David. Like Balls, Austin was irritated that the younger, less experienced Ed was now on the verge of the leadership. But Watson's lobbying skills proved to be more effective; recruiting Michael Dugher, another former adviser to Brown, he succeeded in persuading four other MPs – John Healey, Khalid Mahmood, Iain Wright and Steve McCabe – to back an Ed Balls/Ed Miliband 'slate'. In the final count, of the forty MPs who backed Balls, twenty-two backed Ed with their second preferences, just fifteen went for David.[122]

'Without these second-preference votes,' wrote Patrick Hennessy, a *Sunday Telegraph* journalist known for his close links to Brown and Balls, 'Ed Miliband would not be Labour leader today, and the narrowest of victories would have been David's.'

ooooo

Tony Blair wanted David Miliband to win the leadership race. He may not have believed his former adviser and Cabinet colleague was a true believer in Blairism but reports emerged suggesting that he considered the prospect of an Ed victory to be a 'disaster' for Labour. On 4 September 2010, the *Daily Telegraph* reported on a meeting between the former Prime Minister and the younger Miliband in a hotel room in New York in the run-up to the 2010 general election, at which Blair had grilled Ed on a range of issues and been particularly unimpressed by the latter's reluctance to confront Iran over its nuclear programme.

But who did Gordon Brown want as his successor? Some say the former Prime Minister, who studiously avoided commenting in public throughout the summer-long leadership campaign, and decided early on that he would not vote in the election, privately backed Ed Balls to begin with but switched to Ed Miliband when he knew the former had no chance of winning. Above all else, Brown wanted a 'stop David' candidate. Balls, however, maintains that the former PM had backed Ed from the start – a claim denied by sources close to Brown. Either way, in the final weeks of the campaign, undecided Brownite MPs were well aware which candidate their mentor was supporting – it was Ed M, not Ed B.[123]

The big, unanswered question for the media, however, related to David and Ed's mother: who was Marion supporting?

A deeply private person, Marion resented the media's newfound interest in her life, her past and her political views. Nor, as a mother, did she want to have to choose between her two sons. Unsurprisingly, therefore, she told David and Ed, and her circle of friends, that she had no intention of being involved in the contest in any shape or form. 'This is about the boys and their politics,' she told a close friend during the summer of 2010. 'It's not about me.'[124]

It was a strange position for Marion to find herself in, sixteen years after the death of her husband. Ralph never believed the Labour Party could be a serious vehicle for the socialist transformation of society; Marion, meanwhile, was a Labour member and supporter but on the Old, not New, wing of the party. But here were Ralph and Marion's two sons vying to lead the Labour Party that their parents had spent decades subjecting to scathing criticism – and, in Ralph's case, outright rejection.

Neither David nor Ed had ever tried to influence her politics or persuade her of the merits of New Labour, Blair or Brown. A friend of the family says he remembers asking Marion how strange it must be for her to be the mother of not one but two sons in the Cabinet; the first brothers to sit in Cabinet since the 1930s. 'But they don't talk to me about politics or policies,' replied Marion.[125]

In the final weeks of the Labour leadership contest, Marion decided to fly to New York and visit her sister Hadassa, in order to get away from the media scrum in London. At around the same time, Ralph's old friend and colleague Leo Panitch arrived in New York, from his home in Toronto, to speak at a book launch for the social theorist David Harvey. Panitch had a few moments to talk alone with Marion, who was in the audience, and had come to the front to meet him before the event began. She asked Panitch whether he had spoken to Ed and what he had heard about the campaign's latest twists and turns. Panitch was impressed at her resilience; Fleet Street photographers had been camped outside her sister's doorstep in New York, trying to get a shot of her. She was 'under siege'.

'You must be proud of them,' Panitch said to Marion, referring to the fact that her two sons were the frontrunners for the leadership of the Labour Party. 'Proud?' she replied. 'What do you mean, Leo? One is not proud of adults, one is proud of children. And if they'd asked my advice, I would have told them not get into this ridiculous game.'[126]

It was an important political point from Marion's perspective. Here was a woman from a Marxist background, with a radical view of mainstream, parliamentary politics, watching her only two sons do potentially permanent damage to their relationship for the sake of something relatively trivial and unimportant: the Labour leadership. What was the point? What was being achieved? It was, she believed, a 'ridiculous game'.

'Marion's attitude,' says a friend, was 'Do what you have to do.' 'They're grown-ups, after all, not children.'[127] Marion did not tell Ed that he should not stand against his older brother – but nor did she give him her blessing or explicit support. Her younger son would later joke that she was backing Diane Abbott. (Abbott seems to have missed the joke, telling audiences at leadership hustings that 'Mother Miliband' was backing her with a confidence that suggested she believed it to be the case.)

However, the evidence from family friends, and friends of Ed, suggests her heart may just have been with her younger, more radically inclined son. A longstanding and close friend of Ed, from outside of the world of politics, says he believes Marion 'privately supported Ed'.[128] Why? She saw him as closer to her late husband's beliefs and values. It was the same view that had been expressed by Wendy Carlin to her husband Andrew Glyn at Ralph's funeral in 1994.

Ralph and Marion's old friend, Tony Benn, agrees with this view: 'I suspect she would have been backing Ed.'[129]

David has told friends that such claims are 'total nonsense'. Indeed, one ally of the elder Miliband claims Marion had been annoyed and upset that 'the family would never be the same again' as a result of Ed's decision to stand.[130] It would not.

ooooo

From the moment Ed declared his candidacy at the Fabians on 15 May, his aides and supporters knew the odds were stacked against them. Many of them had risked their political careers in working for the underdog – and against his brother, the frontrunner. It was, as one of Ed's closest advisers now admits, a 'deeply bitter leadership contest'.[131]

'You better win,' Greg Beales was heard telling Ed at one stage, 'or else we better find out what's going on, politically, in Peru.'[132] Ed, however, had no intention of relocating to South America. He believed he would win – and he had a plan.

As the campaign progressed, Ed and his aides became wedded to the idea that they had to fight an 'insurgency campaign'. They would be proud underdogs, self-professed outsiders, a bottom-up movement. 'Powered by people' became one of Team Ed's internal mantras.[133] The role of insurgent, of course, was one that Ed had performed before in his campaign against rent-rises at Oxford, in his battle for the Doncaster nomination and in the run-up to the Copenhagen climate conference.

In contrast, his brother struggled to shake off the label of 'establishment candidate' which did such harm to his campaign for the leadership. And there were 'chinks in David's armour', says a friend of Ed.[134] He wasn't picking up as many endorsements from MPs as he had hoped to, he was struggling to formulate a coherent message and the unions were resolutely opposed to his leadership bid. Despite all this, the elder Miliband's campaign reeked of complacency, rather than inevitability.

'If you're going to be the inevitability candidate,' says a former adviser to Ed, 'be the fucking inevitability candidate. Ultimately, David, with his sense of entitlement, was Hillary Clinton to Ed's Obama.'[135]

The former adviser isn't alone in his invocation of Obama. Numerous members of Ed's campaign staff say they took inspiration from the Obama presidential campaign and pored over books like *Renegade: The Making of a President* by journalist Richard

Wolffe and *The Audacity to Win* by former Obama campaign manager David Plouffe.[136]

Critics of Ed have long ridiculed any comparisons or analogies between the David–Ed race in 2010 and the Hillary–Barack contest in 2007 and 2008. David would later be overheard ridiculing his brother's adoption of an insurgent approach: 'So he thinks he's Obama, does he?'[137]

The Obama analogy, however, ended up reaching the White House. David Muir, the former director of strategy in Downing Street for Gordon Brown who now works as a political consultant, was on a visit to Washington DC in early September, as the Labour leadership race reached its climax. At a meeting in the White House with Rahm Emanuel, President Obama's then chief of staff, and David Axelrod, the President's senior counsel and the chief strategist of the 2008 presidential campaign, the conversation touched on the Labour leadership and the Miliband brothers. The White House officials were more familiar with former Foreign Secretary David than they were with Ed, and assumed the former was going to win. Axelrod asked Muir who he thought would win and the latter said he believed Ed would win a narrow victory. 'Why?' asked Axelrod. 'David is very good but he is running at 100 per cent while Ed is at 70 per cent,' replied Muir. 'Ed has so much more capacity to improve. It's just like Obama when he ran against Hillary.' A wry smile appeared on Axelrod's face.[138]

Like Obama, Ed used the internet and social network sites to harness the energy and enthusiasm of his supporters, build excitement, and mobilise and recruit volunteers for his leadership campaign. His team also exploited advances in mobile phone technology, using the company MASS1 to send out thousands of two-way text messages to Labour Party members in a single, 24-hour period at the beginning of August. These texts – the first of their kind to be used in a British election campaign – didn't just contain a message from the candidate but asked for a response, too. Around half of the recipients replied, of whom 45 per cent said they were supporting the former Energy Secretary. The texts resulted in the campaign recruiting 1,300 potential new volunteers. Meanwhile, those who said they were not supporters were asked via a second two-way text from the team as to why they were backing other candidates – 1,500 people answered, giving Ed's strategists a treasure-trove of information on voting intentions. A campaign spokesman triumphantly told *The Guardian* on 2 August: 'We have said all along we might be outspent throughout this campaign, but we wouldn't be out-organised.'

The end result of the online and text campaigns was a large, Obama-style network of young, idealistic volunteers – more than 5,000 people nationwide. Recognising the importance of a grass-roots campaign, Team Ed's campaign videos focused predominantly on the volunteers and interviews with the volunteers, rather than the candidate himself. David's tended to do the reverse.

Neil Kinnock remembers going to speak at the Oxford University Labour Club in June 2010. The final question from the audience of students – which included Labour and non-Labour voters – related to why he was backing Ed Miliband. His answer – about Ed's capacity to inspire, his 'X-factor', his embodiment of change – prompted two Lib Dem students to hand over their party membership cards to the former party leader and pledge to join the Labour Party then and there. A few weeks later, Kinnock spotted the duo manning phones for the Ed campaign at Unite's offices in London. His wife, Glenys, says she was stunned to see dozens of young people sitting on the floor, some of them using their own mobile phones to make calls on Ed's behalf. 'My God,' she thought to herself, 'This has to be the right thing to do.'[139]

Like Obama, Ed raised large sums of money through small donations – more than £60,000, of which £42,000 was raised through online initiatives from less than a thousand individual donors.

Then there was the distinctive policy platform – living wage, High Pay Commission and graduate tax – that added to the sense of radicalism, boldness and a break from New Labour triangulation and caution. 'For those of us who believed we had to rethink our policies from first principles, Ed was the obvious candidate,' says a Labour strategist normally associated with the Blairite wing of the party. 'He was very clever in colonising [the] space that David left vacant.'[140]

It was also an all-important element of what became Ed's 'change to win' strategy. 'Ed Miliband wrote the manifesto, he was one of Gordon's chief economic advisers in the early years of New Labour, he worked for Harriet as a researcher and yet when the leadership contest kicks off, he is the Year Zero candidate,' says a former adviser to Brown, who backed Balls. 'Ed Balls and David Miliband are weighed down by their association with the past while Ed Mili immediately breaks free of it.'[141]

The key moment in the development of the Ed campaign's insurgency strategy came in early August at a meeting of advisers chaired, in Ed's absence, by the pollster James Morris. Prior to the meeting, Morris had circulated a confidential memo, reiterating the key objective of the Ed campaign: 'We need to make this election *change* versus *continuity*.' The 'change' on offer, suggested Morris, would need to be about style as well as substance but, in a nod to the 'Red Ed' accusations from critics on the party's right, was 'not about a swing to the left'. It was about a 'vibrant, open, volunteer-led campaign that goes out and meets working people', 'standing up for workers and entrepreneurs in the labour market' and 'post-Iraq'.[142]

Other advisers had made similar arguments before. 'You've got to be the change candidate,' Sadiq Khan had told Ed when he signed on as his election agent. 'Your biggest Achilles heel is that you're so associated with Gordon. You've now got to be change.'[143] For Greg Beales, there was no alternative: their campaign had to articulate a change versus continuity message, with 'Ed being change, David being continuity'.[144]

There had been some incoherence in the early months of the campaign – was Ed the 'values' candidate, the 'change' candidate or both? The message was starting to get confused. But the meeting in August, and the Morris memo, was a 'turning point' for the Ed campaign, says a former adviser to the candidate.[145] Change transcended values; differentiation from the past and the rest of the leadership field was the priority.

The strategy was drummed into Ed by Wood and MP Jon Trickett – who had run Jon Cruddas's much-lauded and insurgent campaign for the deputy leadership in 2007 – while he was away on holiday in Cornwall with a pregnant Justine and one-year-old Daniel. Ed agreed.[146] Change was the key but, above all else, changing to win. He had run insurgency campaigns before but knew that this would be the biggest, most intense, most important insurgency of them all.

'I am the head and the heart candidate,' Ed would repeatedly proclaim throughout the latter half of the campaign. Why? 'The heart of the Labour Party beats to the left, the head to the right,' says Trickett. 'But I told Ed he could reconcile both heart and head, and win by building a progressive coalition.'[147] New Labour, according to Trickett's analysis, had been too far to the right to hold onto public sector workers, manual workers and ethnic minorities. The party had lost five million voters between 1997 and 2010.

On 16 August, Team Ed hardened up the head-and-heart message: the change their candidate was advocating was not about returning to left-wing comfort zones but winning back lost Labour voters. This argument was expressed in an essay for the Fabian Society that James Morris, with Jon Trickett's help, wrote on Ed's behalf, and which included an important psychological analysis:

> New Labour's proposition was simple – we need to persuade Tory voters to come to us. The task is very different now. Five million votes were lost by Labour between 1997 and 2010, but 4 out of the 5 million didn't go to the Conservatives. One third went to the Liberal Democrats, and most of the rest simply stopped voting.
>
> It wasn't, in the main, the most affluent, professional voters that deserted Labour either. New analysis has been produced by Ipsos/Mori which shows the scale of loss among lower income groups. Between 1997 and 2010, for every one voter that Labour lost from the professional classes (so called 'ABs'), we lost three voters among the poorest, those on benefits and the low paid (DEs). You really don't need to be a Bennite to believe that this represents a crisis of working-class representation for Labour – and our electability.

In the essay, Ed stated, provocatively: 'It is my rejection of ... New Labour nostalgia that makes me the modernising candidate at this election.'[148]

Of the five candidates, few would now dispute the fact that it was the younger Miliband who gave the clearest articulation to the argument that the Labour Party needed to change its economic and political-reform agendas and own up to its massive, strategic errors on foreign policy. Ed voiced these points in a language, tone and style that Labour members heard and understood more clearly than they did the arguments and talking-points of the other candidates – David included.

'David was just blind to the change issue,' asserts a friend of Ed's. 'He almost defined himself as the candidate of the status quo, especially with his inability to move on Iraq. But that's what happens when you surround yourself with people like Alastair Campbell.'[149]

'You can't be change if you don't articulate a critique of the past,' adds another Ed ally.[150]

By the time his brief holiday was over, Ed was telling Stewart Wood and other key advisers: 'I know I'm the "change candidate". I know how to do "change."' He was in his stride in terms of messaging and narrative; he was 'fizzing', say aides, after his break in Cornwall.[151]

David, meanwhile, had lost his early momentum but continued to pick up endorsements. John Prescott was telling MPs to vote for David, though he stopped just short of naming the older Miliband as his choice. On 10 September, left-wing backbencher Dennis Skinner came out for the elder Miliband. 'The big question is who are the Tories afraid of?' said the 'Beast of Bolsover'. 'For me the best choice is David Miliband and that is why I will be supporting him as next Labour leader.'[152]

David's camp were delighted, briefing friendly journalists that Skinner's endorsement – like Jon Cruddas's – was 'symbolic' and illustrated how their man had transcended left–right divisions inside the party.

But just forty-eight hours later, the David campaign would receive their biggest and nastiest surprise of the contest so far. 'Shock Labour Party leadership poll gives lead to Ed Miliband,' declared the headline on the front page of the *Sunday Times* on 12 September.[153] The You Gov survey – of 1,011 party members and 718 members of Labour-affiliated trade unions – put Ed on 51 per cent and David on 49 per cent, once second-preference votes from the third-placed Andy Burnham, the fourth-placed Ed Balls and the fifth-placed Diane Abbott were redistributed. (David was four points ahead of Ed – thirty-six to thirty-two – on the basis of first-preference votes only.)

Four days later, on 15 September, Alex Smith, the former Labour blogger who had joined Team Ed to run its online campaign, visited the candidate's home. His task was to help Ed prep for his appearance that night on the final debate of the Labour leadership contest – on BBC One's *Question Time*. 'There was a new whole aura to him,' recalls Smith. 'We're going to win, we're going to win,' Ed told his aide, with a beaming smile.[154]

He had every reason to be optimistic. With the publication of the YouGov poll, David's 'inevitability' strategy lay in tatters. 'The race is neck and neck,' wrote YouGov's Anthony Wells on the company's website on 13 September, before concluding: '[B]ut Ed Miliband is now in pole position.'

ooooo

On 11 July 2010, the members of Ed's campaign team gathered upstairs in a private room in the north London Tavern pub in Camden to watch the World Cup final between Spain and Holland. There were around sixty staffers and volunteers crowded into the room. At half time, Ed walked around the tables, chatting to his team members, asking for their feedback on the campaign so far, before giving an impromptu speech. Name checking one of his heroes, Bobby Kennedy, Ed declared: 'I've always seen those programmes and films about political campaigns that have fantastic volunteers working for them. I never dreamed that I would have one myself.'[155] It was a line he used again and again throughout his campaign. He understood the power and potential of what he and his advisers had created. They had succeeded in building an insurgency campaign from the ground up, and had seized the mantle of change from David. Ed himself had inspired and enthused his young supporters, and rallied MPs, party activists and trade union members to his cause.

Win or lose, it was an impressive achievement from the 40-year-old underdog. But it had come at a high price. Ed's hardnosed and ruthless campaign had severely damaged his relationship with his brother. In the space of a single summer, David and Ed had gone from allies and friends to sworn political enemies.

VICTORY

SEPTEMBER 2010

At around 6am on Saturday 25 September, Justine Thornton got up, played with her son Daniel for an hour, and boarded an early morning train for Manchester for the result of the Labour Party leadership contest. With her during the nervous journey, during which there was little conversation, were Ed's aides Rachel Kinnock, Simon Alcock and Alex Smith.

Once in Manchester they headed straight for Ed's hotel room. Justine hugged and kissed Ed, and sat on his knee for a while, while members of the campaign team flitted in and out of the room. The mood was initially tense, and not all of them were as confident that he'd won as the candidate himself. Rachel Kinnock came in and declared that she was convinced David had won: she had been trying to contact party officials to discuss logistics if Ed were to win, and had received radio silence. Then Polly Billington told everyone they should spend the next five minutes thinking as if they had lost. This general apprehension was at odds with a front page story in *The Guardian* the previous day, predicting an Ed victory. But for Ed the defeat scenario was easy to imagine: he would do a round of media interviews unreservedly congratulating his older brother, the only other possible winner. Ed knew he did not need to rehearse a losing speech as no slot had been scheduled for the runner up. Instead, the victor was to give an eight-minute address, and it was this that Ed now practised.[1]

Eventually, Ed and his entourage headed for the conference centre where the result would be announced. Several campaign insiders say that it was at this point they felt certain Rachel Kinnock had been right – that David had won. The body language of senior members of David's camp seemed so confident. 'They were walking around like they owned the place,' recalls an adviser to Ed.[2] The sense of alarm among David's rivals was exacerbated by the older brother's arrival from Euston at lunchtime wearing casual jeans and a dark shirt. 'We were all in suits and David was in casual clothes,' says one of the Miliband brothers' leadership rivals. 'We were all so nervous and he seemed so super-relaxed. He was acting like he'd won.'[3]

Each candidate now had to go to a separate room upstairs with only one person allowed to join them. Ed had chosen his campaign agent Sadiq Khan, but not before his team members had worked out a code for alerting them in advance as to whether or not Ed had won. The plan was for Khan to arrive in the hall without his conference pass on if Ed had lost – but if he was wearing it around his neck, as normal, the team would know their man had won.

Ed's apparent confidence about the result masked his inner turmoil as he awaited it. At one point, around forty-five minutes before the announcement upstairs, Ed bumped into Lisa Tremble, David's press secretary, in a corridor. Tremble found Ed uncharacteristically nervous. 'I need you to know I'm just pleased it's all over,' he said. Tremble agreed: 'We all are.'[4]

Meanwhile, Ed's aides were so anxious that he should avoid bumping into David immediately before the result that at one point they warned Ed against using the gents' toilet after learning that his brother was inside, shaving and getting changed into his suit.[5]

ooooo

After filing into a large room on the top floor of the conference chamber, the five leadership candidates stood next to one another in a semi-circle and waited nervously to hear the result for the first time. As it happened, Ed was at the centre, with David next to him; Balls, Burnham and Abbott stood on both sides of the brothers. Behind them were their agents, Khan for Ed and for David his long-serving special adviser Madlin Sadler. Facing them was Ray Collins, Labour's general secretary and the one man who had known the result since the night before – much to the annoyance of Harriet Harman, the acting leader, who had only been told an hour or so earlier.

The candidates had come such a long way, and taken part in so many hustings together, they now simply wanted to know the result. So when Collins launched into what sounded like a lengthy speech, declaring that the five candidates had 'all been wonderful ambassadors for the party', the tension was momentarily punctured by a collective groan from the quintet. Collins responded by cutting to the chase. Walking towards the middle of the semi-circle, he looked straight at Ed and said what an 'honour' it was to announce that Ed Miliband was the next leader of the Labour Party.

Burnham, Balls, Abbott and Harman's immediate instinct was to congratulate Ed. But quickly they realised how awkward the situation was, as Ed had first to face the brother whose political career he had just wrecked. Ed and David went into an awkward sideways hug, their heads together as they exchanged whispered words. Harman slipped away to practise her impending speech. Khan grinned, as a distraught Sadler stared off into the middle distance. Balls and his agent, the MP Jim Knight, meanwhile, studied the break-down of the result.

The brutally blunt nature of Collins's announcement hid the extremely close and controversial nature of the result. After four rounds of voting, Ed had won with 175,519 votes to David's 147,220.[6] But, crucially, David had won in both the Labour members' and the Labour MPs' sections. Ed had only topped the trade union section – a point not lost on the new Labour leader as he left the room to have a brief and private conversation with his brother in the corridor outside.

The candidates now had to regroup with their agents before making their way into the hall for the official announcement. Ed had not had much time to think about David, though he says now he felt an understandably strange mixture of euphoria for himself and disappointment for his brother. The consensus among those he spoke to in the immediate aftermath of the result was that his overriding emotion was concern for David.[7]

Downstairs on the conference floor meanwhile, the tension was building to almost unbearable levels as delegates and media waited to hear the outcome. Ray Collins spoke briefly, praising all that Labour had accomplished and making special mention of the gay rights legislation that had enabled him to enter a civil partnership. Gordon Brown, largely unseen by the travelling Westminster circus since he left office in May, received a deeply warm ovation for a speech in which he reminded the hall of Labour's achievements and, in an apparent dig at his predecessor, declared: 'I am Labour. I will always be Labour.' Warming up the crowd for the main event, Brown boomed that Labour was 'the keeper of hope, the guarantor of justice, and now, so clearly, the only progressive party that this country has'. He added that whoever the new leader was they would have Brown's 'full, tireless and unequivocal support'.[8] Brown had run through his speech with his aide Kirsty McNeill in a tiny anteroom backstage, with no idea who had won.

During this period, Ed snatched half an hour to practise his victory speech with an ecstatic Khan, before heading down with the four defeated candidates to the packed hall, where party faithful and media alike had been waiting for over an hour.

Contrary to myth no one apart from the candidates, their agents, Collins and Harman knew the results at this stage. Lisa Tremble was having to bat away text messages from journalists begging her for the result, saying that 'Honestly no one knows'.[9] New MPs supporting Ed – Chuka Ummuna, Rachel Reeves and Luciana Berger – huddled together, none the wiser. Douglas Alexander arrived on stage late, utterly inscrutable and ignoring text messages being sent from the floor.

When the candidates entered the room – first David, then Ed, then Balls, Burnham and Abbott – the suspense heightened. David walked across the stage and took his seat looking relaxed and grinning broadly. Ed walked on looking sombre and poker-faced – having decided that the last thing he wanted to do was smile after what had happened to David. Later, Oona King would text him telling him to 'please smile a bit more,' only to get the reply: 'For God's sake, can people please stop telling me to smile.'[10] Whether or not Ed felt guilty, he was astute enough to know that now was not the time to look triumphant. The only clue that Ed may have won came from Ed Balls, who was grinning at and talking to Ed on his right.

The twenty-strong Ed team was standing on tiptoes towards the back of the hall when Khan walked in and took his seat alongside the rest of the shadow Cabinet. Not an overly tall man, Khan was hard to spot. 'I can't see his bloody pass,' muttered an anxious Stewart Wood.[11] Eventually, Khan turned around fully to face the Ed team. The pass was on. They had won!

Almost immediately however, there was fresh doubt. Harriet Harman had followed Brown's address by giving a brief, self-deprecatingly witty speech before handing over to Ann Black, chair of Labour's NEC, who was supposed, finally, to make the announcement. Yet to the collective disbelief of those in the hot and crowded conference hall, she delayed breaking the news still further by opting to run through the complete breakdown of the result. In classic British party conference style, the crucial moment was left to a person who seemed to be the least charismatic and concise figure in the room.

The first round of results were projected onto a screen and read out, showing a total percentage of 37.78 for David and 34.33 for Ed, with the membership section, judged at this point by both camps as key, broken down as 13.9 per cent for David and 10.5 per cent for Ed. For a second, Wood panicked, thinking there had been a terrible mistake and that Khan's 'pass system' had gone wrong. He was not alone in his confusion. Another senior aide to Ed recalls thinking to himself: 'Fuck, something is wrong here.'[12] And in an embarrassing – if unusual – error of judgement, the respected BBC political editor Nick Robinson predicted that David had won. Marcus Roberts, Ed's director of field operations, was sharper. The moment the results of the first round flashed up on screen, he scribbled a line on a piece of paper and passed it down the line of colleagues sitting next to him. It read: 'We've won, but without the members. Sorry.'[13]

What followed was a stomach-churning roller-coaster through the next rounds until at last the full breakdown could be seen. The results were as follows:

First round: Abbott – 7.4 per cent; Balls – 11.8 per cent; Burnham – 8.7 per cent; David Miliband – 37.8 per cent; Ed Miliband – 34.3 per cent.

Second round: Abbott – OUT; Ed Balls – 13.2 per cent; Burnham – 10.4 per cent; David Miliband 38.9 per cent; Ed Miliband – 37.5 per cent.

Third round: Abbott & Burnham – OUT; Balls – 16.0 per cent; David Miliband – 42.7 per cent; Ed Miliband – 41.3 per cent.

As Black announced the fourth round figures, Ed kept up his poker face while David produced a grin:

Fourth round: Abbott, Burnham and Balls – OUT; David Miliband – 49.4 per cent; Ed Miliband – 50.6 per cent.[14]

So finally, at just after 4.50pm, the result was out – all of a sudden everyone knew. There were pockets of wild cheers and cameras flashing, and Ed finally allowed himself a smile. David was the first to his feet. He stepped forward, embraced his brother and patted him on the back some fifteen times while whispering in the new leader's ear. Ed just nodded and thanked David repeatedly. After a few seconds, Ed moved on, hugging Andy Burnham and then making his way onto the stage. Oblivious that he was there, Black carried on speaking – her words buried by the cheers; so Ed patted her on the back, effectively ushering her off the stage. Then he took to the lectern and spoke without notes.

'Conference, can I start by thanking you for the amazing honour you have given me. I first joined this party aged seventeen. Never in my wildest imagination did I believe I would one day lead this party.' In an almost identical echo of what Tony Blair said when he became leader in 1994, Ed went on: 'You have put your trust in me, and I am determined to repay that trust.'

Then he turned to his brother. 'David, I love you so much as a brother and I have so much extraordinary respect for the campaign that you ran and the strength and eloquence that you showed.' Earlier, he had gone through this line with his team, querying any mention of 'love' at all, adamant that he couldn't just say 'I love you' – insisting that in his family, 'We don't say that!'[15]

He went on: 'And you taught us the most important lesson, that we can be a party that reaches out to the community and we can also be a serious party of government again. We all know how much you have to offer this country in the future.'[16]

After the announcement, Ed was to be taken triumphantly backstage. The plan was that he would be greeted by party officials and escorted off to a holding room to gather his thoughts and then do a round of press interviews. Like all the other candidates, he and his team had practised the choreography before the announcement was made. Now, though, something was horribly wrong. The party's personnel had disappeared; they had voted with their feet. Many had headed for the bars to drown their sorrows. One senior party official admits today that 'at least 80 per cent of the party backed David'.[17] Some Labour Party press officers were spotted sobbing outside by members of the Ed campaign.

Surreally, the new party leader was alone backstage – until he was joined by his aides, who rushed over to be at his side.[18] 'A backbench MP wouldn't be that badly looked after,' says an adviser to Ed, who was present. 'The party officials had just pissed off.'[19] It was not the most auspicious of starts for the new Labour leader. His party machine had been meant to help navigate him through the first few chaotic hours of his leadership, protect him from the media pack, and provide him a diary from minute one. But it failed to do so. The insurgent candidate had defeated the establishment candidate and people weren't pleased.

When Wood went through to the cramped Labour press office room behind the conference chamber, he found party workers in tears. Taken aback, he tried to rally the dejected troops: 'I don't care who you voted for, we should all just get on – five years from now we'll be back in power'.[20]

Elsewhere, members of Ed's team immediately noticed a difference when they met former friends from the David campaign. They were either blanked – or pilloried for having won with trade union support. In the first sign that family relations would never be the same again, Ed himself was cut dead by David's wife, Louise, shortly after the result, as he headed back to his hotel room with his entourage, after a meeting with Labour's National Executive Committee.[21]

Ed thanked his people in a brief but generous speech, telling his team members that each of them could individually take credit for the victory, given the closeness of the result – he had beaten David by just 1.2 per cent in the fourth and final round. Marcus Roberts then apologised again for the fact that Ed had failed to win the leadership section, but was shouted down by grateful staff who knew he had done vital work. Now Ed told most of his outer staff to go and have a drink. Lucy Powell asked seven or eight staffers to stay behind.[22] Suddenly, the brief moment of elation and self-congratulation was over. The work of leadership had to begin.

Downstairs, it was not just party officials and press officers who were furious on David's behalf in the bars of the Manchester conference centre that night. Former senior Cabinet ministers were, too. Figures such as Alistair Darling could be heard in the main bar of the Midland Hotel openly expressing their doubts about the new leader, along with key backbenchers such as Jon Cruddas. Darling was not critical of Ed personally, but he felt the party had made a grave mistake. His adviser, the amiable former journalist Catherine MacLeod, agreed, though when Stewart Wood entered the bar of the Midland at 11pm, MacLeod went up to him and said: 'I'm not an Ed fan as you know, but good on you.' She then reminded Wood of the need for Ed to 'reconcile' the party and heal the wounds.[23]

For the likes of Cruddas, of course, it was the personal aspect that rankled. 'You just don't fuck over your older brother,' he was, again, heard saying at a party in Manchester.[24] For most David supporters, however, it was the politics of the result that rankled. Their anger revolved principally around what was widely being seen as the 'union stitch-up'. But Ed's aides were unfazed, sticking to the line that rules are rules and every candidate had signed up to them in advance of the contest. Most members of the Blairite wing of the party viewed the tripartite electoral system as an absurdity – despite the fact that Blair was elected under the same system and chose not to reform or change it during his thirteen years as Labour leader. A few even thought the party should have broken with the unions long ago. What they all believed was that David had won a 'moral victory', having come top in the party, among both members and MPs.

They were also livid that David had been, in the words of a key adviser to the elder Miliband, 'locked out'[25] by the big unions, whose general secretaries endorsed Ed directly in mail shots to their membership. David supporters in Manchester pointed to the example of the GMB, which had sent its 700,000 members ballot papers inside a larger envelope featuring Ed's picture. Labour Party rules say 'affiliates should not include any materials in the ballot envelope indicating support for individual candidates' but they also allow for the ballot envelope to 'be inserted in another union mailing, which may contain a recommendation from the trade union as to which candidate to support'. The GMB had – just – stayed within the letter, if not the spirit, of the law. But Mark Wickham-Jones, a professor of politics at Bristol University, was quoted in *The Guardian* on the eve of the result as saying: 'The GMB appear to have broken the spirit of the rules guiding the conduct of the Labour Party leadership election by sending out a strong recommendation for Ed Miliband together with the ballot paper for political levy payers.'[26]

'Those union mail shots are the reason Ed won,' argues a senior member of the David campaign.[27] Alan Johnson, however, was more sanguine at the time, telling reporters that unions had been 'stretching the rules a bit. But I've got no argument with leaderships making a recommendation. That's what trade unions do for all kinds of areas.'[28]

But it wasn't just the trade union factor. There was a genuine feeling among Blairites that the party had indulged itself by electing a leader who would keep Labour in opposition and abandon the 'centre-ground', election-winning formula of their hero, Blair. According to one friend of the former Prime Minister, it was as if senior Ed backers such as Neil Kinnock had 'got their revenge on Tony'.[29]

A shadow Cabinet minister who backed Ed described the behaviour of David's supporters at the party conference – publicly questioning the legitimacy of the result and then privately briefing the right-wing press on 'Red Ed' – as 'totally disgraceful'.[30] Another key Ed supporter says that Manchester, in hindsight, was like 'occupied territory' for the new Labour leader.[31] The bulk of the delegates – MPs, peers, council leaders, activists – had voted for his brother. There wasn't the usual euphoria that greeted new party leaders. Luckily for Ed, he spent the night of his victory away from the toxic atmosphere in the conference bars, first running through formalities with the party's NEC, and then installed in the leader's suite, talking to aides and MPs.

Early in the evening, while Ed was preparing for an appearance on the *Andrew Marr Show* the following morning, he received a call from David Cameron, who congratulated the new opposition leader. Senior Tories had watched the result on Sky News at Conservative Campaign Headquarters (CCHQ) with interest, cheering when Ed won. Usually, party leaderships bluff about who they fear on the opposite benches. In 2001, Labour briefed that Michael Portillo was the Tory leadership candidate they feared, when in fact it was Ken Clarke. But according to a senior Conservative Cabinet minister, the Tories had genuinely feared a David Miliband victory and were delighted when the Labour leadership result was announced.[32] On top of this, the breakdown of the result – Ed's victory on the back of union votes – was a perfect gift to the Tories. Baroness Warsi, the party chair, was immediately

authorised to hit the airwaves, highlighting the influential role of
the trade unions, at the same time as Cameron was exchanging
warm words with Ed. For Ed's part, he was struck by how 'posh'
Cameron was on the phone, as he later remarked to his staff.[33]

If David Miliband shared any or all of his angry supporters'
opinions, he did not show it. There is no denying that outwardly
at least, he was magnanimous in defeat, even if his people were
openly enraged and – in the word of one senior member of his
team – 'heartbroken'.[34]

During the blood-letting in the bars, senior MPs in David's
team gathered at an Indian restaurant outside the conference's
secure zone for a curry, organised by Keith Vaz. David said a few
words and graciously thanked his staff. He did not encourage any
recriminations.

Douglas Alexander, his campaign chief, was sitting by David,
and after the meal – at about 11.30pm – he reached for his phone
to discover that Ed had texted him half an hour earlier asking for
a meeting. Alexander made his way to the leader's suite of the
Midland Hotel where Ed was now based. The two of them talked
for forty-five minutes, as a conscious first step towards rekindling
the friendship that had been broken by Alexander's decision to
back David. At this point, Ed's mind was turning to his leader's
speech on the Tuesday. Alexander agreed to help.[35]

ooooo

During the next two and a half days Ed focused on his first speech
as leader of the party. His aides, Greg Beales and James Morris,
had sequestered themselves in a room to work on the text, which
they had begun preparing a week earlier in London. As they
hunched over a computer screen until the early hours, fuelled with
caffeine, Ed invited various allies to come in and offer their input
– Hilary Benn, John Denham, Sadiq Khan, Chuka Ummuna and
Jon Trickett, among others. Significantly, he also brought in several
supporters of his brother, notably Philip Collins, the former Blair
speechwriter and *Times* columnist. Collins made one significant change to the structure of the speech, moving the personal
passage on Ed's childhood and parents, which had originally been
in the middle of the address, to the start. Collins understood the

importance of Ed's back-story and the impact it would make to begin with the wartime experiences of Ralph and Marion. Another invitee from his elder brother's camp was Alexander, who had worked on the draft of the speech that David had planned to give had he won, and who now went through Ed's draft speech line by line, making suggestions. In between sessions in front of the computer, Ed was on the phone consulting friends and colleagues. At one point he amused his staff by ringing Ted Sorensen, former speechwriter to President John F. Kennedy, leaving a message saying he would like Sorensen to check over a draft of his leader's speech. Sorensen didn't call back.

He had to, as the cliché goes, give the speech of his life. The sheer number of people involved in the drafting, offering input and advice, as well as conflicting opinions on the tone they believed Ed should strike, left the new leader exasperated. At one stage, he turned to one of his advisers and said: 'Let Miliband be Miliband.'[36] The line was a reference to a famous episode of one of his favourite US television shows *The West Wing*, in which the fictional, liberal President, Josiah 'Jed' Bartlet, is confronted by an aide who challenges him to act boldly and 'raise the level of public debate'. 'You have a strategy for all this?' asks the President. The aide's response is to scrawl a note on a legal pad: 'Let Bartlet be Bartlet.'

Overall, the speechwriting process was as bitty as it was intense. Because of the endless round of receptions hosted by party factions – which Ed was expected to attend – and media organisations looking for sound bites from the newly-crowned Leader of the Opposition, there were prolonged moments of panic amid the core speechwriting group on the Sunday and the Monday.

One of the conference events, which graphically demonstrated the chaotic atmosphere in Manchester that weekend, was a reception for David's 'Movement for Change'. The crowd was largely made up of David's supporters, and not for the first time Ed and his people felt like uninvited guests at a party. Posters emblazoned with David Miliband's name had been hurriedly taken down, but some could be seen scrunched up under seats.[37]

It is impossible to know for sure whether David had believed he had won before the result was revealed. The decision to go to Manchester in casual clothes, which some see as significant, could be interpreted as a sign of confidence – or as a normal element of a weekend train journey from London to Manchester. What is not in doubt is that elements of his team, aided by the party machine, were expecting a David victory. This is partly demonstrated by the collective exodus of party workers from backstage after the result. But there are two other key pieces of evidence. Following the result on the Saturday, members of Ed's entourage found, when they tried to check into hotel rooms around the leader's suite, that some of them had been booked in advance by David's people – seemingly in anticipation of a victory for the elder, and not the younger, Miliband. (There is no evidence, however, that these hotel bookings were organised by party personnel.)

Secondly, on the Sunday, Ed's team were bemused to find that around twenty advertisements for Labour Party jobs had been published in the official conference newspaper – without any consultation with the new leader or his team. This, it seems, had been organised by a combination of David's aides and party officials. An annoyed Lucy Powell promptly ordered that the ads be pulled.

As this was happening Ed was appearing on Andrew Marr's BBC One interview show, broadcast live from Manchester. His aides had been alarmed to wake up that morning to headlines screaming 'Red Ed'. The main thrust of his interview was to try to stamp out this impression. He insisted his leadership was 'not about some lurch to the left, absolutely not'.

By now, however, Ed was facing another major issue: what his brother planned to do. David was refusing to comment at this stage on whether or not he would serve in the shadow Cabinet, but he would have to make up his mind by the following Wednesday, when the formal process of frontbench elections would take place. He said he did not want to 'take anything away' from the new leader by drawing attention and speculation to himself.[38] Swiftly however, this would be the only story in town. Ed told Marr that David 'needs time to think about the contribution he can make'. He added: 'I think he can make a very big contribution to British politics.'[39]

The following day, all eyes were on David as he was scheduled to give his official speech as shadow Foreign Secretary. Whatever the faults in behaviour of his more zealous supporters – and there were many – it is universally acknowledged that David Miliband gave an exceptionally gracious, and moving, speech that day. Walking round the stage without notes, with Ed sitting behind to his right, David described the new leader as a 'special person'.

> I've been incredibly honoured and humbled by the support that you have given me. But we have a great new leader and we all have to get behind him. I'm really, really, really proud. I'm so proud of my campaign, I'm so proud of my party, but above all I'm incredibly proud of my brother.
>
> Ed is a special person to me. Now he is a special person to you and our job is to make him a special person for all the British people.
>
> You don't run for the leadership, you don't do anything like that in politics or in life, unless you are 100 per cent committed to winning.
>
> But I've also learned something else in life – you never go in for something, especially something so important, unless you are sure in yourself that you are reconciled to the prospect that you might lose. That's life.[40]

It was reported that during his speech, David's wife Louise was in tears, backstage (though friends of David have denied this to be the case). There is, however, no denying the fact that members of David's inner circle were in an emotional state throughout the party conference in Manchester. At one point a despondent Lisa Tremble bumped into Polly Billington. Billington was about to say something to try and console her when Tremble intervened: 'Don't be nice to me yet.'[41]

In a later passage in David's speech, he had the whole hall – including his brother – laughing. 'So to those of you who have been coming up to me in the last few days – don't worry, I'll be fine,' he said, adding that there was one thing he could do without. David described how at a reception for the USDAW union some- one had come up to him and exclaimed: '"Ed, congratulations on your victory!" I can do without that.'

Keeping up the show of humour, David joked about the amount of work that had gone into his preparations for victory.

'As it happens, on my computer in a couple of files marked

"Saturday, version seven" and "Tuesday, version twenty-three", it just so happens I've got a couple of speeches to draw on this morning. But don't worry; I'm not going to give them!'[42]

As the brothers embraced on the stage, at the end of the speech, Ed jokingly asked David if he could have a copy of version twenty-three. But his attempt to lighten the mood failed to hide the fact that their relationship had been irrevocably altered. David aides who heard of the exchange later were appalled. 'He just didn't get it,' said one of Ed.

ooooo

By Tuesday morning Ed's own speech was finally ready. The text was set up on the autocue and sent to the party's press office.

In the leader's suite, Ed was remarkably calm. He had had a number of moments of doubt over the years, and even some friends concede he is prone to bouts of anxiety and indecision. But since declaring his candidacy, Ed had never looked back. If there was an act of fratricide, it was standing against David, not beating him. He had always believed he would win, and that he offered something distinctive from David. Now the time had come to show his distinctiveness, to show his party and the public that Labour was entering a new and different era.

Entering the conference hall to Vampire Weekend's 'A-Punk', and prepared to address conference for the first time as leader, Ed was probably more relaxed than most of his predecessors had been before their inaugural speech as Labour leader. 'He was as cool as a cucumber,' says Sue Nye, who had seen Smith, Kinnock and Brown prepare for such speeches.[43]

During the delivery, too, Ed was confident, calm, himself. One of his oldest friends, Marc Stears, was at home in Oxford watching the speech on television. 'The amazing thing watching him was that he's exactly the same as he was when we were students. It's bizarre – the same mannerisms, the same demeanour. It took my breath away.'[44]

Ed began by drawing a line under New Labour. 'Conference, I stand here today ready to lead: a new generation is now leading Labour. Be in no doubt. The new generation of Labour is different. Different attitudes, different ideas, different ways of doing politics.'

Then Ed told his own story, drawing on his parents' past.

In 1940, my grandfather, with my Dad, climbed onto one of the last boats out of Belgium. They had to make a heart breaking decision – to leave behind my grandmother and my father's sister. They spent the war in hiding, in a village sheltered by a brave local farmer. Month after month, year upon year, they lived in fear of the knock at the door.

At the same time, on the other side of Europe, my mother, aged five, had seen Hitler's army march into Poland. She spent the war on the run, sheltering in a convent and then with a Catholic family that took her in. Her sister, her mother and her. My love for this country comes from this story. Two young people fled the darkness that had engulfed the Jews across Europe and in Britain they found the light of liberty. They arrived with nothing. This country gave them everything... The gift my parents gave to me and David are the things I want for every child in this country. A secure and loving home. Encouragement and the aspiration to succeed.

There was of course a sense among David's supporters in the hall that their man would have delivered a similar passage.

Ed then broadened the speech out, thanking the party faithful, many of whom had not in fact voted for him. 'I am so honoured that you chose me to lead your party and I know you share those values. And I am proud that every day, day in and day out, in every village, and every town and city in the land, you work to put those values into practice.'

On the general election result however, there were no platitudes. 'But let's face facts. We had a bad result. We had a very bad result.' In answer to Alastair Campbell's devastating claim that Ed would make Labour 'comfortable' with losing, the new leader went on: 'Let me tell you, there is nothing good about opposition. Every day out of power is another day when this coalition can wreak damage on our communities, another day when we cannot change our country for the better.'

So far, the conference was broadly united in their applause. Ed moved on to a recurring campaign theme: the need for 'painful truths' about what went wrong with New Labour.

You remember. We began as restless and radical. Remember the spirit of 1997, but by the end of our time in office we had lost our way…I tell you, I believe that Britain is fairer and stronger than it was thirteen years ago. But we have to ask, how did a party with such a record lose five million votes between 1997 and 2010? It didn't happen by accident. The hard truth for all of us in this hall is that a party that started out taking on old thinking became the prisoner of its own certainties.

Then, in the clearest critique of Labour in office, and in a passage that ended with him distancing himself from the hubris of his former mentor, Gordon Brown, he said:

Let me say to the country: You saw the worst financial crisis in a generation, and I understand your anger that Labour hadn't changed the old ways in the City of deregulation. You wanted your concerns about the impact of immigration on communities to be heard, and I understand your frustration that we didn't seem to be on your side. And when you wanted to make it possible for your kids to get on in life, I understand why you felt that we were stuck in old thinking about higher and higher levels of personal debt, including tuition fees.

You saw jobs disappear and economic security undermined – I understand your anger at a Labour government that claimed it could end boom and bust.

After a reference to the diminishing effect of the expenses scandal on politics as a whole, Ed echoed his former leadership rival Andy Burnham's key campaign theme of New Labour as an out-of-touch elite. 'We came to look like a new establishment in the company we kept, the style of our politics and our remoteness from people.'

With repeated references to the 'new generation', Ed rattled through passages on the need for a fresh approach to banks and finance, to civil liberties, and – in particular – to crime. In a passage that delighted liberals and angered Blairites, he said:

'When I disagree with the government, as on the deficit, I will say so loud and clear and I will take the argument to them. But when Ken Clarke says we need to look at short sentences in prison because of high re-offending rates, I'm not going to say he's soft on crime. When Theresa May says we should review stop and search laws to prevent excessive use of state power, I'm not going to say she is soft on terrorism.'

Switching tack, Ed sounded a tough note on the trade unions, who many in the hall felt had put him there. He had considered addressing directly the issue of the awkward breakdown of the result, eventually deciding on a more balanced approach instead:[45]

> Responsible trade unions are part of a civilised society, every democratic country recognises that. But all of us in this movement bear a heavy responsibility. We want to win an argument about the danger this coalition government poses to our economy and our society. To do so we must understand the lessons of our own history too. We need to win the public to our cause and what we must avoid at all costs is alienating them and adding to the book of historic union failures. That is why I have no truck, and you should have no truck, with overblown rhetoric about waves of irresponsible strikes. The public won't support them. I won't support them. And you shouldn't support them either.

In the audience, Unite's Derek Simpson – whose union backed Ed Miliband – looked on stony faced. Next to him, Len McCluskey – who would later succeed Simpson and Tony Woodley as general secretary of Britain's biggest union – shouted 'Rubbish', and a row of unimpressed union leaders refused to clap.

Neil Kinnock's spectacular denunciation of the far-left Militant Tendency in 1985 – when Derek Hatton walked out of the conference hall – this was not. But it was a significant statement, nonetheless. A moment of controversy was still to come, however, on foreign policy.

> We are the generation that came of age at the end of the Cold War. The generation that was taught that the end of history had arrived and then saw 9/11 shatter that illusion.
>
> And we are the generation that recognises that we belong to a global community: we can't insulate ourselves from the world's problems. For that reason, right now this country has troops engaged in Afghanistan. They represent the very best of our country...

Then came the key, and provocative, admission:

> But just as I support the mission in Afghanistan as a necessary response to terrorism, I've got to be honest with you about the lessons of Iraq.
>
> Iraq was an issue that divided our party and our country. Many sincerely believed that the world faced a real threat. I criticise nobody faced with making the toughest of decisions and I honour our troops who fought, and died, there.
>
> But I do believe that we were wrong – wrong to take Britain to war – and we need to be honest about that.
>
> Wrong because that war was not a last resort, because we did not build sufficient alliances and because we undermined the United Nations.

Referring to Barack Obama, Ed declared that 'America has drawn a line under Iraq and so must we.'

As Ed soaked up the applause from a Labour Party thirsty for so long to move on from this foreign policy disaster, he had no idea what had happened to his left.

In an exchange that with the help of the media's lip-reading skills would soon be all over the airwaves, overshadowing the speech, David Miliband had engaged in an extraordinary exchange with Harriet Harman. When Ed first referred to Iraq as 'wrong', he had received prolonged applause from the audience, and from some – but far from all – senior Labour politicians on the platform. One of those clapping was Harriet Harman. David Miliband had looked on blank-faced during Ed's Iraq passage. Now he turned to a grinning Harman and said, 'Why are you clapping? You voted for it.' Harman did not falter, kept smiling and replied: 'I'm clapping because I'm supporting him.'[46]

At the time, nobody actually listening to the speech on the floor was aware of this brief dispute, and the moment quickly passed. But it would have major implications for the future of the Labour shadow Cabinet.

In a passage on multilateralism that Ed was determined to keep in during the drafting, Labour's first Jewish leader decided to take a much clearer line against Israel than his predecessors who had tended to just reiterate the need for a 'Palestinian state' alongside a 'secure Israel' and then moved on. Ed declared:

> There can be no solution to the conflicts of the Middle East without international support, providing pressure where it is needed, and pressure where it is right to do so.
>
> And let me say this, as Israel ends the moratorium on settlement building, I will always defend the right of Israel to exist in peace and security. But Israel must accept and recognise in its actions the Palestinian right to statehood. That is why the attack on the Gaza flotilla was so wrong. And that is why the Gaza blockade must be lifted and we must strain every sinew to work to make that happen. The government must step up and work with our partners in Europe and around the world to help bring a just and lasting peace to the Middle East.

The Manchester-based *Jewish Telegraph* would later describe Ed as the first potential British Prime Minister who could not be deemed 'a friend of Israel'.[47]

Ed went on to call for reform to the House of Commons, to fix a 'broken' politics, and paid tribute to the achievements of 'Tony and Gordon'. He ended with a rousing, almost Blair-esque, peroration:

> We are the optimists in politics today. So, let's be humble about our past. Let's understand the need to change. Let's inspire people with our vision of the good society. Let the message go out, a new generation has taken charge of Labour – optimistic about our country, optimistic about our world, optimistic about the power of politics. We are the optimists and together we will change Britain.[48]

As expected, Ed received a standing ovation from the party's grass-roots for his first set-piece speech as party leader. He exited the hall to another indie hit, Kings Of Leon's 'Use Somebody', stopping off to greet Gillian Duffy, the lady at the centre of the 'Bigotgate' row, who had been strategically placed in his route by his aides.[49]

However, in yet another demonstration of the lingering bitterness and division within Labour after the recent result, there was further controversy to come.

Understandably, one member of the audience who was especially delighted with the speech was Neil Kinnock, who had first urged Ed to run in March. He felt, especially on Iraq and the economy, that Ed had at last broken free of some of the more conservative elements of New Labour thinking. Kinnock, ever an emotional man, was grinning broadly and on his feet when from behind him he heard a voice from the crowd. 'Neil, we've got our party back!' said an excited trade union delegate. Kinnock explains now:

> I responded by saying that we had never actually lost it. We have party members, not owners. That's been a theme of mine for forty years, particularly in the [Tony] Benn and Blair years.[50]

Later that evening, Kinnock re-told the story at a Tribune rally. Unfortunately for him, he now says, it was misreported, giving the impression that it had been the former Labour leader himself who had used the phrase. The phrase 'We've got our party back' came to symbolise for die-hard David supporters the self-destructive nature of Ed's candidacy and campaign for the leadership: in their eyes, it seemed to appeal to a streak in the party that preferred the 1980s-style ideological purity of Old Labour in opposition to the power and authority exercised by New Labour in office in the nineties and noughties. Madlin Sadler confronted Glenys Kinnock demanding to know why her husband had said such a thing – and refused to believe the latter's denial.[51]

As Wednesday dawned, the deadline for those standing for the shadow Cabinet elections loomed. But behind the scenes, Ed had an important and bold decision to make. From the moment he planned to stand for the leadership, Ed had – like David – been thinking about who would serve as Labour's chief whip and maintain party discipline in opposition. He was determined to get rid of the incumbent, Nick Brown. Brown had for years been one of Gordon Brown's most loyal and aggressive enforcers. Mistrusted by the Blairites, he was seen as having been responsible for some of the worst briefings against Blair, Mandelson and other perceived 'enemies' of Brown.

Nick Brown arrived at the conference oblivious of what was to come. Getting off the lunchtime train from Euston on the

Saturday of the result, he told one journalist off the record that he would definitely be staying on as chief whip 'whatever happens'.[52] So he was surprised to receive a call on Wednesday morning asking him to see Ed in the leader's suite. Minutes after their meeting, he found himself writing to the leader. 'As you know I intended to stand for election as chief whip. During our meeting earlier today you indicated that you wished me not to do so. The chief whip must have the full confidence of the party leader. I fully respect your wishes and will no longer be standing for the position.'[53]

Ed replied: 'As we discussed, the election of a new leader is a time for a fresh start and that's why I am grateful to you for agreeing to step aside as chief whip.'[54] It was a decisive show of strength from the new leader that confounded – and delighted – many of his critics on the Blairite wing of the party.

ooooo

Speculation was feverish over whether David would stand for the shadow Cabinet, and therefore serve under his younger brother. But most of those who knew David could sense he would not. After the Harman incident, now playing big on the rolling news, Lisa Tremble told a member of Ed's team that such episodes were evidence of why he could not stay on.[55]

David's instinct was to get out of it all. His wife Louise was determined that he should do so. He was still in shock, and needed time to recharge his batteries. It would be damaging to both Ed and him for his every move to be monitored by the media for signs of disloyalty or dissent in the way it had during Ed's speech.

The one positive aspect of the whole sorry business was that he could spend some time with his wife and two young sons after a long, gruelling and bitter campaign against his brother. After brief deliberation, he informed Ed that he was set to stand down. Reflecting his unwillingness to acknowledge the rift between them, Ed urged him to reconsider; he had wanted David as his shadow Chancellor. But it was to no avail.

Back in London, David issued the following statement:

> The party needs a fresh start from its new leader, and I think that is more likely to be achieved if I make a fresh start. This

has not been an easy decision, but, having thought it through and discussed it with family and friends, I am absolutely confident it is the right decision for Ed, for the party, and for me and the family.

Any new leader needs time and space to set his or her own direction, priorities and policies. I believe this will be harder if there is constant comparison with my comments and position as a member of the shadow Cabinet. This is because of the simple fact that Ed is my brother, who has just defeated me for the leadership.[56]

Stepping outside his home in a faintly bizarre floral shirt, David smiled for the cameras, less wholeheartedly perhaps than his wife beside him. They gave a brief photo call before David went inside and conducted a series of interviews with the major broadcasters, explaining his decision to withdraw to the backbenches. Never once did he slip into anything that could be interpreted as an attack on Ed, nor did he attack the electoral system that by now he had concluded was to blame for a wrong turn by Labour. The only line that betrayed his frustrations, as he could feel his political obituaries being prematurely written, was: 'I am not dead.'[57]

Ed, on the other hand, was feeling very much alive.

LEADER OF THE OPPOSITION

SEPTEMBER 2010–

He had done it. Against the odds, he had become the twentieth leader of the Labour Party; Ed was now in charge of Her Majesty's Opposition. Returning from the party conference in Manchester, he rang a childhood friend. 'How does it feel?' asked the friend. 'You have to pinch yourself,' replied the new Labour leader.[1]

Publicly he was, as ever, calm and cool. Just weeks after his first general election victory, in May 1997, Tony Blair had visited his wealthy friend Michael Levy at his home in north London. Standing on Levy's tennis court, out of earshot of his security detail, the exuberant Blair jumped up and down, yelling: 'I really did it. Can you believe it? I'm the Prime Minister! I'm the Prime Minister!'[2]

Ed, of course, has always been a less excitable figure than Blair. 'He's not the sort of person to be jumping up and down going "Yeah",' says a former girlfriend. 'You're more likely to find him thinking through his next move.'[3]

His 'next move' revolved around formulating a coherent strategy with which to challenge the Conservative–Liberal Democrat coalition government. It wasn't just Ed who had been a beneficiary of the summer-long Labour leadership campaign. David Cameron, Nick Clegg and the coalition Cabinet had spent the previous four months rolling out radical reforms to the NHS, the school system and the welfare state, as well as the biggest cuts to public spending in a generation, while the opposition, leaderless and directionless, had turned inwards and preferred to obsess over the melodrama of the Miliband brothers. Despite the best efforts of the acting leader, Harriet Harman, to hold the government to account with a series of impressive performances at the despatch box at Prime Minister's Questions each week, the Labour Party itself had been 'in a form of cryogenic suspension'.[4]

Upon becoming Leader of the Opposition on 25 September, therefore, Ed had one obvious and pressing task: to reinvigorate and refocus a lacklustre opposition and take the fight to David Cameron and the coalition government.

But the new Labour leader hit the ground walking, rather than running. His was a slow and subdued start – as even his supporters have since conceded.

Several factors conspired to blunt Ed's initial impact on the political village of Westminster, as well as on the media and the wider British public. The first related to his preparedness for the top job. Insurgents, almost by definition, tend not to be ready to rule. Ed's own team, says a close ally, 'had a plan for beating David and winning the leadership election but they didn't have a plan for what they would do once they'd won. David and his people had a much more developed plan for the party. I'm not saying it was the right plan but they had one.'[5]

A similar criticism is voiced by a well-connected supporter of Ed's brother: 'The Labour Party spent four months without a clear message during the leadership campaign, and then another two or three months without a clear message as Ed tried to put his team in place. David would have rolled out "the plan".'[6] (The elder Miliband reportedly kept 'a copy [of his plan] on his phone to consult, like a kind of leadership app'.[7])

The problem for Ed wasn't just a lack of a 'plan' but a lack of adequate and experienced staff. 'He had a very small team, some of them quite junior, all of them working eighteen-hour days to begin with,' says a friend of the Labour leader.[8] Some of his aides, struggling to make the transition from campaign mode to leadership mode, now admit they felt like 'square pegs in round holes'.[9]

Ed and his team also had a recalcitrant and sullen party machine and personnel to contend with. Reports have suggested Ray Collins, the party's outgoing general secretary, had backed David, and not Ed, and was subsequently guilty of 'shoring up the party machine against the Labour leader'.[10] Others in the Ed camp have pointed the finger at Roy Kennedy, the party's former director of compliance, and his wife Alicia Kennedy, Labour's deputy general secretary, also rumoured to be David backers and accused of dragging their feet in the wake of Ed's victory.[11] No hard evidence has been produced, however, and Collins and the Kennedys have denied the claims.

'We were left seriously under-supported by Victoria Street,' says a senior member of Team Ed, referring to the party headquarters at 39 Victoria Street, London.[12] Meanwhile, Ed's entourage arrived at the Leader of the Opposition's suite of offices on the top floor of the Norman Shaw South parliamentary building, across the road from the House of Commons, to find the lights not working and the computers not set up. 'It was a very difficult first few weeks. We felt like outsiders in our own palace; we weren't a fully-functioning team with a fully-functioning office.'[13]

Then, of course, there was the matter of another major party vote to deal with: elections for Labour's shadow Cabinet – the first since 1996 – had been scheduled to be held less than a fortnight after Ed's own victory in the leadership contest. (In opposition, the PLP elects the shadow Cabinet from among its number.)

The results of the shadow Cabinet elections, in which forty-nine candidates stood for the nineteen elected posts on offer, were announced on the evening of 7 October, just hours after the ballot closed. In a separate but simultaneous vote, MP Rosie Winterton was elected unopposed as chief whip, having been encouraged to stand by Ed himself after the defenestration of Nick Brown. But the rest of the results were a disappointment for the new leader and his inner circle. None of the MPs who came in the top ten had voted for Ed in the leadership election; the top three MPs were all members of Team Balls – Yvette Cooper, John Healey and Balls himself. Overall, just five out of the nineteen successful candidates had been supporters of Ed's leadership bid.

The new Labour leader's predicament, however, was not unprecedented. Thatcher too had found few supporters on her frontbench upon becoming Conservative Party leader, in opposition, in February 1975; her candidacy had been opposed by virtually every member of Ted Heath's shadow Cabinet. Some supporters of Ed were quick to make the comparison between Ed and the Iron Lady, citing a rather apt quote from the first volume of John Campbell's acclaimed biography of Thatcher: 'She was very conscious of the weakness of her political position, a little frightened of her own inexperience and the heavy responsibility which had suddenly been thrown on her, and well aware of the formidable combination of habit, convention and vested interest that was ranged against her.'[14]

But who would be Ed's Willie Whitelaw and help him consolidate his grip on power? The day after the leadership election in Manchester, Alan Johnson had been called in to see Ed. The former Home Secretary didn't shake the new leader's hand or congratulate him, but instead made clear his criticisms of Ed's leadership campaign and insisted that Ed oppose Nick Brown's candidacy for the position of chief whip. He was taken aback to hear his new leader in full healer mode: 'I know you supported David, but you must come in and tell me frankly when you're worried about how things are going.' A few days later, he was pleasantly surprised to see Ed heeding his advice on Nick Brown.[15]

So what role would Johnson play in a Labour Party led by Ed, and not David, Miliband? The former Home Secretary told friendly journalists at the party conference in Manchester that he hoped the new leader would appoint him to shadow the deputy Prime Minister, Nick Clegg, and put him in charge of Labour's constitutional affairs portfolio.[16]

Ed's biggest conundrum, however, was who he should appoint as shadow Chancellor, by far the most important frontbench post in a parliament that would be dominated by debates over the future of the economy and rows over the coalition's cuts to public spending.

The day after the results of the shadow Cabinet elections, Ed stunned the Westminster village by making Johnson, who had never worked in the Treasury, had no background in economics or finance and had shown scant interest in the economy brief, his shadow Chancellor. It was a risky appointment and Johnson himself was lost for words. Trying to make light of his lack of relevant experience, the former Home Secretary joked that his first task would be to 'pick up a primer – "Economics for beginners"'.[17] It was a throwaway line but one that would come to define his brief, gaffe-prone tenure as shadow Chancellor.

Johnson may have had a limited grasp of economics; Ed didn't. In fact, the extent to which the appointment of Johnson was part of a deliberate and conscious decision by the new Labour leader to take charge of the party's economic – and, in particular, fiscal – policy has been supremely underestimated. One of the reasons Tony Blair had outsourced economics to Gordon Brown in opposition and then in government was because of his lack of knowledge and interest in the subject. Ed, on the other hand, had studied economics at Oxford University and the London School of Economics and spent more than seven years working in the Treasury as a special adviser, including his stint as chairman of the Council of Economic Advisers. He was determined to put his own stamp on economic policy.

But what was to be done with Balls, who had had his eye on the job? Ed had briefly considered his old Treasury colleague for the post of shadow Chancellor but as a senior MP who backed Balls in the leadership race puts it: 'People were saying to Ed Miliband, "Look, you might be able to make it work for a bit but you're going to wake up in ten years, in Downing Street, as Prime Minister, with a madman living next door".'[18]

The other Ed was given the job of shadow Home Secretary. Asked by the BBC whether he was surprised at being handed the home affairs, rather than the Treasury, portfolio, a frustrated Balls replied 'yes' before adding quickly: 'The most important thing is not who's doing what job, but winning the argument.'

It was an unconvincing answer. With Labour languishing in opposition, Balls longed to be shadow Chancellor – just as he had longed to replace Alistair Darling as Chancellor of the Exchequer when Labour was in government.[19] At times during the summer, Balls's campaign for the Labour leadership had felt more like a pitch for the job of shadow Chancellor. The man himself, once described as the 'deputy Chancellor', believed he had done enough to prove his economic credentials during the protracted leadership contest – his speech on deficit reduction at Bloomberg on 27 August 2010, for example, had been hailed not just by centre-left commentators in *The Guardian* and *The Independent*, but by centre-right commentators in *The Times* and the *Financial Times*. His supporters in the PLP had been lobbying for weeks for him to be rewarded with the shadow chancellorship and, by October, even past critics of Balls's so-called statist and bureaucratic approach, like the influential MP Jon Cruddas, had called for him to be made Labour's chief spokesman on the economy.[20]

Ed determinedly ignored these calls, opting for Johnson instead. The priority, given the closeness of the result, 'was to show that I was building a balanced team'. Plus, he says, the former Home Secretary was one of the party's 'best communicators and most experienced performers'.[21] Privately, Balls was fuming. 'I didn't agree with it,' Balls later confessed. 'I wasn't annoyed or disappointed, but I thought it was a mistake. And I said that to Ed.'[22] Some say Balls refused to speak to Johnson at shadow Cabinet meetings[23] – a claim the other Ed flatly denies.

That Ed was able to dispense with the services of Nick Brown in his first few days as leader, and then resist the pressure to appoint Ed Balls to the most high-profile job in the shadow Cabinet in his first few weeks, surprised his critics and spoke volumes about the nature and style of his leadership. First, he couldn't be caricatured by his critics as an unreconstructed Brownite, a card-carrying member of the Brown gang. Second, his ruthlessness and steeliness clearly extended beyond his decision to challenge his brother for the Labour leadership. He was his own man, making his own decisions.

But it didn't all go Ed's way. Mrs Balls, aka Yvette Cooper, had been offered the shadow business portfolio by Ed but angrily refused, demanding that her former flatmate give her the opportunity to shadow one of the 'Great Offices of State' – the Treasury, the Home Office or the Foreign Office. Cooper had topped the shadow Cabinet poll, forty votes ahead of the second-placed candidate, John Healey. A reluctant Ed then gave her the job of shadow Foreign Secretary. (Later, Cooper rung Ed to say she might be willing to reconsider – but it was too late. By then, Ed had already appointed his friend and ally John Denham to the post of shadow Business Secretary.)[24]

A party leader's power of patronage is a double-edged sword – Ed had to ensure his appointments satisfied the various and conflicting factions, interests and personalities in his disoriented parliamentary party. Unsurprisingly, he made a 'strenuous effort to court David's people', says a senior Labour MP and supporter of Ed Balls. 'He was, for example, very conscious that he needed to give Jim Murphy a big job.'[25] Murphy, who had co-chaired the David campaign, was appointed shadow Defence Secretary. David's other co-chair, Douglas Alexander, became shadow Work and Pensions Secretary.

Ed had originally wanted Andy Burnham, his former leadership rival, to take on the job of chief whip – the ex-Health Secretary, understandably annoyed and affronted having gone through the trials of the leadership campaign, turned him down. Ed then cleverly moved Burnham to education, despite the latter wanting to keep his health portfolio, or move to shadow Home Secretary. The new leader stressed to his former rival the importance of having different people in the various frontbench posts – or as a conciliatory Burnham puts it: 'If people are in their old government jobs, they end up defending their old positions.'[26]

Other appointments were less high-profile but no less interesting or important: Jon Trickett, the backbencher and former Compass chair who had played such an influential role in Ed's leadership campaign, despite his first-preference vote for Ed Balls, was made shadow minister of state for the Cabinet Office, and invited to attend shadow Cabinet meetings. Ed's key ally Peter Hain, who had failed to get elected to the shadow Cabinet after falling three votes short of an automatic place, was nonetheless appointed by Ed as shadow Welsh Secretary and chair of Labour's National Policy Forum (where he replaced the ex-Blair aide and David supporter, Pat McFadden). Diane Abbott, the other defeated leadership candidate and a serial critic of previous party leaders, was appointed to the Labour frontbench for the first time, as shadow public health minister and number two to the new shadow Health Secretary, John Healey.

Keen to show his party and the press that his commitment to a 'new generation' was more than a rhetorical device, Ed also broke with Westminster tradition and awarded junior shadow ministerial roles to a third of his party's sixty-six newly elected MPs – promoting, among others, former TV journalist Gloria De Piero (culture), ex-Downing Street press spokesman John Woodcock (transport) and economist Rachel Reeves (work and pensions). He made Chuka Umunna his parliamentary private secretary (PPS). (Umunna has since been promoted to the frontbench as a shadow business minister working under John Denham; Ed appointed Michael Dugher, the Balls supporter, as Umunna's replacement).

But in the leader's own back office, there were still gaps in personnel to be filled, chief among them the role of 'chief of staff'. Lucy Powell had been the 'acting' chief of staff since Ed's election but, despite praise for her role as a tenacious campaign manager, she proved less popular in her new role. There was grumbling inside the PLP that Ed hadn't gone for a bigger figure: 'Where's his Jonathan Powell?'[27] Others worried about her centrist political views. 'She's never done a job like this,' says one of Ed's aides. 'And the really weird thing about Lucy is that she works in this senior role in Ed Miliband's office but she doesn't even remotely share Ed Miliband's politics.'[28]

To the horror of some on the Labour left, it soon emerged that the runners and riders for the post of chief of staff were even more to the right of Ed than Powell. The new leader was reaching out to the Blairites. First, he approached James Purnell to fill the role. But the former Blair aide and supporter of David, who dramatically quit Gordon Brown's Cabinet in June 2009 and then stood down from Parliament in May 2010, turned him down in November 2010.[29] Then, in January 2011 and though his spin doctors would later try and deny this, Ed approached Charlie Falconer, the former Lord Chancellor, and another close ally of Tony Blair and David Miliband. Their discussions hit a brick wall when both men agreed that Falconer lacked the organisational skills required to be an effective chief of staff.[30] The former Lord Chancellor, however, remains one of the few leading Blairites publicly to sing Ed's praises and endorse him as a Prime-Minister-in-waiting. 'He is very impressive,' says Falconer, adding: 'The difference between Tony [Blair] and Ed is that Ed became leader in a post-election landscape that was unfavourable to him, whereas Tony became leader of Labour in a pre-election landscape that was essentially favourable to him.'[31]

This is perhaps an understatement. The intensity and breadth of the hostility that greeted Ed's victory was astonishing, if perhaps inevitable after the dubious and problematic breakdown of the result. Some of it was driven by resentment and anger from disgruntled supporters of David, fuelled by sniping from the ultra-Blairites who had never even believed David, let alone Ed, was committed enough to their version of 'modernisation'. Allies of Ed – who had promised his supporters during the campaign that he would be a 'new broom'[32] ready to sweep away New Labour's dinosaurs – believe that this coalition of interests (David supporters and ultra-Blairites) could not handle the fact that it was no longer in charge of the party, and it wasn't going to take the defeat lying down. 'I think we all might have underestimated the people around David,' says a close friend and political ally of Ed.[33]

Much of the rest of the hostility consisted of a cynical and crude attempt by the right-wing press – led by the Murdoch-owned papers – to paint Ed as a left-wing radical, an Old Labour throwback: 'Red Ed.'

Labour leaders, especially in opposition, have long faced dispro-portionate hostility from the press, the centre of gravity of which is to the right. Think Michael Foot and the mythical 'donkey jacket'. Think Neil Kinnock, the 'Welsh windbag'.

Ed had to endure a barrage of media attacks on his character, his personality, his politics, and – perhaps more justifiably – his links to the unions and his style of leadership. 'Ed Miliband faces being sucked down the plughole,' opined the *Daily Mail*.[34] 'No style, no substance,' declaimed the *Daily Telegraph*.[35] 'Time for Miliband to show us the beef,' said the *Sunday Times*.[36]

'I think that you'll always get the sort of ultra-Blairites, the über-Blairites sniping away because they've got their friends in the media and it suits the media to write this stuff,' says a shadow Cabinet minister who backed Ed in the leadership election.[37]

'From the very beginning, the media narrative was that Ed is going to be a disaster as leader. Why? Because the political journal-ists had all been on the side of David and had all told their editors David was going to win,' says a close friend of Ed. Therefore, argues the friend, they had to set about proving how right they had been, regardless of the result. David became Labour's lost leader; Ed became the illegitimate incumbent struggling to get going.[38]

Meanwhile, the newspaper headlines became increasingly detached from reality. 'Plotters give Ed Miliband until May to prove himself,' declared a headline in the *Evening Standard* on 8 December, less than a hundred days into his leadership, quoting an anonymous Labour MP saying: 'Ed is running out of time to define himself to voters'.[39]

ooooo

Bizarrely, the issue which had brought most of the criticisms to a head was his decision to take paternity leave less than two months after becoming party leader.

On the evening of 7 November 2010, Justine gave birth to their second child, Samuel Stewart Thornton Miliband – named after Ed's grandfather (Samuel) and Justine's father (Stewart) – at UCL Hospital in London. A new pair of Miliband brothers had been formed – their eldest, Daniel, was, by this stage, eighteen months old. Ed and Justine released a statement saying they were 'over-joyed' by their son's birth, and the Labour leader announced he would be taking his two weeks' statutory paternity leave.

The issue of Ed's family life was sensitive territory. He had already faced criticisms for failing to turn up with Justine for the registration of their first child's birth. This, combined with cover-age over the ownership of his house being in Justine's name only led to claims about his lack of organisation and even allegations of commitment-phobia – and, of course, they were not yet married.

On the birth certificate claim, Ed has said: 'It was a mess up on our part. No – it was a mess up on my part.' And he said of his latest child's birth: 'I will be going down to the Register Office straight away this time.'[40]

Ed had admitted he was 'embarrassed' that his name wasn't on Daniel's birth certificate. On the issue of paternity leave however, Ed was in a seemingly impossible position. He was damned when he did take it – but would have been damned if he didn't. Nonetheless, the row took its toll. 'He'd gone away thinking he was in a solid position, having had a great first PMQs but then two weeks later he was suddenly on the defensive,' says an aide. 'He contributed to this negative mood in the office and then very quickly realised that we had to mobilise and take on this latest threat.'[41]

But he wasn't just saddened – he was annoyed. What did he have to apologise for? He had done nothing wrong. Asked by an interviewer upon his return to work if he thought his decision to take a fortnight off had been a mistake, he replied: 'Absolutely not! My first duty is to my family. Paternity leave is really important. I think people outside Westminster completely understand that.'

He claimed to be 'relaxed and phlegmatic' about the sniping, arguing that there were 'no quick fixes here – it is going to take time to build a relationship with the public, and I genuinely don't think people judge you on the day-to-day'.[42]

The one advantage of the ultimately trivial row about paternity leave was that it allowed Ed to sidestep a simultaneous row over Phil Woolas, the former minister stripped of his seat after being found guilty of lying about an electoral opponent and making inflammatory claims about ethnic minorities. Ed's aides told him that he had to wait for a legal verdict from the courts but having seen Woolas's offensive election pamphlets Ed should surely not have retained him on the frontbench as a shadow immigration minister. It was a serious error of judgement.

But the media preferred to focus on more minor issues. As a demonstration of Ed's apparent difficult start as leader, he was widely ridiculed by pundits and bloggers, as well as by the Tories, for an interview on the BBC Radio 4's *Today* programme on 26 November 2010, subsequently described, including among some senior Labour figures, as 'disastrous'.[43] The main complaint was that he gave six different definitions of 'the squeezed middle' – the phrase he had been pushing since becoming leader in September, and the group on whose behalf he claimed to be toiling – to interviewer John Humphreys. Sounding hesitant, he stuttered his way through several descriptions: from 'people who are working hard' to 'those not on six-figure salaries, who are in the middle of the income distribution'.

Asked if he meant those on the median income of £26,000, Ed replied: 'Well, I'm a bit confused now; I'm saying it's above £26,000 and below and you're talking about the poor. I'm talking about the people either side. I'm saying it's either side of the average income.'[44]

It was certainly not Ed at his best. But the same media pack that turned on him that day would later adopt the phrase as it seeped into Westminster parlance. 'Labour winning over "squeezed middle" voters,' proclaimed the headline in *The Independent* on 1 March, reporting on a ComRes poll showing Miliband's party leading the Tories among unskilled workers, skilled manual workers and the lower-middle class.[45] Humphreys himself referred to the 'squeezed middle' live on air the day before the Budget, on 22 March. The reality is that the phrase, pushed by Ed and his team since winning the leadership, is one that resonates with voters.

Ed was also attacked for being vague and even flippant in the same *Today* programme interview in November about whether or not he would join a student protest against an increase in university tuition fees. His office eventually said he wouldn't after Ed said in the interview he was 'tempted' to go and meet the protesters, adding, 'We'll see what happens'.

Buried in the interview, Ed did make an important and revealing point about his approach to politics, something that surely neither Blair nor Brown – and possibly not David Miliband – would have said. Pressed on whether his party needed a new 'Clause IV moment', he said that Labour did not lose the general election because it was 'too left-wing'. The unscripted comment gave an all-too-rare glimpse of how Ed, even as leader, could unashamedly define his politics as distinct from the defensive triangulations of New Labour.

Meanwhile, assaults on Ed's authority and credibility during this crucial, early period weren't just coming from anonymous Blairites on his backbenches or Tory-supporting columnists in the press: Ed was being undermined by his own shadow Chancellor too.

Around the time of Alan Johnson's appointment as shadow Chancellor, one of Tony Blair's closest allies explained the thinking behind the appointment as a holding move which gave Ed more time to work out what to do about Ed Balls. 'I think the appointment of Alan was inspired both on its own terms and because Alan is the ideal foil for George Osborne. But it's also unlikely that Alan will be Chancellor in five years time, if we win the next election, so it defers the decision of who'll be Ed's Chancellor and, in that sense, it's an inspired move.'[46]

Except it didn't turn out that way. It became a source of tension from the very first day, with the duo split on graduate tax – Johnson had been a strong supporter of tuition fees in government and wrote an open letter to the new Labour leader the day after his victory urging him not to 'pursue a graduate tax'[47]– and the 50p top rate tax on income.

Ed had made it clear throughout the leadership race that the 50p top rate of income tax should stay in place, saying it was 'not just about reducing the deficit, it's about fairness in our society'.[48]

But in an interview with *The Times* on 13 November 2010, in which he allowed himself to be described as an 'instinctive cutter' and revealed that he preferred to work out of his own office rather than move in next door to the leader's as he had been requested to, Johnson declared: 'I am only backing 50p for the times we are in. It is not ideal; five years ago [we] wouldn't have done it.'[49]

The next day, in a BBC interview, Johnson was again defiant: 'We are working through these issues – on the graduate tax and on the 50p tax rate – and we will provide a considered policy option at the right time. We are not setting all our policies out now.'[50]

Ed's reaction to Johnson's comment is instructive. 'I went to his house the next day,' says a friend, who worked with him in the Treasury, 'and he was very calm about it. Gordon would have literally been throwing things around the room but Ed just rolled his eyes and said: "Can someone call Alan and remind him what our line is?"'[51]

Johnson, however, persisted in his insubordination. On 4 December, Ed penned a comment piece for *The Guardian* in which he said there was a 'strong case for moving towards a graduate tax'. In a *Daily Telegraph* interview with Johnson published on the same day, however, the shadow Chancellor was asked whether he believed such a tax could be implemented. 'Well, I don't think it could [work]. Frankly, there's a difference of view,' he replied, before adding: 'I feel it's going to be very difficult to make a graduate tax a workable proposition.' In the words of interviewer Mary Riddell, his remarks were 'the clearest indication yet of the depth of division' between the shadow Chancellor and the Labour leader.[52]

Johnson, observed a columnist in *The Guardian*, was 'in the unique position of being inside the tent, pissing in'.[53] As even the right-wing, anti-Ed *Spectator* noted: 'Johnson is abusing the trust placed in him: he's a canny enough politician to know how all these interviews are going to play. Ed Miliband deserves better, much better from his shadow Chancellor.'[54] Meanwhile, other reports in the press suggested Johnson was 'being urged by his supporters to "ready himself" to replace Ed Miliband if the Labour leader succumbed to the growing crisis surrounding the party. The shadow Chancellor is already being talked up as a stand-in leader...'[55]

There was no truth to these reports. If Johnson had wanted to be leader, he would have joined the numerous coup attempts against Gordon Brown ahead of the general election or he would have stood himself for the leadership in the summer of 2010. But the irony was not lost on Ed: he had appointed Johnson not Balls because he and his close allies had worried that the latter would disloyally undermine him. Balls, however, had been loyal and on-message as shadow Home Secretary; it was Johnson who kept rocking the boat.

Then there were the shadow Chancellor's embarrassing gaffes on the economy, which were piling up. He suggested that the coalition's VAT rise would affect food bills, when food VAT seldom affects food; he said Labour would eradicate the structural Budget deficit by 2015, before saying he 'probably' meant 2016; he claimed in a live television interview that employers' National Insurance contribution was going up 'from 20 per cent to 21 per cent' when the correct figures were 12.8 per cent to 13.8 per cent.[56]

Senior Labour figures wondered aloud: was Johnson on top of his brief? Or did he perhaps need that economics primer he'd joked about? 'Alan's a great guy and a good communicator but he is a lazy fucker,' says a former adviser to Gordon Brown.[57] A former shadow Cabinet colleague of Johnson's agrees: 'A. J. just didn't put any effort in.'[58]

In the end, however, it wasn't his incompetence or his insubordination that cost Johnson his job barely three months after he'd started. The shadow Chancellor resigned suddenly on 20 January 2011 citing 'personal issues in my private life'; it subsequently emerged in the press that his wife had been having an affair with Johnson's former police bodyguard.

It came as a shock to Ed. 'He spent several hours just sitting on his own, contemplating what he was going to do,' says a shadow Cabinet minister. 'He was really down.'[59] The Murdoch-owned *Sun* described Johnson's departure, and the associated political sex scandal, as a 'bitter blow for Ed Miliband … after a dire first three months'.

Johnson had informed Ed that he planned to stand down a week before his resignation was publicly announced; Ed and his aides persuaded him to keep the news to himself until they perfected their first reshuffle.

Johnson's personal tragedy was to be Balls's professional gain. The night before Johnson's resignation was revealed, on 19 January, the shadow Home Secretary had been in the midst of a deferred Christmas dinner with former civil service colleagues from the Department of Education at Brown's restaurant near Westminster when he received a text from Lucy Powell: 'Can you meet Ed tonight?' Balls, blissfully ignorant of Johnson's decision to stand down, demurred and tried to reschedule for the next morning before being told 'firmly' in another text from Powell that his presence was required. He left the restaurant for an 8.30pm meeting with Ed at his Commons office, grabbing a cab and not returning to the staff dinner till after 10pm to find his steak cold and congealed.

Balls arrived at Norman Shaw South to discover Ed and Powell waiting for him in the Leader of the Opposition's large, rectangular, wood-panelled office overlooking the Thames. Ed shared with Balls the news of Johnson's resignation and then said he wanted the other Ed to replace him. 'But do you really want this?' asked Balls. 'You have to want this otherwise you shouldn't do it.' Sources close to both Eds have denied there was a Granita-style deal in which conditions were applied or concessions extracted – but it has been suggested that a minute of the meeting was written and circulated among the leader's closest colleagues. Balls told Ed he was willing to sign up to the Darling plan on deficit reduction – that is, halving the Budget deficit over four years. Ed told Balls that the two of them should go away and 'reflect overnight' before making a final decision in the morning.[60]

The next day, as he was being driven up the M1 to Wolverhampton, the Labour leader rang Balls to confirm the appointment. The then shadow Home Secretary was busily preparing to ask an Urgent Question in the chamber on the coalition's counter-terrorism policy, frantically typing out questions on his computer, his office heaving with aides. With less than fifteen minutes to go before his appearance at the Despatch box, and without wanting to let on to his team that he was being promoted to shadow Chancellor, Balls's response to Ed's job offer was brief and blunt: 'Yes, that's great. Fine. Cheers. I'm happy with that.' A confused Ed put the phone down wondering why the other Ed seemed so indifferent to being awarded the job he'd always wanted – it wasn't until an hour later, after he had completed his Urgent Question in the Commons, that Balls called Ed back to explain his earlier and strange behaviour on the phone.[61]

Overnight, Balls became de facto number two to the Labour leader. But inside the party, his appointment provoked an array of positive and negative responses. Some of Balls's former critics have been keen to give him the benefit of the doubt – and even praise Ed's bold appointment of the other Ed.

'Ed Balls seized his opportunity as shadow Home Secretary; he was like a dog with a bone,' says a senior shadow Cabinet minister who believes Balls's tenacity will serve him in good stead over the course of this parliament as Labour's spokesman on the economy.[62]

Elated by the move, the so-called 'dark side' of Balls and his history of negative briefings is now said by some to be a thing of the past. 'Ed Balls is now completely loyal to Ed Miliband' says another shadow Cabinet minister who had been one of Balls's biggest critics until the start of 2011. 'He always name checks Ed in all of his major speeches and interviews.'[63]

That is not to say 'the Balls problem' has totally been put to bed. Others are much more suspicious of the shadow Chancellor and fear Ed may live to regret his promotion of Balls. 'A leopard doesn't change his spots,' says a senior Brownite who worked with both Eds in the Treasury. 'I'm worried about what Balls as shadow Chancellor means for Labour, as Ed's now got to go much further in distancing himself from the past than he might otherwise have done.'[64] A Blairite ex-Cabinet minister, now serving in Ed's shadow Cabinet, say that Balls's colleagues on the Labour frontbench will be 'watching him like a hawk'.[65] In fact, there are MPs and shadow ministers on all wings of the Labour Party who continue to believe that Balls, given his record at the Treasury and beyond, could pose as Ed's biggest challenge in the coming years.

The Labour leader knew from the moment he made the appointment that he could not afford to have the same relationship with Balls that Blair had with Brown. He insisted that his former Treasury colleague report directly to him, with a clear line of accountability; there would be no scenario in which the shadow Chancellor would behave as if he was a co-equal leader.

'We had front-row seats at the Blair–Brown movie and we are not about to repeat it,' Ed said in an interview in April 2011, in which he also referred to Balls as a 'mate'.[66] One would assume that the clever and ambitious Balls, who now says that his 'mission is to get Ed Miliband into Downing Street',[67] surely knows his fortunes in the immediate term, at least, are tied to his leader's.

As Ken Livingstone, who backed Ed Balls over Ed Miliband, puts it: 'Balls knows that if he can win the economic debate against the Tories he will be the number two in the next Labour government.'[68]

'He's got the job he wants: shadow Chancellor. The next job he wants is Chancellor of the Exchequer. If he still harbours any leadership ambitions, then those are a long way down the line, in the distant future,' says a friend of Balls, who adds: 'And if Ed [Balls] is going to ever have any chance in the distant future of becoming leader he has to show that he has been a loyal, team player because the PLP will never again reward someone who behaved as disloyally as Gordon did towards Tony.'[69]

The Blair–Brown analogy isn't right, says one of Ed's closest allies in the shadow Cabinet: 'The difference this time is that there was a leadership election. Ed won. Ed Balls lost.'[70]

Personality issues aside, there is no denying the fact that Balls was the strongest candidate for the job of shadow Chancellor. He is the best-qualified and most experienced economist on the Labour frontbench, with links to the City and the trade unions, and he has, says a senior Labour figure, 'a 24/7 relentlessness with which he can hurt the Tories on the economy'.

Balls, as even his most vociferous critics on the right acknowledge, is a 'ferocious attack dog' and the most 'able fighter' on Labour's frontbench.[71] Since he assumed the role of shadow Chancellor, he has sharpened Labour's economic message and landed blows on George Osborne over the hike in VAT, rising fuel prices and sluggish growth.

The drawbacks of the two Eds leading Labour are obvious, however. Their presence at the top of the party has enabled the Tories to claim the 'sons' of Brown are now in charge of Labour's economic policy, with other 'Brown children' – Cooper, Alexander – also in senior positions on the frontbench. In the words of a *Times* headline: 'Watch out – Gordon's gang are back in town.'[72]

ooooo

By the New Year, Justine was telling friends that she felt Ed had 'grown into the role of leader'.[73] Her own role in providing support, strength and advice should not be underestimated.

Friends say they find the idea of Justine being the wife of a Prime-Minister-in-waiting 'strange' and 'bizarre'. But Justine is signed up to Ed's political project. She has been described as 'the sort of person who gathers information about something, processes it and then works out what she wants to do – then she is decided'.[74] This stands her in good stead as a barrister, but applies equally to her private life. In the early days of her relationship with Ed Miliband, a friend says that the couple never discussed the Labour leadership but 'Justine did expect that he might become a Cabinet minister and be in politics for a long time, and she thought through the pros and cons. She decided that she was willing to make whatever sacrifices were necessary.'[75]

Though she has little to say about the ups and downs of British politics and policy and tends to defer to Ed on such issues, Justine is very much her own person. Like her old Cambridge friend Frances Osborne, wife of George, she is averse to being typecast as a 'political wife'. She is hugely supportive of Ed's career – he has called her 'my best counsel' – but he likewise is genuinely supportive of hers. One friend of Ed and Justine talks about their 'strikingly consensual relationship... It is so equal: neither dominates at all.'[76]

One of Ed's former girlfriends is clear in her mind about the importance of Justine in Ed's life: 'She is essential to him, and to understanding him, because she has grounded him.'[77] Despite her support for his career, however, Justine has also made it clear to friends that she is of a different generation to political wives of yesteryear and, like the deputy Prime Minister Nick Clegg's wife Miriam González Durántez, has no plans to parade around behind Ed.

Friends attest to the changes she has wrought in Ed. 'Justine has definitely had a positive influence [on him], helped humanise him, taken him out of the high-flying economics world and brought him into the real world. He was an urban intellectual, a wonk but she has got him into the countryside, going walking, moving outside his wonk world.'[78]

Meanwhile, domestically, Justine is undoubtedly the organiser and always has been – she handled their move in March 2008 from his flat in Primrose Hill to a spacious house in Dartmouth Park (and, as the press has been keen to point out, it is her name on the house deeds). A friend comments: 'The house looks imposing but it's not glamorous, and it's not a very swanky neighbourhood.' As to Justine's credentials as a domestic goddess: 'She doesn't swan around effortlessly producing three-course meals. She's more likely to be on her way to the kitchen and start a conversation with someone.'[79] Another friend of Justine agrees that 'the striking thing about their home is the normality of it – it's a relaxed, informal family home'.[80] A Labour MP, however, who has visited their home says it is 'a family house but you're not quite sure Ed is the creator of it. It feels like a house he inhabits which has been made by his wife.'[81] Asked by a journalist in 2010 what was on the walls of his new house, Ed replied, 'Something white'.[82]

Perhaps the most important role Justine has played is in supporting Ed through his struggle with David for the Labour leadership. Justine was one of those who supported his decision to stand – 'Life's an adventure. And you've got to seize the day'[83] – and told him he had nothing to be guilty about. Since David's defeat at the hands of Ed in September 2010, Justine herself is believed to have fallen out with David's wife Louise who, only a few years earlier, she had been 'in awe of' over the latter's musical prowess and career success as a violinist. 'Louise has been nasty towards Ed and Justine can't handle that,' says a friend of the couple.[84]

But Justine is also a calming person in Ed's life – especially since he became party leader. 'She encourages him to trust his instincts,' says a friend of hers.[85] A close confidant of Ed says Justine can always be relied upon to reduce her husband's stress, rather than exacerbate it. She is a sensitive person and deeply aware of Ed's emotional state and his need to discuss and reflect on his feelings. Before he met Justine, Ed's world had been a rational, intellectual and political world – Justine helped bring out the emotional and empathetic side that the rest of us have seen in Ed in recent years. As the friend observes: 'She is engaged with his political life but easily his greatest refuge from it too.' Her attitude is 'this is where we are and we'll deal with it'.[86] Another friend has said, 'She's a great political wife, because while everyone is talking, she just gets on with things.'[87]

But Justine has the tough task of being the public figure she never planned or wanted to be. 'While Glenys at least was a political activist,' says Neil Kinnock, a friend of the couple, 'Justine just has a totally normal background.'[88]

ooooo

One of the persistent criticisms of Ed's leadership so far has been his failure to define himself. At a press conference in January 2011, Ed was asked how he would sum himself up. He replied that he was someone who was 'passionate about this country' and stressed the power and importance of politics.[89] It was a weak and unoriginal answer to an important if predictable question.

So far, however, Ed may be held back by his admirable disdain for political stunts. 'You know, I don't think huskies are really the answer,' said Ed in one of his first newspaper interviews as leader, referring to David Cameron's famous decision to be photographed in the Arctic with huskies at the start of his leadership in 2006.[90] 'It was a mistake to say he wouldn't do huskies,' says a former Labour strategist who has known Ed since the 1990s. 'People understand who you are by looking at you rather than reading about you and it drives me mad that I can't think of a single iconic picture of Ed since he's become leader.'[91]

Mischievous critics of the Labour leader have suggested there is such a snap: Ed hugging his defeated brother on stage in Manchester on the day of his leadership victory in September. The perceived void over what Ed stands for risks being filled by a definition probably most recognisable to the public: that he is the man who 'shafted' his brother.

One of the low points of Ed's leadership came on 6 January, when Ed appeared on Jeremy Vine's BBC Radio 2 show. 'What sort of man stands against his own brother?' asked Vine at the outset of the interview before later claiming that 'the only thing they [the public] know about Ed is that he is the guy who shafted his brother'. Among the callers was a former RAF serviceman named Darren who asked the Labour leader: 'What chance do I stand as a person in the country if you're quite happy to tread all over your brother to get to the top?' It was a disastrous broadcast, with caller after caller berating Ed for his refusal to get married, his failure to put his name down on his son's birth certificate and his supposed lack of passion. The only respite for the Labour leader came with the occasional musical interlude.[92]

Ed emerged from the BBC studios psychologically bruised. 'That was the moment that he finally realised that what he'd done to his brother would continue to define him in the eyes of voters for a long time to come,' says a shadow Cabinet ally of David's.[93]

It hasn't just been members of the public – or allies of his brother – who have castigated Ed for his decision to run against David – the Prime Minister and his advisers have also spotted an opportunity to embarrass the Labour leader on this front. At PMQs, Cameron has delighted in dodging Ed's questions and, instead, making not-so-coded references to his elder brother. On 2 March, Ed noted Cameron's tendency to 'ditch a policy and dump a colleague in it' (referring to the Prime Minister's earlier U-turn on the sell-off of state-owned forests and the assigning of blame to the Environment Secretary, Caroline Spelman). Cameron hit back: 'In a minute, he is going to give me a lesson on family loyalty.' A few moments later, he jibed: '[W]hen the Opposition considers the Rt Hon. Gentleman's performance it could be time for a bit of "Brother, where art thou?"'[94]

The following week, at PMQs, when Ed challenged the Prime Minister on his 'silence' over William Hague and the botched SAS incursion into Libya, Cameron responded: 'I think we have an excellent Foreign Secretary. There is only one person around here I can remember knifing a Foreign Secretary and I am looking at him.' The PM went on to loudly quote from a *Times* column by the elder Miliband, in which David had decried the 'deficit of ideas' on the left on the same day he delivered a speech on the decline of the left in Europe to a packed hall at the LSE.[95]

Of course, one obvious area where Ed has had the chance to make an impact in the country, via the nightly news bulletins, is at Prime Minister's Questions – despite the fact that Ed has privately told friends he finds the weekly joust takes up an absurdly disproportionate amount of time and effort, and believes its format should be rethought.

Ed's PMQs preparation team includes his two parliamentary private secretaries, the MPs Anne McGuire and Michael Dugher (and before him, Chuka Umunna). Others who are on hand to help are Ayesha Hazarika, the comedienne and former aide to Harriet Harman who now works as a press officer to the leader, Polly Billington and Bruce Grocott, the former Labour MP and PPS to Tony Blair who now sits in the House of Lords. All contribute, but Ed's trademark way of preparing himself in the final minutes before the sessions is to clear the room and take time on his own to think through his best attack lines.

Ed approached his first PMQs in a more confident and relaxed mood than his predecessors, telling friends he was 'nervous, but not horrifically so'.[96] Taking on David Cameron seemed less daunting than taking on David Miliband. 'Nothing is as difficult as doing a live TV hustings against your brother. People told me that I would be so nervous before Prime Minister's Questions that my legs would be shaking but, let me tell you, it is less awkward to debate with David Cameron than it is to debate with David Miliband. Not least because I don't love David Cameron,' he later remarked.[97]

Ed made a solid start to PMQs, striking a measured and mature tone, and focusing on the 'fairness' of the coalition government's cuts to child benefit – but even a sympathetic commentator couldn't help but notice that 'his voice is still slow, and his lisp seems to be exaggerated by the Commons microphones'.[98] To make matters worse, *The Times* published a briefing memo that was either leaked or – some of his team suspect – stolen from his unlocked suite of offices in the Norman Shaw South wing of the parliamentary estate.

He was told to develop 'cheer lines' to help to secure a slot on broadcast news bulletins. The 'big prize', though, according to the memo, was to make the Prime Minister appear 'evasive' by asking him simple questions that he would struggle to answer.[99] To make matters worse, the briefing was published on the day of PMQs – and used to devastating and hilarious effect by the Prime Minister in his final answer to the Leader of the Opposition that afternoon in the House.

But Ed handles PMQs in a far more grown-up manner than his insecure and often short-tempered predecessor, Gordon Brown. A former Brown aide who now works in the Leader of the Opposition's office says 'it is remarkable nothing seems to faze him. He does get angry but he doesn't slam doors or bang on the table like Gordon.' The aide points to the PMQs session on 2 December when Ed was dismissed by Cameron as the 'son of Brown'. 'It was his worst PMQs and he recognised that he'd had a bad day but he just lets it bounce off him.' Ed's response, says the aide, is to shrug his shoulders and tell colleagues: 'You have good days, you have bad days.'[100]

'Ed's greatest gift is equanimity,' says Douglas Alexander. 'When he has a good Prime Minister's Questions, he's very calm. If he has a less good one, he's just as calm.'[101]

It hasn't been all bad for Ed in the chamber. By common consent, his performance at PMQs improved over the course of his first nine months as leader and he succeeded in landing several blows on Cameron in the Commons, using his questions each week to force the Prime Minister into embarrassing U-turns and volte-faces: from the sell-off of the forests to Downing Street's appointment of a 'vanity photographer' to the removal of ring-fenced funding for sport in schools.

On 16 March 2011, at PMQs, Cameron was left floundering at the Despatch box as Ed held a copy of the coalition's controversial Health and Social Care Bill aloft and quoted various technical clauses at him. 'Why does the Prime Minister not answer the question?' asked the Labour leader. 'Does he even know whether the health service will now be subject to EU competition law?' It was a confident, impressive performance from the Leader of the Opposition that left Labour MPs behind him – even those who had backed his brother – cheering loudly.[102]

A fortnight later, the Health Secretary Andrew Lansley announced a 'pause' to the pace of the NHS reforms. It was a mini-victory for the Labour leader whose attention to detail and wonkish obsession with facts and figures serves him well against a Conservative leader notoriously weak on detail and heavily reliant on those around him for support and guidance on policy.

But March also saw Ed's much-discussed address at the TUC rally against the cuts in Hyde Park. The Labour leader debated the pros and cons of going with his various advisers and allies, recognising the risks of being perceived to be, in a phrase favoured by the Tories, 'in the pocket of the trade unions'.

Ed's speech to the tens of thousands of protesters gathered in the park was panned by the press, as well as by the Prime Minister at PMQs just days later, for its bombastic references – seen as comparisons – to the suffragettes and Martin Luther King.[103] Yet Ed, never overly burdened by regret, maintains it was the right thing to do. It certainly offered him an opportunity to speak directly to hundreds of thousands of people from all walks of life – despite his speech being overshadowed on the television news channels by the antics of the anarchist fringe on Oxford Street. But there was a bigger prize for Ed: the Labour leader has often argued that authenticity is what matters most to voters in an age of superficiality and spin, yet there is a danger that he himself, as leader, will allow his own character and personality to be lost in positioning and triangulation. At key moments in his career, he has deliberately and self-consciously fought insurgency-style campaigns but has yet to emerge as an insurgent or populist Leader of the Opposition. In associating himself with a rally which saw hundreds of thousands of people from all walks of life assembled in the heart of the nation's capital, as his instincts told him to do, he at least was being himself. 'Would David have come?' a trade union leader mused aloud at Hyde Park. 'I very much doubt it.'[104]

Nonetheless, Ed's association with the unions will continue to haunt him, in the eyes of Blairites inside his party as well as the Tories and the right-wing press. In fairness, he may have pleased the trade union movement with his decision to attend the anti-cuts rally on 26 March 2011 but he has also taken steps to distance himself from union bosses. His first conference speech as leader condemned 'waves of irresponsible strikes', and when activists from the media union, BECTU, threatened to 'black out' Cameron's own party conference speech on television by going on strike the following week, Ed urged the union to show restraint. 'Whatever the rights and wrongs of the dispute', he said, 'my speech was seen and heard on the BBC and in the interests of impartiality and fairness, so the Prime Minister's should be.' BECTU described his intervention as 'not helpful' and 'dismissive'.[105]

Ed is also thinking long and hard about party reform. Some on the right of the party have long craved for Labour to break altogether with the unions. Ed is having none of that. But he may yet change the system by which he got elected. The former SDP founder and Labour Cabinet minister, Lord Owen, who is an admirer of Ed, believes 'it is perfectly possible to have a different electoral system for electing a Labour leader in opposition and a Labour leader in government.' He adds: 'I told him that he must look at the electoral college.'[106]

So far, Ed, a long-standing believer in movement politics and community organising, has indicated that he wants the public to play a bigger and more formal role in Labour's policy formation – and allow them to become 'registered supporters' free of charge. It is no coincidence that a project headed by his shadow Cabinet ally, Peter Hain, and charged with transforming the party into a more outward-looking and dynamic organisation, is rather grandly called 'Refounding Labour'.

But union leaders are ready for battle with the new Labour leader they helped elect. 'If people are seeking to reduce the influence of the trade unions either in the election of the Labour leader or at party conference, we will resist that,' says Len McCluskey, the general secretary of Unite, Britain's biggest union. He adds: 'I've no intention of giving a blank cheque to the Labour Party as we move forward.'[107] Given the fact that Unite provided nearly a quarter (23 per cent) of all Labour Party funding in 2010, with the trade union movement as a whole responsible for 62 per cent of all donations,[107] whether or not Ed can ignore or overcome the resistance from the 'brothers' to his party reform plans will be a key test of his leadership.

ooooo

Perhaps the biggest issue for Ed is how far he is willing to go in disassociating himself from New Labour, in general, and the Brown government, in particular. Here is a politician who has spoken repeatedly of breaking with both – and yet he emerged from the heart of New Labour and was blooded as a Cabinet minister in the Brown government.

'The big strategic question for Ed,' says his friend Spencer Livermore, who worked in Number 10 as Brown's director of political strategy before leaving in 2008 to work in corporate communications, 'is whether or not to disown the past. If you disown everything, voters will ask why they should trust you again. If you disown nothing, voters will wonder why you haven't learned from your mistakes in office.' He adds: 'My view on communications is you have to start where the audience is.'[108]

Livermore is right. A balance has to be struck by the new leader. Even his critics inside the party unconsciously accept this point. Those on the Labour right, for example, who urge Ed to apologise for the record Budget deficit and Brown's 'overspending' tend to be those who also criticise him for apologising for Iraq. The same applies to the Labour left – but in reverse. So far, on the economy, Ed, bolstered by his shadow Chancellor Ed Balls, has rightly resisted pressure from Blairites, the Tories and the right-wing media to disown Labour's fiscal record. The two Eds continue to insist that the deficit was not caused by reckless or chronic Labour overspending but by a global financial crisis that resulted in the worst recession in living memory, a collapse in tax receipts and a massive bailout of the banking sector. It is a message that is slowly getting through to the British public, as the coalition's spending cuts begin to bite and polls show the Tories' lead on the economy narrowing.

Ed's shake-up of his communications team has been a significant factor in the improvement of the party's messaging and narrative. In mid-December 2010, nearly three months after winning the leadership, Ed unveiled his new directors of strategy and communications. They were, respectively, Tom Baldwin, chief reporter at *The Times*, and Bob Roberts, political editor of the *Daily Mirror*.

The combative Baldwin, a close ally of Alastair Campbell, was hired on Campbell's advice to cause problems for the Conservatives while the very straight and affable Roberts's role was to appease and charm his former colleagues in the lobby. In the words of a headline in *PR Week* magazine: 'Labour adopting "Good cop, bad cop" PR strategy with hires of Tom Baldwin and Bob Roberts'.[110]

Even a long-standing critic of the former *Times* journalist concedes: 'Since they've got Baldwin, they've got sharper. He is ruthless.' Meanwhile, one former adviser to Blair described it as a 'pretty imaginative appointment', adding: 'What Ed needed more than anything else was someone to shake things up and be quite aggressive and therefore Tom is a good choice.' And an admiring member of Team Ed now refers to Baldwin and Roberts as the 'yin and yang' of the inner circle, a combination of energy, enthusiasm and eccentricity (Baldwin) and calm, composure and charm (Roberts).

When he was tapped up by Stewart Wood for the job of director of strategy, Baldwin went to discuss the role with Ed in his office in Norman Shaw South. Ed's opening remark to *The Times* journalist at that meeting is worth quoting: 'I spent fifteen years trying to avoid having lunch with you.' 'That natural caution of yours got you where you are today,' replied Baldwin.[111]

But did Ed take a risk in bringing Baldwin on board? While the latter is widely regarded even by his many critics as an effective attack dog against the Tories, he is a deeply divisive figure among his former journalistic colleagues. This is partly because of his controversial role in reporting briefings from Alastair Campbell over Iraq and the late weapons scientist Dr David Kelly, as exposed by the Hutton Inquiry in which Baldwin was a bit-part player. But it is also because despite his title – director of 'strategy' – some would argue that strategy is not his strong suit.

Then there are the darker allegations about Baldwin. The former Tory deputy chairman and billionaire donor Lord Michael Ashcroft, in his 2005 book, *Dirty Politics, Dirty Times*, had made a series of controversial claims about Baldwin's private life. 'Meet the champagne (and coke snorting) socialist who is Labour's new Alastair Campbell,' proclaimed the provocative headline in the *Daily Mail*, just days after his appointment to Ed's inner circle.[112] In fact, since the resignation of Andy Coulson as Cameron's director of communications over the *News of the World* phone-hacking affair, there have been rumours in the Westminster village that Tory sympathisers have hired private detectives to dig up dirt on Baldwin.[113]

Meanwhile, some of Ed's supporters have been disturbed by the idea that a former employee of the Murdoch media empire should be advising Ed on press strategy in the wake of one of the most damaging scandals in the history of the Murdoch-owned News International. Baldwin's colleagues in the leader's office claim he has been pushing Ed to raise the issue of phone-hacking and the lack of regulation in the British press but the evidence seems to suggest otherwise. In an email forwarded to Labour frontbenchers on behalf of Baldwin, and leaked to the *New Statesman* website, shadow Cabinet ministers and party officials were instructed to avoid linking Murdoch's proposed takeover of BSkyB to the phone-hacking controversy surrounding the Murdoch-owned *News of the World*: 'These issues should not be linked'.

Despite Labour having publicly raised questions about the Culture Secretary Jeremy Hunt's claim to be neutral and impartial on Murdoch-related issues, and emerging evidence of contacts between the Prime Minister and various senior members of Murdoch's News Corp, the memo continued: 'Downing Street says that Cameron's dinners with Murdoch will not affect Hunt's judgement. We have to take them at their word.'

The email concluded with the warning, 'We must guard against anything which appears to be attacking a particular newspaper group out of spite.'[114]

By April, however, in the wake of News International's surprise confession over phone-hacking, Ed had shifted the party's position and called for an independent review of the regulation and practices of newspapers. 'I think the review needs to have some independence, both from government and from those involved in the day-to-day running of newspapers. I think that would help the industry... Wider lessons have to be learned,' he said.[115] The boldness may have been belated but it was welcome: few party leaders have been willing to confront newspaper proprietors and, in particular, Rupert Murdoch, in recent years.

Whether or not Ed has the courage to refuse to bow to the pressures all Labour leaders encounter from the Murdoch-owned media that tries to drag them to the right, remains to be seen. It will be another key test of his leadership.

ooooo

One major strategic dilemma that Ed knows he must resolve before the next election, scheduled for May 2015, is how to deal with the Liberal Democrats. During his leadership campaign, Ed tore into the Lib Dems at every opportunity, delivering perhaps the most misjudged statement of the contest during a tour of Scottish constituencies in August 2010: 'We have to make the Lib Dems an endangered species and then extinct,' he told cheering Labour Party members in Kilmarnock.[116] In that same month, he also said that he would most likely insist on the resignation of Nick Clegg before considering any alliance with the Liberal Democrats in the future: 'Given what he is supporting, I think it is pretty hard to go into coalition with him.'[117]

Since becoming leader, however, Ed's tone and attitude towards the Lib Dems have changed. In his conference speech in Manchester, he proclaimed: 'Wisdom is not the preserve of any one party. Some of the political figures in history whom I admire most are Keynes, Lloyd George, and Beveridge, who were not members of the Labour Party.' The tribal leadership candidate from the summer had disappeared – replaced by a pluralist and progressive party leader.

And, despite refusing to share a platform with Nick Clegg in the Yes2AV referendum campaign, and maintaining that it would be difficult to work with Clegg in the future, Ed also said that if the Lib Dem leader were to be a 'sinner repenteth' then things might change between them.[118] Reports emerged of secret conversations between the two men on a range of issues, including the possibility of collaboration on House of Lords reform.[119]

Ed's approach to the Lib Dems did not fall on deaf ears. On 12 December 2010, *The Observer* led on its front page with astonishing remarks from Richard Grayson, a leading Liberal Democrat activist, parliamentary candidate and the party's former director of policy: '[I]n the past, common ground with Labour leaders has been hard to find... With the election of Ed Miliband as Labour leader, that has changed... since he became leader he has acted as a genuine pluralist.'[120]

Ed spotted an opportunity. The next morning, at 7.30am, as he sat in his lounge watching a pre-recorded game of American football, Grayson received a phone call from the Labour leader inviting him to contribute to the party's policy review that was being led by the shadow Cabinet minister, Liam Byrne. He agreed to do so.[121]

Later that same morning, in the first of his monthly press conferences, Ed called on disillusioned Lib Dems to work with him against the Conservative-led coalition government, before moving on to his main announcement. 'To those who are reluctant to abandon ship but are concerned about the direction of their party, I invite them to work with us on issues of common interest,' he said, in front of the assembled television cameras at Church House in Westminster. 'I have asked Liam Byrne to work with Richard Grayson [a former Lib Dem policy director] to draw up areas where our policy review can be informed by submissions and ideas of Liberal Democrats who want to contribute.'[122]

Grayson has since revealed that seven other former Lib Dem parliamentary candidates had agreed to join him in making contributions to Labour's policy reviews on issues such as public service reform, crime and the environment. 'Calling on people from outside Labour to engage in Labour's policy process, while remaining in their own parties, is nothing less than revolutionary,' wrote Grayson in February.[123]

ooooo

Ed is keen to stress his pluralist credentials, and his ability to unify different strands of thought and tradition on the liberal-left. Here is a Labour leader who has united behind him Tony Benn and David Owen, Ken Livingstone and Jon Cruddas, Maurice Glasman and Neil Kinnock.

But what does he believe?

In late December 2010, Jon Cruddas was invited to the office of the Leader of the Opposition for a chat with Ed. 'He was a good listener like everyone says,' recalls the Labour backbencher. 'He was courteous and responsive; he had a nice manner.'

In the midst of their conversation about Labour's future, Cruddas suggested Ed should join him on a visit to Billingsgate Fish Market, in east London, where the Corporation of London, the governing body of the City, was on the verge of withdrawing trading licenses – or 'badges' – from the 120 porters (whose role has been recognised by the Corporation since 1632). He had assumed Ed would decline the offer but, to Cruddas's surprise, the Labour leader agreed. It was as if his bluff had been called.

A couple of days later, at the crack of dawn, Cruddas arrived in his Freelander at Ed's Dartmouth Park home to pick him up for the trip to Billingsgate, where they were greeted by Cruddas's friend and ideological soul mate, the academic and London Citizens activist Maurice Glasman. (Cruddas had insisted that there be no media; Ed had not demurred and, in the words of one commentator, 'may himself have realised that a photo call with a dead fish would avail him little'.[124])

Ed met the porters and heard their concerns. He listened to their stories, took their questions, showed interest in their lives and career challenges.

The trip to Billingsgate illustrated two important facets of Ed's leadership. First, it is a reminder of how personable a politician he is. 'He was absolutely brilliant at reacting to people,' says Cruddas. 'We met some really tough guys and he just talked to them and listened to them; he didn't look out of place at all. He was bloody good at it.' The former David supporter adds: 'I am much more impressed with him as leader than I thought I would be.'[125]

Second, it shows the political direction in which he is travelling; Billingsgate is evidence of his desire to find ways of enhancing the meaning of people's lives, of stressing 'the centrality of life beyond the bottom line' and of building a 'good society' – based around the concepts of greater equality, solidarity, community and social justice.

In his conference speech in Manchester, Ed referred to the 'good life' and proclaimed: 'We must be on the side of communities who want to save their local post office, not be the people trying to close it. We must be on the side of people trying to protect their high street from looking like every other high street, not the people who say that's just the forces of progress.'

He concluded this particular section of his address with the line: '… the good life is about the things we do in our community and the time we spend with family'.[126] It wasn't the type of rhetoric often used by Labour frontbenchers – least of all Labour frontbenchers of the Brownite, statist, and interventionist variety. 'Red Ed', the caricature promoted by right-wing media commentators and Blairite supporters of his brother, had morphed into 'Blue Ed', highlighting the value of local communities and neighbourhoods, of human relationships above economic relationships.

It is a theme he has been keen to build on as his leadership has progressed. In a major speech to the Fabian Society in January 2011, Ed said Labour had to 'recognise the way our managerialism took us away from the instincts and values of the broad progressive majority in Britain. That our communities came to see us as the people who put markets and commerce before the common good. And many citizens came to see us also as the people who did not understand that the state could be intrusive as well as empowering.'

He contrasted the dysfunctional extremes of the 'bureaucratic state and the overbearing market' before referring to his Billingsgate trip:

'Just before Christmas, I went with Jon Cruddas to Billingsgate Fish Market and met a porter there who told me that the best day of his life was when he got his porter's badge and that there has not been a day since when he has not woken up feeling proud to be doing the job he does.

'That is why politicians should not shrug and walk away when they hear that traditional ways of life are under threat. We should seek to defend ways of life which give people self-respect.'[127]

Some in the party worry about the nostalgia and social conservatism inherent in the so-called 'Blue Labour' communitarian project pushed by, among others, Jon Cruddas and Maurice Glasman – who, less than a year after meeting Ed, had become an influential member of the leader's inner circle (and was rewarded by the new leader with a peerage).

But Ed rejects the idea that he has blindly or uncritically embraced Blue Labour as his political philosophy or as the theoretical underpinning of his leadership. 'There seems to be one model of leadership which says, "I'm going to come along and tell you all what to think, and these will be my tablets of stone handed down, and you're all going to obey",' says Ed. 'And yet there's another model of leadership which says "I want to create some space for debate and I'm going to look on as an interested observer, having created this space for debate, and then take it in a particular direction". That's what I'm doing.'[128]

The youngest son of Ralph Miliband, Ed is a thinker who values ideas and understands the importance of fostering debate – whether in the corridors of Harvard or at the top of the Labour Party.

Ultimately, however, friends and colleagues agree that Ed, deep down, is a classic European-style social democrat – though, like his father, he calls himself a 'socialist' – who is grappling with the central challenge that confronts European social democracy in the twenty-first century: the balance between the state and the market. The Labour leader has written how:

> Historically, debates within Labour have often been conducted on the basis of a choice between 'more state and less market' or 'more market and less state'. That approach needs revisiting for three fundamental reasons. First, because Labour's approach to prosperity and fairness should rely on an effective combination of both strong, good government, and efficient, well-regulated markets. Second, because a twenty-first century Labour project must pledge to be reformers of both the state and the market. And third, because in Labour's debates of the past, both the statists and the pro-market voices underplayed the importance of the aspects of our lives and our communities that must be protected from the destructive effects of both markets and the unresponsive state.[129]

His open-mindedness and his desire for debate, however, should not be confused with vacillation or triangulation. His politics are not a case of 'all things to all men'. Ed, in this sense, is not Blair – nor is he trying to be Blair (though friends have noticed how, in private, he has adopted Blair-esque glottal stops and other mannerisms of the former Prime Minister in recent months).

He sees himself as 'blending'[130] the best aspects of the various progressive traditions and philosophies – Fabianism, Croslandism, social liberalism, communitarianism and the rest. He sees the state as a benevolent but not infallible force, in need of reform and democratisation but, above all else, a crucial instrument for achieving social justice. And the issue that transcends all of these debates, drives his leadership and defines his social democracy is the issue of inequality.

'Ed is an egalitarian,' says a close friend. 'He does believe that the gap between rich and poor really matters. He's famously not relaxed about that.'[131]

'Britain is grossly unequal – in class, income, wealth – and that is what troubles me most about this country,' says the Labour leader.[132] He has read and re-read *The Spirit Level*, by academics Richard Wilkinson and Kate Pickett, which forcefully argues that income inequality is the root cause of most social ills – murder, obesity, teenage pregnancy, depression.

Ed's unashamed focus on inequality has policy implications. 'Ed wants to deal with intergenerational inequality and that will require a radical policy programme,' says a senior Labour strategist. 'The commentariat have yet to recognise what is involved in tackling intergenerational inequality.'

In a speech to the Resolution Foundation think tank in London on 28 February 2011, in which he expanded on his concept of the 'squeezed middle' and referred to a 'cost-of-living crisis for ordinary families ... squeezed wages, squeezed prospects, squeezed aspirations', Ed referred to his mission as being to combat inequality – 'It's why I am in politics' – and a desire to build a 'fairer' and 'more prosperous' capitalism.[133]

'He is,' says Nick Pearce, 'a modern social democrat who, in a liberal age, is instinctively more liberal than his predecessors.' Pearce adds: 'His challenge is turning those values, intuition and intellectual abilities into a clear and concise definition of what he is and what he stands for.'¹³⁴

It would be wrong to see Ed as opposing New Labour on ideological grounds only. As he made clear in his Fabian essay in August 2010, in the midst of his leadership campaign, one of the main reasons Ed rejects a great deal of the assumptions that were at the heart of the New Labour project is because they are no longer electorally successful. In the wake of the financial crisis, for example, the public are much more sceptical about the role of the banks, much more angry about the bonus culture and much more concerned about the gap between the rich and the rest ('the squeezed middle'). Given the authoritarianism of the New Labour years, and the various rows over policing and counter-terror policies, there is genuine and widespread concern about civil liberties. After Iraq, voters want the country to behave less like an extension of America in the international arena.

Such positions reflect a distinct and different ideology to both Blair and Brown but they are based on Ed's robust analysis of what Labour needs to do in order to win back voters and be re-elected.

Ed understands that the centre ground of politics is not a fixed, georgraphical location; it shifts and morphs from generation to generation. His agenda, say his allies, is 'Thatcher-esque' in its ambition – and based on deeply-held beliefs about the nature of society and state.

Ed's view is that people of his father's generation and outlook may have had a political perspective that was wrong, impractical and unsustainable but what motivated them was not wrong. He shares with Ralph a desire to intellectually and morally explain the purpose of politics. Few of his contemporaries could say the same – even his brother.

'Ed has radical sensibilities,' says a family friend who has known him since he was a child. 'He would like to live in a very, very different world. David long ago accommodated himself to the difficulty of changing the world; Ed less so.'¹³⁵

ᴏᴏᴏᴏᴏ

Ed Miliband has not had a sympathetic press in his first year as Labour leader. He told friends that he has the 'difficult task of trying to make a case for progressive politics in a relatively hostile climate'.¹³⁶

Nonetheless, by any objective measure, he had a solid start. He won three by-elections with ease. In Oldham East and Saddleworth, the seat vacated by the disgraced frontbencher Phil Woolas, Labour secured a bigger majority in January 2011 than it did in May 2010 – and in May 1997. In Barnsley Central, the seat vacated by another disgraced ex-Labour MP, expenses cheat Eric Illsley, Labour again received a bigger majority in March 2011 than it did in May 2010 – with the Tories slipping to third place, behind the UK Independence Party. In Leicester South, Ed's aide Jonathan Ashworth romped home with 58 per cent of the vote.

Cameron has been denied a Blair-like honeymoon while Labour has benefited from the transformation of Cleggmania into Cleggphobia.

But it hasn't all been good news for Ed or for Labour. Thursday 5 May 2011 marked the first nationwide electoral test for the new Labour leader, as it did for the coalition government. Cameron's Conservatives emerged as the winner – their vote share held up and the party gained seats from the Liberal Democrats. Although the front pages in the immediate aftermath of the local elections and AV referendum were dominated by the humiliating disaster for Nick Clegg's Lib Dems, Ed had his own problems. Labour picked up more than 800 seats but the party failed to gain crucial swing voters in the south of England and, more importantly in the long term, suffered a heavy defeat at the hands of the SNP in Scotland, which won the first overall majority since the creation of the Scottish Parliament in 1999. The Scottish Labour leader Iain Gray – who Ed had praised for doing a 'fantastic' job – had had an awful campaign symbolised in the Scottish press by an episode in which he hid in a branch of Subway, the sandwich shop, while cuts protesters surrounded him. Ed himself came under fire for his failure to treat the election as a devolved contest; in a speech to the Scottish Labour conference in March 2011 he had proclaimed: 'We need to win at these elections and we need to send a message to the government at Westminster.'[137] But the people of Scotland had their own, rather negative, message for him.

Has Ed grasped the magnitude, or significance, of the Scottish crisis? Some of his allies are unsure. The day after the elections, Ed's office issued a statement claiming a 'root and branch review' of Scottish Labour. But with Salmond promising a referendum on independence in the coming term of office, the Union is facing its biggest threat since its inception 300 years ago. And with the Tories on the verge of perpetual rule in England in the event of a separation – even Michael Howard managed to win a majority of 'English votes' in 2005 – Cameron has less of an interest in fighting against independence. Ed, however, needs Scotland in order to be Prime Minister – Labour cannot win a Commons majority without Scottish votes.

The 70–30 per cent victory for the No campaign in the AV referendum was also a blow to Ed. He had taken a risk by siding with the Yes campaign, despite sizeable and vocal opposition to electoral reform among the more tribal and conservative members of his party's front and back benches. Ed was therefore associated with a campaign that failed to excite the electorate – and was heavily defeated by a Cameron-led and Tory-funded campaign. And Ed, a passionate believer in a 'progressive majority' and a 'new politics' had been unable to persuade the British public to vote for a small reform that would have hugely empowered progressives and modernised our political system.

More broadly, critics point to Ed's weak personal poll ratings, which have failed to match his party's. A year on from the general election, Cameron outpolls his party; Ed's party outpolls him. (Defenders of the Labour leader, however, point to data from Ipsos Mori from April 2011 showing how 'satisfaction' with Miliband is in line with Cameron a year into his leadership of the opposition.[138])

Even Ed's most ardent advocates would struggle to describe Labour's shadow Cabinet as a government-in-waiting or Ed himself as a Prime-Minister-in-waiting. And asked by Jon Sopel on the BBC if he was ready to be Prime Minister in the event of the coalition collapsing, Ed himself merely replied: 'Of course we can be ready'.[139]

But if Ed is to stand a chance against the assured and self-confident Cameron at the next election, he has to look sufficiently authoritative and prime ministerial; he has to overcome what a senior Labour peer and former frontbencher refers to as the 'Kinnock issue'. Affable, popular, constantly ahead in the opinion polls, Kinnock was beaten in consecutive general elections: first by Margaret Thatcher and then by John Major. He was never deemed to be a plausible Prime Minister by the British public.

As of April 2011, only a quarter of the public would say that Ed would make 'the most capable PM'. But, as Ed supporters point out, it was up from a fifth in September 2010.[140] And, as an aide to the Labour leader says: 'He has more experience at the top of government, and of international negotiations, than Tony Blair or David Cameron had before either of those two men walked through the door of Number 10.'[141]

His biggest challenge now is to define a direction of travel for his party. So far, he has been unable to do so. Friends say he has lacked time and space. He went from winning the election to writing his conference speech, choosing his shadow Cabinet, staffing his back office, replacing his shadow Chancellor and then fighting the local elections and the AV referendum campaign.

So is it fair to describe Ed as an indecisive ditherer? He himself answers this question by pointing out that he stood against his brother. Others still have their doubts.

Predictably, the Tories published a dossier to mark the Labour leader's first hundred days in office entitled: '100 days of dithering and disarray'. The same charge, of course, has been levelled at Barack Obama in the US by the President's voluble critics – and the response of Obama's supporters could apply equally to Ed: first, the messianic certainty of Bush (read Blair) is worse; second, it is a mistake to confuse deliberation and reflection for dithering and indecisiveness.

In meetings, the Labour leader is often the first to say: 'Hang on a minute. Let's think this through.' As one senior party figure who has observed Ed very closely over the years says: 'The thing about Ed Miliband is he's got this ridiculous reputation for vacillation and not being able to make up his mind. That isn't actually true. What he does is, he tests all propositions and he will ask – it's quite disconcerting – he will ask loads of people what they think and that gives the impression that actually he doesn't know what he's thinking. But what he's doing is gathering a whole lot of information and then when he makes his mind up, he's made his mind up.'[142]

In fact, throughout his life, Ed has always looked at all the options before taking a position on an issue, big or small. Recall the words of his tutor Adam Swift at Oxford: 'He was noticeably cautious – but then when he did end up arguing a position, it was very well-argued.'

Ed's closest allies believe his reflective nature, his proclivity for deliberation and contemplation doesn't hinder him – it strengthens him as a leader and bolsters his judgement. There have been few Cameron-esque U-turns on his watch.

'The alpha-male style of leadership that we've seen in British politics in recent years isn't the only model,' says one of Ed's allies inside the shadow Cabinet, who cites the example of Clement Attlee.[143] Labour's most successful post-war Prime Minister – referred to by Ed on countless occasions as one of his inspirations and role models – is considered to have been a chairman and a facilitator rather than a decider or dictator.

Ed is by no means a chairman but he is, by nature, a more measured and methodical figure than the party leaders that we have become used to in recent years – but, as Leader of the Opposition, he cannot afford to be characterised by caution. A close ally says: 'I think Ed felt weighed down by the sense of responsibility after he'd won. He couldn't afford to fuck up and he became cautious – whereas caution had been the last thing on his mind during the leadership campaign.'

'He needs to find a way to be disruptive,' says a gloomy friend. 'Cameron and Blair disrupted politics and attracted the attention of the media by taking on their parties. Ed has made it clear that he doesn't see the need to 'take on' the modern Labour Party in the same way. So how and what does he disrupt to capture people's imagination?'[144]

Other friends of the Labour leader are more confident in his political future. His university friend Marc Stears says: 'I think he is much tougher than people imagine and he won't back away from a fight if one's needed. He beat his brother to become leader and yet people still think he's not up for a scrap.'[145]

Ed's advisers claim he is playing the long game because 'opposition is a marathon not a sprint'. Or, in the words of the Labour leader: 'Opposition is a long haul. It's about digging in.'[146]

But Ed can't afford to get stuck in the mud. He won the leadership partly through being nimble and flexible, eager to embrace change, break from the past and take bold decisions. Caution didn't deliver him victory against David Miliband and it won't deliver him victory against David Cameron.

Nor should Ed, a former TV researcher, forget that in a 24-hour media culture impressions are formed fast. Just ask Nick Clegg.

And, given the implosion of the Lib Dems in the local council elections, and the ongoing tensions between the coalition partners, there is no guarantee that the government will last until 2015. Time is not necessarily on Ed's side.

Further worries that Ed is prone to opportunism and short-term tactics over strategy came with the Ken Clarke rape row on 18 May. In the late morning, Clarke went on Victoria Derbyshire's Radio 5 Live phone-in programme to discuss his plan for a sentence 'discount' – including halving sentences – in the event of early admissions of guilt. The programme ended up focusing on rape, with several callers, including a rape victim, emotionally remonstrating with the Justice Secretary. Clarke, a plain-speaking politician, fumbled his words throughout and in later interviews, in which he was seen to have distinguished between different types of rape, referring to some as 'classic', 'serious' and 'proper' while pointing out that sex between two teenagers is also called 'rape' if it is consensual. When Derbyshire put it to him that 'rape is rape', Clarke replied 'no it's not'.

Though he may have been correct in terms of sentencing policy, Clarke's language was ill-advised, and created a media frenzy at Westminster.

Ed and his team were preparing for PMQs in his office while the furore erupted. They were planning to 'go on' a different topic altogether before deciding, at 11.10am – fifty minutes before the Commons clash – to go on Ken Clarke. Though there was clear excitement among Ed's media team that the story was taking off, and their man should 'get in' on it, it was in fact Ed himself who decided it was right to call for Clarke to go. Some in the room disagreed, but Ed was determined. In the chamber, he started by saying that Clarke cannot 'represent the women of this country' using the type of language he had that morning. But then he went a step further, telling Cameron that Clarke should be removed from his post by the end of the day.

It was a bad mistake. Not only did Clarke stay, and the liberal press disagree with Ed the following day, with *The Guardian* and *The Independent* arguing he should stay, but Ed had targeted his first call for a minister to resign at a man who he had singled out after becoming leader as one he would not opportunistically attack. In what could be interpreted as a failure to see the wood for the trees, Ed's team may have judged that Clarke would be gone by the end of the day and that Ed could therefore claim credit. But the call for Clarke to go was not made with the best interests of the country in mind. For whatever Clarke's faults, Ed knows he is, in his own blustering way, a relatively progressive member of the Cabinet, a crucial counter-balance to the Tory right. Had he gone, the government would have tilted rightwards, the very direction Ed likes to criticise it for heading in.

Though the Labour leader is unrepentant about his decision to call for Clarke to be fired, the episode showed Ed at his weakest and most ineffective. There are lessons to be learned here.

ooooo

In his defence, Ed has put the party back on its feet after its second-worst defeat in a general election since 1918. Talk of splits, divisions and plots has slowly been brought under control. His leadership is focused, say aides, on three strong pillars: 'the squeezed middle', 'life beyond the bottom line' (the Blue Labour agenda) and the 'British promise' (the expectation that children should have more opportunities in life than their parents). He spends a great deal of time working through his options, deciding on strategy and thinking about what distinguishes him from others.

Meanwhile less partisan figures on the right have recognised Ed's political skills and the potential danger he poses to Cameron and the coalition. The Tory-supporting columnist Iain Martin coined the phrase 'DUEMA' (the Don't Underestimate Ed Miliband Association). And the *Telegraph*'s chief political commentator Peter Oborne confessed:

'It is growing increasingly hard to resist a grudging admiration for Edward Miliband. He has emerged as a ruthless, talented and effective Labour leader... Above all, he is the master of interest-group politics, one of the acknowledged keys to electoral victory in the twenty-first century: nobody at Westminster does this half as well.'

Oborne is right to use the word 'ruthless'. For that is what Ed has proved to be – from his decision to stand against David to his sacking of Nick Brown to his appointment of Alan Johnson over Ed Balls. 'One of the ways in which Ed has been underestimated by the media and by the Tories is the extent to which he's capable of being ruthless – and ruthless in acquiring political power,' says a former colleague of Ed who worked with him at the heart of New Labour. The ex-colleague adds: 'That's why it is so dangerous for his opponents to fall into the caricature that Ed is somehow too ideological, too idealistic, that he isn't interested in being in government, that he wants to lead a movement rather than a serious party of power.'[147]

'What he has actually shown if you look at his record over the past year is great ruthlessness and great decisiveness,' says a senior Labour peer and former Cabinet minister, who voted for David.[148]

But his enemies continue to underestimate this calm, clever and talented politician. Indeed Ed has been underestimated throughout his life: from the dons of Corpus Christi, who he battled over the rent hikes in 1991 to Ed Balls, who thought he would always be the senior of the two Eds, to his brother David, who had assumed Ed wouldn't challenge him and, when he did, assumed he wouldn't win.

He is far from perfect: occasional naïvety and a tendency to be swayed can stray over into cautiousness; he can come across as wooden on television; he needs to shed an obsession with journalists – and learn to take more risks. Then there is his voice, described by some as 'chronically adenoidal'. In April, Team Ed announced that their man would undergo surgery on his nose – but they claimed the procedure was not aimed at changing or improving his voice. 'Ed Miliband has been diagnosed with sleep apnoea made worse by a deviated septum,' a party spokesman confirmed. 'On medical advice he is having a routine operation ... at the end of July with the NHS.'[149]

Fundamentally, however, Ed has the potential to lead a reformed and rejuvenated Labour Party back to power in 2015. As the Labour strategist David Muir told David Axelrod in the White House, during the Labour leadership campaign: 'Ed is at 70 per cent. [He] has so much more capacity to improve.' Or, in the confident words of one of the Labour leader's key advisers: 'What he has got can't be taught, what he hasn't got can be learned.'[150]

Some of his supporters in Parliament are effusive. 'I knew Kinnock and Smith pretty well. And I worked for Blair and Brown in the Cabinet Office and Number 10,' says Jon Trickett. 'But Ed, potentially, is the best of the lot – intellectually, ideologically and in terms of his engaging personality.'[151] Political opponents disagree. As SNP leader Alex Salmond told one of us, 'Ed is the worst Labour leader I've seen in my political career. He is no Neil Kinnock, who was actually a great motivator.'[152]

The pressure now is on Ed to deliver. He emerged from New Labour and then broke with New Labour but can he succeed at the polls as New Labour did? Perhaps, as his supporters argue, he is the right man at the right time for Labour; the embodiment of change and a break with the past. The right-wing media pack, the Conservative leadership and even some in his own party were slow to recognise the significance of his emergence. After sacrificing so much for the sake of securing the Labour crown – including his relationship with his brother, for now at least – Ed has yet to put his own stamp on the party But his passion for politics is undimmed, his ambition for power undiminished. It would be unwise for a new set of opponents to underestimate him again.

EPILOGUE

In December 2010, David and Louise Miliband hosted a birthday party at their home in Edis Street for their elder son, Isaac, who had just turned six. Friends and relations, including mother Marion, gathered to celebrate with tea and cake. But there were some crucial absentees. Ed did not attend the party. Nor did Justine or their two children, Daniel and new baby Samuel. Ed's family live a ten-minute drive away from David's.

Guests who attended the party were unclear as to whether Ed was invited and declined the invitation, or was not asked to begin with. It remains a mystery.[1]

Perhaps understandably, both brothers have refused to comment on the episode. But for friends of the Miliband brothers, Ed's absence confirmed one of their worst fears: that the relationship between David and Ed had so deteriorated that it was now impacting on the entire family. This, of course, had been Marion's biggest worry and she was said to have aged by several years since the summer.

The once tight-knit Miliband clan would not be together for Christmas either. Despite Ed optimistically telling the press he was looking forward to spending it with his brother – and quipping that 'no peacekeeping forces will be needed'[2] – David headed off to America to spend the holidays with his in-laws. Meanwhile, the regular Sunday lunches where the two brothers would gather with their families and their mother are a distant memory.

ooooo

Despite singlehandedly having ended his brother's long-standing leadership ambitions, Ed looked remarkably breezy as he emerged from the Midland Hotel in Manchester for an organised media doorstep to cheers from supporters on the day David announced his decision to quit frontline politics. In a comment that was interpreted as remarkably 'patronising' by many David supporters, still reeling from their man's downfall, Ed said that his brother had done the right thing for himself but added: 'My door is always open for him to serve in the future.'[3]

In fact, that door has rarely been approached by David.

There is no doubt that although Ed today puts on a brave face, and tells friends his bond with David is 'on the mend', relations are in fact far worse than is widely assumed. Some who know both brothers believe that Ed is 'in denial' about the implications for his relationship with David, blocking the issue out. But in reality the brothers barely speak these days, and communicate if at all largely through their offices and aides. Ed sought David's advice on how to handle the crisis in Libya in April 2011, and received it, but that was an exception and general brotherly chatter is gone.[4]

One stark demonstration of the bizarre relationship came with the announcement of Ed's wedding to Justine. Immediately there was speculation on Ed's dilemma over whether or not to ask David to be his best man. The *Mail on Sunday* reported a rumour that the reason Ed was reluctant to offer David the role was for fear of being rebuffed.

Ed had been best man at David's wedding to Louise in 1998, albeit a rather straight and serious one. But now the nature of the relationship had changed. Ed has insisted that he and Justine wanted a 'different' kind of wedding, a non-traditional ceremony in which there would be no father of the bride speech either. Yet there is surely little doubt that had the brothers not gone head to head in the Labour leadership contest, Ed would have opted for a best man and it would have been David.

There was another curious element to Ed and Justine's decision to marry. For six years, they had chosen not to, despite having had two children in that time period. Ed is known to disapprove of the view that the traditional family model is somehow superior to every other model, and some believe that his decision to wed was cynical, part of his attempt to ingratiate himself with a hostile and suspicious right-wing press. The singer Lily Allen summed up the view of many on the liberal left when she tweeted: 'Ed Miliband is getting married. Ha, they got to him in the end then?'

In the end, the wedding on Friday 27 May was a happy and emotional one. It was free from speculation about David, who was the only politician present at the intimate gathering and who deliberately kept a low profile after arriving by car with his wife and children. 'Great day for Ed and Justine,' David wrote on Twitter. 'They look very happy. Congratulations from all the Milibands.'

The event itself was low key but elegant, with the civil ceremony at Langar Hall, a Georgian house in Nottinghamshire near where Justine grew up.

After a dinner of asparagus and lamb washed down with champagne and wine, Ed made a moving speech in which he told his new wife: 'You are the most beautiful, generous and kind person that I've ever met in my life. You are my rock and I'm so lucky to have you and Daniel and Sam. I love you with all my heart.' Justine wept. In her own speech, she said: 'When I was growing up I thought when I was thirty I would be married and have two kids. It might be a decade late but it was worth the wait for Ed.'[5]

There were distinctly personal touches. Guests were instructed to make donations to Barnado's and Methodist Homes for the Aged, instead of bringing presents for the couple. And, in an acknowledgement of the Milibands' Jewish background, Ed smashed a glass with his foot in a symbolic tradition marking the last time the groom can put his foot down before marriage. After the gathering in Nottingham, the couple had some friends round for drinks and music at their London house before escaping on a five-day honeymoon.

But, perhaps following a new pattern, David did not turn up at the post-wedding party that night in Ed and Justine's home. And, if the Labour leader could not see how his decision to avoid having David as his best man would look to the outside world, or how it would lead to further damaging speculation about the brothers' relationship, then he is guilty of a lack of self-awareness.

Because of their age gap, David and Ed had always moved in slightly different circles, lived slightly different lives. But they would always speak, at the very least on the phone, several times a week. Now, with the exception of occasional requests for advice from Ed, they hardly speak at all.

Shortly after Ed and Justine's second son was born on 7 November 2010, the new Labour leader received a visit from his shadow Cabinet colleague, Tessa Jowell. Though a David supporter, the sociable Jowell took a gift round to Ed's home for new-born Samuel. But according to one friend of Ed's, she also used the visit to issue some 'home truths' about how upset David was. Ed, it is said, was annoyed and taken aback by her comments. Though his political ally Maurice Glasman would later claim that Ed was 'racked with guilt' over what he had done to David he appeared to believe he had nothing to reproach himself for; certainly he has yet to face up to the chasm in their relationship.

David has tried to keep himself busy by taking on a range of roles, from part-time teaching at Haverstock to non-executive positions at Sunderland FC as well as in business. He has started blogging again, as he did at the Foreign Office and during his leadership campaign, but his posts are almost all confined to foreign affairs. He still talks to a few favoured journalists, and did a round of lunches and meetings with editors towards the end of 2010. More earnestly, he continues his work with the grassroots 'Movement for Change' organisation, a cause now adopted by his brother too. And he has made three major speeches, one at the LSE on why the left is losing ground in Europe, one on a political solution to the Afghanistan war at the Massachusetts Institute of Technology in Boston in April, and one in Poland in May. Hundreds attend his talks, especially students: in May he attracted some 300 at Sussex University. But he remains 'trapped', says a friend, unable to comment on Labour and British politics for fear of being hounded by a press pack looking for another Harman moment. He cuts a lonely figure on the fifth floor of the modern Portcullis House building in Westminster where his Commons office is now situated next to that of his old campaign chief Douglas Alexander.

Though he wants Ed to do well, David is said to genuinely believe that his party is heading in the wrong direction. He is said to feel that Ed's leadership campaign approach of revisionism over areas like civil liberties and fees, does not translate easily into an agenda for government. And he has told friends that Ed's personnel are not strong enough and are made up of people who are interested in self-promotion rather than a desire for Labour to win again.

Ed and his advisers have made a number of approaches to David – direct, through David's office and floated through the media – urging him to come back into the party leadership fold in some way. David has made it clear he will not be returning to the party's frontbench in the near future – the next shadow

Cabinet elections are scheduled for the autumn of 2012 – and the likelihood remains he never will under Ed. Aides to the Labour leader have come up with other ideas, such as a policy review role, but David has rejected these on the grounds he has 'been there, done that'. One Ed ally even suggested, outlandishly, that perhaps David could fill the chief of staff vacancy turned down by a series of targets including Charlie Falconer and James Purnell.[6]

David recently told a confidant that he finds it difficult being in Westminster at all. He wishes he could travel more but wouldn't want to leave his young family behind in London for long. David and Louise did take the kids to the US before Easter, when he caught up with old contacts, including at Harvard. The fundamental dilemma David now faces is whether to hold out in the Commons for a possible role in Labour's leadership – including the top job – in the future, or to quit British politics for good. His friends are divided on this question. Friends of Tony Blair believe that there remains a 'window' for David to come back, albeit a window that is slowly but surely closing. Other, more personal friends believe that for the sake of David's psychological wellbeing he should make a clean break out of Westminster and focus on something completely different. At present, David feels no obligation to decide his future quickly. At some point, however, the decision will need to be made.

ooooo

Meanwhile, the success of Ed Miliband's leadership of Labour ironically depends, in part, on him remaining distinct from his brother, and reminding MPs and party members that there were valid political and ideological reasons for his controversial decision to run in May 2010. This unquestionably ruthless politician has to show his party and the country why he was prepared to do whatever it took – including political fratricide – to become leader. There is no time to waste.

But he also needs somehow to resolve the David issue which could come to haunt his leadership. He may not, as Glasman claims, be overburdened with guilt. But he cannot afford to ignore the breakdown of relations between them, and his share of responsibility for it.

As one senior former Cabinet minister close to David observes: 'I don't understand the dynamics between the two of them. Have you met anyone who can properly explain it to you? I just simply don't understand it.' The dynamic is all the harder to understand given Ed's tendency to be so warm to almost everyone he meets, an approach that makes him popular but could occasionally be misconstrued as verging on superficial.

The Miliband brothers are the two most talented Labour figures of their generation. It is right that one of them should be leader. But it would have been better for Labour to have had them both at the top of the party, serving in the frontline of the war against the coalition, rather than just one of them.

By all accounts, Ed genuinely wishes his brother would return to frontline politics. He is fortunate to have other talented figures, like Douglas Alexander and Ed Balls, on his frontbench – but he believes he would benefit from David's presence too.

Almost everyone interviewed for this book agrees that one of Ed's strengths is his ability to empathise with others, to listen and to learn. Yet when it came to communicating and empathising with his own brother he fell woefully short.

Politically, Ed and David had been heading in different directions for several years; personally, however, there is more that unites them than divides them. 'My impression is that they were profoundly close in the sense that there was a real bond between them,' says one senior Labour figure who knows them both well. 'I quite often saw them together, casually or at meetings and it's obvious when you saw them together that they knew how each other thought, they'd know each other's opinions on everything.'[7] A female friend of Ed observes: 'The thing about David and Ed that you have to realise is that they come from a very unusual family. And whereas I might speak to my sister twice a day or my mother three times a day, they never had that relationship to start off with. That doesn't mean that they don't love each other, it doesn't mean that they're not close.'[8]

Ed Miliband could well be the country's next Prime Minister. There is every sign he could be an effective one. But first he has to develop and ripen. He must apply the same sense of urgency and insurgency that characterised his leadership campaign to the job of party leader. He must be true to his own values and not be swayed by more cynical figures. At the same time, given the ongoing distrust between his own circle and that around David, Ed must do everything he can to make peace with his brother, who secured more votes than him among party members and MPs. Only then will the Labour Party fully be at peace with itself.

No longer 'the other Miliband' or 'the other Ed', he has now fully emerged from the shadows. Though he has done so with some ruthlessness, he may well be, as David said so memorably after his own defeat, 'a special person'. Ed's challenge now is to prove this to a sceptical country.

ENDNOTES

Ralph 1969–1981

1. Ed Miliband, speech to Labour Party conference, Manchester, 28 September 2011
2. Michael Newman, *Ralph Miliband and the Politics of the New Left* (Merlin Press, 2002), p.6
3. Michael Newman, *Ralph Miliband and the Politics of the New Left*, p.9
4. Michael Newman, *Ralph Miliband and the Politics of the New Left*, p.11
5. Michael Newman, *Ralph Miliband and the Politics of the New Left*, p.14
6. Michael Newman, *Ralph Miliband and the Politics of the New Left*, p.23
7. Michael Newman, *Ralph Miliband and the Politics of the New Left*, p.12
8. Ed Miliband, speech to Labour Party conference, Manchester, 28 September 2011
9. Michael Newman, *Ralph Miliband and the Politics of the New Left*, p.146
10. Michael Newman, *Ralph Miliband and the Politics of the New Left*
11. 'Ralph Miliband, Socialist Intellectual, 1924-1994', *The Socialist Register* 1995, pp.1-21
12. 'In the house of the rising sons', *The Guardian*, 28 February 2004
13. Ed Miliband, speech to Labour Party conference, Manchester, 28 September 2011
14. Michael Newman, *Ralph Miliband and the Politics of the New Left*, p.72
15. Michael Newman, *Ralph Miliband and the Politics of the New Left*, p.72
16. Michael Newman, *Ralph Miliband and the Politics of the New Left*, p.52
17. Ralph Miliband, *Parliamentary Socialism: A Study in the Politics of Labour* (Merlin Press, 1972) p.13
18. 'David and Ed Miliband – if you really want to move on, listen to your father', *Guardian* website, 5 August 2010
19. 'Ralph Miliband, Socialist Intellectual,

1924-1994', *The Socialist Register* 1995, pp.1-21
20. Michael Newman, *Ralph Miliband and the Politics of the New Left*, p.77
21. Ralph Miliband, *Parliamentary Socialism: A Study in the Politics of Labour*, p. 376
22. Interview with Leo Panitch
23. Michael Newman, *Ralph Miliband and the Politics of the New Left*, p.107
24. Michael Newman, *Ralph Miliband and the Politics of the New Left*, p.107
25. Michael Newman, *Ralph Miliband and the Politics of the New Left*, p.108
26. Ed Miliband, speech to Labour Party conference, Manchester, 28 September 2011
27. Ed Miliband interview with Mary Riddell, 10 June 2010
28. Interview, Ed Miliband
29. Interview, Leo Panitch
30. Ed Miliband speech, 'Why I'm standing', Leeds, 10 June 2010
31. Interview, Tony Benn
32. Michael Newman, *Ralph Miliband and the Politics of the New Left*, p.108
33. Ed Miliband, eulogy for Ralph Miliband, 27 May 1994
34. Private interview
35. 'Ed and David Miliband: the battle of the brothers', *The Observer*, 5 September 2010
36. Interview, Leo Panitch
37. Robin Blackburn interview on *Newsnight*, BBC2, 23 September 2010
38. Interview, Richard Kuper
39. Ed Miliband interview with Mary Riddell, 10 June 2010
40. Michael Newman, *Ralph Miliband and the Politics of the New Left*, p.227
41. Michael Newman, *Ralph Miliband and the Politics of the New Left*, p.225
42. Interview, Ed Miliband
43. Michael Newman, *Ralph Miliband and the Politics of the New Left*, p.258

44. Michael Newman, *Ralph Miliband and the Politics of the New Left*, p.258
45. Interview, Ed Miliband
46. Interview, Ed Miliband
47. Private interviews
48. Private information
49. Interview, Norma Dolby
50. Ed Miliband, 'Why I'm standing' speech, Leeds, 10 June 2010
51. Private interview
52. Ed Miliband, speech to Labour Party conference, Manchester, 28 September 2011
53. Michael Newman, *Ralph Miliband and the Politics of the New Left*, p.127
54. Interview, Ed Miliband
55. Ed Miliband interview on BBC Five Live, 29 September 2010
56. 'My family values: Ed Miliband', *The Guardian*, 7 August 2010
57. Michael Newman, *Ralph Miliband and the Politics of the New Left*, p.339
58. Interview, Ed Miliband
59. Michael Newman, *Ralph Miliband and the Politics of the New Left*, p.299
60. 'In the house of the rising sons', *The Guardian*, 28 February 2004
61. Ed Miliband interview with Mary Riddell, 10 June 2010
62. Robin Blackburn, 'Ralph Miliband, 1924-1994', *New Left Review* 206, July/August 1994, p.15
63. Ed Miliband, speech to Labour Party conference, Manchester, 28 September 2011

Haverstock 1981–1989
1. 'The London comprehensive that's schooled Labour's elite', *The Guardian*, 2 August 2010
2. Interview, Nikki Haydon
3. 'The London comprehensive that's schooled Labour's elite', *The Guardian*, 2 August 2010
4. Interview, Oona King
5. 'Haverstock alumni in the spotlight!', *Camden New Journal*, 27 May 2010
6. Interview, Vivian Jacobs
7. Interview, Andrew Turnbull
8. Interview, Nikki Haydon
9. Interview, Nikki Haydon
10. Interview, Vivian Jacobs
11. Interview, Ed Miliband

12. Interview, Ed Miliband
13. 'Ed Miliband called me a Turkish b****** ... so I hit him: Former schoolmate claims racist abuse was real reason Labour leader was beaten up', *Mail on Sunday*, 6 February 2011
14. 'Ed Miliband called me a Turkish b****** ... so I hit him: Former schoolmate claims racist abuse was real reason Labour leader was beaten up', *Mail on Sunday*, 6 February 2011
15. Interview, Oona King
16. 'Ed Miliband called me a Turkish b****** ... so I hit him: Former schoolmate claims racist abuse was real reason Labour leader was beaten up', *Mail on Sunday*, 6 February 2011
17. Interview, Ed Miliband
18. Interview, Nikki Haydon
19. Interview, Oona King
20. Interview, Oona King
21. 'The London comprehensive that's schooled Labour's elite', *The Guardian*, 2 August 2010
22. Interview, Clive Bull
23. Interview, Vincent Graff
24. Private information
25. 'In the house of the rising sons', *The Guardian*, 28 February 2004
26. Interview, Tony Benn
27. Interview, Ruth Winstone
28. Interview, Ed Miliband
29. 'From the intern pen to Her Majesty's Government', *The Nation Associate*, Fall 2007
30. Interview, D.D. Guttenplan
31. 'From the intern pen to Her Majesty's Government', *The Nation Associate*, Fall 2007
32. Private information

Oxford 1989–1992
1. Interview, Marc Stears
2. Gautam Mody
3. Interview, Catherine O'Rawe
4. Interview, Gautam Mody
5. Interview, Marc Stears
6. Private interview
7. Interview, Gautam Mody
8. Interview, Marc Stears
9. Interview, Adam Swift
10. 'Obituary: Andrew Glyn, *The Guardian*, 1 January 2008

11. Interview, Marc Stears
12. Private interview
13. Interview, Marc Stears
14. Interview Marc Stears
15. Private interview
16. Prime Minister's Questions, 10 December 2010
17. Interview, Marc Stears
18. Interview, Gautam Mody
19. Interview, Gautam Mody
20. Private information
21. Interview, Marc Stears
22. Private information
23. 'The Lady who turned to nationalisation', *Times Higher Education Supplement*, 20 October 1995
24. Interview, Marc Stears
25. Private interview
26. 'Band of brothers', *The Guardian*, 12 July 2008
27. Private information
28. Interview, Marc Stears
29. Interview, Marc Stears
30. Private interview
31. Private interview
32. Interview, Catherine O'Rawe
33. Interview, Gautam Mody
34. Interview, Catherine O'Rawe
35. Interview, Marc Stears
36. Private interview
37. Private interview
38. Interview, Marc Stears
39. Interview, Marc Stears
40. Interview, Marc Stears
41. Private information
42. Interview, Marc Stears
43. Interview, Marc Stears
44. Private interview
45. Interview, Catherine O'Rawe
46. Interview, Catherine O'Rawe
47. Private interview
48. Interview, Catherine O'Rawe
49. Private interview
50. Interview, Gautam Mody
51. Interview, Gautam Mody
52. Interview, Catherine O'Rawe
53. Interview, Gautam Mody
54. Private interview
55. Interview, Gautam Mody
56. Interview, Martin Conway
57. Interview, Catherine O'Rawe
58. Interview, Martin Conway
59. Interview, David Leopold
60. Interview, Adam Swift
61. Interview, Neil Kinnock
62. Interview, Adam Swift
63. Private interview
64. Interview, Gautam Mody
65. Private interview

Into Opposition 1992–1997

1. '"Bright boy" Mili's big break', *Evening Standard*, 29 September 2010
2. Interview, Anne Lapping
3. Interview, Andrew Rawnsley
4. Interview, Anne Lapping
5. Interview, Anne Lapping
6. Interview, Harriet Harman
7. Private information
8. Interview, Harriet Harman
9. '"Bright boy" Mili's big break', *Evening Standard*, 29 September 2010
10. Interview, Andrew Rawnsley
11. Private information
12. Interview, Harriet Harman
13. Interview, Andrew Rawnsley
14. Interview, Anne Lapping
15. Interview, Marc Stears
16. 'The New Statesman Politics Interview — Yvette Cooper', *New Statesman*, 27 April 2011
17. Private interview
18. Private information
19. Interview, Ed Miliband
20. 'Simple arithmetic and Tory taxes: Why does the burden seem to go up and up, under both parties?', *The Independent*, 25 January 1994
21. Private information
22. 'You created this job, David. You should do it', *The Times*, 11 November 2009
23. Interview, Sue Nye
24. Interview, Harriet Harman
25. 'In the house of the rising sons', *The Guardian*, 28 February 2004
26. Interview, Harriet Harman
27. Private interview
28. Interview, Neal Lawson
29. Private information
30. Private information
31. 'In the house of the rising sons', *The Guardian*, 28 February 2004
32. Interview, Gautam Mody
33. Private interview

34. Ed Miliband interview with Mary Riddell, 10 June 2010
35. Private information
36. Ed Miliband, eulogy for Ralph Miliband, 27 May 1994
37. Ralph Miliband, *Socialism for a Sceptical Age* (Polity Press, 1994)
38. Michael Newman, *Ralph Miliband and the Politics of the New Left*, (Merlin Press, 2002) p.331
39. Private information
40. Ralph Miliband, *Socialism for a Sceptical Age* (Polity Press, 1994), pp.194-95
41. Interview, Philip Collins
42. Interview, Philip Collins
43. Steve Richards, *Whatever It Takes: The Real Story of Gordon Brown and New Labour* (Fourth Estate, 2010), p.67
44. 'Mandelson admits Labour "fissure"', BBC website, 26 September 2006
45. Steve Richards, *Whatever It Takes: The Real Story of Gordon Brown and New Labour* (Fourth Estate, 2010), p.81
46. Private information
47. Interview, Paul Gregg
48. Interview, Ed Balls
49. Private information
50. Hugh Pym & Nick Kochan, *Gordon Brown: The First Year in Power* (Bloomsbury, 1998), p.87
51. Private interview
52. Hugh Pym & Nick Kochan, *Gordon Brown: The First Year in Power* (Bloomsbury, 1998), p.88
53. Interview, Ed Balls
54. 'Brown pledges 10p tax, but no top rate rise', *The Independent*, 21 January 1997
55. Private information
56. 'Gordon Brown's reign is a "family affair"', *The Times*, 6 January 2008
57. Steve Richards, *Whatever It Takes: The Real Story of Gordon Brown and New Labour* (Fourth Estate, 2010), p.99

Treasury 1997–2002
1. *New Statesman* Labour Leadership Hustings, 9 June 2010
2. Private interview
3. Hugh Pym & Nick Kochan, *Gordon Brown: The First Year in Power* (Bloomsbury, 1998), p.4

4. Interview, former Treasury permanent secretary
5. 'In the house of the rising sons', *The Guardian*, 28 February 2004
6. Private interview
7. Geoffrey Robinson, *The Unconventional Minister: My Life Inside New Labour* (Penguin, 2001), pp.32-33
8. Private interviews
9. 'Brown's mechanics behind the machinations of government', *The Guardian*, 9 November 1999
10. Private information
11. Private interview
12. Private information
13. Private interview
14. Private interview
15. Private interview
16. Private interview
17. Private information
18. Interview, Ed Miliband
19. Interview, former Treasury official
20. Private interview
21. Private interview
22. Interview, former Cabinet minister
23. 'Brown's mechanics behind the machinations of government', *The Guardian*, 9 November 1999
24. Hugh Pym & Nick Kochan, *Gordon Brown: The First Year in Power* (Bloomsbury, 1998), p.55
25. Interview, Deborah Mattinson
26. Interview, Andrew Turnbull
27. Interview, former Treasury official
28. Interview, Charles Falconer
29. Andrew Rawnsley, *The End of the Party: The Rise and Fall of New Labour* (Penguin Books, 2010), p.12
30. Andrew Rawnsley, *The End of the Party: The Rise and Fall of New Labour*, p.62
31. Andrew Rawnsley, *Observer*, 18 January 1998
32. Interview, former Cabinet minister
33. Interview, former Downing St official
34. 'Inside the brotherhood: meet David and Ed Miliband', *The Times*, 1 August 2008
35. '"Red Ed" Miliband lives in £1.6m house after shrewd property moves', *Daily Telegraph*, 4 October 2010
36. Private information

37. 'In the house of the rising sons', The Guardian, 28 February 2004
38. Private information
39. Private interview
40. Private interview
41. Private interview
42. 'An unimaginably big tent', New Statesman, 3 February 2003
43. Interview, Downing
44. Private interview
45. Private information
46. Private information
47. Andrew Rawnsley, Servants of the People: The Inside Story of New Labour, (Penguin, 2001), p.338
48. 'Tax-funded NHS "offers fairest and best value way ahead"', Daily Telegraph, 29 November 2001
49. Private information
50. Derek Wanless, Securing our future health: taking a long-term view (HM Treasury, 2002)
51. Budget speech, 17 April 2002
52. Andrew Rawnsley, The End of the Party: The Rise and Fall of New Labour, p.76
53. Steve Richards, Whatever It Takes: The Real Story of Gordon Brown and New Labour (Fourth Estate, 2010), p.153
54. Interview, Ed Miliband
55. Andrew Rawnsley, The End of the Party: The Rise and Fall of New Labour, p.76
56. 'Popularity of Budget halts Tory revival', The Guardian, 23 April 2002
57. Private interview
58. Interview, Ed Balls
59. Private interview
60. Private interview
61. Polly Toynbee & David Walker, Did Things Get Better? An Audit of Labour's Successes and Failures (Penguin, 2001), p.21
62. 'Brown's mechanics behind the machinations of government', The Guardian, 9 November 1999
63. Andrew Rawnsley, The End of the Party: The Rise and Fall of New Labour, p.69
64. Polly Toynbee & David Walker, The Verdict: Did Labour Change Britain? (Granta Books, 2010), p.206
65. 'Labour's tax and benefits strategy has closed the income gap, thinktank says', The Guardian, 26 March 2010
66. Private interview
67. 'Can the brothers give Labour family therapy?', The Times, 20 May 2010
68. Private interview
69. Interview, Stewart Wood
70. Private information
71. Private interview
72. 'It will deprive Labour of one of its strongest assets', The Scotsman, 26 July 2002
73. Private information

Harvard 2002–2004
1. Interview, Peter Hall
2. Interview, Trisha Craig
3. Interview, Martin O'Neill
4. Interview, George Ross
5. Michael Newman, Ralph Miliband and the Politics of the New Left, (Merlin Press), p.255
6. 'The Ed Miliband Interview', Labour Uncut website, 21 July 2010
7. Private interview
8. Interview, Martin O'Neill
9. Interview, Peter Hall
10. Interview, Archon Fung
11. Interview, Archon Fung
12. Interview, Peter Hall
13. Private interview
14. Private interview
15. Interview, Trisha Craig
16. Interview, Trisha Craig
17. Interview, Martin O'Neill
18. Interview, Trisha Craig
19. Interview, Peter Hall
20. Interview, Ed Miliband
21. Interview, Trisha Craig
22. Interview, Martin O'Neill
23. Tony Blair interview. Newsnight, BBC2, 4 June 2001
24. Private interview
25. Private interview
26. Interview, David Blackbourn
27. Interview, Martin O'Neill
28. Interview, Trisha Craig
29. Interview, Trisha Craig
30. Interview, Martin O'Neill
31. Private interview
32. Interview, Spencer Livermore
33. Interview, Peter Hall
34. Interview, Spencer Livermore

35. Interview, Stewart Wood
36. Interview, Trisha Craig
37. Interview, Peter Hall

Iraq 2003
1. George Bush speech to the United Nations General Assembly, 12 September 2002
2. *Iraq's Weapons of Mass Destruction: The Assessment of the British Government*, 24 September 2002
3. 'The double standards of Mr Blair's promotion of human rights', *The Independent*, 19 September 2003
4. Private information
5. Interview, Richard Sennett
6. Interview, Gautam Mody
7. Private interviews
8. Interview, Trisha Craig
9. Interview, George Ross
10. Interview, Spencer Livermore
11. Interview, Spencer Livermore
12. Interview, Spencer Livermore
13. Private interview
14. Private information
15. Private interview
16. 'Adviser regrets pushing Edwards on Iraq', MSNBC website, 13 March 2007
17. Andrew Rawnsley, *The End of the Party: The Rise and Fall of New Labour* (Penguin Books, 2010), p.168
18. Anthony Seldon, *Blair Unbound* (Pocket Books, 2008)
19. Interview, Paul Gregg
20. Interview, Trisha Craig
21. Interview, former adviser to the Treasury
22. Private interview

Council of Economic Advisers 2004–2005
1. Private interview
2. 'Brown's kitchen cabinet costs £1m a year', *Daily Telegraph*, 23 February 2007
3. Private interview
4. Interview, former Treasury official
5. Private interview
6. Interview, Paul Gregg
7. Private information
8. Private information
9. Private interview
10. Interview, former Treasury official
11. Interview, former Treasury official

12. Interview, Nicholas Stern
13. Interview, Naomi Eisenstadt
14. Interview, Nicholas Stern
15. John Prescott, *Prezza, My Story: Pulling No Punches* (Headline Review, 2008), p.308
16. Andrew Rawnsley, *The End of the Party: The Rise and Fall of New Labour*, p.270
17. 'How the bloody anarchy of Iraq broke the spirit of Tony Blair', *The Observer*, 28 February 2010
18. 'Blair team denies smear campaign in new war of words with Brown', *Daily Telegraph*, 29 June 2004
19. Private interviews; Andrew Rawnsley, *The End of the Party: The Rise and Fall of New Labour*, p.270; Anthony Seldon, *Blair Unbound* (Pocket Books, 2008), pp.276-77
20. Private interview
21. Private interview
22. Interview, former Treasury official
23. Interview, Geoffrey Robinson
24. Interview, former Treasury official
25. Interview, Spencer Livermore
26. Interview, former Treasury adviser
27. 'The anger and hurt of Brown', *The Guardian*, 2 October 2004
28. Private information
29. Private interview
30. Interview, former Treasury official
31. Private information
32. Private information
33. Interview, friend of Justine Thornton
34. Interview, friend of Justine Thornton

Doncaster 2005
1. Private information
2. Private information
3. Interview, David Muir
4. Interview, Jonathan Ashworth
5. Private information
6. 'Ed Miliband: Welcome to my world', *The Guardian*, 19 March 2011
7. Private information
8. Interview, Jon Trickett
9. 'Row erups over MP shortlist', *Doncaster Free Press*, 21 March 2005
10. Interview, Michael Dugher
11. Private interview
12. Private information
13. Interview, Michael Dugher

14. Private information
15. Private interview
16. Private interview
17. Private interview
18. Private information
19. Private information
20. Private interview
21. Private information
22. Private interview
23. Interview, Michael Dugher
24. Interview, John Healey
25. 'Oh brother, a star in the making',
    Yorkshire Post, 26 March 2005
26. Private information
27. 'Oh brother, a star in the making',
    Yorkshire Post, 26 March 2005
28. Interview, Michael Dugher
29. Interview, Michael Dugher
30. Interview, George Ross
31. Private interview
32. 'Oh brother, a star in the making',
    Yorkshire Post, 26 March 2005
33. Private interview
34. Private information
35. Ed Miliband letter to Doncaster Free
    Press, 30 September 2010
36. Ed Miliband letter to Doncaster Free
    Press, 30 September 2010

Into Parliament 2005–2007

1. Private information
2. Private information
3. Interview, Lyn Brown
4. Interview, Sadiq Khan
5. Interview, Lyn Brown
6. Inteview, Sadiq Khan
7. Private information
8. Private information
9. Interview, Sadiq Khan
10. Francis Elliott & James Hanning,
    *Cameron: The Rise of the New
    Conservative* (Harper Perennial, 2009)
11. Interview, friend of Justine Thornton
12. Interview, Quincy Whitaker
13. Ed Miliband, maiden speech in the
    House of Commons, 23 May 2005
14. Private information
15. 'New Socialist Entrepreneur - Ed
    Miliband, minister for the third
    sector', *Regeneration & Renewal*, 6
    April 2007
16. 'New Socialist Entrepreneur - Ed
    Miliband, minister for the third

sector', *Regeneration & Renewal*, 6
April 2007
17. 'Miliband's plan for power is putting
    his party back on course', *Daily
    Telegraph*, 1 April 2011
18. Private interview
19. Private information

Into Cabinet 2007–2008

1. Private information
2. Peter Watt, *Inside Out: My story of
   betrayal and cowardice at the heart of
   New Labour*, (Biteback, 2010), p.173
3. Private interviews
4. 'The Politics interview: Douglas
   Alexander', *New Statesman*, 16 July
   2009
5. 'How 'the election that never was'
   turned political allies into bitter
   rivals', *The Independent*, 17 September
   2010
6. Private information
7. Interview, Ed Miliband
8. Private information
9. 'How 'the election that never was'
   turned political allies into bitter rivals',
   The Independent, 17 September 2010
10. Private interview
11. Private interview
12. Private information
13. Ed Miliband speech to the Labour
    Party spring conference, Birmingham,
    2 March 2008
14. Private information
15. 'Against all odds we can still win, on
    a platform for change', *The Guardian*,
    29 July 2009
16. Private information
17. Private information
18. Private information
19. Private interview
20. Private information
21. Private information
22. Private information
23. Private information
24. Private information

Climate Change 2008–2010

1. Interview, Ed Miliband
2. Private interview
3. Private information
4. 'Government pledges to cut carbon
   emissions by 80% by 2050', *The*

Guardian, 16 October 2008
5. Interview, DECC civil servant
6. Private information
7. Interview, former Downing St official
8. Private information
9. Private interview
10. Interview, Gavin Kelly
11. Interview, former Downing St official
12. Private information
13. Interview, Gavin Kelly
14. Private information
15. Private information
16. Interview, former Cabinet minister
17. Private information
18. 'Conflict, compromise and the rise of the "Milibenn" tendency', *The Guardian*, 16 January 2009
19. Private information
20. Interview, former Downing St official
21. 'Heathrow third runway reaction', BBC website, 15 January 2009
22. Private information
23. Ed Miliband speech, 'The Politics of Climate Change', London School of Economics, 19 November 2009
24. Private interview
25. Private interview
26. Interview, Mark Lynas
27. Private interview
28. Interview, Mark Lynas
29. Interview, former Cabinet minister
30. Interview, Richard Darlington
31. Interview, Richard Darlington
32. Private information
33. Private interview
34. 'Lord Mandelson has set up rival "energy and climate change unit"', *The Guardian*, 26 April 2009
35. 'Clean coal push marks reversal of UK energy policy', *The Guardian*, 23 April 2009
36. 'Getting warm on coal', *Guardian* Comment is Free, 24 April 2009
37. 'Ed Miliband's live-in girlfriend is nuclear lawyer', *Daily Telegraph*, 14 March 2009
38. Interview, Quincy Whitaker
39. Interview, former Downing St official
40. Private interview
41. Interview, senior climate change adviser to coalition government
42. 'Ed Miliband declares war on climate change sceptics', *The Observer*, 31 January 2010
43. 'Ed Miliband: Tories are "climate saboteurs"', *The Times*, 4 December 2009
44. 'Opposing wind farms should be socially taboo, says Ed Miliband', *The Guardian*, 24 March 2009
45. Interview, former Downing St official
46. 'The US and China Joined Forces Against Europe', *Der Spiegel*, 12 August 2010
47. Interview, former Foreign Office minister
48. Interview, Ed Miliband
49. 'Climate Crunch', *The Guardian*, 21 November 2009
50. 'Rich nations accused of Copenhagen "power grab"', *The Guardian*, 9 December 2010
51. Private information
52. Private information
53. Ed Miliband statement to the House of Commons, 5 January 2011
54. 'Copenhagen deal reaction in quotes', BBC website, 19 December 2009
55. 'Copenhagen: The last-ditch drama that saved the deal from collapse', *The Guardian*, 20 December 2009.
56. 'Copenhagen closes with weak deal that poor threaten to reject', *The Guardian*, 19 December 2009.
57. '"Don't wreck conference" pleas Miliband', BBC website, 19 December 2009
58. Interview, Michael Jacobs
59. 'Did Ed Miliband save the Copenhagen summit from complete failure?', *The Guardian*, 23 December 2009
60. 'Copenhagen cuts corners on climate change safeguards', *The Times*, 19 December 2009
61. Private interview
62. 'The road from Copenhagen', *The Guardian*, 21 December 2009.
63. Private interview
64. Interview, former Cabinet minister
65. Interview, former Cabinet minister
66. Interview, Sadiq Khan
67. Interview, Nick Pearce
68. Interview, former Downing St official
69. Private information

General Election 2010
1. Private information
2. Interview, Patrick Diamond
3. Private information
4. Private information
5. Private interview
6. 'Will they, won't they launch a coup?', *The Independent*, 1 January 2010
7. 'In full: Text of Brown letter', BBC website, 6 January 2010
8. Private information
9. Private information
10. Private information
11. Private information
12. Private interview
13. Private interview
14. Private information
15. Private interview
16. Private interview
17. Private information

Decision to Run May 2010
1. Private information
2. Interview, Marc Stears
3. Private information
4. Interview, Oona King
5. 'Alan Johnson backs David Miliband for Labour leader', BBC website, 12 May 2010
6. Private information
7. 'David Miliband is first to declare leadership hopes', *Daily Mail*, 13 May 2010
8. Private information
9. Interview, Ed Miliband
10. Private information
11. Private information
12. Private information
13. Private information
14. Private information
15. Private information
16. Ed Miliband speech to the Fabian Society, London, 15 May 2010
17. Private information
18. Private information
19. Private information
20. Private interview
21. Private information
22. Private information
23. Private interview
24. Private information
25. Private information
26. Private interview

27. Interview, Neil Kinnock
28. Private interview
29. Private information

Leadership Campaign May–September 2010
1. Private interview
2. Private interview
3. Interview, Peter Hain
4. Private information
5. Private information
6. Private interview
7. Interview, Stewart Wood
8. Interview, Stewart Wood
9. Interview, adviser to Ed
10. Private information
11. Interview, senior Labour strategist
12. Interview, adviser to Ed
13. Private interview
14. Private information
15. Private interview
16. Interview, former Cabinet minister
17. Private information
18. Private information
19. Interview, Tom Watson
20. Interview Tom Watson
21. 'In conversation with...Peter Mandelson', *Total Politics*, 21 November 2010
22. 'The favourite – David Miliband', *New Statesman*, 26 July 2010
23. Interview, Sadiq Khan
24. 'Ed Miliband blasts back at Peter Mandelson as Labour leadership contest heats up', *Daily Record*, 31 August 2010
25. 'Miliband hits back at criticism from Lord Mandelson', BBC website, 30 August 2010
26. Private information
27. Private interview
28. Private interview
29. Ed Miliband, opening remarks, *New Statesman* Labour Leadership Hustings, 9 June 2010
30. Private interview
31. Interview, Hilary Wainwright
32. Interview, union general secretary
33. Private information
34. Interview, senior Labour MP
35. Interview, adviser to Ed
36. Interview, Ed Miliband
37. Private interview

38. Private information
39. Private information
40. Private information
41. 'Campbell: Ed Miliband isn't up to leading Labour', *Independent on Sunday*, 6 June 2010
42. Private information
43. Private interview
44. Private interview
45. Private information
46. Private information
47. Private information
48. Private information
49. Private interview
50. Private information
51. Private interview
52. Private information
53. David Miliband speech, London, 25 August 2010
54. Private information
55. Private interview
56. Private interview
57. Private interview
58. Private interview
59. Interview, Neil Kinnock
60. Private interview
61. Private information
62. Private information
63. 'How much is your Labour leadership vote worth?', *New Statesman* website, 26 August 2010
64. 'How David Miliband "lurched" to the centre-left', *Next Left* blog, 22 July 2010
65. Private interview
66. Interview, adviser to Ed
67. Interview, adviser to Ed
68. Private interview
69. Private information
70. Private information
71. Private information
72. Interview, adviser to Ed
73. Private information
74. Private information
75. Interview, shadow Cabinet minister
76. Private interview
77. Interview, former Foreign Office minister
78. Private information
79. Private interview
80. Private interview
81. Private information
82. Private interview
83. Private information
84. Private interview
85. Interview, Jon Cruddas
86. Private information
87. Interview, Jon Cruddas
88. 'David Miliband attacks Gordon Brown for failing to renew Labour Party', *Guardian* website, 9 July 2010
89. 'Cruddas: Why I'm backing David Miliband', *New Statesman* website, 26 August 2010
90. Interview, Jon Cruddas
91. Interview, Neal Lawson
92. Interview, Neal Lawson
93. Interview, shadow Cabinet minister
94. *New Statesman* Labour Leadership Hustings, 9 June 2010
95. Private information
96. 'Labour leadership hopefuls attack Ed Miliband on Iraq war stance', *Guardian* website, 16 June 2010
97. Private information
98. 'Milibands battle it out over Iraq war', *The Guardian*, 30 July 2010
99. Interview, shadow Cabinet minister
100. 'New Labour is like the Monty Python Parrot... Dead', *Daily Mirror*, 11 September 2009
101. '"I told David Cameron's man to get lost"', *New Statesman*, 8 March 2010
102. Private interview
103. Private information
104. Interview, union general secretary
105. Private information
106. Interview, union general secretary
107. Interview, union general secretary
108. Private information
109. Private interview
110. Private information
111. Private information
112. Private interview
113. Interview, friend of Ed Balls
114. Interview, Ken Livingstone
115. Private interview
116. Interview, Ken Livingstone
117. Interview, former Downing St official
118. Private information
119. 'Will Balls drop out to back David Mili?', *Evening Standard* blog, 23 July 2010
120. Private information
121. Private interview
122. 'Charlie Whelan: The puppet master who "won it for Ed"', *Sunday*

Telegraph, 3 October 2010
123. Private information
124. Private information
125. Interview, Miliband family friend
126. Interview, Leo Panitch
127. Interview, friend of Marion Kozak
128. Private interview
129. Interview, Tony Benn
130. Private interview
131. Interview, senior adviser to Ed
132. Private information
133. Private information
134. Private interview
135. Private interview
136. Private interviews
137. Private information
138. Interview, David Muir
139. Interview, Neil and Glenys Kinnock
140. Private interview
141. Private interview
142. Private information
143. Interview, Sadiq Khan
144. Interview, Greg Beales
145. Private interview
146. Private information
147. Interview, Jon Trickett
148. Ed Miliband chapter in 'The Labour Leadership', (Fabian Society, August 2010)
149. Private interview
150. Private interview
151. Private information
152. 'David Miliband boosted by Dennis Skinner's endorsement', *New Statesman*, 10 September 2010
153. 'Shock Labour Party leadership poll gives lead to Ed Miliband', *Sunday Times*, 12 September 2010
154. Interview, Alex Smith
155. Private information

Victory September 2010
1. Private information
2. Private interview
3. Interview, Labour leadership contender
4. Private information
5. Private information
6. 'Ed Miliband is elected leader of the Labour Party', BBC website, 25 September 2010
7. Private information
8. Gordon Brown, speech to the Labour Party conference, Manchester, 25 September 2010
9. Private information
10. Private information
11. Private information
12. Private information
13. Interview, Marcus Roberts
14. 'Labour Leadership Election 2010', Labour Party website
15. Private information
16. Ed Miliband, speech to the Labour Party conference, Manchester, 25 September 2010
17. Private information
18. Private information
19. Private interview
20. Private information
21. Private information
22. Private information
23. Private information
24. Private information
25. Private information
26. 'Ed Miliband union backers accused over Labour ballot mail-out', *The Guardian*, 25 September
27. Private interview
28. 'Ed Miliband union backers accused over Labour ballot mail-out', *The Guardian*, 25 September
29. Private interview
30. Interview, shadow Cabinet minister
31. Private interview
32. Interview, Conservative Cabinet minister
33. Private information
34. Private interview
35. Private information
36. Private information
37. Private information
38. 'Will humiliated David now walk away, or stay and spark civil war?', *Daily Mail*, 27 September 2010
39. Ed Miliband interview, *The Andrew Marr Show*, BBC1, 26 September 2010
40. David Miliband, speech to the Labour Party conference, Manchester, 27 September 2010
41. Private information
42. David Miliband, speech to the Labour Party conference, Manchester, 27 September 2010
43. Interview, Sue Nye
44. Interview, Marc Stears

45. Private information
46. 'David sees Red Ed mist', *The Sun*, 29 September 2010
47. 'Mixed views among Jews', *The Guardian*, 1 October 2010
48. Ed Miliband, speech to the Labour Party conference, Manchester, 28 September 2010
49. Private information
50. Interview, Neil Kinnock
51. Private information
52. Private information
53. 'Chief whip is forced to step down', *Financial Times*, 30 September 2010
54. 'Ed Miliband asks chief whip Nick Brown to step aside', BBC website, 29 September 2010
55. Private interview
56. 'Extracts from David Miliband's letter', BBC website, 29 September 2010
57. 'Exit David ... but will he be back?', *Daily Mail*, 30 September 2010

Leader of the Opposition
September 2010 –
1. Private interview
2. Andrew Rawnsley, *The End of the Party: The Rise and Fall of New Labour*,
3. Private interview
4. 'Labour leadership', *Financial Times*, 1 September 2010
5. Private interview
6. Private interview
7. 'Playing the long game: Miliband shuns quick fixes in first 100 days', *The Guardian*, 4 January 2011
8. Private interview
9. Private information
10. 'Coalition search for some killer apps', *The Guardian*, 3 March 2011
11. Private information
12. Private interview
13. Interview, adviser to Ed
14. 'Ed's leadership will be lonely, but his politics are sound', *The Guardian*, 8 October 2010
15. 'From the sublime to the ridiculous', *The Independent*, 4 April 2011
16. Private information
17. 'Miliband snubs Balls and Cooper by picking Johnson', *Daily Telegraph*, 9 October 2010
18. Interview, senior Labour MP
19. Private information
20. Interview, Jon Cruddas
21. Interview, Ed Miliband
22. 'Ed Balls – man in a hurry', *New Statesman*, 4 April 2011
23. 'From the sublime to the ridiculous', *The Independent*, 4 April 2011
24. Private information
25. Interview, senior Labour MP
26. Interview, Andy Burnham
27. Interview, Labour MP
28. Interview, adviser to Ed Miliband
29. Private information; 'Miliband offered senior role to Purnell', Labour Uncut website, 12 November 2010
30. Private information
31. Interview, Charles Falconer
32. Private information
33. Private interview
34. 'Miliband faces being sucked down the plughole', *Daily Mail*, 2 December 2010
35. 'No style, no substance', *Daily Telegraph*, 4 December 2010
36. 'Time for Miliband to show us the beef', *Sunday Times*, 21 November 2010
37. Interview, shadow Cabinet minister
38. Private interview
39. 'Plotters give Labour leader until May to prove himself', *Evening Standard*, 8 December 2010
40. 'No "mess-ups" this time as Labour leader Ed is listed as the father of Milibaby No 2', *Daily Mail*, 12 November 2010
41. Private interview
42. 'Miliband plots the daddy of all fightbacks', *Sunday Times*, 12 December 2010
43. Private information
44. Ed Miliband interview, *Today* programme, BBC Radio 4, 26 November 2010
45. 'Labour winning over "squeezed middle" voters', *The Independent*, 1 March 2010
46. Interview, former Cabinet minister
47. 'A letter to the new Labour leader', *Independent on Sunday*, 26 September 2010
48. '50p supertax should stay for ever, says Ed Miliband', *Evening Standard*, 16 June 2010

49. 'No more Mr Nice Guy (but Harriet can boss me around)', *The Times*, 13 November 2010
50. 'Johnson still at odds with Miliband over tax', BBC website, 14 November 2010
51. Private interview
52. 'I'd be delighted if David Miliband decided to join us', *Daily Telegraph*, 4 December 2010
53. 'We can't keep treating party leaders like football managers', *The Guardian*, 9 December 2010
54. 'Alan Johnson's degree in making life difficult for Ed Miliband', *Spectator* website, 4 December 2010
55. '"Ready yourself" Johnson told as Miliband falters', *Mail on Sunday*, 5 December 2010
56. 'Off message', *The Guardian*, 21 January 2010
57. Private interview
58. Interview, shadow Cabinet minister
59. Interview, shadow Cabinet minister
60. Private information; 'Labour has to raise the stakes – and Ed Balls is a very good bet', *Daily Telegraph*, 25 January 2011; 'Exit the charmer, enter the hardman', *Sunday Times*, 23 January 2011
61. Private information
62. Interview, shadow Cabinet minister
63. Interview, shadow Cabinet minister
64. Private interview
65. Interview, shadow Cabinet minister
66. 'Coalition "has sold Middle England down the river"', *Sunday Telegraph*, 10 April 2011
67. '"Forget voters" aspirations at your peril, Balls warns Labour', *Financial Times*, 18 February 2011
68. Interview, Ken Livingstone
69. Private interview
70. Interview, shadow Cabinet minister
71. 'Renaissance Balls', *Spectator* website, 20 January 2011
72. 'Watch out – Gordon's gang are back in town', *The Times*, 29 January 2011
73. Private information
74. Private information
75. Private interview
76. Private interview
77. Private interview
78. Private information
79. Private interview
80. Private interview
81. Interview, Labour MP
82. 'Anguish of the Mili-women', *Evening Standard*, 28 September 2010
83. Private information
84. Private interview
85. Private interview
86. Private interview
87. Private interview
88. Interview, Neil Kinnock
89. Ed Miliband press conference, Westminster, 10 January 2011
90. 'No huskies, no north pole - but Miliband is in for the long haul', *The Guardian*, 22 November 2010
91. Private interview
92. Ed Miliband interview, *The Jeremy Vine Show*, BBC Radio 2, 6 January 2011
93. Interview, shadow Cabinet minister
94. Prime Minister's Questions, 2 March 2011
95. Prime Minister's Questions, 9 March 2011
96. Private information
97. 'Miliband plots the daddy of all fightbacks', *Sunday Times*, 12 December 2010
98. 'PMQs verdict: Ed Miliband beats David Cameron on points', *FT* Westminster Blog, 13 October 2010
99. 'Memo to Miliband: use humour against Cameron', *The Times*, 27 October 2010
100. Private interview
101. 'I'm keeping it real', *Sunday Times*, 1 May 2011
102. Prime Minister's Questions, 16 March 2011
103. 'Mandela and Miliband. Spot the difference', *The Times*, 30 March 2011
104. Private information
105. 'Ed Miliband issues BBC strike plea', BBC website, 1 October 2010
106. Interview, David Owen
107. Interview, Len McCluskey
108. 'Labour's growing dependence on the unions', *New Statesman* website, 23 February 2011
109. Interview, Spencer Livermore
110. 'Labour adopting "Good cop, bad cop" PR strategy with hires of Tom Baldwin and Bob Roberts', *PR Week* website, 16 December 2010

111. Private information
112. 'Meet the champagne (and coke snorting) socialist who is Labour's new Alastair Campbell', *Daily Mail*, 18 December 2010
113. Private information; 'Bring Me the Head of Thomas Baldwin', *New Statesman* website, 24 January 2011
114. 'Leaked Labour email: lay off Murdoch', *New Statesman* website, 2 February 2011
115. 'Ed Miliband calls for press review after phone hacking', BBC website, 19 April 2011
116. 'Kennedy in talks to join Labour', *Daily Mail*, 21 August 2010
117. '"I won't be defined by the right-wing press"', *New Statesman*, 22 August 2010
118. Ed Miliband interview, *The Andrew Marr Show*, BBC1, 16 January 2011
119. Private information; 'A dangerous liaison for Cameron – an emerging Lib Lab pact', *Daily Telegraph*, 18 January 2011
120. 'Liberal Democrats should engage with like-minded members of Labour', *Guardian* Comment is Free, 11 December 2010
121. Interview, Richard Grayson
122. 'Ed Miliband appeals to disenchanted Lib Dems to work with the Labour Party', *Daily Telegraph* website, 13 December 2010
123. 'Is this supping with the devil?', *The Liberator*, 10 March 2011
124. 'Can Ed Miliband find an antidote to the politics of fear and loathing?', *Daily Telegraph*, 11 January 2011
125. Interview, Jon Cruddas
126. Ed Miliband, speech to Labour Party conference, Manchester, 28 September 2011
127. Ed Miliband speech to the Fabian Society, London, 15 January 2011
128. Interview, Ed Miliband
129. Foreword, *The Labour Tradition and the Politics of Paradox* (The Oxford London Seminars, 2010), pp.6-7
130. Private information
131. Private interview
132. Interview, Ed Miliband
133. Ed Miliband speech to the Resolution Foundation, London, 28 February 2011
134. Interview, Nick Pearce
135. Private interview
136. Private information
137. Ed Miliband speech to the Scottish Labour Conference, Glasgow, 21 March 2011
138. Bobby Duffy and Helen Cleary, *The Coalition's First Year: the public's verdict* (Ipsos MORI, 2011), p.20
139. Ed Miliband interview, *The Politics Show*, BBC1, 1 May 2011
140. Bobby Duffy and Helen Cleary, *The Coalition's First Year: the public's verdict* (Ipsos MORI, 2011), p.22
141. Private information
142. Private interview
143. Interview, shadow Cabinet minister
144. Private interview
145. Interview, Marc Stears
146. 'No huskies, no north pole - but Miliband is in for the long haul', *The Guardian*, 22 November 2011
147. Private interview
148. Interview, former Cabinet minister
149. 'Ed Miliband to have nose operation for sleep disorder', BBC website, 22 April 2011
150. Private information
151. Interview, Jon Trickett
152. 'The curse of victory', *Prospect*, Issue 183, June 2011

Epilogue
1. Private information
2. 'David escapes Christmas lunch with Ed', *Daily Telegraph*, 22 December 2010
3. 'Door still open as a "massive talent" departs to the back benches', *The Independent*, 30 September 2010
4. Private information
5. '"You are my rock and I'm so lucky to have you and the kids"', *Daily Mirror*, 28 May 2011
6. Private interview
7. Private interview
8. Private interview

SELECT BIBLIOGRAPHY

Blair, Tony, *A Journey* (Hutchinson, 2010)

Boulton, Adam, & Jones, Joey, *Hung Together: The 2010 Election and the Coalition Government* (Simon & Schuster, 2010)

Campbell, Alastair, *The Blair Years* (Arrow, 2008)

Cowley, Philip, & Kavanagh, Dennis, *The British General Election of 2010* (Palgrave Macmillan, 2010)

Laws, David, *22 Days in May: The Birth of the Lib Dem–Conservative Coalition*, (Biteback, 2010)

Macintyre, Donald, *Mandelson and the Making of New Labour* (Harper Collins, 2000)

Mandelson, Peter, *The Third Man* (HarperPress, 2011)

Mattinson, Deborah, *Talking to a Brick Wall: How New Labour stopped listening to the voter and why we need a new politics* (Biteback, 2010)

Miliband, David, *Reinventing the Left* (Polity Press, 1994)

Miliband, Ralph, *Parliamentary Socialism: A Study in the Politics of Labour* (Merlin Press, 1972)

Miliband, *Ralph Socialism for a Sceptical Age* (Polity Press, 1994)

Miliband, Ralph, *The State in Capitalist Society* (Quartet Books, 1973)

Newman, Michael, *Ralph Miliband and the Politics of the New Left* (Merlin Press, 2002)

Pym, Hugh, & Kochan, Nick, *Gordon Brown: The First Year in Power* (Bloomsbury, 1998)

Powell, Jonathan, *The New Machiavelli: How to Wield Power in the Modern World* (Bodley Head, 2010)

Radice, Giles, *Trio: Inside the Blair, Brown, Mandelson Project* (I.B. Tauris, 2010)

Richards, Steve, *Whatever It Takes: The Real Story of Gordon Brown and New Labour* (Fourth Estate, 2010)

Rawnsley, Andrew, *Servants of the People* (Penguin, 2001)

Rawnsley, Andrew, *The End of the Party: The Rise and Fall of New Labour* (Penguin, 2010)

Robinson, Geoffrey, *The Unconventional Minister: My Life Inside New Labour* (Penguin, 2001)

Seldon, Anthony, *Blair Unbound* (Pocket Books, 2008)

Seldon, Anthony, & Lodge, Guy, *Brown at 10* (Biteback, 2010

Toynbee, Polly, & Walker, David, *Did Things Get Better? An Audit of Labour's Successes and Failures* (Penguin, 2001)

Toynbee, Polly, & Walker, David, *Better or Worse? Has Labour Delivered?* (Bloomsbury, 2005)

Toynbee, Polly, & Walker, David, *The Verdict: Did Labour Change Britain?* (Granta Books, 2010)

Watt, Peter, *Inside Out: My story of betrayal and cowardice at the heart of New Labour* (Biteback, 2010)

Wilson, Rob, *5 Days to Power: The Journey to Coalition Britain* (Biteback, 2010)

INDEX

TONY BENN
A Biography

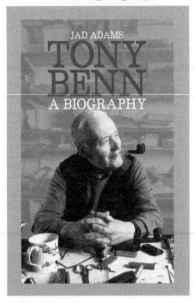

'Told with considerable grace and style' SUNDAY TIMES

'Fascinating reading' DAILY EXPRESS

'Benn's character shines through this... very readable biography'
DAILY TELEGRAPH

This comprehensively revised edition of Jad Adams's classic biography is written with unparalleled access to Benn's private records, and chronicles the behind-the-scenes story of Benn's bitter battles with every leader of the Labour Party since Gaitskell.

It details his service in the governments of Wilson and Callaghan, his role as a champion of the left during the Labour Party's long period in opposition, his retirement from Parliament to 'devote more time to politics' in 2001, and his subsequent emergence as a leading figure of the British opposition to the war in Iraq.

560pp paperback, £14.99
Available from all good bookshops
www.bitebackpublishing.com

BROWN AT 10

Anthony Seldon & Guy Lodge

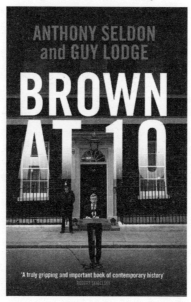

'A must-read for anyone who wants to know what really happened in the final three years of the Labour government.' GUARDIAN

Updated with new material, the paperback edition of the most complete account of Gordon Brown's turbulent premiership. This is a frank, authentic and penetrating account of a remarkable political era by one of Britain's foremost political and social commentators.

'Superbly well-informed.' PETER OBORNE, DAILY TELEGRAPH

'Seldon and Lodge's book is the product of deep historic research and sheds fresh light on both Gordon Brown and his extraordinarily problematic premiership. It is the definitive history and will be read for years to come.' DENNIS KAVANAGH

502pp hardback, £20
Available from all good bookshops
www.bitebackpublishing.com

IN DEFENCE OF POLITICIANS
(IN SPITE OF THEMSELVES)

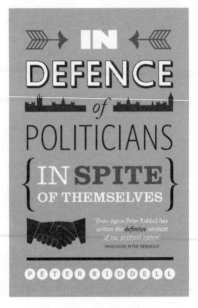

PETER RIDDELL

'In their hour of acute need, the British political class have found a true and candid friend in Peter Riddell – part historian; part anthropologist; and part psychotherapist.'
PETER HENNESSY

We may have a low opinion of politicians but we can't do without them, and here Peter Riddell, for decades one of the most astute and respected of all observers of the Westminster scene, presents the case for their defence, offering a series of recommendations for rehabilitating the political class in the eyes of voters.

192pp paperback, £9.99
Available from all good bookshops
www.bitebackpublishing.com